The Bible in Music

The Bible in Music

A Dictionary of
Songs, Works, and More

Siobhán Dowling Long
John F. A. Sawyer

ROWMAN & LITTLEFIELD
Lanham • Boulder • New York • London

Published by Rowman & Littlefield
A wholly owned subsidary of The Rowman & Littlefield Publishing Group, Inc.
4501 Forbes Boulevard, Suite 200, Lanham, Maryland 20706
www.rowman.com

Unit A, Whitacre Mews, 26-34 Stannary Street, London SE11 4AB

British Library Cataloguing in Publication Information Available

Library of Congress Cataloging-in-Publication Data

Dowling Long, Siobhán.
  The Bible in music : a dictionary of songs, works, and more / Siobhán Dowling Long,
John F. A. Sawyer.
     pages cm
  Includes bibliographical references and index.
  ISBN 978-0-8108-8451-9 (cloth : alk. paper) — ISBN 978-0-8108-8452-6 (ebook)
  1. Bible in music—Dictionaries. 2. Bible—Songs and music–Dictionaries. I. Sawyer,
John F. A. II. Title.
  ML102.C5L66 2015
  781.5'9–dc23

                                                            2015012867

Printed in the United States of America

Contents

Acronyms and Abbreviations

GENERAL

A.	alto, contralto (voice)
AGO	American Guild of Organists
AV	*Asow-Verzeichins*, catalog of Richard Strauss's works by Mueller von Asow
B.	bass, bassus (voice)
b.	born
Bar.	baritone (voice)
B-Bar.	bass-baritone (voice)
BBC	British Broadcasting Corporation
BC F	Bach Compendium: *Choräle und geistliche Lieder*
BCP	*Book of Common Prayer*
Bib. Nat.	*Bibliothèque Nationale*
BVN	catalog of Langgaard's works by Bendt Viinholt Nielsen
BWV	*Bach-Werke-Verzeichnis*, catalog of J. S. Bach's works by Wolfgang Schmieder
ca.	circa
CA	California
CCM	contemporary Christian music
CCTV	closed-circuit television
CD	compact disc
CE	Common Era
cf.	*confer*, compare
CG	catalog of Gounod's works by Gérard Condé
Ct.	contratenor, countertenor
CT	Connecticut
d.	died
D.	catalog of Schubert's works by Otto Erich Deutsch
DVD	digital video disc or video versatile disc
ed.	edited
e.g.	*exempli gratia*, for example
EH	*English Hymnal*
F	catalog of Arthur Bliss's works by Louis Forman

FA	Football Association
FP	catalog of Poulenc's works by Carl Schmidt
FWV	*Franck Werke Verzeichnis*, catalog of Franck's works by Wilhelm Mohr
H.	catalog of Berlioz's works by D. Kern Holoman
H.	catalog of Charpentier's works by Hugh Wiley Hitchcock
H.	catalog of Honegger's works by Harry Halbreich
H.	catalog of Leo Sowerby's works by Ronald M. Huntington
Heb.	Hebrew
HM	Her Majesty
Hob.	*Hoboken-Verzeichnis*, catalog of Haydn's works by Anthony van Hoboken
HRH	Her Royal Highness
HWC	Healey Willan Catalogue
HWV	*Händel-Werke-Verzeichnis*, catalog of Handel's works by Bernd Baselt
i.e.	*id est*, that is
J.	catalog of Peter Maxwell Davies's works by Judy Arnold
Jr.	Junior
K.	catalog of Mozart's works by Ludwig Ritter von Köchel
KJV	King James (Authorized) Version
JPS	Jewish Publication Society, New York
L.	catalog of Debussy's works by François Lesuré
Lat.	Latin
LXX	Septuagint
Mez.	mezzo-soprano (voice)
Movt.	movement
Movts.	movements
MS	manuscript
MS Bodl.	Manuscript Bodley
MS NAL	Manuscript *Nouvelles Acquisitions Latines*
MTV	American basic cable and satellite television channel
NAB	New American Bible
NBC	National Broadcasting Company
NIV	New International Version
No.	number
Nos.	numbers
NT	New Testament
Op.	opus
OT	Old Testament
OUP	Oxford University Press
P.	catalog of Respighi's works by Potito Peddara
PA	Pennsylvania

POW	prisoner of war
R.	catalog of Alfvén's works by Jan Olof Rudén
rev.	revised
RSV	Revised Standard Version
RV	*Ryom-Verzeichnis*, catalog of Vivaldi's works by Peter Ryom
S.	soprano (voice)
S.	catalog of Liszt's works by Humphrey Searle
Schleifer	catalog of Gilchrist's works by Martha Furman Schleifer
St.	Saint
SV	*Stattkus-Verzeichnis*, catalog of Monteverdi's works by Manfred H. Stattkus
SWV	*Schütz-Werke-Verzeichnis*, catalog of Schütz's works by W. Bittinger
T.	tenor (voice)
TN	catalog of Rachmaninoff's works by R. Threlfall and G. Norris
TV	television
TWV	*Telemann-Werke-Verzeichnis*, catalog of Telemann's works by Werner Menke and Martin Ruhnke
UK	United Kingdom
Univ. Lib.	university library
US	United States
v. (pl. vv.)	verse(s)
Vulg.	Vulgate
WoO	*Werke ohne Opuszahl*, Spohr's works "without opus number"
WWI	World War I
WWII	World War II
WWV	*Wagner-Werk-Verzeichnis*, catalog of Wagner's works by John Deathridge, Martin Geck, and Egon Voss
Z.	catalog of Purcell's works by Franklin Bershir Zimmerman

BIBLICAL LITERATURE

Hebrew Bible/Old Testament

Gen.	Genesis
Exod.	Exodus
Lev.	Leviticus
Num.	Numbers
Deut.	Deuteronomy
Josh.	Joshua
Judg.	Judges
Ruth	Ruth

1–2 Sam.	1–2 Samuel
1–2 Kgs.	1–2 Kings
1–2 Chron.	1–2 Chronicles
Ezra	Ezra
Neh.	Nehemiah
Esth.	Esther
Job	Job
Ps. (pl. Pss.)	Psalm(s)
Prov.	Proverbs
Eccl.	Ecclesiastes
Cant.	Canticles (Song of Songs or Song of Solomon)
Isa.	Isaiah
Jer.	Jeremiah
Lam.	Lamentations
Ezek.	Ezekiel
Dan.	Daniel
Hos.	Hosea
Joel	Joel
Amos	Amos
Obad.	Obadiah
Jonah	Jonah
Mic.	Micah
Nah.	Nahum
Hab.	Habakkuk
Zeph.	Zephaniah
Hag.	Haggai
Zech.	Zechariah
Mal.	Malachi

New Testament

Mt.	Matthew
Mk.	Mark
Lk.	Luke
Jn.	John
Acts	Acts
Rom.	Romans
1–2 Cor.	1–2 Corinthians
Gal.	Galatians
Eph.	Ephesians
Phil.	Philippians
Col.	Colossians
1–2 Thess.	1–2 Thessalonians

1–2 Tim.   1–2 Timothy
Titus   Titus
Philem.   Philemon
Heb.   Hebrew
Jas.   James
1–2 Pet.   1–2 Peter
1–2–3 Jn.   1–2–3 John
Jd.   Jude
Rev.   Revelation (Apocalypse)

Apocrypha

Bar.   Baruch
2 Esdr.   2 Esdras
Jud.   Judith
1 Macc.   1 Maccabees
2 Macc.   2 Maccabees
Sir.   Sirach (or Ecclesiasticus)
Tob.   Tobit
Wisd.   Wisdom of Solomon

Chronology

CE   New Testament references to singing Psalms, hymns, and spiritual songs (Col. 3:16: cf. Mt. 26:30)

Mishnah (ca. 200) includes rules for Jewish worship

Apostolic Constitutions (375–380): eight books on early Christian worship, including hymns and doctrine

Niceta of Remesiana (ca. 335–414), author of the *Te Deum Laudamus*

Ambrose, bishop of Milan (ca. 339–397), preacher, theologian, and hymn writer

Jerome's Latin Vulgate (382–ca. 410): 80 books (39 Old Testament, 14 Apocrypha, 27 New Testament)

Prudentius (349–ca. 410), poet, author of *Corde natus ex parentis* ("Of the Father's Love Begotten")

500   Romanos the Melodist, one of the greatest Greek hymnographers (d. 510)

Benedict of Nursia (ca. 480–550), Rule of Benedict, Divine Office

Text of the Gregorian vespers hymn *Vexilla Regis* ("The Royal Banner") written by the poet Venantius Fortunatus (530–609 CE)

Lindisfarne Gospels (ca. 696–698) written by the monk Eadfrith, later bishop

Andrew of Crete (650–740), exponent of the Canon, a series of nine odes or canticles interspersed with the nine biblical canticles

Bede (ca. 673–735) composes two of the earliest treatises on Gregorian chant

Early codification of plainchant (eighth century)

Musica enchiriadis, an anonymous ninth-century musical treatise to establish a system of rules for counterpoint

Gregorian hymn *Veni Creator Spiritus*, attributed to Rabanus Maurus (ca. 780–856)

Earliest musical notation of plainchant and polyphony (850–900)

Winchester Troper (10th century); the earliest collection of two-part music in Europe, it includes the *Quem quaeretis*

1000   Guido of Arezzo (ca. 980–1050), inventor of staff notation and a method of sight singing using solemnization syllables

Hildegard of Bingen (1098–1179), *Symphony of the Harmony of Heavenly Revelations*

1200   Leoninus (d. ca. 1201), Notre Dame de Paris, *The Great Book of Organum* (1170), a collection of two-voiced settings of music for the liturgical year

Fleury Playbook (1200)

Play of Daniel (*Ludus Danielis*), 13th-century liturgical drama

The Great Book of Organum revised by Perotinus Magnus (d. ca. 1205), Notre Dame de Paris

Francis of Assisi (ca. 1181–1226), *The Canticle of the Creatures*

Jacopone da Todi (ca. 1230–1306), author of the *Stabat mater*

Cantigas de Santa Maria (1260–1280), a collection of Spanish songs in praise of the Virgin Mary

Dublin Troper (1361), Christ Church Cathedral, Dublin

John Wycliffe (ca. 1330–1384), first translation of the New Testament into English (1361)

John Wycliffe, first translation of the Old Testament into English (1380)

1500   Ottaviano dei Petrucci (1466–1539), Venice, prints music using movable musical type

Martin Luther posts "Ninety-Five Theses" (1517)

Publication of Luther's first hymnbook, *Achtliederbuch* (Hymnal of Eight) (1524)

Martin Luther, "Christ Lag in Todesbanden," hymn, published in the *Erfurt Enchiridion* (1524)

Geystlich gesangk-Buchleyn published by Johann Walter, the first cantor of the Lutheran Church (1524)

William Tyndale's New Testament printed in English in Hamburg (1525)

Martin Luther, "Ein Fest' Burg ist Unser Gott," hymn (ca. 1529)

Martin Luther's *Geistliche Lieder* published in Wittenberg (1535)

Myles Coverdale Bible, first complete Bible, printed in English (1535)

Council of Trent (1545)

Thomas Tallis, *If Ye Love Me*, anthem (ca. 1547–1548)

Book of Common Prayer (1549)

1550   Orlando de Lassus, *Prophetiae Sibyllarum* (ca. 1550)
Christopher Tye, *The Actes of the Apostles* (1553)
Anglo-Genevan Psalm Book (1556)
The Wode Psalter (1562–1592)
Orlando de Lassus's *Thesauras Musicus* published (1564)
Alessandro Striggio, *Ecce beatam lucem* (ca. 1565)
Ane Compendious Buik of Godlie and Spiritual Sanges (Edinburgh, ca. 1567)
Archbishop Parker's *Psalter* published (1567)
Thomas Tallis, *Spem in alium* (1568)
Giovanni Pierluigi da Palestrina's *Liber primus motettorum* published (1569)
Translation of the Geneva Bible, the Bible of the Protestant Reformation (1570)
William Byrd and Thomas Tallis, *Cantiones sacrae* ("Sacred Songs") (1575)
Thomas Este, *The Whole Book of Psalmes*, published (1582)
Orlando de Lassus, *Psalmi Davidis Poenitentiales*, motet cycle (1584)
Giovanni da Pierluigida Palestrina, *Canticum Canticorum* (1584)

1600   William Byrd, *Sing Joyfully*, the composer's last surviving anthem
Claudio Monteverdi's monumental choral work *Vespro Della Beata Vergine* (1610)
King James Authorized Bible (1611)
John Dowland's fourth book, *A Pilgrimes Solace*, published (1612)
Johann Hermann Schein, *Cymbalum Sionium sive Cantiones sacrae* (1615)
Heinrich Schütz, *Psalmen Davids* (1619)
Johann Hermann Schein, *Israelsbrünnlein*, sacred madrigals (1623)
The Hymnes and Songs of the Church (1623), earliest hymnal of the English Church
Heinrich Schütz, *Symphonae sacrae*, Book 1, Venice (1629)
The Bay Psalm Book (1640)
Claudio Monteverdi, *Selva Morale e Spirituale* (1641)
Book of Common Prayer banned in England and all church music except metrical Psalm singing (1645)
Heinrich Schütz, *Symphoniae sacrae*, Book 2, Dresden (1647)
Heinrich Schütz, *Symphoniae sacrae*, Book 3, Dresden (1648)

1650   *The Scottish Metrical Psalter* published (1650)
Horatius Bonar, the "prince of Scottish hymn writing," *The Bible Hymn Book* (1660)
Heinrich Schütz, *Die Weihnachtshistorien* (ca. 1660)

The Restoration of the English Monarchy (1660)

Book of Common Prayer (1662)

Münster Gesangbuch (1677)

Alessandro Scarlatti, *Davidis Pugna et Victoria* (ca. 1679–1682)

Alessandro Scarlatti, *Agar et Ismaele Esiliati* (1683)

Henry Purcell, *Hear My Prayer*, anthem, performed at the funeral service of Charles II (1685)

Arcangelo Corelli, *Christmas Concerto* (ca. 1690)

Nicholas Brady and Nahum Tate, *New Version of the Psalms of David* (1696)

1700   Johann Kuhnau, *Biblical Sonatas* (*Biblische Historien*) (1700)

J. S. Bach, *Aus der Tiefen rufe ich* ("Out of the depths I cry to thee, O Lord"), earliest extant cantata by Bach (1707)

Elisabeth-Claude Jacquet de la Guerre, *Cantates Francoises Sur Des Sujets Tirez De L'Ecriture* (1708)

B. H. Brocke, *Brocke's Passion* (1712)

Antonio Lucio Vivaldi, *Juditha Triumphans Devicta Holofernis Barbarie*, sacred military oratorio (1716)

Antonio Lotti, *Crucifixus* (1717–1719)

G. F. Handel, *Chandos Anthems* (1717–1718)

William Billings, *The Shepherd's Carol*, one of the earliest American carols by Billings (1778)

G. F. Handel, *Esther*, oratorio (1718)

Isaac Watts, *The Psalms of David* (1719)

G. F. Handel, *Joseph and his Brethren*, oratorio (1722)

William Croft's *Funeral Sentences* published in *Musica Sacra* (1724)

J. S. Bach, *St. John Passion* (1724)

J. S. Bach, *Easter Oratorio* (1725)

G. F. Handel's coronation anthems *Zadok the Priest, The King Shall Rejoice, Let thy Hand be Strengtened,* and *My Heart is Inditing* composed by Handel for the coronation of George II and Queen Caroline in Westminster Abbey (11 October 1727)

J. S. Bach, *St. Matthew Passion* (1727)

J. S. Bach's cantata *Wachet Auf* first performed in Leipzig (1731)

G. F. Handel, *Athalia*, oratorio (1733)

J. S. Bach, *Christmas Oratorio* (1734)

J. S. Bach, *Ascension Oratorio* (1735)

William Boyce, *David's Lamentation over Saul and David* (1736)

G. F. Handel, *Israel in Egypt*, oratorio (1738)

Charles Wesley, *Hymns and Sacred Poems* (1739)

G. F. Handel, *Samson*, oratorio (1741)

G. F. Handel's *Messiah* first performed in Dublin, Ireland (1742)
Scottish Paraphrases (1745; rev. Michael Bruce, 1781)
G. F. Handel, *Judas Maccabaeus* (1746), one of the most popular oratorios during the composer's lifetime
G. F. Handel, *Joshua*, oratorio (1747)
G. F. Handel, *Alexander Balus*, oratorio (1747)

1750   G. F. Handel, *Jephthah*, his last oratorio (1751)
John Francis Wade, *Cantus Diversi pro Dominicis et Festis per annum* (1751)
Isaac Watts, *Psalms, Hymns and Spiritual Songs* (1751)
Karl Heinrich Graun, *Der Tod Jesu* (1755)
Philip Doddridge, *Hymns Founded on Various Texts in the Holy Scriptures* (1755)
William Billings, *The New England Psalm Singer* (Boston, 1770)
W. A. Mozart, *La Bethulia Liberata* (1771)
J. C. F. Bach, *Die Kindheit Jesu* (1773)
Joseph Haydn, *Il Ritorno di Tobia* (1775)
Augustus Montague Toplady, *Rock of Ages*, popular hymn first published in "The Gospel Magazine" (1776)
William Billings, *The Singing Master's Assistant* (1778)
William Billings, *David's Lamentation* (1778)
William Billings, *The Psalm-Singer's Amusement* (1781)
Joseph Haydn, *The Seven Last Words of Our Redeemer on the Cross* (1783)
The first performance of *Davide Penitente* by W. A. Mozart (13 March 1785)
William Billings's *The Suffolk Harmony* published (1786)
Simon Mayr, *David in Spelunca Engaddi* (1795)
Josef Haydn, *The Creation* (Die Schöpfung) (1798)
John Newton, *Olney Hymns* (1779)
Charles Wesley, *A Collection of Hymns for the Use of the People Called Methodists* (1779)
Joshua Smith, *Divine Hymns or Spiritual Songs* (1784)
W. A. Mozart's *Requiem* (1791; completed by Franz Xavier Süssmayr)

1800   William Billings's *The Continental Harmony* published (Boston, 1794)
Ludwig van Beethoven, *Christus am Ölberge* (1803–1804)
Thomas Kelly, *Hymns on Various Passages of Scripture* (1804)
Text of *Silent Night* by Xavier Gruber (1816) set to music by Joseph Mohr (1818)

Gioachino Rossini, *Moses in Egypt*, opera (1818)

Anna Bartlett Warner's popular hymn "Jesus Loves Me" (1819–1885)

Louis Spohr, *Die Letzten Dinge* (1826)

William Crotch, *The Captivity of Judah*, oratorio (1834)

Louis Spohr, *Des Heilands Letzte Stunden* (1834–1835)

Henry Francis Lyte, *The Spirit of the Psalms* (1834)

Felix Mendelssohn, *St. Paul*, oratorio (1834–1836)

Giuseppe Verdi, *Nabucco* (1841)

William John Fox, *Hymns and Anthems* (1841)

Richard Wagner, *The Love Feast of the Apostles* (1843)

Felix Mendelssohn, *Elijah*, oratorio, first performed at the Birmingham Music Festival (1846)

Felix Mendelssohn, *Christus* (1847)

Cecil Frances Alexander (née Humphreys), *Hymns for Little Children* (1848)

Hector Berlioz, *Enfance du Christ* (1850–1854)

1850   John M. Neale, *Mediaeval Hymns* (1851)

Michael Costa, *Eli* (1855)

William Batchelder Bradbury, *Esther the Beautiful Queen* (1856)

Horatius Bonar, *The Bible Hymn Book* (1860)

Julie W. Howe, "Battle Hymn of the Republic" (1861)

William Henry Monk, ed., *Hymns Ancient and Modern* (1861)

Franz Liszt, *Christus* (1862–1866)

Johannes Brahms, *A German Requiem* (*Ein Deutsches Requiem*) (1865–1868)

George Frederick Bristow, *Daniel* (1866)

Horatius Bonar, *Hymns of Faith and Hope* (1866)

William Sterndale Bennett, *Woman of Samaria*, cantata (1867)

Otto Goldschmidt, *Ruth*, sacred pastoral (1867)

Hymns Ancient and Modern published (1868)

Johannes Brahms performs *German Requiem* in Leipzig (1869)

César Franck, *Les Béatitudes* (1869–1879)

Jules Massenet, *Marie-Magdaleine*, one of the most popular oratorios by the composer (1871–1872)

Fisk Jubilee Singers tour the United States singing spirituals to raise funds for college (1871)

John Knowles Paine, *St. Peter*, oratorio (1872)

Theodore F. Seward's *Jubilee Songs as Sung by the Jubilee Singers of Fisk University* published (1872)

Sunday School Book for the Use of Evangelical Lutheran Congregations (1873)

Karl Goldmark, *The Queen of Sheba* (*Die Königin von Saba*), opera, first performed in Vienna (1875) and New York (1885)

Jules Massenet, *Ève*, one the most sensuous oratorios of the genre (1875)

Franz Lizst, *Via Crucis*, oratorio (1876–1867; published in Leipzig, 1936)

Camille Saint-Saëns, *Samson et Dalea*, grand opera (1877)

John Stainer, *The Daughter of Jairus* (1878)

Max Bruch, *Kol Nidre* (1881)

Liber usualis (1883)

Sir Charles Villiers Stanford, *Three Holy Children*, oratorio, dedicated to Queen Victoria (1885)

Gabriel Fauré's *Requiem* (1887–1890)

First British Folk Revival (1890–1920)

Sir Charles Villiers Stanford, *Eden* (1891)

Hubert Parry, *King Saul* (1894)

Antonin Dvořák, *Biblical Songs (Biblické písne)* (1894)

Johannes Brahms, *Vier Ernste Gesänge*, song cycle, the composer's last choral composition before his death in 1897 (1896)

1900   Edward Elgar, *Dream of Gerontius* (1900)

Hubert Parry, *I Was Glad*, coronation anthem (1902)

Vaughan Music Publishing Company (1903)

Florent Schmitt, *Psaume XLVII* (Psalm 47) (1904)

George Ratcliffe Woodward and Charles Wood, eds., *Songs of Syon: A Collection of Hymns and Sacred Poems* (1904)

Richard Strauss, *Salome*, opera (1905)

Edward Elgar's *The Kingdom* performed at the Birmingham Festival (1906)

Percy Dearmer and Vaughan Williams, eds., *English Hymnal* (1906; rev. ed., 1933)

Edward Elgar, *The Apostles* (1907)

R. Nathaniel Dett, *Folk Songs of the American Negro* (1907)

Florent Schmitt, *La Tragédie de Salomé*, ballet (1907)

John Truman Wolcott, *Hezekiah* (1908)

Charles Villiers Stanford, *Biblical Songs* (1909)

Birth of southern gospel in the southeastern United States (1910)

Alexander Tikhonovich Grechaninov, *Seven Days of the Passion* (1911)

Granville Bantock, *Vaniety of Vanieties*, choral symphony, written before the outbreak of World War I (1913)

Herbert Howells, *Three Psalm Preludes* (set 1), tone poems for organ (composed between 1915 and 1916)

Hubert Parry, *Jerusalem* (1916)

Public School Hymnal (1919)

Development of country-and-western music in Atlanta, Georgia (1920s)

Harry Dixon Loes, *"This Little Light of Mine,"* children's gospel song (ca. 1920)

Gustav Holst, *The Hymn of Jesus* (1920)

Paola Gallico, *The Apocalypse* (1920)

Marcel Dupré improvises on Gregorian chant in Wanamaker's Department Store (currently Macy's) in Philadelphia (1921)

Arthur Honegger, *Le Roi David,* symphonic Psalm (1923)

Zoltán Kodály, *Psalmus Hungaricus* (1923)

1925 Mario Castelnuovo-Tedesco, *Le Danze del Re David* (1925)

Arnold Schoenberg, *Moses und Aron,* opera (unfinished; completed 1928)

Rued Langgaard, *The Antikrist,* opera (1921–1923; rev. 1926–1930)

R. Nathaniel Dett, *Religious Folk Songs of the Negro* (1927)

Sergei Prokofiev, *Fils Prodigue,* ballet (1928–1929)

Oxford Book of Carols (1928)

Luther G. Presley and Virgil Oliver Stamps, "When the Saints Go Marching In," American gospel hymn, popularized by Louis Armstrong (1930s)

Marcel Dupré, *Le Chemin de la Croix,* tone poem for organ (1931)

William Walton, *Belshazzar's Feast* oratorio (1931)

Ottorino Respighi, *Belkis Queen of Shebai,* ballet suite (1932)

The Clarendon Hymn Book (1936)

Thomas A. Dorsey, the "father of gospel," "Precious Lord, Take My Hand" (1937)

Kurt Weill's *The Eternal Road* first performed at the Manhattan Opera House (7 January 1937)

Sir Granville Bantock's *King Solomon* composed for the coronation of George VI (1937)

Herbert Howells, *Three Psalm Preludes* (Set 2), tone poems for organ (1938)

Florent Schmidt, *Das Buch mit sieben Siegeln* ("The Book with Seven Seals") (1938)

First album of Sister Rosetta Tharpe, the original "soul sister" (1938)

Sir Michael Tippett, *A Child of Our Time* (1939–1941)

Development of rock and roll (1940s)

Brother Roger founds Taizé Community in Burgundy (1940)
Randall Thompson, *Alleluia.* Motet (1940)
William Walton, *The Wise Virgins,* ballet, premieres at Sadler's
  Wells Theatre, London (26 April 1940)
Olivier Messiaen, *Quatuor Pour la Fin du Temps* (1941)
Leonard Bernstein, *Jeremiah,* Symphony no. 1 (1942)
Benjamin Britten, *A Ceremony of Carols* (1942)
Olivier Messiaen, *Vingt Regards Sur l'Enfant Jésus,* one of the
  the most important works of the 20th century for piano (1940)
Frank Martin, *In Terra Pax,* oratorio, performed to mark the end
  of World War II (May 1945)
Genesis Suite commissioned by Nathaniel Shilkret (1945)
Second British Folk Revival (1945–1969)
Randall Thompson, *The Last Words of David,* anthem (1949)

1950   Gian Carlo Menotti, *Amahl and the Night Visitors,* children's
             Christmas opera (1951)
             Wayne Shanklin, "Jezebel," popular song (1951)
             Gian Carlo Menotti, *The Apocalisse* ("Apocalypse") (1951–1952)
             Gélineau Psalmody (1953)
             Carlisle Floyd, *Susannah,* opera, premiered at Florida State Uni-
             versity (1955)
             Davis Sisters's hit song *Twelve Gates to the City* featured on al-
             bum by the same name (1955)
             Karlheinz Stockhausen, *Gesang Der Jünglinge,* the first master-
             piece of electronic music (1956)
             Lennox Berkeley, *Ruth,* lyrical opera, performed at the Scala The-
             atre, London (1956)
             Daniel Rogers Pinkham, *Christmas Cantata* (1957)
             Bob Ferguson, "Wings of a Dove," country song (1958)
             Perry Como sings "Whither Thou Goest" by Guy Singer (1954)
             on the album *When You Come to the End of the Day* (1958)
             Igor Stravinsky, *Threni, Id Est Lamentationes Jeremiae Prophe-
             tae,* cantata, one of the composer's first and longest works in
             twelve-tone serialism (1958)
             Robert Starer, *Ariel: Vision of Isaiah* (1959)

1960   American Jesus movement begins on the West Coast of the United
             States (early 1960s); development of Jesus music/gospel beat
             music
             Neil Sedaka and Howard Greenfield, songs "Run, Samson, Run"
             (1960) and "Stairway to Heaven" (1960)

Benjamin Britten's *War Requiem* first performed in Coventry Cathedral (1961)

Kay Roger, Luther Dixon, and Bob Elgin, hit song "A Hundred Pounds of Clay" (1961)

Mahalia Jackson sings before Martin Luther King Jr.'s speech "I Have a Dream" (1963)

Olivier Messiaen, *Couleurs de la Cité Céleste* (1963)

Leonard Bernstein, *Chichester Psalms* (1963)

Michael Perry, *Calypso Carol* (1964)

William Walton, *The Twelve*, anthem and mini-cantata, premiered at Christ Church, Oxford (May 1965)

First sacred concert by jazz musician Duke Ellington (1965)

Bob Dylan, *Highway 61 Revisited*, album (1965)

Darius Milhaud, *Cantata from Job* (1965)

Chuck Berry, song "The Promised Land" on the album *St. Louis to Liverpool* (1965)

Duke Ellington's *Concert of Sacred Music Live from Grace Cathedral* recorded at Fifth Avenue Presbyterian Church, New York City (26 December 1966)

Elvis Presley wins a Grammy for second gospel album, *How Great Thou Art* (1966)

Pete Seeger's song "Turn Turn Turn" (1965) reaches number 1 on the American Billboard charts (1966)

Benjamin Britten, *The Burning Fiery Furnace* (1966)

Samuel Barber, *Agnus Dei* (1967)

Samuel Hans Adler, *The Binding* (Hebrew Akedah) (1967)

Bob Dylan, *John Wesley Harding*, album (1967)

Billy Ray Hearn, the "father of contemporary Christian music," *Good News*, musical (1967)

Andrew Lloyd Webber and Tim Rice, *Joseph and the Amazing Technicolor Dreamcoat*, musical (1968)

Dave Brubeck, oratorio *The Light in the Wilderness* (1968)

Development of heavy metal (late 1960s and early 1970s)

1970   Irish Rovers's album *The Unicorn* (1968) sells over 8 million copies worldwide

New Zealanders David and Dale Garrett, *Scripture in Song*, first of 30 albums (1968)

Larry Norman, the "father of Christian rock," releases first solo album, *Upon This Rock* (1969)

Development of hip-hop in New York City (1970s)

Jesus Christ Superstar, composed by Andrew Lloyd Webber, lyrics by Tim Rice (1970)

John Tavener's *The Whale: A Biblical Fantasy* released by the Beatles' Apple Records label (1970)

Brent Dowe and Trevor McNaughton of the Melodians, *Rivers of Babylon* (1970)

Ralph Carmichael and Kurt Kaiser's musical *Tell It Like It Is* released on LP (1970)

Penderecki's *Utrenja Part I*, inspired by the Eastern Orthodox Holy Saturday Liturgy, composed (1970)

Gene MacLellan, "Put Your Hand in the Hand," gospel song (1970)

Stephen Schwartz and John-Michael Tebelak's *Godspell* opens off-Broadway, and *Jesus Christ Superstar* opens on-Broadway (1971)

Argentine rock band Vox Dei's album *La Biblia* ("The Bible") widely regarded as a masterpiece (1971)

The band 2nd Chapter of Acts founded in Los Angeles (1971)

Dolly Parton, *Coat of Many Colours*, album (1971)

Elvis Presley, *He Touched Me*, album (1972)

Bob Hartman founds Christian rock band *Petra* (1972)

Jean Langlais, *Cinq Meditations sur L'Apocalypse* (1973)

Johnny Cash, *The Gospel Road*, album (1973)

Resurrection Band (Rez Band) formed in Milwaukee, Wisconsin (1973)

Graduale Romanum published (1974)

Schola Gregoriana, Cambridge, United Kingdom, founded by Mary Berry CBE for the study and performance of Gregorian chant (1975)

Brian May (from the band Queen), "The Prophet Song," on the album *A Night at the Opera* (1975)

Sir Elton John's song "Tower of Babel" featured on the album *Captain Fantastic and the Brown Dirt Cowboy* (1975)

Folk-rock artist Don Francisco, *Forgiven*, album (1977)

Górecki, *Beatus Vir* (1979)

1980   Bob Marley's album *Uprising* features the song "Zion Train" (1980)

U2, *Boy*, album (1980)

Steve Reich, *Tehillim* ("Psalms"), minimalist work, composed (1981)

Rock band Burning Sensations, "Belly of the Whale," MTV hit
(1982)

John Tavener, *The Lamb*, anthem (1982)

Karel Goeyvaerts, *Aquarius*, opera (1983–1992)

Michael Card's "El Shaddai" wins Gospel Music Association
Dove Award for Song Writer and Song of the Year (1983)

Hymns and Psalms, Methodist hymnal (1983)

Heavy metal band Metallica, song "The Four Horsemen," on the
album *Kill 'em All* (1983)

Heavy metal band Metallica, *Ride the Lightning*, album (1984)

1990   Leonard Cohen's ballad "Hallelujah" published in the *Book of
Mercy* (1984)

Henk Badings, *Cain and Abel*, electronic ballet (1986)

Philip Glass, *In the Upper Room*, ballet (1986)

John Rutter's *What Sweeter Music* commissioned for the annual
Festival of Nine Lessons and Carols (1987)

Sting's carol "The Angel Gabriel" featured on the album *A Very
Special Christmas* (1987)

Lawrence Goldberg's pulpit opera *The Test of Faith* wins competition by Jewish Music Commission of Los Angeles (1987)

U2 album *The Joshua Tree* is the fastest-selling album in U.K.
Album Chart history (1987)

Rich Mullins, "Awesome God," on the album *Winds of Heaven
Stuff of Earth* (1988)

Steve Reich, *The Cave*, multimedia opera (1990–1993)

"Star of Bethlehem," Christmas hymn, composed for the movie
Home Alone II (1990)

Arvo Pärt, *The Beatitudes*, oratorio (1991)

Cristóbal de Morales's "Emendemus in Melius" featured in the
horror movie *The Pit and the Pendulum* (1991)

John Rutter, *Psalmfest* (1993)

Folk singer Joni Mitchell, "The Sire of Sorrow: Job's Sad Song"
(1994)

Coolio's album *Gangsta's Paradise* sells over 5.7 million copies
worldwide (1995)

Krzysztof Penderecki commissioned to compose Symphony no.
7, "Seven Gates of Jerusalem," to celebrate the Holy City's
third millennium (1996)

Irish musical and dance production *Lord of the Dance* created and
choreographed by Irish American Michael Flatley, who also
starred in the show (1996)

Mark Lowry's song "Mary Did You Know?" performed by Wynonna Jude and Kenny Rogers on the album *The Gift* (1996)

John Tavener's "Song for Athene" performed at the funeral service for Diana, Princess of Wales (1997)

Vladimir Martynov's *The Beatitudes* (1998) performed in a concert for the 10th anniversary of the 9/11 terrorist attacks in New York City (2011)

Stephen Schwartz, song "When You Believe," for the animated movie *The Prince of Egypt* (1998)

The Residents, *Wormwood: Curious Stories from the Bible*, concept album (1998)

Eric Whitacre's choral work *When David Heard That Absalom Was Dead* premieres (26 March 1999)

Ralph McTell, song "Jesus Wept," on the album *Travelling Man* (1999)

John Tavener, "Fall and Resurrection" (1999)

2000   Arvo Pärt's choral work *Which Was the Son of . . .* commissioned by the Reykjavík European City of Culture 2000 for Voices of Europe (2000)

"Hinne ma Tov" popularized by the Miami Boys Choir (2000)

Wolfgang Rihm, *Deus Passus* (2000)

Michael Isaacson, *A Covenant of Wonders: The Giving and Receiving of the Ten Commandments* (2002)

Johnny Cash, "The Man Comes Round," one of the last songs written before his death in 2003 (2002)

Josh Groban popularizes the hit song "You Raise Me Up" (2003)

John Tavener's *Veil of the Temple* (All Night Vigil) premiered at the Temple Church, London (27 June and 1 July 2003)

James Macmillan, *Chosen* (2003)

American heavy metal band Avenged Sevenfold, "Beast and the Harlot" (2005)

Bruce Springsteen, song "Jesus Was an Only Son," on the album *Devils and Dust* (2005)

Todd Agnew, *Do You See What I See?*, Christian rock album (2006)

Brooke Fraser, song "Hosea's Wife," on the album *Albertine* (2006)

Regina Spektor, song "Samson," on the album *Begin to Hope* (2006)

The Manchester Passion, a modern passion play (2006)

The Liverpool Nativity, a modern musical (2007)

The Margate Exodus (2007)

Pioneer of gospel and contemporary Christian music Amy Grant named the best-selling contemporary Christian music artist (2007)

James McMillan, *St. John Passion* (2007)

Ståle Kleiberg, *David and Bathsheba* (2007)

Sinéad O'Connor, *Theology*, album (2007)

Coldplay, song "Viva la Vida," included on their fourth album, *Viva la Vida or Death and All His Friends* (2008)

Howard Goodall, *The Beatitudes* (2009)

Heavy metal band W.A.S.P., *Babylon*, their 14th studio album (2009)

Zad Moultaka, *The Passion according to Mary* (2011)

Lady Gaga, song "Judas," on the album *Born This Way* (2011)

John Rutter's wedding anthem "This Is the Day" performed at the wedding of Prince William to Kate Middleton at Westminster Abbey (2011)

"In Dulci Jubilo," carol, performed at the opening ceremony of the London Olympic Games (2012)

Choirbook for the Queen (2012)

Purcell's anthem "Hear My Prayer" performed at the funeral service of British Prime Minister Margaret Thatcher (2013)

Bobby McFerrin, *Spirityouall*, album (2013)

Acknowledgments

The idea for this volume was first suggested more than 20 years ago by the sociologist Jon Davies, at the time a colleague in the Department of Religious Studies at Newcastle University, where a successful conference, "The Sociology of Sacred Texts," was held in 1991. But it was not until 2010, when circumstances brought together an aging biblical scholar in Perugia and a young musicologist in Cork, that the idea began to take shape.

But it would not have been possible to get to where we are today without the help and advice of many people, too many to mention here, and we gratefully acknowledge how much we owe them all. In particular, we would single out for special mention Cillian Long, Bláthnaid Long, Joseph Sawyer, David Baker, Paul Laird, Cosette Damiano, Martin O'Kane, David Chalcraft, Eric Cross, Monica Dowling, and Betty Lanigan; the staff of the School of Education, University College Cork, especially Professor Kathy Hall and Angela Desmond; Bennett Graff, Monica Savaglia, Lara Graham, and the staff at Rowman & Littlefield; Alexander Sawyer for invaluable expertise, particularly in the final stages; and Fiachra Long and Jean Sawyer for invaluable support and encouragement at every stage.

Introduction

There have been numerous publications in the past decade or two on the Bible in literature, the Bible in art, the Bible in film, and other aspects of the reception history of the Bible but nothing comparable on the Bible in music. Many highly successful oratorios, operas, musicals, and other works based on biblical themes, although originally written for the liturgy, Jewish or Christian, are more often performed for secular audiences than in churches or synagogues and are thus one of the chief ways in which the Bible interacts with culture. Furthermore, biblical language and imagery are present not only in music specifically written for Jewish or Christian audiences but also in numerous secular works, including ballets, operas, folk songs, and rock music.

Musical works often contain innovative applications of biblical texts (Isa. 66:13 in Brahms's *German Requiem*), variations in the original plot (Handel's *Jephthah*), and striking modern interpretations (The Residents's "Burn Baby Burn" on Judg. 11:31–40). There are also some pieces written for instruments alone, such as Kuhnau's six *Bible Story Sonatas* for keyboard (1700), in which biblical characters and themes are dramatically portrayed in music without words. The marriage of the Bible with music, ranging from the sublime (Allegri's *Miserere*) and the ceremonial (*Zadok the Priest* [1 Kgs. 1:38–40]) to the militaristic (*Mine eyes have seen the glory*) and the subversive (*The Margate Exodus*), is so much part of its reception history as to make it almost impossible to separate them.

Yet the Bible in music lags far behind the Bible in literature and the Bible in art. Two recent works by the American cantor Helen Leneman, *The Performed Bible: The Story of Ruth in Opera and Oratorio* (2007) and *Love, Lust, and Lunacy: The Stories of Saul and David in Music* (2010) are conspicuous exceptions, as are our own publications, J. F. A. Sawyer, *The Fifth Gospel: Isaiah in the History of Christianity* (1996), which has a chapter entitled "Isaiah in Literature and Music," and Siobhán Dowling Long, *The Sacrifice of Isaac: The Reception of a Biblical Story in Music* (2013). Several reference works now give some prominence to the Bible in music: J. F. A. Sawyer, *A Concise Dictionary of the Bible and Its Reception* (2009), the *Blackwell Companion to the Bible and Culture* (ed. Sawyer, 2006), the *Oxford Handbook of the Reception History of the Bible* (ed. Lieb et al., 2011), and the 30-volume *Encyclopaedia of the Bible and Its Reception* (ed. Allison et al., 2010–). The same is true of two new series of biblical commentaries: first, the Blackwell Bible Commentary series, of which 11 volumes have so far been published (www.bbibcomm.net), including the first volume of Susan Gillingham's Psalms commentary, where musical interpretations of the text are naturally prominent, and, second, the Eerdmans Illuminations series (https://illuminationscommentary.wordpress.com), of which the first part of C. L. Seow's Job commentary, already published, nicely demonstrates the exegetical value of music. But in all these, music is just one among many other contexts alongside art, literature, film, drama, politics, theology, and so on. There is nothing comparable, for example, to the very popular *Dictionary of Biblical Tradition in English Literature*, edited by D. L. Jeffrey (1992), or the more recent *Blackwell Companion to the Bible in English Literature* (2010).

It is the aim of the present volume to make a small contribution toward filling this gap and, for the first time, to do justice to the vast range and frequency of musical settings of biblical texts and texts inspired by the Bible, ancient and modern, Christian and Jewish, classical (e.g., oratorios and operas) and nonclassical (e.g., musicals, hymns, spirituals, pop, and rock). The material is arranged in such a way as to enable biblical scholars and other readers with an interest in the Bible to access as many musical uses and interpretations of the Bible as possible while at the same time providing, for the benefit of choirs, musicians, musicologists, lecturers, teachers, and students of music and religious education, a convenient reference tool covering the biblical, liturgical, and theological information that contributes to the appreciation of the music. For example, it will be a valuable resource for teachers of the Bible curriculum in U.S. public schools, as it contains entries on every reference to music in the textbook *The Bible and Its Influence* (2005) by Cullen Schippe and Chuck Stetson.

Alongside examples of classical music from the Middle Ages down to our own day, there is a deliberate emphasis on popular culture in the numerous entries on hymns, spirituals, musicals, film music, contemporary rock, and the like. Special attention has also been given to works by women composers, such as Camilla de Rossi and Elisabeth Jacquet de la Guerre, who have been neglected until quite recently, as well as to contemporary songwriters and performers, such as Sinead O'Connor and Debbie Friedman.

In the main part of the volume, musical works inspired by the Bible or containing interpretations of biblical texts are arranged alphabetically by title or first line. In some cases, titles are given in the original Latin (*Ave Maria*), German (*Ein fest' Burg*), French (*Quatuor pour la fin du temps*), Hebrew (*Hinne ma tov*), or the like, but English translations and cross-references to other entries are provided where appropriate. Oratorios (*Creation*), operas

(*Nabucco*), ballets (*Cain and Abel*), and the like are included, as are hymns ("Jesus Loves Me"), popular songs ("Turn Turn Turn"), and musicals (*Godspell*). Some significant collections, such as hymnbooks (*Olney Hymns*) and albums (*Wormwood*), are also covered. Obviously, readers will notice omissions, as it would clearly have been impossible, in one volume, to cover every piece of music that contains a reference to the Bible. We have had to be selective and decided to concentrate, first, on works that are often played or have been particularly influential in some way and, second, on those that are exegetically interesting, that is, musical works in which biblical themes or stories or personalities, some very familiar, others more obscure, have been given a particularly interesting interpretation.

Each entry contains essential information about the original context of each composition (date, composer, and so on) and, where relevant, its afterlife in literature, film, politics, liturgy, or the like. But the focus throughout is on the use and interpretation of the Bible, and to help readers locate musical interpretations of particular biblical texts and topics, there is an index of biblical references as well an index of biblical names. A chronology is provided at the beginning to give the reader some idea of what is to follow. While it doesn't contain every work listed in the dictionary, it picks out some key events, works, and publications and indicates their historical context. There is also a bibliography, a glossary of technical terms, and a list of artists, authors, and composers.

Finally, it may be worth pointing out that a printed book, however comprehensive and detailed, is not a substitute for the music itself, performed by a choir or an orchestra or a band or listened to on radio, a CD, or YouTube. Furthermore, scores of most of the oratorios and other choral works discussed can be accessed online at www3.cpdl.org/wiki/index.php or http://imslp.org/wiki/Category:Composers. We hope our dictionary will encourage people to discover and perform some less well known pieces and help them listen to familiar music with a fresh awareness of what it is about.

The Dictionary

Note: boldface text indicates relevant entries elsewhere in the dictionary.

1 CORINTHIANS 15:55. Song by American country music legend Johnny Cash from the posthumous album *American VI: Ain't No Grave* (2010). Based on a gentle country gospel melody, it is the last song written before his death from Parkinson's disease in 2003 and addresses the angel of death in the words of 1 Cor. 15:55: "Where O death, is thy victory? Where, O grave is thy sting?" (KJV) as he accepts his impending death and looks to the Resurrection.

23RD PSALM, THE. Work for male a cappella chorus by Bobby McFerrin from the album *Medicine Man* (1990). Dedicated to the songwriter's mother, feminine pronouns are substituted for the original masculine to portray an image of God as Mother, and the work concludes with a doxology. It has been performed by many choirs, including "Singing Quaker Women Plus Other Faithful Friends" at the Hyattsville Mennonite Church in Hyattsville, Maryland.

40. Song by U2 also known as "40 (How Long)" from the album *War* (1983). A paraphrase of Psalm 40:1–3 with the chorus "I will sing, sing a new song," based on verse 3, and "How long to sing this song," reputed to have been 40 minutes (10 to compose, 10 to record, 10 to mix, and 10 to perform). It closed every concert of the 1983 War Tour and featured the audience singing "How long to sing this song" to drum accompaniment by Larry Mullan Jr. after Bono and The Edge left the stage.

119TH PSALM OF THE KING AND PROPHET DAVID, THE. "THE SWANSONG." (*Königs und Propheten Davids hundert und neunzehnter Psalm. "Der Schwanengesang"*). A cycle of 13 motets in German for double chorus and basso continuo (1671) by Heinrich Schütz based on Psalm 119 (*SWV 482–492*) and concluding with a joyful rendition of Psalm 100, "Shout with joy to the Lord" (SWV 493) and the German **Magnificat** (*SWV* 494) (Lk. 1:46–49, 51–55). Psalm 119, the longest Psalm in the Psalter, is an alphabetic acrostic and was arranged by Schütz in 11 16-verse polychoral motets, each one entitled with two letters of the Hebrew alphabet. Each motet begins with an intonation and concludes with a setting of the lesser doxology. An extended setting of verse 54 in motet no. 4 ("Thy statutes have been my song in the house of my pilgrimage") was chosen by Schütz as a text for a funeral motet, later set to music by his student Christoph Bernard and performed at Schütz's funeral service.

• A •

A BOY WAS BORN. Choral variations for unaccompanied SATB chorus with boys' voices written by Benjamin Britten and dedicated to his father (op. 3, 1934; rev. 1955). The libretto comes from 10 poetic texts, mainly from the 15th and 16th centuries. Opening with a hymn-like theme "A Boy Was Born," it is followed by six variations, including "Lullay Jesu," based on a rocking figure of descending fifths sung initially by the two sopranos and later by other voices; "In the Bleak Midwinter" by Christina Rossetti, sung by the upper voices against the boys' choir singing the anonymous "Corpus Christi Carol"; and the Finale, an extended rondo that combines another anonymous carol "Noel Welcome Yule," with "Christmas" by Thomas Tusser, and "A Christmas Carol" by Francis Quarles.

A COVENANT OF WONDERS: THE GIVING AND RECEIVING OF THE TEN COMMANDMENTS. One-act music drama for narrator, soloists, and ensemble by Michael Isaacson to a libretto by Marcia Hain Engle (2002). Inspired by the biblical story of the Exodus, the **Ten Commandments**, and the Golden Calf, the work explores the emotional lives of the characters on their epic journey such as "Egyptian Chase," "We've Crossed the Red Sea," "Free Is Such a Scary Thing," "Make Us a Golden Calf," "Free Is Such an Awesome Thing," and "Free Is Such a Wondrous Thing." The audience participates in the drama by singing a song of thanksgiving, "To Reach This Day," learned in a preperformance rehearsal.

A HUNDRED POUNDS OF CLAY. Hit song (1961) by Kay Roger, Luther Dixon, and Bob Elgin, performed by American singer/songwriter Gene McDaniels. It sold over 1 million copies. Inspired by the account of the creation of man from clay (Gen. 2:7), the chorus suggests that God created woman not from the rib of man (Gen. 2:21–22) but from a hundred pounds of clay. The songwriter gives thanks to God for creating woman who has brought a "lot of lovin'" and has made life "worth livin'."

A NEW SONG. Anthem for SATB and organ by James MacMillan, commissioned by Nicholas Russell for the choir of St. Bride's Episcopal Church, Glasgow (1997). Based on verses from Psalm 96, it is divided into three sections, the last section featuring a majestic postlude for organ expressing the grandeur and majesty of God's reign on earth (v. 13).

A SAFE STRONGHOLD OUR GOD STILL IS. Hymn by Martin Luther. *See* EIN FEST' BURG IST UNSER GOTT.

A SERMON, A NARRATIVE AND A PRAYER. Cantata for two soloists (AT), speaker, chorus, and orchestra by Stravinsky, dedicated to Paul Sacher (1961). Inspired by the story of the stoning of St. Stephen, the first Christian martyr and deacon, and considered Stravinsky's New Testament equivalent to his Old Testament–inspired work **Threni**, it is noted for its serialism and use of canons. In three movements, the narrative of St. Stephen's trial and stoning (Acts 6:8–7:59) is framed by a sermon (Rom. 8:24; Heb. 11:1; 12:2) and a prayer by the Elizabethan writer Thomas Dekker (1570–1631), beginning with "Oh My God, if it be thy pleasure to cut me off before night" and ending with a mournful **Alleluia**.

A SPACEMAN CAME TRAVELLING. Christmas song inspired by Mt. 2:2–12 from the album *Spanish Train and Other Stories* by Chris de Burg (1976). The **Star of Bethlehem** is represented by the light of a spacecraft hovering over the stable and the Magi by an extraterrestrial being who sings a simple chorus that audiences generally sing in live performances and then carries the good news across the universe. In recent times, the song has been recorded by the German band Gregorian (2006) and in a live concert, "Believe," described as "Riverdance for the Voice" by the Irish group Celtic Woman (2011).

A VIRGIN UNSPOTTED. Christmas carol by William Billings adapted from a 16th-century traditional English carol set to a new tune, "Judah," and published in *The Singing Master's Assistant* (Boston, 1778). The verses are sung in the tempo of a "sprightly dance," and the refrain, scored in compound duple time, invites listeners to "be merry" and "put sorrow away."

ABENDLIED. ("Evening Song"). One of three hymns (*Drei Geistliche Gesänge*) for SSATTB a cappella chorus by Josef Rheinberger (op. 69, no. 3, 1873) based on the disciples' words to Jesus on the road to Emmaus (Lk. 24:29). Hauntingly beautiful with contrapuntal and homophonic textures, the diminuendo at the end signifies the fading light at the end of the day. It has been arranged as an instrumental for cello ensemble and saxophone sextet.

ABIDE WITH ME. Most famous hymn of the Scottish Anglican Henry Francis Lyte, published in *The Spirit of the Psalms* (1834) and usually sung to the tune *Eventide* by William H. Monk. It is based on Jesus' appearance to the two disciples at Emmaus (Lk. 24:29) but also alludes to Paul's teaching on the Resurrection (1 Cor. 15:55). Said to have been a favorite of King

George V and Mahatma Gandhi, it features in numerous films and popular music albums and is traditionally sung at funerals and various annual events, including the Football Association Cup Final at Wembley.

ABIMELECH. Oratorio in three acts by Samuel Arnold retelling the story of Gen. 20, where Abraham passed his wife off as his sister for fear of his life. It was first performed in the Theatre Royal in Haymarket, London, in 1768 and later in Covent Garden in 1772. The oratorio is set for the characters of Abraham, Sarah, King Abimelech, Chief Captain Phichol, Sarah's handmaiden Hagar, and the queen of Gerar, and the chorus sings the parts of officers, soldiers, and other attendants. It concludes with a duet celebrating the blissful union of Abraham and Sarah and a grand chorus with Phichol and the soldiers, who invite the faithful to proclaim love and peace.

ABRAHAM. Oratorio in two parts for SATB soloists, chorus, and orchestra by Bernhard Molique (op. 65, 1860), inspired by events in the life of Abraham as told in Gen. 12–22, including his call, the Promises, Sodom and Gomorrah, the expulsion of Hagar and Ishmael, and the sacrifice of Isaac. The text of the meditative airs and choruses sung by the narrator, Abraham, Isaac, God, Hagar, and the chorus is taken from Pss. 23, 46, 51, 98, 114, and 149 and other biblical texts, including, Deuteronomy, Job, Isaiah, Jeremiah, Lamentations, and Revelation.

ABRAHAM AND ISAAC. Canticle by Benjamin Britten (1952), based on a 15th-century Chester mystery play (Gen. 22) and later incorporated into the *Offertorium* of his **War Requiem**. Scored for two solo voices, tenor (Abraham) and alto (Isaac), and the combined voices of alto and tenor (God), it retells the biblical story (Gen. 22) in a series of dialogues and one dramatic internal monologue sung by Abraham. Listeners gain an imaginative insight into Isaac's character prior to and after the sacrifice as he pledges to become patriarch elect of Israel in the "Song of Obedience" at the end of the work. Britten employs a variety of musical rhetorical devices to sound paint the text, including rests to suggest fretting and sobbing, minor intervallic leaps to express pathos, and a contrasting use of major and minor tonalities to signify a character's change of mood. The entire composition revolves around the interval of the tritone (E-flat–A) to represent the horrific nature of the sacrificial act demanded by God.

ABRAHAM AND ISAAC. Sacred ballad for baritone and chamber orchestra by Stravinsky (1963), commissioned by the Israel Festival Committee and dedicated to the people of the state of Israel, where it premiered in 1963. With no knowledge of Hebrew, Stravinsky sought the assistance of Sir Isaiah Berlin (1909–1997), who transliterated the Hebrew text into phonetic Russian to enable the composer to grasp its natural accents, stresses, and pronunciation. Melismas, ululations, and reiterated notes in the melodic line evoke the sound of Jewish chant, and while there is no overt dramatization of the text, changes of tessitura and dynamic markings distinguish the biblical characters, most notably a high tessitura for God and the angel, whose speeches are characterized by the repeated note C sharp.

ABRAHAM AND ISAAC. Folk song from the album *Play Me Backwards* (1992), cowritten by Jewish American folk artist Joan Baez and producer/ songwriters Wally Wilson and Kenny Greenberg. Based on Gen. 22, the first stanza, sung a cappella and followed by a rhythmic berimbau accompaniment, captures Abraham's loneliness and the chilling atmosphere of the unfolding story. The song tells how the angels, whose tears fell from heaven, failed to comprehend the ritual killing of the "righteous boy," but concludes that Isaac's memory will shine on "this mountain high and never never fade away."

ABRAHAM: A CONCERTO FOR HOPE. Concerto for violin and orchestra by British composer Roxanna Panufnik, commissioned by the Savannah Music Group (Georgia, USA) and premiered in 2005. Based on the story of **Abraham and Isaac** (Gen. 22:1–19), it incorporates Roman Catholic plainsong, Anglican bell patterns, an Ashkenazi chant, a Shofar horn, Sufi drum patterns, and elements from the traditional Islamic call to prayer. Later adapted as a short orchestral prelude entitled "Three Paths to Peace," it was performed by the World Orchestra for Peace in Jerusalem in 2008.

ABRAHAM JOURNEYED TO A NEW COUNTRY. A hymn, sung to the tune "Bunessan" (**"Morning Has Broken"**), written for immigrants by Carolyn Winfrey Gillette. It is inspired by words from Gen. 12; Ruth; Mt. 2:13–16; 10:40; 25:31–46; Heb. 11:13–19; and Lev. 19:18, 33–34.

ABRAHAM'S DAUGHTER. Sound track for blockbuster teen movie *The Hunger Games* by Arcade (2012). The story of the **sacrifice of Isaac** (Gen. 22) is told from the perspective of Abraham's daughter, a nonbiblical character invented by the songwriter, who secretly followed her father and brother up a "lonesome hill" and raised her bow in an attempt to save Isaac's life. In binary form (AB), the chilling narration, sung by a plaintive female voice and scored mostly in crotchets in the A section, expresses the horror of the story.

ABRAM IN EGYPT. Cantata for baritone solo, chorus, and orchestra by American composer Elinor Remick Warren, commissioned by Chicago baritone and music patron Louis Sudler and premiered in its orchestral form at the Los Angeles Music Festival on 7 June 1961. Cast in a neoromantic style, the composer compiled the libretto from texts from the Bible (Gen. 12:10–17; 13:14) and the Dead Sea Scrolls (Gen. Apocryphon 19–20). The story of Sarah's abduction by Pharaoh Zoan, king of Egypt, is told in the first person by Abram (Bar), as in the Dead Sea Scrolls text, and narrated by the chorus who sings Pharaoh's words to Abram.

ABRAMO ED ISACCO. ("Abraham and Isaac"). Oratorio *volgare* by Josef Mysliveček (1776), misattributed for a time by musicologists to Mozart despite the fact that Mozart himself attended a performance in Munich and told his father in a letter that "all Munich" was talking about it. The libretto, known throughout the Holy Roman Empire and beyond as *Isacco figura del Redentore* ("Isaac figure of the Redeemer"), is by the renowned Habsburg court poet Pietro Metastasio. As well as numerous biblical references (e.g., Gen. 12:1–3; 15:4–18; 17:1–8; 22:1–18; Lam. 1:1–2, 17; 5:15; Prov. 1:7; Jn. 8:56; 14:1, 18, 27–28; 20:26; Heb. 6:13, 17), Metastasio included references to the church fathers and in the spirit of the Counter-Reformation interpreted Gen. 22 typologically. Thus, Isaac is a type of Christ, Sarah a type of Mary, Abraham a type of God the Father, Isaac's friend Gamari a type of John, the beloved disciple, the shepherd's types of the other disciples, and the Abrahamic family as a whole a type of the Holy Family, who consented to the sacrifice but did not want the beloved son to die. Sarah plays a pivotal role by re-enacting, like Mary (Lk. 2:35), the details of the sacrifice in her imagination. Composed in the *style gallant*, the entire oratorio is set in the major tonality to highlight the fulfillment of the Old Testament in the New, with the exception of two passages expressing the emotional pain of Abraham and Sarah. The beginning and the end of the oratorio are set in C major to symbolize Christ as the Alpha and the Omega (Rev. 1:8; 21:6; 22:13). *See also* ABRAHAM AND ISAAC; SACRIFICE OF ISAAC; SACRIFICIUM ABRAHAE.

ABSALOM FILI MI. ("Absalom My Son"). Motet for four voices (SSAT) attributed to Josquin des Prez although ascribed to Pierre de la Rue, commemorating the death of Giovanni Borgia, son of Pope Alexander VI (1497). Inspired by David's lament for his son Absalom (2 Sam. 18:33) and texts from Job and Genesis, it is scored in imitative counterpoint with repetitions and melismas on "Absalom fili mi," punctuated by *quis det ut moriar pro te* ("would that I could die for you") with melismas on *pro te*. David's lamentations are compared to those of Job (*non vivam ultra* ["let me live no longer"]) (Job 7:16) and Jacob (*sed descendam in infernum plorans* ["but I shall descend into hell, weeping"]) (Gen. 37:35), with descending melismas on *descendam* and *infernum*. There is also a cantata by Heinrich Schütz based on this text, published in *Symphonae sacrae* 1 (SWV 269, 1629).

AC-CENT-TCHU-ATE THE POSITIVE. Song composed by Harold Arlen to lyrics by Johnny Mercer and first performed in 1944 by Mercer with the Pied Pipers and Paul Weston's orchestra. It was inspired by the stories of Jonah (Jonah) and Noah (Gen. 6:11–14), interpreted as characters who accentuated the positive during times of adversity. Subsequent performances include those by Bing Crosby and the Andrews Sisters, Dolly Mitchell, Artie Shaw, Johnny Green and Connie Francis, Perry Como, Ella Fitzgerald, Aretha Franklin, and, more recently, Paul McCartney on the album *Kisses on the Bottom* (2012). It has appeared in the movies *Here Come the Waves* (1944) starring Bing Crosby, *Bugsy* (1991), and *The Mighty Ducks* (1992).

ACHTLIEDERBUCH. ("Hymnal of Eight"). Oldest Lutheran hymnal compiled and published by Jobst Gutknecht in Nuremberg (Wittenburg, 1524), it comprises eight hymns, four of which were composed by Luther, three by Paul Speratus, and one by an unnamed composer (later attributed to Justus Jonas). Hymns written by Luther are *Nun Freut euch, lieben Christen g'mein* ("Dear Christians, Let us Now Rejoice") (Rom. 7:7–24), *Ach Gott, vom Himmel sieh darein* ("Oh God, look down from heaven") (Ps. 12), *Es spricht der Unweisen Mund* ("Although the fools Say with their Mouth") (Ps. 14), and *Aus Tiefer Not schrei ich zu dir* ("From deep affliction I cry out to you") (Ps. 130).

ACHTUNG BABY. Seventh studio album by U2 published in 1992. Songs with allusions to biblical themes include "The Fly" (Lk. 10:18), "**Until the End of the World**," and "She Moves in Mysterious Ways," which is accompanied by a video showing distorted images of Bono and a Moroccan belly dancer, referring to Salome's dance before Herod (Mk. 6:21–29; Mt. 14:6–11).

ACTES OF THE APOSTLES, THE. Fourteen songs in four parts (1553) based on Acts 1–14. It is the only published work of Christopher Tye and dedicated to King Edward VI. Sung in the manner of a hymn to lute accompaniment, it was intended for performance at home rather than at church. The music of two compositions derives from it: the a cappella anthem "O come ye servants of the Lord" (Acts 4) and the hymn tune "Winchester Old," similar to the Christmas carol "**While shepherds watched their flocks by night**," published in Este's Psalter *The Whole Book of Psalmes* (1592).

ADAM AND EVE. Reggae song by Rastafarian Bob Marley from the album *The Very Best of Bob Marley: 25 Classic Songs* (2011). Inspired by the story of Adam and Eve from Gen. 3:1–6, it identifies the woman as the root of all evil and blames her for humanity's sinfulness.

ADAM AND EVIL. Song from the musical film and comedy *Spinout* (1966), later recorded on an album with the same name, sung by Elvis Presley to words and music by Fred Wise and Randy Starr. Based on Gen. 3, the music sets the mood with a drum roll ("every time you kiss me, my heart pounds like a drum"), followed by a saxophone melody evoking the sound and image of an oriental snake charmer, though there's no explicit mention of the serpent. The song portrays Eve as the temptress, called "Evil" and the "Devil," and Adam as too ready to give in to her.

ADAM LAY Y BOUNDEN. An anonymous 15th-century English carol in four verses portraying Adam in limbo for 4,000 years for "an apple that he took" (Gen. 3) and humanity's redemption, which would not have been possible if it had not been for the apple. The final verse is a call to thank God for that blessed sin (Thomas Aquinas's *felix culpa*). It became popular in England after a setting by Boris Ord was performed at the Festival of Nine Lessons and Carols in King's College Chapel, Cambridge. Other notable settings include those by Peter Warlock, John Ireland, and Benjamin Britten as "Deo Gracias" in his **Ceremony of Carols**.

ADAM RAISED A CAIN. Song by Bruce Springsteen from the album *Darkness on the Edge of Town* (1978), digitally remastered as part of a boxed set in 2010. A play on the words "Cain" and "cane" in the song's title and the chorus suggests that Cain suffered corporal punishment at his father's hands and was a victim of violent outbursts of rage. The song points to this experience, along with Adam's absence from home because of heavy work commitments (Gen. 3:17), as possible explanations of Cain's subsequent murder of his brother Abel (Gen. 4:8). Springsteen's emotive rock-and-roll performance highlights the violence of Cain's childhood and perhaps also of his own.

ADAM'S RIB. Fanfare for brass quintet (1995) by Scottish composer James MacMillan, commissioned for the ceremonial opening of the first session of the modern Scottish Parliament in 1999. The title draws an analogy between the story of the woman's creation from Adam's rib (Gen. 2:21–23) and the rebirth of the Scottish Parliament out of the British Parliament in Westminster. Based on a melodic fragment from his opera *The Confession of Isobel Gowdie* (1990), the fanfare begins quietly from low pedal tones on the tuba to signify God's creative act (Gen. 2:21) and gradually crescendos with a fanfare to announce the birth of the woman (Gen. 2:22–23). The piece ends in the same quiet manner as it began, this time with a barely audible melody played on a muted trumpet. A song by the same title was written by English folk artist Ian Campbell and performed by the Ian Campbell Folk Group and the songwriter's sister, Lorna Campbell, on the album *Adam's Rib* (1976). It was also the title of a movie (1949) starring Spencer Tracy and Katharine Hepburn with music by Miklós Rózsa and Cole Porter.

ADESTE FIDELES. Well-known Latin Christmas carol, attributed to John Francis Wade, first published in his *Cantus Diversi pro Dominicis et Festis* (1751), and translated into English by Frederick Oakeley as "O Come All Ye Faithful" (1841). It celebrates the Incarnation as much as the Nativity with references to the Nicene Creed and the "Word made flesh" (Jn. 1:14) as well as the angel's chorus (Lk. 2:14).

AFRICA UNITE. Song by reggae singer/songwriter Bob Marley from the album *Survival* (1979) performed by Marley and the Wailers. It is inspired by Ps. 133 and calls for the unification of Africa ("How good and pleasant it would be before God and man, yeah, to see the unification of all Africans!") and Africa's liberation from the control of Babylon (Western governments) and a return to Zion (a united Africa). *See also* HINNE MA TOV.

AGAR ET ISMAELE ESILIATI. ("Hagar and Ishmael in Exile"). Oratorio in two parts for five soloists (SSSAB), mixed chorus, string orchestra, and continuo by Alessandro Scarlatti (1683). Based on a libretto adapted by Giuseppe Domenico de Totis, it retells the story of the banishment of Hagar and Ishmael by Abraham and Sarah (Gen. 21). Operatic in form and style, it comprises duets, a trio, recitatives semplice, and arias that focus on interactions between the four characters along with the angel who intervenes to save the lives of Hagar and Ishmael in the desert. *See also* HAGAR IN THE WILDERNESS; HAGAR'S LAMENT.

AGNUS DEI. ("Lamb of God"). There are numerous musical settings of this prayer from the Mass Ordinary in plainchant, polyphony, and settings by composers from every period in the history of music. The text comes from Jn. 1:29, where it is addressed to Jesus by John the Baptist. One of the best-known settings is that of Samuel Barber for eight-part a cappella chorus (1967), originally the second movement of his highly successful String Quartet op. 11 (1936) and described as the saddest music ever composed (BBC Radio 4 online survey, 2007). The arch form of the composition, with its melodic chant rising in stepwise movement to an impassioned fortissimo climax, is made all the more dramatic by a silence that follows, surely denoting the sacrificial death of Christ the Lamb, while the prayer for mercy **Dona Nobis Pacem** ("Grant Us Peace") seemingly fades away to another realm. It features in a number of movies dealing with the themes of war, sacrifice, suffering, and death, including *The Elephant Man* (1980), *El Norte* (1983), *Platoon* (1986), *Lorenzo's Oil* (1992), *Les Roseaux sauvages* (1994), *Crime of the Century* (1996), *Amélie* (2001), and *S1mOne* (2002). It accompanied the radio announcement of the death of President Roosevelt (1945) and has been played at numerous funeral services of dignitaries and royalty and memorial services, most notably those commemorating the victims of 9/11. *See also* CHRISTE, DU LAMM GOTTES; LAMB OF GOD, THE.

AGNUS DEI. ("Lamb of God"). Mass setting for 60 individual voice parts by Alessandro Striggio. The voices enter one by one in imitative counterpoint and form an impressive climax with all 60 voices singing together for the remainder of the work. Grouped together in five separate choirs, the surround-sound effect appeals to Christ the Lamb of God for mercy (Jn. 1:29). It was influenced by Striggio's 40-part motet *Ecce beatam lucem* (1566) and features as the largest-known polyphonic work of the Renaissance.

AGNUS DEI. ("Lamb of God"). The fifth movement of Fauré's Requiem in D Minor for chorus, soloists, orchestra, and organ (op. 48, 1887–1890). It begins with an orchestral introduction in F major, featuring a delightful theme in triple meter played by the violas. The *Agnus Dei* is repeated three times, by the tenors, the chorus (sung with greater intensity and dynamic contrast), and the tenors again, with a recurrence of the viola theme this time on the organ. The reference to *Dona eis requiem* ("Give them rest") is surely a reference to Fauré's parents, who died in 1885 and 1886 shortly before the composition of the requiem.

AGNUS DEI. ("Lamb of God"). The final movement of Mozart's unfinished Requiem in D Minor (K. 626) written by Mozart's friend and student Franz Xavier Süssmayr after the composer's death. It is not known whether Mozart left instructions or sketches for him to work on. Scored in triple meter, there is a marked contrast between the *Agnus Dei qui tollis peccata mundi* ("Lamb of God who takes away the sins of the world"), sung fortissimo and in homophony, and the sublime prayer of supplication *dona eis requiem* ("give them rest"). The *Agnus Dei* is accompanied by the funereal sound of the timpani and woodwind punctuating every phrase in the first rendition and the strings' foreboding melody in all three repetitions, while *Dona eis pacem*, introduced first by the basses, then sopranos, and finally the basses, is sung pianissimo and accompanied by the heavenly sound of strings. Carl Czerny composed a four-hand piano accompaniment for this setting.

AHAB. Oratorio for six soloists, chorus, and orchestra by George Benjamin Arnold to a libretto by F. H. Arnold, first performed by the National Choral Society, Exeter Hall, London, in 1864. Based on the story of Elijah and Naboth's vineyard, the death of **Jezebel**, and the defeat of Ahab at Ramoth Gilead (1 Kgs. 21–22), the words sung by the various characters and the chorus representing "Believers," the Elders, and the People, are taken from the Psalms; Exod. 15:11; Lev. 25:23; 1 Chron. 16:11, 12, 14, 26–29, 36; 2 Chron. 6:30; Job 7:1, 9; 34:15; Song of Solomon (Cant. 3:1–4); Lam. 5:19; Ezek. 46:18; and Ecclesiasticus (Sir. 34:13, 16, 17). There are instrumental quintets, including an overture at the beginning of part 1, an instrumental introduction in part 2, and a "War March" before the battle.

ALABASTER BOX. Gospel song and album, written by Janice Sjostrand and performed by award-winning gospel singer CeCe Winans (1999). Inspired by the story in Matthew's Gospel (Mt. 26:6–13), the chorus and second stanza are sung in first-person narration by the believer, who, like Mary, pours her praise on Christ like oil "from Mary's alabaster box."

ALEXANDER BALUS. Oratorio in three acts for soloists, chorus, and orchestra by Handel, with a libretto by Thomas Morell (HWV 65, 1747). Based on 1 Macc. 10–11, it tells the story of the involvement of High Priest Jonathan the Maccabee, chief of the Jews, in the wars between Alexander Balus, King of Syria (Mez), and Ptolomee, king of Egypt (B). Act 2 ends with Alexander's wedding to the Egyptian king's daughter Cleopatra (S), comprising a duet sung by the newlyweds ("Hail Wedded Love") and two Wedding Choruses ("Triumph, Hymen, in the Pair" [added 1754] and "Hymen, Fair Urania's Son"). Act 3 turns to Ptolomee's devious attempt to acquire Alexander's kingdom and the abduction of Cleopatra by some ruffians during her aria "Here amid the shady woods." When news of the war between Alexander and Ptolomee and their subsequent deaths reaches Cleopatra, she sings a moving lament in the *accompagnato* "Calm thou my Soul" and the air "Convey me to some peaceful shore." The work concludes with an upbeat chorus sung by Jonathan and a chorus of Israelites praising God with exuberant **alleluias** and **amens**.

ALL ALONG THE WATCHTOWER. Song by Bob Dylan from the album *John Wesley Harding* (1967), inspired by Isaiah's mysterious vision of the "wilderness of the sea" (Isa. 21:1–9) and described as "the first biblical rock album." Written while Dylan was convalescing after a motorcycle accident, it was later famously covered by Jimi Hendrix on the album *Electric Ladyland* (1968), which replaced Dylan's original as the definitive version.

ALL CREATURES OF OUR GOD AND KING. English version by W. H. Draper of St. Francis's "Canticle of the Creatures," known also as "The Canticle of Brother Sun," inspired by Ps. 148 and composed shortly before his death in 1226. Sung to the German hymn tune *Lasst uns erfreuen* (1623), it first appeared in the *Public School Hymn Book* (1919), later harmonized by Vaughan Williams in the **English Hymnal** (rev. ed. 1933).

ALL GLORY, LAUD AND HONOR. Processional hymn celebrating Christ's triumphant entry into Jerusalem (Mt. 21:9), originally written in Latin (*Gloria, laus et honor*) by the ninth-century bishop of Orleans, St. Theodulph, and translated into English by John Mason Neale. Sung to the tune *Valet will ich dir geben* by Melchior Teschner (1613), it features in two chorale preludes by Bach (BWV 735 and BWV 736) as well as in his Cantata no. 3, *Christus, der ist mein Leben* (BWV 95), and the **St. John Passion**.

ALL MY HOPE ON GOD IS FOUNDED. Well-known hymn originally written in German by Joachim Neander (1680) and sung to the chorale tune *Meine Hoffnung* ("My hope") and later translated into English by Robert Bridges (1899). It was set to the tune *Michael* written by Herbert Howells in memory of his son and first performed in the chapel at Charterhouse school (1930). First published in *The Clarendon Hymn Book* (1936), it gained popularity following its inclusion in the Church of England's "100 Hymns for Today" supplement to **Hymns Ancient and Modern** (1969) and the Methodist hymnal *Hymns and Psalms* (1983). It was arranged with descant for mixed choir and congregation with organ accompaniment by John Rutter (1980).

ALL PEOPLE CLAP YOUR HANDS. Anthem for five-part chorus (SAATB) by Thomas Weelkes based on Ps. 47. Verse 5 is sung to an ascending melody line (**"God is gone up"**), and an ascending and descending leap of a perfect fourth/fifth depicts the sound of the trumpet (Ps. 47:5). The work ends with a seven-measure **Amen**. In recent times, this text has been set as a rap with parts for horn by Christian music artist Timothy Smith.

ALL THINGS BRIGHT AND BEAUTIFUL. Anglican hymn written by Christina Rossetti, first published in *Hymns for Little Children* (1848) to the 17th-century melody "Royal Oak," adapted by Martin Shaw, and to a more popular tune by William Henry Monk. The song, based on the second article of the Apostles' Creed, "God the Father maker of heaven and earth," is inspired by the creation story from Gen. 1:1–2:3. In recent times, a version by John Rutter for mixed voices (SATB) and piano accompaniment has been popularized by British choirboy Thomas Gesty (BBC Radio 2 Choirboy of the Year in 2004) and Libera on the album *Angel Voices 2* (1996).

ALL WOMEN ARE BAD. Song by the Cramps from the albums *Bad Music for Bad People* (1984) and *Stay Sick!* (1990). Based on the stories of **Adam and Eve** (Gen. 3) and **Samson and Delilah** (Judg. 16), each verse imagines a dialogue in which the woman's ulterior motive is followed by her partner's derisive response. The chorus, sung first by Adam and then by Samson, describes all women as "bad," as a type of devil with "groovy wiggly tails" and "horns on their heads" and as "a wolf dressed up like sheep."

ALL YOU ZOMBIES. Song written by Rob Hyman and Eric Bazilian from the Hooters, originally released as a single and included on their albums *Amore* (1983) and *Nervous Night* (1985). Based on the stories of Noah's Ark (Gen. 6–7), Moses before Pharaoh (Exod. 4:27–6:11), the Golden Calf, and Moses breaking the Tablets of the Law (Exod. 32), the catchy chorus condemns all idol worshippers, including Egyptians, Israelites, the people who derided Noah, and unbelievers today. Written in D minor, the blend of ska, reggae, and rock and roll produces a haunting, almost hypnotic effect that stays in listeners' memories long after the performance.

ALLELUIA. Motet composed in 1940 for SATB a cappella chorus by Randall Thompson that became one of the most popular choral compositions in the United States. It was commissioned by Serge Koussevitzky, director of the Tanglewood Festival, who requested a choral "fanfare" for the opening of the new Berkshire Music Centre. But with the outbreak of World War II, Thompson felt it was inappropriate to compose joyful and triumphant music, and the subdued mood and slow tempo of this hauntingly beautiful setting were inspired by Job 1:21. Apart from a final **Amen**, the six-minute setting is based entirely on the word *Alleluia* (cf. Rev. 19:1, 3–6), its four syllables stressed through a variety of devices combining rhythmic emphasis, melodic interest, and vocal part arrangement. In 2012, another American composer, Eric Whitacre, composed a nine-minute Alleluia for SATB a cappella chorus on the album *Water Night*. *See also* HALLELUJAH.

ALSO HAT GOTT DIE WELT GELIEBT. ("God So Loved the World"). Cantata by J. S. Bach composed for the second day of Pentecost on 21 May 1725 (BWV 68). The libretto, inspired by the Epistle and Gospel readings for the day (Acts 10:42–48; Jn. 3:16–21), is by the poet Christiana Mariana von Ziegler. Scored for SATB chorus, soprano and bass soloists, and orchestra and continuo, the work is in five movements, beginning unusually with the first stanza of a hymn and concluding with a magnificent chorus, a double fugue, on two contrasting themes: "He who believes will not be judged" and "Who does not believe is already judged."

AMAHL AND THE NIGHT VISITORS. Christmas opera for children in one act by Gian Carlo Menotti (1951), commissioned by NBC and first performed by the NBC Opera Theatre on 24 December 1951. Inspired by the story of the Adoration of the Magi (Mt. 2:1–12), it tells of their stopover at the home of Amahl, a shepherd boy (Tr), and his widowed mother (S) ("Have you seen a child?"). Later, when the **three kings** are asleep, Amahl's mother attempts to steal the gold ("All that gold") but is intercepted by the kings, who tell her the king they are seeking does not need gold but will establish a kingdom based on love ("O woman, you may keep the gold"). When Amahl offers his crutch as a gift for the Christ child, his crippled legs are miraculously healed ("I walk Mother"), and the work concludes with Amahl leaving with the kings to visit the Christ child in Bethlehem.

AMAZING GRACE. The most famous of John Newton's compositions, published in **Olney Hymns** (1779) and popularized in a Mahalia Jackson version (1947); several films, including *Alice's Restaurant* (1969); and an arrangement for bagpipes. It is based on 1 Chron. 17:16–17 with allusions to Lk. 15:24 and Jn. 9:25.

AMEN. Song based on the spiritual of the same name, arranged by African American singer, songwriter, actor, and choral director Jester Hairston for the film *Lilies of the Field* (1963). The song telling of the life of Jesus is sung by a soloist alongside a chorus singing the ever-popular Amens from the spiritual. It was a hit for the Impressions in 1963.

AMNON UND TAMAR. Chamber opera in one act by Israeli composer Josef Tal for mezzo-soprano (Tamar), tenor (Amnon), bass-baritone (Absalom), bass (Jonadab), male chorus (Slaves and Shepherds), and orchestra, premiered in Jerusalem in 1961. Based on 2 Sam. 13, the libretto is by Recha Freier, translated into English by Rahel Vernon. The work was inspired by Professor Hermann Scherchen, who asked the composer to compose a short opera, not exceeding 20 minutes, for four soloists, a small chorus, and an orchestra limited to 15 players. Unlike Tal's earlier avant-garde electronic and atonal operas, this one ends in a typically dramatic fashion with the death of Amnon.

AND ONE OF THE PHARISEES. Work for three a cappella voices or three-part choir by Arvo Pärt (1992), based on the story of Simon the Pharisee (Lk. 7:36–50). Singing in the manner of Gregorian chant, the biblical narrator (CtTB) introduces the dialogue between Simon (Ct) and Jesus (T). Dissonances prevail throughout, in particular in the internal monologue of those sitting at the table (CtTB) saying, "Who is this that forgiveth sins also?," and the work ends with a unison chant, "Thy faith hath saved thee; go in peace."

AND WHEN THE BUILDERS. Anthem for mixed choir and organ by Edmund Rubbra, dedicated to the provost and fellows of Worcester College, Oxford, on the occasion of its 250th anniversary (1964). Inspired by Ezra 3:10–13, a sustained pedal note in the organ accompaniment suggests the foundation of the Second Temple in Jerusalem, trumpets and cymbals represent the celebrations of the priests and Levites, and the choir sings in unison, "praising and giving thanks to the Lord . . . because the foundations of the house of the Lord were laid." The work concludes with a lament in which soprano and alto voices sing "aah" to represent the cries of those who remembered the first Temple, but these are concealed by tenors and basses representing the people who "shout aloud with joy."

ANGELUS AD VIRGINEM. ("The Angel to the Virgin," also known as "Gabriel from Heven-King/Sent to the Maide Sweete"). Medieval song of French or English origin that enjoyed widespread popularity in the Middle Ages. It is sung by Nicholas to the accompaniment of a psaltery in Chaucer's *The Miller's Tale*. A version in three-part *fauxbourdon* is preserved in the "Dublin Troper" manuscript (1361) in Christ Church Cathedral, Dublin. It begins with a dialogue between the Virgin Mary and the angel Gabriel (vv. 1–3) and then looks forward to Christ's crucifixion (v. 4) and the salvation of humanity (v. 5). It was arranged as a cheerful Advent carol for choir and organ by David Willcocks.

ANTIKRIST. Mystery opera in two acts by Rued Langgaard (BVN 170, 1921–1923; rev. 1926–1930). Subtitled "Church Opera" and "Judgement Day Scenes," the work is based on verses from the Letters of John (1 Jn. 2:18, 4:2; 2 Jn. 7) and the image of the Antichrist in Rev. 13. The language of the opera, set "in the time around World War I," is obscure to express the uncertain, decadent mood of the Antichrist period, and the musical style was influenced by Wagner, Strauss, Schoenberg, and Korngold. The five names for Christ corresponding to five names for the Antichrist appear together on the score at the beginning of the relevant scene, each supported by biblical quotations. Scene 6 features the destruction of the Antichrist and ends with the moral: "Only God has the power to give man peace, harmony and insight."

APOCALISSE. ("Apocalypse"). Symphonic poem for orchestra by Gian Carlo Menotti (1951–1952) commissioned by the conductor Victor de Sabata. A synthesis of the vast corpus of Jewish and Christian writing on the Apocalypse, it is in three movements. Movement 1, *Improperia*, features a trumpet fanfare repeated throughout the movement to represent the seven trumpets sounded by the seven angels (Rev. 8–11). The title comes from the **Reproaches** (*improperia*) in the Good Friday liturgy. Movement 2, *La città celeste*, is based on a recurring circular musical theme suggesting "the celestial city" suspended in midair (Rev. 21). Movement 3, *Gli angeli militanti* ("The angels of war"), repeats the trumpet fanfares from movement 1 and celebrates the victory of the triumphant angels in their war against Satan (Rev. 12:7–9).

APOCALYPSE, THE. Dramatic oratorio composed by Paola Gallico in the aftermath of World War I (1920) to texts in English taken from Daniel and Revelation and arranged by Pauline Arnoux MacArthur and Henri Pierre Roché. The prologue, **"Belshazzar's Feast,"** features a bacchanal dance for male voices, scored in triple meter and featuring trills in the upper registers of instruments, and soloists representing the spirits of Drunkenness, Gluttony, and Idolatry. It ends with the chorus singing in homophony the mysterious words written on the wall: "Mene, Mene, Tekel, Upharsin" (Dan. 5:25). Part 1 describes war since the murder of Abel by Cain (Gen. 4:8) and despite the cries of the chorus for peace (Lk. 2:14), and a lone soprano voice ("Where is the good will of men?"), the seven bowls of God's wrath (Rev. 16:1–26), and the gathering of the multitude in Armageddon (Rev. 16:16). In part 2, the role of "Babylon . . . mother of harlots and of earth's abominations" (Rev. 17:1–6) is sung by a soprano in first-person narration. The final movement, "The Millennium," is composed of many well-known texts about the Second Coming of Christ, including "And I saw a new heaven and a new earth" (Rev. 21:1), sung by a heavenly chorus of boys, a tenor solo with descending quintuplets in the accompaniment to paint the movement of "the water of life" (Rev. 22:1, 17), and a choral fugue proclaiming the joyful news of the reign of the Lord God omnipotent (Rev. 19:6, KJV). The work concludes with a blessing sung by the baritone ("The grace of our Lord Jesus be with you all") and a choral **Amen** (Rev. 22:21; also 2 Thess. 3:18; Rom. 16:24; Phil. 4:23).

APOSTLES, THE. Oratorio in two parts by Elgar, scored for six soloists, double chorus, orchestra, and organ, with the addition of a shofar or flugelhorn (op. 49, 1903), first performed on 14 October 1903 at the Birmingham Triennial Festival. Based on biblical texts selected and arranged by Elgar and built around a number of recurring leitmotifs, such as "Christ the Man of Sorrows," it tells the story of Jesus' ministry, passion, death, resurrection, and ascension from the perspective of the apostles, including Peter (B), Judas (B), and Mary Magdalene (A), identified as the woman who anointed Jesus' feet with her tears (Lk. 7:36–50). After a prologue based on Isa. 61:1–3 (cf. Lk. 4:18), the first section, "The Calling of the Apostles," begins at night with "The Voice of thy Watchmen" (Isa. 52:9), an aria sung by the angel Gabriel (S), and "The Dawn" is heralded by a rising sixth on the shofar and the chorus "Morning Psalm (within the Temple)" (Ps. 92:1–12) to the accompaniment of traditional Hebrew melodies. In the second section, "By the Wayside," Jesus (Bar) intones the **Beatitudes** (Mt. 5:3–12) with comments from Peter, John, Judas, Mary Magdalene, the Virgin Mary, and the chorus. Section 3, "By the Sea of Galilee," tells of Mary Magdalene's conversion and the miracle of Jesus walking on water, ending in Caesarea Philippi with Jesus' words to Peter "Thou art Peter and upon this rock I will build my Church" (Mt. 16:13–20) and an aria by Mary Magdalene, "Thy face O Lord, will I seek" (Ps. 27:8). Part 2 begins with 4, "The Betrayal of Jesus," focusing on Judas and Peter and ending with the chorus "He went out and wept bitterly"; 5, "Golgotha," depicts the scene of the Crucifixion, followed by 6, "At the Sepulchre," in which a narrator tells the story of the Resurrection; and finally, 7, "The Ascension," is scored for the full forces of soloists, chorus, and orchestra.

AQUARIUS. Opera in two acts and eight languages for 16 soloists (eight sopranos and eight baritones), orchestra, and ballet dancers by Karel Goeyvaerts (1983–1992). Inspired by a number of sources, including Rev. 21–22, it was regarded by the composer as "a drama of society, which traces humanity's search for a more harmonious society in the Age of Aquarius." In the final scene, this search leads to the Holy City, a place of peace and radiant harmony.

ARIEL: VISIONS OF ISAIAH. Cantata in six movements for soprano, baritone, chorus, and orchestra by Robert Starer (1959). The words are from the Book of Isaiah, beginning with his prophecies of judgment on sinful Jerusalem ("Woe to Ariel") (Isa. 29:1–4; 1:4, 7) and the wantonness of "The Daughters of Zion" (Isa. 3:16–24), described in a flighty scherzo (movement 3). In the fourth movement, the male-voice chorus "Fear and the Pit, and the Snare" (Isa. 24:17) is followed by a soprano lament (Isa. 22:4–5) and the chorus singing in upbeat fashion, "Let us eat and drink; for tomorrow we shall die" (Isa. 22:13). The fifth movement for small-chorus a cappella is meditative, beginning, "The Lord shall give thee rest" (Isa. 14:3), and ending in unison, "The Lord will wipe away tears from all faces" (Isa. 25:8). The final movement for orchestra and chorus ("Break forth into joy") (Isa. 52:9) celebrates the restoration of Jerusalem ("Awake, awake, stand up O Jerusalem") (Isa. 51:17) and concludes with the words "Let us walk in the light of the Lord" (Isa. 2:5). Special effects include the chorus whispering, "and their speech shall whisper out of the dust" (Isa. 29:4), and the baritone's announcement in *Sprechstimme*, "Behold joy and gladness, eating flesh and drinking wine" (Isa. 29:15). Other musical interpretations of the Book of Isaiah include the oratorio *Das Gesicht Jesajas* ("The Face of Isaiah") by Willy Burkhard (1936). *See* ISAIAH'S PROPHECY

ASCENSION ORATORIO, THE. (*Himmelfahrts-Oratorium/Lobet Gott in seinen Reichen*). Oratorio (1735) in two parts for SATB soloists, SATB chorus, orchestra, and continuo by J. S. Bach (BWV 11), first performed in Leipzig at the Feast of the Ascension in 1735. By an unknown librettist inspired by the readings for the day (Acts 1:1–11; Mk. 16:14–20), the work contrasts Christ's Ascension into heaven with the intense suffering and loss of three unnamed characters living on earth (SAB). A tenor voice narrates text based on Mk. 16:19, Lk. 24:50–2, and Acts 1:9–12 in recitative secco, while the alto aria *Ach bleibe doch, mein liebstes Leben* ("Ah stay, my dearest life"), which uses almost the same music as the **Agnus Dei** in Bach's B Minor Mass, imagines the words and sentiments of Mary Magdalene. The juxtaposition of ascending and descending motifs contrasts the joyful ascension (*Wenn soll es doch geschehen* ["When shall it happen"]) with the sorrowful lamentations of Christ's followers (*Ach, Jesu, ist dein Abschied* ["Ah Jesus, is your farewell so near"]). The soprano's aria in G major at the end, *Jesu, deine Gnadenblicke* ("Jesus, your merciful gaze"), illustrates musically Christ's departure from the earth through the absence of a continuo part, symbolizing the earth, and the high tessitura of flutes, oboes, and strings, symbolizing the heavens. There are two chorales based on Ascension hymns: *Nun lieget alles unter dir* ("Now everything is subject to you") from the fourth verse of *Du Lebensfürst,*

Herr Jesu Christ ("Lord Jesus Christ, you prince of life") by Johann Rist (1641) and *Wenn soll es doch geschehen* ("When shall it happen?") based on the seventh verse of the hymn *Gott fähret auf den Himmel* ("God ascends into heaven") by Gottfried Wilhelm Sacer (1697), which provides the triumphant finale of the oratorio.

ASCRIBE UNTO THE LORD. Verse anthem by Samuel Sebastian Wesley, believed to have been written for the Church Missionary Society's annual service in Winchester Cathedral (1853). Based on verses from Pss. 96 and 115, the opening chorus for full choir (Ps. 96:7–8) is followed by a setting for women's voices (SSAA) of the words "Worship the Lord in the beauty of holiness" (Ps. 96:9) and a chorus, beginning with a lively fugue, ridiculing idols who "have mouths but do not speak" (Ps. 115:3–8). The final chorus ("The Lord hath been mindful of us") ends fortissimo with "Ye are the blessed of the Lord who made heaven and earth" (Ps. 115:12–15).

ATHALIA. English oratorio in three acts by Handel (HWV 52) to a libretto by Samuel Humphreys, commissioned for the Encaenia ceremonies in the Sheldonian Theatre, Oxford, England, in 1733. Based on Racine's tragedy *Athalie* (1691), it tells the story of Athalia (S), who ordered the murder of all the males of the royal household, and her grandson Joash (Tr), who escaped and remained hidden in the Temple for six years (2 Kgs. 11:1–3). The well-known arioso "My Vengeance Awakes Me" is sung by Athaliah's mother (Jezebel) in a dream in which she foretells her daughter's death (cf. 2 Kgs. 9:10, 30–37). The oratorio concludes with the brutal death of Athaliah, treated offstage, followed by a duet, "Joys in gentle trains," sung by Joad, the high priest (Jehoiada) (Ct), and Josabeth (S) and a chorus of Israelites praising God's name. From the 16th century, the figure of Jezebel, the false prophetess who led believers astray (Rev. 2:20), was understood to represent the Catholic Church. Mendelssohn also composed a work based on this narrative, *Athalie: Incidental Music to Racine's Play* (op. 74, 1845), scored for three soloists, chorus, orchestra, and two orators, which includes the well-known instrumental *Kriegsmarch der Priester* ("War March of the Priests").

AUDIVI VOCEM DE CAELO. ("I Heard a Voice from Heaven"). A respond for matins on the Feast of All Saints' Day inspired by the Gospel reading for the day (Mt. 25:1–13), set as a motet by Thomas Tallis, Willam Byrd, and others. The Tallis motet for four-part a cappella chorus opens with imitative polyphony on *audivi* ("I heard") (Rev. 14:13), followed by plainchant on *vocem de caelo* ("a voice from heaven") and in the speech of the foolish virgins (Mt. 25:6) and then a return to imitative polyphony for the announcement of the arrival of the Bridegroom (Mt. 25:10). It concludes with a reiteration of the plainchant section with a warning to all who hear to keep oil in their lamps.

AUS DEN PSALMEN DAVIDS. ("From the Psalms of David"). Choral suite in four parts for mixed chorus (SATB), two pianos, percussion, double bass, and harp by Penderecki (1958). Based on the first verses of Pss. 28:1, 30:1, 43:1–2, and 143:1 in a Polish translation by Jan Kochanowski (1579), the work expresses the feelings conveyed by the Psalms; for example, whispered choral fragments represent the cry of the people (Ps. 28:1), and a steady *crescendo* depicts the people's anguished invocation (Ps. 143:1).

AUS DER TIEFEN RUFE ICH. ("Out of the Depths I Cry to Thee"). Cantata for SATB soloists, SATB chorus, violin, viola, oboe, bassoon, and continuo by J. S. Bach (BWV 131). It was the first cantata composed by Bach, possibly written for a penitential service following a great fire that destroyed a large part of the town of Mühlhausen in May 1707. The text from Ps. 130:1–8 is juxtaposed with two strophes from the chorale *Herr Jesu Christ, du höchstes Gut* ("Lord Jesus Christ, O highest good") by Bartholomäus Ringwaldt. The work opens with a sinfonia scored in a mournful minor tonality that moves without a break into *Aus der Tiefen* ("Out of the depths") sung by the chorus with word painting on *Flehen* ("supplications"). The fear of the Lord (*fürchte*) in the next two verses (v. 4) is expressed by semiquavers, while the "waiting" in the next two sections (vv. 4–5) is depicted by melismas on *harren* ("waiting . . . for the Lord") and *wartet* ("wait"). The work ends with the aria *Israel, hoffe auf den Herrn* ("Israel, hope in the Lord") (Ps. 130:7–8) with an oboe obbligato and an elaborate choral fugue *und er will Israel erlösen* ("he will redeem Israel").

AVE MARIA. ("Hail Mary"). Prayer to the Blessed Virgin Mary based on the angel Gabriel's salutation to Mary at the Annunciation (Lk. 1:28) and Elizabeth's greeting (Lk. 1:42). The petition "Holy Mary, Mother of God, pray for us sinners now and at the hour of our death, **Amen**" was added by the Council of Trent (1545–1563). There are numerous settings, most notably *Ave Maria . . . Virgo serena* ("Hail Mary . . . gentle Virgin") by Josquin des Prez, which was regarded as one of the most famous compositions of the 15th century, featuring early imitative counterpoint. Other well-known 15th- and 16th-century settings include those by Ockeghem, Taverner, Palestrina, Orlando de Lassus, Byrd, and Victoria. Gounod's well-known setting, published in 1853, features a superimposed melody sung or played over Bach's Prelude no. 1 in C Major (BWV 846). Verdi's ethereal four-part setting (1889) is based on the "enigmatic scale" of C–D-flat–E–F-sharp–G-sharp–A-sharp–B–C. Other well-known 19th- and 20th-century settings include those of Bruckner (1856, 1861, 1882), Mendelssohn (1830), Liszt (1883), Franck (1863), Brahms (1861), Rachmaninoff (1915), and Holst (1900). Twentieth-century settings include sublime works by Bruno Bettineli (1918), Franz Biebl (*Angelus Domini*, 1964), Arvo Pärt (1990), Morten Lauridsen (1997), Philip W. J. Stopford (2007), and Kevin Memley (2007). Schubert's popular *Ave Maria* (1826) was originally a setting for voice and piano of "Hymn to the Virgin" or "Ellen's Song," a poem from Sir Walter Scott's *The Lady of the Lake* (1810), translated into German by Adam Storck (1780–1822), although now very frequently sung with the traditional Latin words.

AVODATH HAKODESH. ("Sacred Service"). Work in Hebrew and spoken English for soloist (cantor), chorus, and orchestra by Ernest Bloch (1933), who studied Ashkenazi Hebrew for a year when commissioned to write it. Based on the Sabbath Morning Service, it is in five parts, unified around a six-note leitmotif based on the Gregorian "**Magnificat**" (GACBAG). After a Symphonic Prelude, part 1 contains settings of texts from the Torah and Psalms (Num. 24:5; Ps. 69:13; Deut. 6:4; Exod. 15:12, 15, 18) and incorporates an arrangement of the traditional melody *Tzur Yisrael* ("Rock of Israel") by Cantor Reuben Rinder (1887–1966) of Temple Emanu-El in San Francisco. Part 2 is a setting of the "Kedushah" (**Sanctus**; Isa. 6:3), and part 3 ("silent devotion") includes a setting of Ps. 19:14 ("Let the words of my mouth") sung a cappella and "Lift up your heads, O ye, gates" (Ps. 24:7–10). Part 4, "Returning the Scroll to the Ark," includes a peace song about the "Tree of Life" (Prov. 3:11–18), and the work concludes with the Priestly Blessing (Num. 6:24–26).

AWAKENING, THE. Chancel opera in one act and five scenes for three soloists (SMezBar) and piano/organ accompaniment by American composer Susan Hulsman Bingham (1944). Featuring traditional harmony, with short arias and recitatives, the work is designed for performance during a service in a church or a synagogue and premiered at Trinity Church on the Green, New Haven, Connecticut, in 1980. The libretto by Neil Olson highlights the participation of women in the ministry of Jesus at the wedding at Cana (Jn. 2:1–11), in the house of Mary and Martha (Lk. 10: 38–42), at the foot of the cross (Mt. 27:55–61), and after the Resurrection (Jn. 20) and depicts Jesus as having a "gentle sense of humour."

AWESOME GOD. Contemporary worship song (1988) by Christian singer/songwriter Rich Mullins, it first appeared on the album *Winds of Heaven Stuff of Earth* (1988). It is full of loose allusions to biblical stories, such as the Creation, the Garden of Eden, Sodom and Gomorrah, and the Second Coming (Rev. 22:7), and phrases such as "awesome God" (Deut. 7:21, NIV; cf. Pss. 47:2; 68:35) and "lightning in his fists" (Job 36:32–33, NIV). Reaching number 1 on the list of 100 Greatest Songs in Christian Music published by *CCM Magazine* in 2006, it has been performed by American contemporary musician Michael W. Smith and sung in a variety of styles, including hip-hop, ska, and rap.

• B •

BABEL. Cantata for male narrator, male chorus, and orchestra by Stravinsky (1944), the last work in the **Genesis Suite**. A musical retelling of the Tower of Babel story (Gen. 11:1–9), it is based on the structure of a passacaglia in four sections, opening with the narrator speaking (vv. 1–5) against a ground bass in the strings and low woodwind accompanied by an oboe obbligato, flute, and trumpet. In the second section, the chorus enters singing God's words ("nothing they plan to do will be impossible for them") (vv. 6–7) to an orchestral accompaniment. The third section recounts the narrator's words (v. 8), "So the Lord scattered them abroad . . . ," and the work concludes with a fast and furious orchestral fugue with a coda returning to the tranquil mood of the opening section (v. 9).

BABYLON'S BURNING. Song by Blackie Lawless, a member of American heavy metal band W.A.S.P., published on the group's 14th studio album, *Babylon* (2009). Based on St. John's vision of the Four Horsemen (Rev. 6:1–8), with references to the Whore of Babylon (Rev. 17, 18) and the 10-horned beast with seven heads (Rev. 17:7–13), the song is performed by lead vocalist Blackie Lawless on rhythm and lead guitars, Doug Blair on lead and rhythm guitars, Mike Duda on bass and vocals, and Mike Dupke on drums. The chorus contains references to the song's title; to the number of the beast, 666 (Rev. 13:17–18); and to the seven seals (Rev. 5–8), which are projected onto a big screen along with other images of dictators, war, children, and fires and an image of the Tower of Babel.

BALM IN GILEAD. Traditional African American spiritual based on Jer. 8:22 (cf. Jer. 46:11). The outpouring of the Holy Spirit's soothing balm is represented by the song's slow, meditative tempo; major tonality; and gentle, undulating melody. An all-time favorite of gospel singer Mahalia Jackson, it was classically arranged for the Fisk Jubilee Singers and African American opera singers Kathleen Battle and Jessye Norman.

BALULALOW. Cradle song adapted from Martin Luther's *Vom Himmel hoch* ("From Heaven High") (1535) and translated into Scottish dialect by James, John, and Robert Wedderburn under the title "Ane Sang of the Birth of Christ," published in *Ane Compendious Buik of Godly and Spiritual Sangis* (1567). The last two verses, originally scored for solo, chorus, and strings by Peter Warlock (1923), are a lullaby sung by the Virgin Mary to the Christ child. There is also a setting by Britten in **A Ceremony of Carols**, and it features on Sting's album *A Winter's Night* (2009).

BATTLE HYMN OF THE REPUBLIC, THE. ("Mine Eyes Have Seen the Glory of the Lord"). Well-known hymn written by social activist and abolitionist Julia W. Howe (1819–1910) after a visit to a Union army camp on the Potomac River in 1861. It was set to the tune of the marching song "John Brown's Body," which she had heard the soldiers singing, and published in the *Atlantic Monthly* in 1862. The verses are from Isa. 63:3 and Rev. 19:15, and the chorus, "Glory! Glory! **Hallelujah!**," is from Rev. 19:1. Stanza 5, which is the climax of the hymn, "As he died to make men holy, let us die to make men free," alludes to John Brown, the radical abolitionist who was hanged for his raid on the Harpers Ferry arsenal to arm a slave rebellion in 1859. Regarded as an American patriotic song and a favorite of Winston Churchill, it is regularly sung at American presidential inaugurations and at funerals of heads of state.

BAY PSALM BOOK, THE. Known also as "The Whole Booke of Psalmes Faithfully Translated into English Metre," it was the first book written and printed in colonial America (1640). Dissatisfied with the translation of existing Psalters, 30 ministers of the Puritans in Plymouth, Massachusetts, undertook a new translation to familiar tunes in strophic verse. Before the ninth edition of 1698, which contained 13 tunes at the back, the music was not notated, and the entire Psalter was sung to a handful of familiar tunes or to tunes found in 17th-century English settings of the Psalms. There were 27 editions of the Bay Psalter printed in New England, 20 in England, and six in Scotland.

BE NOT AFRAID. ("You Shall Cross the Barren Desert"). Well-known Catholic hymn by Robert J. Dufford (1975). Sung at funerals, it is inspired by Isa. 43:1–5. The verses allude to the journey through the wilderness (vv. 1–2) and the **Beatitudes** (v. 3), while the chorus ("Be not afraid; I go before you always/Come follow me and I will give you rest") recalls the words of Jesus (Jn. 21:19; Mt. 4:19; Mk. 1:17; Lk. 18:22). *See also* DO NOT BE AFRAID.

BE-TZET YISRAEL. ("When Israel Went Out"). Psalm 114, one of the Hallel Psalms (Pss. 113–18), traditionally sung in Hebrew as part of the Passover Haggadah celebrating the liberation of the Israelites from slavery. There are several popular Israeli settings and one by the Canadian World Music Group Jaffa Road on the album *Sun Place* (2009). *See also* IN EXITU.

BEAST AND THE HARLOT, THE. Song by American heavy metal band Avenged Sevenfold taken from their third album, *City of Evil* (2005), it was released as a single and reached number 1 on the U.K. Rock Chart in 2006. Based on the account of the fall of Babylon from Rev. 17–18, the song's title is a reference to the woman arrayed in purple and scarlet sitting atop a seven-headed, 10-horned, scarlet-colored beast (Rev. 17:3–18). Noted for its guitar and drum solos, pulsing bass line, and fast riffs, the accompanying video illustrates the fall of Babylon and the spread of evil in the inhabitants as they succumb to sin and lose their souls.

BEATI MORTUI. ("Blessed Are the Dead"). Motet for four-part a cappella male chorus (TTBB) by Mendelssohn (op. 115, no. 1). A slow, meditative work in three sections, noted for its rich sonorities, fluid melodic lines, and alternating soloist and chorus in sections 1 and 3, it poignantly expresses the sentiments of two biblical texts (Rev. 14:13; Mt. 5:4), used also by Brahms at the beginning of his **German Requiem**.

BEATI QUORUM VIA. ("Blessed Are Those Whose Way"). One of three Latin motets for a cappella chorus by Charles Villiers Stanford (op. 38, no. 3, 1905). Based on Ps. 119:1, the overall mood is reflective with flowing phrases of great beauty to suggest "those who walk in the law of the Lord."

BEATITUDES. Twelve works in Latin for sopranos, solo cello, organ, synthesizer, and hand bells by Howard Goodall (2009). In addition to the eight biblical Beatitudes, beginning with the word "Beati" ("Blessed") (Mt. 5:3–12), Goodall has added four new ones ("for those that care for others, those that are cared for, the lonely and the stateless"). Featuring on Howard Goodall's album *Enchanted Voices* (2009), they are a fusion of ancient and modern styles, evoking the sound of plainchant.

BÉATITUDES, LES. Oratorio (1869–1879) for eight soloists, chorus, and orchestra by César Franck to a libretto by Joséphine Colomb, considered one of the composer's greatest masterpieces. It is a meditation on the eight Beatitudes (Mt. 5:3–10), each one preceded and followed by dramatic or reflective poetry. The work is unified by a Christ motif that appears either complete or in part in every movement and the chromatic Satan motif in movements 7 and 8. In movement 7, Satan proclaims himself king of the world, supported by choruses of tyrants, (basses), pagan priests (tenors and basses), and the crowd, but then recoils in fear on hearing Christ proclaiming, "Blessed are the peacemakers" (movt. 7) with a chorus (SATBB) of Peacemakers. The last movement ("Blessed are those who are persecuted . . .") opens with Satan asserting his power against a chorus of the Just who sing about their suffering, followed by a soprano solo in which Mary laments her son's death on the cross. Satan begins to lose his power, Christ sings the last Beatitude, and the work ends with a celestial chorus singing **Hosanna**.

BEATITUDES, THE. Choral work by Russian composer Vladimir Martynov (1998), arranged for the Kronos Quartet and played in their "Awakening" concert in San Francisco on the fifth anniversary of the 9/11 terrorist attacks (2006) and later in New York for the 10th anniversary (2011). Combining American minimalism and Russian Orthodox chant, it is a poignant meditation on the eight Beatitudes (Mt. 5:3–12).

BEATITUDES, THE. Popular choral work by Arvo Pärt (1991). Based on the Beatitudes (Mt. 5:3–12), it is characterized by dissonances, tintinnabuli, and reflective pauses, ending with an empathetic **Amen** and an arpeggiated organ solo.

BEATUS VIR. ("Blessed Is the Man"). Work subtitled "Psalm for baritone, mixed chorus and large Orchestra" by Górecki (op. 38, 1979), commissioned by Cardinal Karol Wojtyla (Pope John Paul II), and premiered in Krakow, Poland, in June 1979 to commemorate the 900th anniversary of the death of Bishop Stanislaw. The text is taken from Pss. 143:1, 6–10; 31:16; 88:2; 67:7, and 34:8, the title from the last of these. The four-measure ostinato repeated 11 times represents the day and month of St. Stanislaw's death on 11 April, highlighted by tubular bells and glockenspiel.

BEATUS VIR. ("Blessed Is the Man"). Motet for soloists, six-part chorus, organ, basso continuo, and two obbligato violins in *stile concertato* by Monteverdi, composed around 1630 and published in *Selva Morale e Spirituale* (1641). The words come from Ps. 112:1–10 (Vulg. 111), and the music borrows material from a duet, *Chiome d'oro*, published in his seventh book of madrigals (1619). The work concludes with repeated "Glorias" and a final **Amen**. There are also settings by Victoria, Vivaldi, and a number of other composers. *See also* VESPERAE SOLENNES DE CONFESSORE

BEAUTIFUL SAVIOUR. Anonymous hymn, also known by the title "Fairest Lord Jesus," inspired by verses from Isa. (40:28), 1 Tim. (1:17; 6:16), and elsewhere. The text first appears in the *Münster Gesangbuch* (1677) and was set to an 18th-century Silesian folk tune, published as *Schönster Herr Jesu* ("Most beautiful Lord Jesus") in *Schlesische Volkslieder* ("Silesian Folksongs") (1842). It is sometimes known as the "Crusaders' Hymn," and Liszt introduced it into the Crusaders' March in his oratorio *St. Elizabeth* (1873). Richard Storrs Willis published an English version in *Church Chorals* (1850), and another version, entitled "Beautiful Saviour," by Joseph A. Seiss (1823–1940), a Lutheran pastor from Maryland, appears in a *Sunday School Book for the Use of Evangelical Lutheran Congregations* (1873). "Beautiful Saviour" was later arranged for SSAATTBB chorus by Frederick Melius Christiansen (1919), and Lilian Stevenson's translation "Fairest Lord Jesus" was published in the World Student Christian Federation hymnbook *Cantate Domino* (1924).

BEHOLD THE MOUNTAIN OF THE LORD. Metrical version of Isa. 2:2–5, first published in *Scottish Paraphrases* (1745) and revised by Michael Bruce (1781). It is most frequently sung to the tune "Glasgow" by Thomas Moore (1756).

BEHOLD THE TABERNACLE OF GOD. Anthem for chorus and orchestra or organ by John Rutter, composed for the consecration of a new transept in St. Anne's Cathedral, Belfast (1981). Based on the text of a Sarum antiphon, it opens with words from Rev. 21:3, sung after a brass fanfare by the chorus in unison. First recalling the imagery of the Tabernacle in the Wilderness, the building of Solomon's Temple, and the building of the Second Temple after the Babylonian exile, the music moves on to the dulcet tones of unison voices, first female, then male, singing about a spiritual temple (1 Cor. 3:16–17). The work ends with an air of festivity in which unison voices, first male, then female, sing "**Alleluia**" in simple triple meter and then "Behold the Temple of God is with Men," together in unison, in a rapturous return to the opening theme.

BELKIS, QUEEN OF SHEBA. Ballet suite in four movements by the Italian composer Ottorino Respighi (P. 171), choreographed by Leonide Massine and first performed in La Scala, Milan, in 1932. Originally conceived as an opera by Claudio Guastall, it was later set as a ballet for large orchestra, including an offstage band, a wind machine, and several Indian sitars and featuring ancient Hebrew melodies and Arabic rhythms. Respighi later decided to create two suites from the ballet, but failing health resulted in the extraction of only one suite. It tells the story of the erotic union between King Solomon and the queen of Sheba, known as Belkis in Islamic tradition. In the opening movement, augmented seconds evoke an oriental atmosphere, while a solo cello depicts the loneliness of King Solomon as he awaits the arrival of the queen of Sheba to Jerusalem. Movement 2 features Belkis's sensual dances in her palace by the Red Sea, and in the third movement, a ceremonial war dance on drums, with nearly naked dancers, thunders out the rhythm to announce the queen's arrival in Jerusalem. The suite concludes with an "Orgiastic Dance" by Solomon and Belkis.

BELL ANTHEM, THE. ("Rejoice in the Lord Alway"). Popular verse anthem for ATB soloists, chorus, strings, and/or organ by Henry Purcell (Z. 49, ca. 1685). A setting of four verses of Paul's Letter to the Philippians (Phil. 4:4–7), it is characterized by alternating sections for soloists and chorus and contains more repetition than any other anthem by Purcell. In the instrumental introduction, it features an imitation of pealing bells.

BELLY OF THE WHALE, THE. Best-known song of the short-lived rock band Burning Sensations from Los Angeles (1982). An MTV hit, it appeared as a title track in the Disney cartoon *Jonah and the Whale* distributed on the Disney Channel. Inspired by the story of Jonah, the songwriter likens himself to Jonah in the belly of the whale, at first enjoying the opportunity to have fun but after a while feeling lonely. An accompanying video shows a party taking place in the belly of the whale, and viewers then realize that this is the place he longs to escape from.

BELSHAZZAR. Oratorio in three acts for soloists, chorus, orchestra, and continuo by Handel (HWV 61, 1745, 1751, 1758), first performed in King's Theatre, Haymarket, London, on 27 March 1745. The libretto by Charles Jennens is based on the story of Belshazzar's Feast and the fall of Babylon as told in the Bible (Dan. 5) along with other works, including Humphrey Prideaux's *The Old and New Testament Connected in the History of the Jews and Neighbouring Nations* (1716). In addition to biblical characters Daniel (Ct), Belshazzar (T), and Cyrus (Ct), Jennens wrote parts for Belshazzar's mother, Nitocris (S), and a chorus of Persians, Babylonians, Jews, and Wise Men. The work includes a Martial Symphony with trumpets and timpani in act 3, scene 2, depicting a battle with Cyrus in which Belshazzar and his attendants are slain. The work concludes with a chorus based on Ps. 145:1–2.

BELSHAZZAR. Gospel song by Johnny Cash, recorded in 1955 and released nine years later on the album *The Original Sun Sound of Johnny Cash* (1964). A cover version of the song was released by Bob Dylan and the Band on *The Basement Tapes* (1988). Inspired by Dan. 5, a lightly syncopated melody paints the wanton behavior of Belshazzar and his guests and, in the final two quatrains, Belshazzar's terror on seeing the mysterious handwriting on the wall. The chorus describes the king as "weighed in the balance and found wanting" (Dan. 5:27–28a) and likens him to the foolish builder who built his house on sand (Mt. 7:24–27). A change in the rhyming scheme from AABB to ABAB in the chorus focuses attention on the gravity of God's judgment.

BELSHAZZAR'S FEAST. Oratorio in three continuous parts by William Walton for baritone solo, mixed chorus, and orchestra, first performed at the Leeds Festival on 8 October 1931. The libretto by Osbert Sitwell is made up of texts from Daniel, Isaiah, Psalms, and Revelation. Part 1 opens with a trombone fanfare and the male voices a cappella intoning Isaiah's prophecies (Isa. 39:7, 13:6) in discordant harmonies, followed by the lament of the Hebrew slaves in exile and the prophecy of Babylon's fall (Ps. 137), sung by a mixed chorus in poignant, flowing harmonies. Part 2 begins with an unaccompanied recitative by Belshazzar in which he alludes to the fulfillment of Isaiah's prophecy to Hezekiah (Isa. 37:7) and boasts of the riches of Babylon (Rev. 18:12–13). The chorus, accompanied by the orchestra, then describes Belshazzar's decadent feast, his desecration of the drinking vessels stolen from the Jerusalem Temple, and his call to the Babylonians, preceded by a three-trumpet fanfare, to praise the idols. In *tempo di Marcia*, first, "the god of gold" is praised with golden-colored instruments, then "the god of silver" with piccolo, glockenspiel, triangle, and bells; "the god of iron" with an anvil; "the god of wood" with a xylophone, woodblocks, and strings *col legno*; the "god of stone" with a whip and short staccato rhythms; and "the god of brass" with brass instruments. The music builds to a climax above an ostinato for cellos, basses, and piano as the choir sing repeatedly, "Praise ye, Praise ye the gods," and Belshazzar is proclaimed "King of Kings" (Rev. 17:4; 19:16). After a brief silence, the baritone soloist, singing a cappella to a slow, eerie accompaniment alternating on cymbal, bass drum, kettledrum, and gong with rattlings from the castanets, describes the appearance of the disembodied fingers of a human hand and the mysterious writing on the wall announcing the death of Belshazzar and the division of his kingdom (Dan. 5:25–30). Part 3 consists of a song of praise sung by the chorus of exiles (Ps. 81:1–3), with exuberant dance-like rhythms in the orchestra, a quieter semichorus telling of the weeping and wailing of kings and merchants at the fall of Babylon (Rev. 18:11, 22–23), and finally a blazing chorus of joyful **Alleluias** (Rev. 19:1, 3, 4, 6). There is an orchestral suite with the same title by Sibelius (op. 51, 1907).

BENEDIC ANIMA MEA DOMINUM. ("Bless the Lord O My Soul"). Motet for SATB by Claudin de Sermisy (1535) based on Ps. 103:1–3. There are also two settings by Orlando de Lassus for STTB and SAATBB a cappella chorus, a grand motet by Henri Du Mont (1684), and a more recent setting by David Bevan/Walter Parratt that features on the album *The Psalms of David* (2002).

BENEDICITE. Liturgical canticle deriving from "The Song of the Three Children," Shadrach, Meshach, and Abednego, who glorified and praised God while in the fiery furnace (Dan. 3:35–88). Vaughan Williams's setting for soprano, SATB chorus, or female voices and orchestra (1929) opens with a brief orchestral introduction in D major, the tonality of "Glory." This is followed by the sopranos *divisi* and altos *divisi* singing "Praise him" in unison, like a choir of angels, against the tenors and basses unison "O ye heavens, bless ye the Lord." The *Lento* section featuring oboe obbligato and soprano soloist beginning "O let the earth praise the Lord: yea . . ." is subdued and reflective in mood, while the final section, which includes the last stanza of John Austin's hymn "Hark My Soul" (1760), returns to the spirited mood of the opening.

BENEDICTUS. Canticle sung at Lauds (Latin rite) or Morning Prayer (Anglican rite), also known as the "Song of Zachariah," father of John the Baptist (Lk. 1:68–79). A setting for two voices, cello, and guitar by Simon and Garfunkel, based on a motet by Orlando de Lassus, first appeared on their album *Wednesday Morning 3 A.M.* (1964). The Welsh composer Karl Jenkins includes an instrumental setting on the album *Karl Jenkins and Adiemus: The Essential Collection* (2006).

BETHULIA LIBERATA, LA. ("The Liberation of Bethulia"). *Azione sacra*, "sacred action," in two parts for six soloists (SSSATB), chorus, and orchestra by the 15-year-old Mozart (K. 118/74c, 1771) to a libretto by Pietro Metastasio (1734), it was commissioned by Giuseppe Ximenes, prince of Aragon. Inspired by the story of how **Judith** defeated the Assyrians in the valley of Bethulia (Jud. 8–16), memorable moments include the aria "Quel occhier che in gran procella" ("The helmsman who in a great tempest") and Judith's recitative relating how she beheaded Holofernes. The oratorio concludes with the conversion of the Assyrian Achior (*Te solo adoro, mente infinita/*"Thee alone I worship, infinite mind") and the rejoicing of the Bethulians. Other notable settings include works by Niccolò Jommelli (1743), including Ignaz Holzbauer (1752) and Antonio Salieri (1821), among others.

BIBLE HYMN BOOK, THE. A collection of hymns (1860) by the "prince of Scottish hymn writing" Horatius Bonar. Arranged in biblical order, it begins with "In the Beginning was the Word (Gen. 1:1) and concludes with

"The Church has Waited Long" (Rev. 22:20). Well-known hymns include "I was a Wandering Sheep" (1 Pet. 2:25).

BIBLIA, LA. ("The Bible"). Concept album by Argentine rock band Vox Dei, widely regarded as a masterpiece (1971). The lyrics were written by Ricardo Souléhad to music by fellow band members Willy Quiroga, Juan Carlos "Yody" Godoy, and Ricardo Soulé. Tracks include "*Génesis,*" "*Moisés,*" "*Las Guerras*" ("The Wars"), "*Profecías*" ("Prophecies"), "*Libros Sapienciales*" ("Wisdom Books"), "*Cristo y Nacimiento,*" "*Cristo—Muerte y Resurrección,*" and "*Apocalípsis.*"

BIBLICAL GRAFFITI. Fifth album by Christian parody band ApologetiX featuring songs such as "Twins Came Out" (Gen. 25:24–6), a parody of "Twist and Shout" by the Top Notes; "Second Timothy" (2 Tim. 3:16), a parody of "Sex and Candy" by Marcy Playground; "Donkey Talked with Him" (Num. 22:28–30), a parody of "Honky Tonk Women" by the Rolling Stones; and "Dancing Dave" (2 Sam. 6:14), a parody of "Dancing Days" by Led Zeppelin.

BIBLICAL SONATAS. (*Biblische Historien*). Six sonatas for harpsichord, Johann Kuhnau's last set of keyboard works, published in 1700. Characterized as programmatic works, each sonata depicts an episode from the Old Testament: "The Battle between David and Goliath" (1 Sam. 17), "The Melancholy of Saul Assuaged by David's Music" (1 Sam. 16), "The Wedding of Jacob" (Gen. 29), "Hezekiah, who being sick unto death, is restored again to health" (2 Kgs. 20), "Gideon the deliverer of Israel" (Judg. 6–8), and "The Death and Burial of Jacob" (Gen. 50). Within each sonata, sections are given their own titles, for example, in Sonata 2, "Saul's Affliction and Madness," "The Refreshing Music of David's Harp," and "The King's Mind once more at peace." Saul's melancholy is depicted with longer note values and chromaticisms, and his affliction with hemidemisemiquavers (64th note) and demisemiquavers (32nd note). David's harp playing is more lyrical and harp-like, and the last section is more upbeat with dotted quavers and semiquavers to illustrate a change in Saul's mood brought about by David's harp playing.

BIBLICAL SONGS. (*Biblické písne*). Ten songs in Czech by Dvořák based on texts from the Psalms in the 16th-century Kralitz Bible translation. They include "Clouds and Darkness are round about him" (Ps. 97:2–6), "The Lord is my Shepherd" (Ps. 23:1–4), "By the Rivers of Babylon" (Ps. 137:1–5), and "O Sing unto the Lord a New Song" (Pss. 98:1, 4, 96:12, 11). The others are settings of the following: Pss. 119:114–15, 117, 120; 55:2–3, 5–9; 144:9; 145:2–3, 5–6; 61:2, 4–5; 63:2, 6; and 121:1–4.

BIBLICAL SONGS. A cycle of six songs for baritone and organ by Charles Villiers Stanford (op. 113, 1909), dedicated to the composer's son-in-law, baritone Harry Plunkett Greene, and the wife of fellow Irish composer Hamilton Harty, Agnes Nicholls (no. 4). Four are settings of "Songs of Ascents" (Ps. 120–134): "A Song of Freedom" (Ps. 126), "A Song of Trust" (Ps. 121), "A Song of Hope" (Ps. 130), and "A Song of Battle" (Ps. 124). Song no. 4, "A Song of Peace," in C major, is based on Isa. 11:1–6, 9–10, and incorporates the tune **O Come, O Come Emmanuel**, while the final song, "A Song of Wisdom" (no. 6), inspired by Sir. 24, contains many instances of word painting, such as semiquavers, to represent the flowing waters of the stream (v. 43).

BINDING, THE. (Hebrew *Akedah*). Oratorio in three parts for soloists, mixed chorus, and orchestra by American Jewish composer Samuel Hans Adler to a libretto by Hugo Chaim Adler, translated by Albert Friedlander; commissioned by Temple Emanu-El, Dallas, and the Dallas Chamber Music Society (1967); and dedicated to the "thousands of sons" who have fallen and who will continue to fall because of this legend. It is based on Gen. 22:1–17b with textual additions from the Midrash and Aggadah. Of particular interest is part 2, which recounts Abraham and Isaac's dialogue sung as an accompanied recitative (vv. 7–8), and the pair's encounter with Satan, who mimics God's command to Abraham to a sound reminiscent of medieval plainchant. The voice of Satan is characterized by an angular, jagged melody based on the twelve-tone scale. *See also* ABRAHAM AND ISAAC.

BLACKMAN REDEMPTION. Roots reggae song by Rastafarian Bob Marley from the album *Confrontation* (1983). The song alludes to Haile Selassie I, emperor of Ethiopia (1930–1974), whom Rastafarians believe was the reincarnation of Christ, that is, the Black Redeemer, descended from King Solomon and the queen of Sheba. Selassie is referred to in the song as "coming from the root of David (Rev. 5:5) through to the line of Solomon" (Mt. 1:6; cf. Isa. 11:1).

BLESSED ASSURANCE. Hymn by Fanny Crosby, first published in 1873. Based on Heb. 10:22 and set to music by Phoebe Knapp, it features in the Academy Award–winning movies *Places in the Heart* (1984) and *Trip to Bountiful* (1985).

BLESSED BE THE GOD AND FATHER. Verse anthem by Samuel Sebastian Wesley, based on verses from 1 Pet. 1. Originally written for performance on Easter Sunday (1834), an opening chorus celebrating the resurrection of Christ (1 Pet. 1:3) is followed by a soprano solo ending with Isaiah's words

"For all flesh is as grass" and a triumphant chorus, "but the word of the Lord endureth for ever" (Isa. 40:8; 1 Pet. 1:24–25).

BLESSED VIRGIN'S EXPOSTULATION, THE. Soprano solo by Henry Purcell to a text by Nahum Tate, published in volume 2 of *Harmonia Sacra* (Z. 196, 1693). Also known by the title "Tell me, some pitying angel," it was inspired by the story of Jesus lost in the Temple (Lk. 2:41–52) and explores, in first-person narration, the Virgin Mary's distress as she seeks her "soul's sweet darling." The music captures the Virgin's change of mood from moments of great tenderness as she reflects fondly on Christ's "little footsteps" to a sense of urgency as she contemplates his loss, foreshadowing his death on the cross. The work alludes, with poignant use of melismas, to Herod's "cruel" slaughter of the innocents and the flight of the Holy Family to Egypt ("Unregarded through the Wilderness"), and the Virgin's sob can be heard on "Oh!" in the final line, "I trust the God, but oh! I fear the child."

BLESSING AND HONOUR AND GLORY AND POWER. Hymn by Horatius Bonar published in *Hymns of Faith and Hope* (1866). Also known as the "Song of the Lamb," it is a paraphrase of Rev. 5:11–14. It is regularly sung to the tune "*O Quanta Qualia*," or "*Trisagion*."

BLEST PAIR OF SIRENS. Work for double choir and orchestra composed by Hubert Parry for Queen Victoria's Golden Jubilee in 1887 and a setting of John Milton's ode "At a Solemn Music" (1645), in which the "Blest Pair of Sirens" unite with the heavenly choirs of Seraphim (Isa. 6:2–3) and Cherubim in praise of God. Milton equates discord with the Fall (Gen. 3) and the restoration of harmony with salvation (Rom. 8:38–39; Phil. 3:4–11; Rev. 22:17), and the work concludes with the hope that humanity will unite with the heavenly court and sing their eternal song of praise. It was performed at the marriage of the duke and duchess of Cambridge on 29 April 2011.

BLOODY MARY. Song by DJ White Shadow, Lady Gaga, Fernando Garibay, and William Grigahcine on Lady Gaga's second studio album, *Born This Way* (2011). Written from the perspective of Mary Magdalene, portrayed as a seductress who prophesies Christ's death and speaks of her readiness to receive a public stoning, the title calls to mind the legend of Bloody Mary, who appeared in different guises to reveal the future.

BLOW UP THE TRUMPET IN SION. Anthem for seven soloists, eight-part chorus, and continuo by English composer Henry Purcell (Z. 10 before 1679), based on Joel 2:15–17. The work opens with a choral fanfare in C major sung by soloists and later repeated by the chorus (v. 15). Male voices sing the command to "assemble the elders," and female voices sing of "the children" and "the bride" (v. 16). In "Spare the people," dissonances and suspensions paint the distress of the priests, while homophonic singing highlights their petition for God's mercy, and references to "the Lord" and "God" are sung mainly on a C major chord. At the end, the phrase "Wherefore shall they say among their people" is sung repeatedly in polyphony, followed by the question in homophony, "where is their God?"

BLOW YE THE TRUMPET. Work for chorus and piano or orchestral accompaniment from the opera *John Brown* (1989) by American composer Kirke Mechem. Inspired by the biblical law of the Jubilee (Lev. 25:8–28), it is based on a hymn by Charles Wesley (1750) that was a favorite of the American abolitionist John Brown. The words, which were adapted and set to a new melody in the style of an early 19th-century American folk hymn, refer to Brown's belief in the abolition of slavery through armed insurrection and to his death as a martyr. Orchestrated versions include trumpets and percussion.

BLUTIGE UND STERBENDE JESUS, DER. ("The Bleeding and Dying Christ"). Early Protestant passion oratorio by Reinhard Keiser (1704), one of the first to use the term *oratorio*. It is a setting of a poetic text by Christian Friedrich Hunold based freely on the Gospel accounts of the passion of Christ. In place of a narrator, it features an allegorical character, the Daughter of Zion (Isa. 62:11; Lam. 1–2; Mic. 4; cf. Lk. 23:28), who comments on emotional events in the drama in the manner of a Greek chorus.

BOBBLE. Opera for a cappella voices, based on the story of the Tower of Babel (Gen. 11:1–9), produced and staged by Bobby McFerrin (2009). Regarded as a new form of opera with wordless libretto and audience participation, it comprises three acts ("Building," "Abusing," and "Rebuilding"). Following its premiere in New York, it made its European debut at the Stimmen Festival in Basel, Switzerland, in 2009 with a cast of 20 singers chosen from a variety of ethnic and cultural backgrounds, reflecting the confusion of languages and scattering of the peoples of the earth (Gen. 11:9). The act of composition is spontaneous, based on improvisation led by McFerrin, until the concluding act, when the people learn to listen and sing a joyful song of celebration.

BOOK OF PROVERBS, THE. Work for soprano, baritone, chorus, and orchestra (1996) by American composer Michael Torke, it was premiered in Holland in September 1996 with the Netherlands Philharmonic Orchestra and Choir, conducted by Edo de Waart. Characterized as a postminimalist work, it is structured in a fashion similar to Torke's other work, *Four Proverbs* (1993), with the words of the text broken up into shorter, identifiable rhythmic and melodic segments. Similarly, the syntax of each proverb is jumbled to emphasize individual words, such as "house a strife better than with full feasting crust with of dry piece a" (Prov. 17:1). After an instrumental introduction, repetition in the second movement, "The Door Turns" (Prov. 26:14), sung by altos and tenors, lulls listeners almost into a state of hypnosis. "Better a Dry Crust" (Prov. 17:1) is sung to a lilting animated melody by sopranos and altos and "The Whip for the Horse" (Prov. 26:3, 7, 11) by tenors and basses to the accompaniment of a whip. The fifth movement, "The Way of an Eagle" (Prov. 30:18–19), sung by a soprano solo, sopranos, and altos, paints the flight of a soaring eagle and is followed by "Drink our fill of Love" (Prov. 37:7–10, 13, 15–23; 30:20), sung by baritone solo, tenors, and basses, reminiscent of "Drink Water" from the composer's earlier work *Four Proverbs*. The work ends with "Like the Man who Seizes" (Prov. 28:17), sung by sopranos, altos, and tenors, and "Boast Not of Tomorrow" (Prov. 27:1) with a full chorus.

BOSOM OF ABRAHAM. Gospel song/spiritual by William Johnson, George McFadden, and Philip Brooks inspired by Lk. 16:22, performed by Elvis Presley on the contemporary gospel music album *He Touched Me* (1972) as well as on one of the *The Jubilee 4 Greatest Spirituals* (1996).

BREADTH OF HEAVEN. ("Mary's Song"). Christmas song by Chris Eaton from the album *Breadth of Heaven*, in which Mary prays for mercy and strength after the Annunciation (Lk. 1:26–35). Performed as a track in the movie *The Nativity Story* (2006), it has been covered by many artists, including Amy Grant, Vince Gill, Sara Groves, and Melissa Manchester.

BRINGING IN THE SHEAVES. Popular gospel song by American preacher and hymn writer Knowles Shaw (1834–1878), inspired by the last verse of Ps. 126. First published in the *Golden Gate: A Collection of New Songs for Sunday School* (1874), it was later arranged to the tune "Harvest" by George Minor. Dotted rhythms, repetitions, and an upbeat tempo combine to evoke the sound of a traditional work song, together with short phrases and a major tonality to capture the joyful mood of Ps. 126. Sung by Tennessee Ernie Ford on one of the best-selling albums of all time, *Hymns* (1956), the song featured in popular television series in the 1960s and 1970s, including *The Beverly Hillbillies* and *Little House on the Prairie*, and, more recently, in an episode of *The Simpsons*.

BROCKES' PASSION. (*Der für die Sünde der Welt gemarterte und sterbende Jesus* ["The Story of Jesus, Suffering and Dying for the Sins of the World"]). A meditation on the passion and death of Jesus Christ, written in German by B. H. Brockes (1712) as a passion oratorio libretto, without dialogue, dramatic personages, or references to specific biblical passages. The most famous setting is by Handel (HWV, 48, 1746). Others include those of Reinhard Kesier (1712), Georg Philip Telemann (1716), and Johann Mattheson (1718). Other meditative oratorio passion libretti include Pietro Metastasio's dramatic oratorio/opera seria *La passione di Gesù Cristo* ("The Passion of Jesus Christ") (1730) set to music by Caldara, Jomelli, and Paisiello, among others, and Carl Wilhelm Ramler's *Der Tod Jesu*, set by Karl Heinrich Graun (1755) and Georg Philip Telemann (1755). *See also* DER TOD JESU; LA PASSIONE DI GESU CRISTO.

BUONA NOVELLA, LA. ("Glad Tidings"). Controversial album by the Italian singer/songwriter Fabrizio de André (1970), based on the apocryphal Gospel of James and the Arabic Infancy Gospel. The story of the birth, passion, and death of Jesus is recounted in 10 songs, beginning with *Laudate dominum* ("Praise the Lord") and ending with *Laudate hominem* ("Praise the Man"). Mary features prominently, notably in "The infancy of Mary" and the "Three Mothers" by the cross, and de André's strong views about the Catholic Church are prominent throughout, especially in "The Testament of Titus," the best-known song on the album, in which one of the thieves on a cross criticizes the Ten Commandments and then tells his mother how he learned about love from "this dying man."

BURIAL SENTENCES. *See* FUNERAL SENTENCES.

BURNING FIERY FURNACE, THE. Chamber opera/parable for church performance for male soloists, male chorus, and instrumental ensemble and organ by Benjamin Britten (op. 77, 1966), first performed in Orford Church on 9 June 1966 at the Aldeburgh Festival. The libretto by William Plomer tells the story of the three children who were thrown into the fiery furnace because they refused to bow down and worship Merodak, the golden image of Nebuchadnezzar. Toward the end of the performance, the three Israelites sing the **Benedicite** with an angel while incarcerated in the fiery furnace. Performed in the manner of a medieval mystery play, it begins and ends with a procession of monks singing the *Salus aeterna* ("eternal salvation"), an 11th-century Advent sequence from the Sarum Missal, of which segments appear at other moments in the opera. The work is set for seven soloists, a chorus, and instruments corresponding as closely as possible to those mentioned in the biblical text (Dan. 3:4, 7, 15): flute, viola, glockenspiel, little harp, horn, alto trombone, Babylonian drum, and small cymbals. At the end of the performance, the monks resume their habits, the Abbot reminds the congregation of the moral of the story, and the work concludes with the recessional chant *Salus aeterna.*

BY THE POOL OF SILOAM. Chancel opera for six soloists (SMezBar-BarBarBar) and SATB chorus by Susan Hulsman Bingham (1944). Based on the story of the healing of the blind man (Jn. 9), it includes acting parts for members of the chorus, traditional harmonies, some chant, and recitative.

BY THE WATERS OF BABYLON. This text, from Ps. 137, has enjoyed numerous settings through the centuries in Latin (**Super Flumina Babylonis**) and other languages. At the end of the 16th century, it was set in Hebrew for four voices by the Jewish composer Salamone Rossi, *Al naharot bavel* ("There by the streams we sat"), and in the 17th and 18th centuries, it was scored by Heinrich Schütz, *An den Wassern zu Babel saßen wir und weinten* (SWV 37, 1619), and as an anthem by English composers Pelham Humfrey (1647–1674) and William Boyce (1740). In the 19th century, it features in the "Chorus of the Hebrew Slaves" (*Va, pensiero*) in Verdi's opera **Nabucco** (1841) and in the second movement of Joseph Nicholds's oratorio *Babylon* (1856). Liszt's *An den Wassern zu Babylon* (S. 17, 1859) is a setting of a German text by J. G. Herder. In the 20th century, it was composed as a rhapsody, *By the Waters of Babylon*, for baritone solo, violin, cello, and organ, by Herbert Howells (1917), and it features in Walton's **Belshazzar's Feast** (1931). American composer Henry Partch composed a setting in 1931 and later adapted it for viola and intoning voice with kithara and "chromeloeon" (1955); it was also set for soprano solo and female chorus by fellow American composer David Amram (1969). There is a chorale for organ by Marcel Dupré (op. 28/6, 1931) and two choral settings by Arvo Pärt (1984/1991), reworked for wind quintet and string orchestra with the title *In Spe* ("In hope") (2010). The text frames five of seven cycles in *Lament for Jerusalem* by John Tavener, described by the composer as a "mystical love song" (2002). The lyric "On the Willows" features in the musical *Godspell* (1971) and in the songs **Rivers of Babylon** by Brent Dowe and Trevor McNaughton of the Melodians (1970) and "By the Rivers Dark" on the album *Ten New Songs* by Leonard Cohen (2001). *See also* ON WILLOWS AND BIRCHES; RIVERS OF BABYLON; SUPER FLUMINA BABYLONIS.

• C •

CAIN AND ABEL. Ballet set to music by Andrzej Panufnik (1968) and choreographed by Sir Kenneth Macmillan (1969) and, more recently, by Emil Wesolowski (2012). Inspired by the story of Cain and Abel (Gen. 4:1–16), the first murder is precipitated by Cain's jealousy over his mother's affection for Abel. The story was also set for the DeBasil Ballet Russe in 1946, choreographed by David Lichine to "Siegfried's Rhine Journey" from Wagner's *Götterdämmerung* and arranged by William McDermott. The first scene caused a sensation with the birth of Cain and Abel rolling onto the stage tangled up with two scantily dressed women representing good and evil.

CAIN AND ABEL. Electronic ballet by Henk Badings (1986), inspired by the story of Cain's murder of Abel (Gen. 4), the music captures the violence, destruction, and madness of the scene with atmospheric sine-wave generators, multivibrators, noise generators, an electronic clavichord, a photoelectric siren, and other instrumental sounds processed through electrical filters, reverberation machines, tape recorders, and a ring modulator.

CAIN AND ABEL. Grand-chamber opera in five scenes for soloists, dancers, and 18-piece chamber orchestra by Tsippi Fleischer (op. 57, 2001) to a libretto in Hebrew by Yossefa Even-Shoshan, premiered at the Israeli music festival "Now Time" in 2002. In avant-garde style, it is scored for Cain (Bar), Abel (Bar), and the two lambs they offer to God (MezS), portrayed as women. God is named Tzafon ("North") (cf. Jer. 1:14) as the God of Nature during the time of chaos before monotheism and after Abel's murder (scene 4). The final scene depicts the separation of the heavens from the earth (Gen. 1:1): the heavenly home of Abel and his lamb ("Abel's Soul Ascends to Heaven") and the earthly domain of Cain, cursed for ever. Other works include the oratorio *Cain e Abel* by Bernardo Pasquini (1637–1710), the *historia Cain* by Giacomo Carissimi, and the cantata *Cain and Abel* by Darius Milhaud in the **Genesis Suite** (1945). *See also* ADAM RAISED A CAIN; CHAPTER FOUR; CHILDREN OF EDEN; WHEN CAIN KILLED ABEL IN A FIGHT.

CALL OF WISDOM, THE. Anthem for four voices by Will Todd with words by Michael Hampel, commissioned for Queen Elizabeth's Diamond Jubilee in 2012 and first performed in St. Paul's Cathedral, London. Inspired by Prov. 8:1–21, a prayer is addressed to "Lord of Wisdom, Lord of Truth" and answered in the refrain "I am here, I am with you . . . those who love me know my love" (Prov. 8:17) with allusions to "wisdom is better than jewels" (Prov. 8:11) and "by me kings reign" (Prov. 8:15).

CALYPSO CAROL. Well-known Christmas carol with words and music by Canon Michael Perry (1964) composed while he was a student at Oak Hill Theological College. Based on the Nativity story and inspired by music from the West Indies, the first line opens, "See him lying on a bed of Straw." It was sung by Cliff Richard and is included in various hymnbooks, including *Youth Songbook 2* (1969). In 2005, it was voted in the top 10 of all-time favorite carols by British audiences of the popular BBC weekly program *Hymns of Praise.*

CANTATA FROM JOB. Cantata in four movements for baritone soloist, SATB chorus, and organ by Darius Milhaud (1965), commissioned in memory of Eugene and Nellie B. Warner to be sung in either English or Hebrew. The first movement is a choral setting of Elihu's final speech (Job 37:1–13), opening with bare octaves in C major as he describes how his heart trembles before the power of God who governs not only the storms of nature but also the storms of life. In movement 2, God the Creator questions Job, "Where were you when I laid the foundation of the earth?" (Job 38:4–7, 8–11), and movement 3 describes the enigmas of creation with music descending in stepwise movement to paint the descent to "the deep" (Job 38:16–21). The work ends with chorus and speaker telling Job about the limitations of human knowledge and that it is God's prerogative alone to save humanity (Job 38:16–21).

CANTATA FROM PROVERBS. Cantata for three-part women's chorus, with oboe, cello, and harp accompaniment, by Darius Milhaud (1953), dedicated to the United Temple Chorus. The libretto is based on three passages from the Book of Proverbs: "Who Crieth: Woe?" (Prov. 23:29–35), "The Woman Folly" (Prov. 9:13–18), and "A Woman of Valour" (Prov. 31:10–31).

CANTATA PASTORALE PER LA NASCITA DI NOSTRO SIGNORE. ("A Pastoral Cantata for the Birth of Our Lord"). Christmas cantata in seven movements for soprano, strings, and basso continuo by Alessandro Scarlatti (1695) to a text by Cardinal Antonio Ottoboni. After a two-part instrumental introduction, alternating recitatives and arias tell the Nativity story with allusions to Christ's passion, ending with a delightful pastorale in which Mary invites the shepherds to join in the adoration of the Christ child (*Toccò la prima sorte a voi* ("The greatest fortune was yours")).

CANTATES FRANÇOISES SUR DES SUJETS TIREZ DE L'ECRITURE. ("French Cantatas on Subjects Drawn from Scripture"). Twelve cantatas composed by Elisabeth-Claude Jacquet de la Guerre, published in two volumes (Paris, 1708, 1711). Inspired by Old Testament subjects, the first volume contains six works for solo voice (S/T): "Esther," "The Crossing of the Red Sea," "Jacob and Rachel," "Jonah," "Susanna," and "Judith." The second volume contains four cantatas for solo voice ("Adam," "The Temple Rebuilt," "Joseph," and "Samson") and two for a vocal duo ("The Flood [SB] and "Jephthah" [SS]). Three cantatas feature expressive instrumental interludes: "Tempest" (Jonah 1), "Sound of War" (Exod. 15), and "Sleep" (Judg. 16:19). The last movement of each work contains a moral drawn from the biblical story.

CANTICUM CANTICORUM. ("The Song of Songs"). A cycle of 29 motets for five voices a cappella by Palestrina from his fourth book of motets (1584), dedicated to the composer's patron and employer, Pope Gregory XI. Divided into four modally distinct groups (nos. 1–10, 11–18, 19–24, 25–29) and scored for SATTB (nos. 1–18, 29), SAATB (nos. 19–22, 27–28), and SSATB (nos. 23–26), the sensual biblical text, interpreted allegorically as an expression of Christ's love for the Church or the Soul, is vividly illustrated with madrigalian effects, such as copious word painting and mood setting. Well-known examples include *Vineam meam non custodivi* ("Mine own Vineyard have I not kept well") (Cant. 1:5–6), *Si ignoras te, o pulchra inter mulieres* ("If thou know not, O fair one among women") (Cant. 1:7–8), and *Pulchrœ sunt genœ tuœ* ("Thy cheeks are beautiful as doves") (Cant. 1:9–11).

CANTICUM CANTICORUM SALOMONIS. ("Solomon's Song of Songs"). Work for 16-voice mixed chorus and orchestra by Krzysztof Penderecki (1970–1973) commissioned by the Gulbenkian Foundation and premiered in Lisbon on 5 June 1973. Based on verses from the Song of Songs (1:1–2, 13, 15, 16; 2:4–9), it is regarded as one of the composer's most sensuous and alluring vocal works, featuring the sound of erotic moaning, multivoice speech, and whispered phonemes interspersed with crashing percussion, pizzicato strings, and bells.

CANTIONES SACRAE. ("Sacred Songs"). The first major printed collection of music published in England in 1575 to celebrate the 17th year of the reign of Queen Elizabeth I. It comprises 17 motets by Tallis and 17 by Byrd. *See also* EMENDEMUS IN MELIUS; IN JEJUNIO ET FLETU.

CANTIQUE DES CANTIQUES, LE. ("The Song of Songs"). Work in seven movements for twelve-part a cappella chorus and solo voices by Jean Yves Daniel-Lesur, commissioned by French Radio (1952). Based on texts from the Song of Songs interpreted allegorically as a celebration of Christ's marriage to the Church, the first movement is characterized by colorful vocal orchestration, wordless singing, and humming by male and female voices, scored in dialogue to suggest the conversation of the bride and bridegroom. The last movement, entitled "Épithalame" ("Wedding hymn"), is a setting of the antiphon *Veni Sponsa Christi* ("Come Bride of Christ"), sung as an ostinato combined with upper voices singing, *Pose-moi comme un sceau sur ton coeur, comme un sceau sur ton bras. Car l'amour est fort comme la Mort* ("Set me as a seal upon your heart, as a seal upon your arm. For love is as strong as Death") (Cant. 8:6–7), ending with a succession of **Alleluias.**

CANZONETTA SPIRITUALE SOPRA ALLA NANNA. ("Little Spiritual Cradle Song"). Song for soprano solo and basso continuo by Tarquinio Merula (1594–1665). The hypnotic two-note figure in the accompaniment is suggestive of the Virgin Mary's gentle rocking of the Baby Jesus as she envisages his passion and death on the cross (Lk. 2:35).

CAOINEADH NA DTRÍ MUIRE. ("Keening of the Three Marys"). Traditional Irish lament (*sean nós*) inspired by the three Marys—the mother of Jesus, his mother's sister, and Mary Magdalene—who stood at the cross of Jesus (Jn. 19:25), it was sung in the past at funerals by keening women and every Friday of Lent. There are many versions of this song in Ireland, some bearing the title "Lament of the Passion" (*Caoineadh na Páise*) or "Lament of the Virgin" (*Caoineadh na Maighdine*). The refrain *Ochón agus ochón ó!* ("Alas and woe to me!"), sung by the Virgin, is typical of the vocables of lament used by keening women. It is performed by traditional folk singer Iarla Ó Lionáird on the DVD *The Complete BBC Highland Sessions*, a program that highlights the links between Scottish and Irish Gaelic traditions.

CAPTIVITY OF JUDAH, THE. Oratorio for SATB soloists, mixed chorus, and orchestra by William Crotch (1834), written for the installation of the Duke of Wellington as chancellor of the University of Oxford. Drawing on texts from Isaiah and Jeremiah, act 1 recalls the lamentations of the prophets in solos, duets, and choruses, and act 2 foretells the destruction of Babylon and the coming of the Messiah. Popular numbers included the soprano recitative "Israel is as scattered sheep" (Jer. 50:17) and the air "But he shall feed on Carmel" (Jer. 50:19).

CARO MEA VERE EST CIBUS. ("My Flesh Is Truly Food"). Motet for two sopranos and continuo by Antonio Caldara (1715) based on Jn. 6:55–56 and sung as a communion motet. Scored in counterpoint for much of the work, the voices unite in homophony on *Et ego in illo* ("and I in him") to highlight Christ's presence in the Eucharist. Other settings of this passage include those of Andrea Gabrieli and Giovanni Bassano.

CAVE, THE. Multimedia opera/theater work in three acts for vocal quartet (SSTBar), four woodwinds, percussionists, three keyboards, and five-piece string ensemble by Steve Reich (1990–1993) to a libretto by the composer's wife, Beryl Korot, first performed in Vienna in 1993. The title refers to the Cave of Machpelah, the burial place of the patriarchs Abraham, Isaac, and Jacob (Gen. 49:29–32) and the only place on earth where Jews and Muslims worship together. Lacking the narrative drama and staged action of an opera, much of the work is derived from recorded interviews with Israeli, Palestinian, and American interviewees in West Jerusalem/Hebron (act 1), East Jerusalem/Hebron (act 2), and New York/Austin (act 3), projected on a large screen and accompanied by Reich's electroacoustic music and translating the speech melodies and rhythms into the instrumental. The work includes settings of Gen. 12, 18, 21, and 25 chanted in Hebrew (act 1), Surah 3 of the Qur'an chanted in Arabic, and the popular *Al Khalil Commentary* (act 2). Each act concludes with a sound recording of the ambient sounds found in the building that surrounds the ancient site of Machpelah in modern Hebron (Arabic *Al Khalil*).

CEREMONY OF CAROLS, A. Choral work for three-part treble chorus, solo voices, and harp by Benjamin Britten (op. 28, 1942). It comprises several anonymous medieval and Tudor poems inspired by the Nativity, along with the Gregorian chant *Hodie Christus Natus Est*, which is sung at the beginning (Procession) and end (Recession). The harp "Interlude" (no. 7) is a pastoral movement based on the chant and the first poem, "Wolcum Yole," calls to mind the heavenly music played by choirs of angels on that holy night (Lk. 2:13–14).

CHANDOS ANTHEMS, THE. Eleven large-scale anthems based on Psalms for chorus, soloists, and orchestra by Handel written between 1717 and 1718, when he was composer in residence to James Brydges, first duke of Chandos. The first anthem in D major (HWV 246), a setting of the *Jubilate* (Ps. 100) scored for a small chorus, derives from the **Utrecht Jubilate** and is characterized by a jubilant fugal chorus at the beginning and the end;

no. 2 in D minor (HWV 247) and no. 9 in E-flat major (HWV 254) are settings of verses from the Psalms in the New Metrical Version by Nahum Tate and Nicholas Brady; no. 6a in E minor for three voices (STB) (HWV 251b) is based on Ps. 42 and includes the moving soprano aria "Tears are my daily food," and the duet for soprano and tenor, "Why so full of grief, O my soul?"; no. 7 (HWV 252), in G major, based on Ps. 89, figures in Handel's concerto grosso in G major (op. 3, no. 3); no. 8 (HWV 253), based on verses from Pss. 95, 96, 97, 99, and 103, is the longest of the anthems, and the soprano aria in no. 10 (HWV 255) appears in the oratorio *Israel in Egypt* (1739). The last of the anthems in B-flat major (HWV 251a) is a setting of Pss. 68:1 and 76:6 in 11 movements, concluding with unison voices and strings on "Blessed be God" before a joyful chorus of **Alleluias**.

CHAPTER FOUR. Song by Avenged Sevenfold taken from their album *Waken the Fallen* (2003). Performed throughout with clean, hard vocals, it is a dramatic retelling of the biblical story of Cain and Abel (Gen. 4:8–16), beginning with Cain's murderous intentions and a comment that one was born of light, "the other born black night," and ending with Abel's blood crying out from the soil, "Murder, liar, vengeance, deceit," and the exile of Cain. The band's name comes from Gen. 4:15. This song features as a sound track in the video games *NASCAR Thunder 2004*, *Madden NFL 2004*, and *NHL 2004*.

CHERRY TREE CAROL, THE. Multiple versions of this English ballad/ carol exist, and a spoken version of the story is found also in the Coventry mystery play from the 15th century. Loosely based on the apocryphal Gospel of Pseudo-Matthew, the lyrics contrast Joseph's anger at Mary's pregnancy (cf. Mt. 1:18–19) with Christ's miraculous works in utero. The music, with its gentle, undulating melody; triple meter; and strophic form, imagines the Virgin's lullaby to her unborn child. Highlighting Joseph's old age, the song tells of his marriage to the Virgin Mary, "the Queen of Galilee," and recounts the couple's dialogue as they walk through a cherry orchard. Mary's request for fruit is followed by Joseph's angry response "Let the father of the baby gather cherries for thee." Then the Christ child intervenes and, alluding to Mary as the Second Eve, the most blessed among women (Lk. 1:42), instructs the trees to bow down and touch his mother's hand. Other versions include additional verses telling of Joseph's repentance, his dialogue with the unborn child, the angel's revelation to Joseph, and a dialogue between Mary and the Christ child whose prophetic words foretell his death and resurrection. Popular renditions include versions by folk singers Joan Baez, Judy Collins, Shirley Collins, the Clancy Brothers, and various cathedral choirs from around the world.

CHICHESTER PSALMS. Choral setting of Hebrew Psalm texts by Leonard Bernstein, scored for a countertenor or boy soprano, mixed chorus, and orchestra (brass, percussion, two harps, and strings). Each of the three movements is inspired by a significant portion of one Psalm text and a fragment of another that is either complementary or contrasting. The musical setting highlights the mood of each text, in particular the contrast between violence and peace. It was commissioned for the annual Festival of Three Choirs in 1963 by the dean of Chichester, Walter Hussey, known as the "last great patron of art in the Church of England." Movement 1 opens with the crash of a cymbal to sound paint the text of Ps. 108:2, the awaking of the psaltery, harp, and dawn. An exuberant setting of Ps. 100 ("Make a Joyful Noise to the Lord") follows with an array of percussive instruments in 7/4 dance meter to reflect the Psalm's triumphant mood. Movement 2 is a sublime setting of the first three verses of Ps. 23 sung by a high male voice to harp accompaniment, suggestive of King David, later joined by upper voices of the choir. The dream-like atmosphere of this section is broken with a loud interjection of male voices singing, *allegro feroce*, Ps. 2:1–4 (*lama rag'shu goyim*? ["Why do the nations rage?"]) to a musical adaptation of a passage from the prologue to *West Side Story*. This is followed by the choir and soloist singing the last two verses of Ps. 23:5–6 to the sublime melody set in counterpoint against the ferocious rhythmic melody of the male voices, with an instruction on the score to sing as if "blissfully unaware of threat." The male voices gradually disappear, and the soloist continues, followed by the upper voices, to the accompaniment of the organ. As the last note is held, the rhythmical theme of Ps. 2 (*lama rag'shu goyim*) is heard again in the organ accompaniment as a reminder of the pervading violent threat in the world. Movement 3 carries on this theme with a dissonant orchestral prelude based on movement 1, after which the chorus enters singing Ps. 133 (**Hinne ma tov**) to a soothing melody in 10/4 meter reminiscent of the sublime melody in movement 2. The work concludes with a repetition of verse 1 sung a cappella to emphasize its message of peace.

CHILD OF OUR TIME, A. Oratorio in three parts by Michael Tippett (1939–1941) modeled on Handel's **Messiah** and Bach's **Passions**. It was inspired by *Kristallnacht*, a violent Nazi pogrom organized in November 1938 against Jews in Central Europe. In a powerful sequence of arias and chorus, the composer tells in his own words a contemporary story of man's inhumanity to man. He also introduced five spirituals—"Steal Away," "Nobody Knows the Trouble I've Seen," "**Go Down Moses**," "O, By and By," and "**Deep River**"—songs of universal significance that call to mind oppression and hope, while "the moving waters that renew the earth," along with references to the **Promised Land** and heaven in the spiritual Deep Water, conclude the work.

CHILDREN OF EDEN. Musical in two acts with music and lyrics by Stephen Schwartz, based on a book by John Caird (1991) and inspired by the stories of Adam, Eve, Cain, and Abel (Gen. 2–4) (act 1) and the story of Noah's flood (Gen. 6–9) (act 2). It was premiered in the West End, London (1991), and later at the Paper Mill Playhouse, New Jersey (1997). Popular numbers include "The Spark of Creation," "Stranger to the Rain," and the ballad sung as a duet by Japheth and his wife, Yonah, "In Whatever Time We Have."

CHILDREN OF GOD. Choral work for soprano and mezzo-soprano soloists, two-part children's choir, string quartet, and piano by Daniel Kellogg (2004). It is a celebration of biblical references to children (Mt. 18:3–4; Gen. 22:1–19; Judg. 11–12; 1 Sam. 1–3; Lk. 1; Isa. 11:6–10) interspersed with hymns and poetry by the Cuban American writer Jill Palaez Baumgaertner and concluding with a joyful **Alleluia**.

CHOIRBOOK FOR THE QUEEN. A two-volume collection of contemporary anthems dedicated to Queen Elizabeth in celebration of her Diamond Jubilee (2012). Inspired by Peter Maxwell Davies and Robert Ponsonby and developed by Ian Richie and Carol Butler, the 44 works include James Macmillan's "Canticle of Zachariah" (Lk. 1:68–79), "These Three" (1 Cor. 13) by Rodney Bennett, "As the Father" (Jn. 15:9–10, 12–13) by Philip Moore, "My Beloved Spake" (Cant. 2:10–12; 5:16) by Julian Anderson, and settings of various Psalms by David Matthews (Ps. 23), Francis Pott (Ps. 61), Andrew Simpson (Ps. 98), and Robin Holloway (Ps. 121).

CHOSEN. Carol/anthem for SAATTB chorus and organ by James Macmillan (2003) with words by British poet Michael Symmons Roberts from *Her Maker's Maker.* It is inspired by the story of the Annunciation (Lk. 1:26–38, 46–55) and tells, in first-person narration, of Mary's shock at the angel's announcement and Joseph's distress and unanswered question, "Why was my beloved chosen?," inspired by Mt. 1:18–21.

CHRIST LAG IN TODESBANDEN. ("Christ Lay in the Bonds of Death"). Chorale cantata for Easter Sunday in eight movements for SATB soloists, chorus, two violins, two violas, and continuo by J. S. Bach (BWV 4, ca. 1708). Based on Luther's hymn (1524), an adaptation of the 12th-century hymn *Christ ist erstanden* ("Christ is Risen") from the Easter sequence *Victimae paschali laudes* ("Praise to the paschal victim"), it is one of Bach's earliest cantatas and therefore includes no recitatives or arias. Inspired by the Epistle and the Gospel readings for the day (1 Cor. 5:6–8; Mk. 16:1–8), the first movement opens with a 14-measure instrumental sinfonia, followed by seven movements comprising the seven stanzas of the chorale, each ending with a **Hallelujah**. The third stanza, *Jesus Christus, Gottes Sohn* ("Jesus Christ, God's Son"), refers to the "sting of death" (1 Cor. 15:55), and a dramatic pause follows *Da bleibet nichts* ("Thus nothing remains [of death's sting"]), and a section marked "adagio" follows in which a *circulatio*, Bach's characteristic sign for the cross, appears on "Tod," highlighting Christ's victory over death.

CHRISTE, DU LAMM GOTTES. ("Christ, the Lamb of God"). Chorale cantata for SATB chorus and strings by Mendelssohn (1827), dedicated to the composer's sister, Fanny. Based on Martin Luther's German translation of the **Agnus Dei**, the chorale tune is placed in the soprano line as a cantus firmus over imitative counterpoint in the other vocal parts.

CHRISTEN, ÄTZET DIESEN TAG. ("Christians, Engrave This Day"). Cantata in seven movements for soloists (SATB), chorus (SATB), and orchestra by J. S. Bach (BWV 63, 1714). The libretto is not explicitly biblical, and the work, scored for four trumpets, three oboes, bassoon, timpani, strings, and basso continuo, includes neither arias nor a chorale. Characterized throughout by lively dance rhythms depicting the joy brought about by Christ's birth, it opens with a festive chorus in C major, scored in triple meter, and closes in the same jubilant manner with a double fugue, *Höchster, schau in Gnaden* ("Highest, behold with grace").

CHRISTMAS CANTATA. *Sinfonia sacra* in three movements for chorus, brass ensemble, and optional organ by Daniel Rogers Pinkham (1957). Sung in Latin, it opens with a question to the shepherds, *Quem vidistis pastores. Dicite* ("Whom did you see, shepherds. Tell us."), and their reply, *Natum vidimus* ("We saw him who was born"). A chant-like setting of the *O Magnum Mysterium*, sung by female voices, follows together with a song praising the virgin (*Beata virgo*) introduced by the men's voices and then joined by the women with a crescendo leading up to the iteration of Christ's name, which is sustained for five measures. It concludes with a joyful syncopated *Gloria in Excelsis Deo* and a series of celebratory **Alleluias**.

CHRISTMAS CONCERTO. Well-known concerto grosso, structured as a *sonata da chiesa*, in G minor by Arcangelo Corelli (op. 6/8, ca. 1690), commissioned by Pietro Ottoboni and published posthumously in 1714.

Inscribed *Fatto per la notte di Natale* ("Composed for Christmas Night"), this regal-sounding work, scored in six movements for an ensemble of two concertino violins, cello, ripieno strings, and continuo, is a celebration of the birth of Christ the King. Its origins hark back to an Italian folk tradition where shepherds and local peasants reenacted the scene of the shepherd's adoration of the Christ child during a Novena, a nine-day period of prayer preceding Christmas Day. Corelli follows this tradition by including the well-known pastoral *Pastorale ad libitum* in G major scored in compound quadruple time.

CHRISTMAS ORATORIO. (*Weihnachts-Oratorium/Oratorium tempore Nativitatis Christi*). A cycle of six cantata-like compositions for SSATTBB solo, SATB chorus, and orchestra by J. S. Bach (BWV 248), first performed over six days from Christmas to Epiphany 1734–1735. The music is based on three earlier "birthday cantatas" composed for various members of the Saxon royal family—*Herkules auf dem Scheidewege* ("Hercules at the Crossroads") (BWV 213, 1733), *Tönet ihr Pauken* ("Resound ye drums") (BWV 214, 1733), and *Preise dein Glücke* ("Praise your good fortune") (BWV 215, 1734)—with a new text most likely written by Picander. The six pieces are Christ's birth (Lk. 2:1–7), the angel's announcement to the shepherds (Lk. 2:8–14), the adoration of the shepherds (Lk. 2:15–20), the circumcision and naming (Lk. 2:21), the journey of the Magi (Mt. 2:1, 3–6), and the adoration of the Magi (Mt. 2:7–12). The popular chorale tune *Vom Himmel hoch* ("From Heaven High") by Martin Luther appears on three occasions, and Leo Hassler's passion chorale tune *Herzlich tut mich verlangen* appears at the end of part 1 and most notably in an elaborate setting as the triumphant finale of the whole work.

CHRISTUS. ("Christ"). Incomplete oratorio for soloists, SATB chorus, and orchestra by Mendelssohn (op. 97, 1847), published posthumously and entitled *Christus* by the composer's brother Paul, who identified 13 movements in the work. The libretto, inspired by the birth and passion of Christ, was written by the German diplomat and ambassador to Great Britain Baron Christian Karl Josias von Bunsen. Well-known pieces from the work include a trio (TBB) representing the Three Wise Men asking about the whereabouts of the new king, scored to a walking pizzicato bass line, and the answer they receive, sung by the chorus: "There Shall a Star from Jacob" (Num. 24:17). It concludes with Philipp Nicolai's chorale *Wie schön leuchtet der Morgenstern* ("As bright the star of morning gleams"), beginning a cappella and concluding with an instrumental.

CHRISTUS. ("Christ"). Oratorio in Latin for soloists, chorus, organ, and large orchestra, in three parts and 14 movements (tone poems), by Liszt (S. 3/R. 4778, 1862–1866), premiered in Weimar on 29 May 1873. An orchestral introduction, **Rorate Caeli** (Isa. 45:8), based on the plainchant melody, is followed by *Angelus Domini* for soprano, tenor, and a women's chorus representing the choirs of angels announcing the Nativity to the shepherds, with atmospheric woodwind, English horn, and horn in E and the addition of strings and trumpets for the triumphant Gloria and **Alleluia** (Lk. 2:10–14). Movement 3 is a hymn, ***Stabat Mater** speciosa*, sung a cappella by the chorus (SSATTB) with intermittent organ accompaniment, describing Mary's delight as she watches and plays with her infant son but also her sorrowful vision of his passion and death. Part 1 ends with "Pastoral Music at the Manger" for woodwind and strings and a march in compound duple time depicting the journey of the Three Wise Men (Mt. 2:9, 11). Part 2, *Nach Epiphania* ("After Epiphany"), opens with a setting of the **Beatitudes** (Mt. 5:3–10), each sung a cappella by the baritone and repeated by the chorus with intermittent organ accompaniment. The choir sings **The Lord's Prayer** (Mt. 6:9–13), *Tu es Petrus* ("Thou art Peter") (Mt. 16:18), and the "The Miracle" (Mt. 8:23–26), and part 2 ends with the "Entrance into Jerusalem" (**Hosanna, Benedictus**) (Mt. 21:9) for soloists and chorus. Finally, "Passion and Resurrection" begins with the baritone solo *Tristis est anima mea* (Mk. 14:34–36) and ***Stabat mater dolorosa*** and ends with the Easter hymn *O filii et filiae*, for women's chorus, and *Resurrexit*, a jubilant movement for soloists, chorus, and full orchestra proclaiming Christ's victory over death.

CHRISTUS AM ÖLBERGE. ("Christ on the Mount of Olives"). Oratorio in three parts for three soloists, chorus (SATTBB), and orchestra by Beethoven (op. 85, 1803–1804) to a libretto by Franz Xaver Huber. Beethoven's only oratorio inspired by the story of Christ in the Garden of Gethsemane and written after the completion of *Heiligenstadt Testament* (6 October 1802), the work most likely draws parallels between the despair felt by Beethoven over his impending deafness and Christ before his crucifixion. After an orchestral introduction marked "grave," a poignant recitative, *Jehova, du mein Vater* ("God, Thou my Father"), in which the tenor sings a cappella for the first few measures, leads into the aria *Meine Seele ist erschüttert* ("My Soul within me trembles") with intermittent accompaniment and an appeal to God to take the cup away (Mt. 26:38–39). Part 2 opens with a recitative followed by an aria sung by the Seraph (S) declaring the purpose of Christ's death, combined with a chorus of angels, *Preist des Erlösers Gute* ("Praise the Redeemer's goodness"), and tells of Jesus' personal agony (*Willkommen, Tod* ["Welcome, death"]) and his arrest by the soldiers. Part 3, "Christ's glorification," comprises choruses of soldiers, disciples, and angels, ending with Christ's declaration of victory over hell and a triumphant song of praise from the chorus of angels.

CHRISTUS FACTUS EST. ("Christ Became"). Motet by Bruckner for four-part a cappella choir, dedicated to Benedictine Father Otto Loidol (1884). Based on Phil. 2:8–9, it is his third setting of the Holy Week gradual for Maundy Thursday and is characterized by rich, complex harmonies, chromatic intensity, and a wide variety of dynamics.

CHURCH HYMNARY. Hymnbook recommended by the General Assembly of the Church of Scotland for use in churches. The first edition was published in 1898 to be used alongside the *Scottish Metrical Psalter* (1650), and contained 650 hymns. This was revised in 1927, accompanied by a valuable *Handbook to the Church Hymnary* (ed. J. Moffatt), and again in 1973, also with a *Handbook* (ed. J. Barkley) published in 1979. The fourth edition (CH4), published in 2007, is considerably larger and contains many works by contemporary writers and musicians, some with guitar accompaniment.

CINQ MEDITATIONS SUR L'APOCALYPSE. ("Five Meditations on the Apocalypse"). Organ composition in five movements by Jean Langlais composed in 1973 following a nearly fatal heart attack and a stay in hospital during which he read the entire Book of Revelation. Movement 1, entitled "He that has ears, let him hear," is based on the concluding words of the angel's messages to each of the seven churches (Rev. 2:7, 11, 17, 29; 3:6, 13, 22) and comprises a short theme in the Hypophrygian mode (the Gregorian fourth mode) played on the pedal organ seven times on a four-foot *Clarion* (trumpet) stop in slightly different rhythms. Movement 2, "He is, He was, He is to come" (Rev. 1:4), represents the eternity of Christ, "Alpha and Omega," through a tied whole note, F, held down at the beginning, middle, and end, while the plainchant **Vexilla Regis** from the Good Friday Service, played loudly on the *Trompette du Grand Orgue*, points to Christ's sacrifice on the cross. Movement 3 opens with a trumpet melody (Rev. 1:10) and then describes the horrific visions of the Apocalypse (Rev. 9:11), depicted musically through a theme consisting of discords on full organ. The angel standing with one foot on the earth and the other on the sea (Rev. 10:1–3) is represented by a short sequence on the pedal organ with very wide three-note chords. In movement 4 ("Even so, come, Lord Jesus") (Rev. 22:20), the flight of the soul heavenward is represented by a melody soaring into the high range of the organ's register, but the final movement ("The Fifth Trumpet") returns to the terrors of hell with low, dark chords for the bottomless pit and rising melodies for the sprawling movements of the locusts (Rev. 9:1–11).

CLEMENCY. One-act chamber opera for five singers (STTBarBar) and string orchestra by James Macmillan to a libretto by Michael Symmons Roberts (2011). It is a contemporary reworking of the story of the visit of the three angels to Abraham and Sarah (Gen. 18) on their way to seek vengeance on Sodom and Gomorrah. They pronounce that Sarah will bear a child within a year, singing in close harmony with an otherworldly sound, and reveal their identity with fire and speaking in tongues. Sarah contemplates the news of her impending pregnancy in an ecstatic solo, and when the couple hear of the divine retribution, Abraham pleads for clemency but to no avail. The opera finishes quietly with Abraham rushing after the three visitors and Sarah contemplating her baby's future amid the destruction of the Twin Towns.

COAT OF MANY COLOURS. Song by Dolly Parton (1969), the title track on the album *Coat of Many Colours* (1971). Described as one of her all-time favorites, the song tells how Parton's mother stitched together a coat from rags as she told the story of Joseph's coat from Gen. 37:3. After wearing the coat to school, Parton tells how she could not understand why the other children laughed at her. The coat now appears in the Chasing Rainbows Museum in the Dollywood theme park in Tennessee. It has been popularly covered by many artists, including Eva Cassidy on the posthumous album *Somewhere* (2008) and Shania Twain on the album *Just Because I'm a Woman: Songs of Dolly Parton* (2003).

COELOS ASCENDIT HODIE. ("He Ascended into Heaven Today"). One of Stanford's three Latin motets for a cappella double chorus (SSAATTBB) (op. 38, no. 2, 1905). Ascending melodic lines amid bursts of joyful **Alleluias** portray the Ascension of Christ as described in Lk. 24:50–52 and Acts 1:9–11.

COLLECTION OF HYMNS FOR THE USE OF THE PEOPLE CALLED METHODISTS. A collection of 525 hymns, mostly by Charles Wesley, first published with a preface by his brother John in 1779 and then in numerous later editions, notably the 1876 edition with a new supplement. Among all-time favorites included in the earliest editions were "Hark, the herald angels sing" and "Love divine, all loves excelling." Major revisions were published under the title *The Methodist Hymn-book* in 1904 and 1933 and *Singing the Faith: The New Methodist Hymn-Book* in 2011. The *United Methodist Hymnal* (1989), following the merging of the Methodist Church and the Evangelical United

Brethren in 1968, used inclusive language and included Native American hymns, black spirituals, and Duke Ellington's "Come Sunday."

COME, O THOU TRAVELLER UNKNOWN. Hymn by Charles Wesley based on the story of Jacob wrestling with the angel at Peniel (Gen. 32:22–32). Originally with 14 verses, it has been described as the greatest of Wesley's hymns and "more a philosophical poem than a hymn." Published with the title "Wrestling Jacob" in *Hymns and Sacred Poems* (1742), it is sung to a number of tunes, including two specially composed for it: "Peniel" (Gen. 32:30) by Wesley's grandson S. S. Wesley (1810–1876) and "Jabbok" (Gen. 32:22) by Cyril V. Taylor (1907–1991).

CONCERT OF SACRED MUSIC LIVE FROM GRACE CATHEDRAL, A. Concert by American jazz legend, composer, bandleader, and pianist Duke Ellington, premiered in Grace Cathedral, San Francisco (1965), and subsequently recorded at Fifth Avenue Presbyterian Church on 26 December 1966. It includes the well-known song "In the Beginning, God," sung by bass-baritone/narrator Brock Peters to the accompaniment of piano, punctuated with instrumental jazzy interludes depicting the void that existed in the beginning (Gen. 1:1–2) and concluding with vocalists chanting the names of the books of the Bible, one by one, to the accompaniment of saxophone and jazz orchestra. This song won a Grammy in 1967 as the best original jazz composition. Other biblical songs on the LP include a setting of **The Lord's Prayer** sung by Esther Marrow and "David danced before the Lord with all his might" (2 Sam. 6:14), performed by tap dancer Bunny Briggs and accompanied by the jazz orchestra with singing by vocalists and soloist Brock Peters. The concert was followed by a Second Sacred Concert in 1968 and a Third in 1973.

CONFITEBOR TIBI DOMINE. ("I Will Give Thanks to You, O Lord"). Motet *alla francese* ("in the French style") by Monteverdi (SV 267, 1641) scored either for five voices (SSATB) and continuo or for four *viole da braccio* and soprano. It is the last of three settings of Ps. 111 and is in C major in homophony, alternating between solo and tutti sections. *Sanctum*, in the phrase *Sanctum et terribile nomen ejus* ("Holy and awesome is his name") (v. 9), is set in whole notes and the phrase *et terribile* in 16ths (semiquavers) to suggest fear and trembling. There are many other settings of the Psalm, including those by Vivaldi (ca. 1732), Pergolesi (1732), and Mozart in his **Vesperae Solennes de Confessore** (K. 339, 1780).

CONVERSION OF SAUL. Anthem for a cappella SSAATTBB chorus (2005) in Latin and English by Z. Randall Stroope. Inspired by Acts 9:1–18, the first section, describing Saul's violent persecution of the Christians, is dominated by the Latin words *Caedite, vexate* ("murder, harass") and *ligate vinculis* ("bind with chains"), sung to a fast tempo (*molto agitato*) in compound duple time, and features octave leaps, glissandos, and foot stomping. Unison altos and basses chant Christ's words "Why do you persecute me, Saul?" (Acts 9:4) in sharp notation to signify pain. In the second section, lush harmonies in softer, flat tonalities and a slower tempo denote Christ's command to Saul to turn "darkness to light" and "hatred to love."

COULEURS DE LA CITÉ CÉLESTE. ("Colors of the Heavenly City"). Work for solo piano, brass, woodwind, and percussion by Messiaen (1963), inspired by five texts from the Book of Revelation (Rev. 4:3; 8:6; 9:1; 21:11, 19–20). The melodic and rhythmic material derives from plainsong **Alleluias**, Greek, and Hindu rhythms and birdsongs from different parts of the world.

COVENANT, THE. (The Rainbow). Sixth movement in the **Genesis Suite,** based on Gen. 9:1–17, scored for orchestra and narrator by Ernst Victorio (ca. 1943). The orchestrations from the existing sound recording are reconstructed by Patrick Russ.

COVENTRY CAROL. Christmas carol, first performed in Coventry in the 16th century as part of the English pageant play of the Shearmen and Tailors. Hauntingly beautiful, it is inspired by the story of the Massacre of the Holy Innocents by Herod (Mt. 2:13–18) and sung as a lullaby by the children's mothers who attempt to quieten the cries of their children in a last effort to save them from slaughter, as indicated by the *Tierce de Picardie* (Picardy third) at the end.

CREATION, THE. (*Die Schöpfung*). Oratorio in three parts for SATB chorus, soloists (STBar), and orchestra by Haydn (Hob XX1/2, 1796–1798). The English text, based on Gen. 1 and 2, Pss. 19 and 54, and Milton's *Paradise Lost*, is said by Haydn to have been written by "an Englishman by the name of Lidley." After the overture in C minor depicting the chaos before the Creation, parts 1 and 2 describe the six days of creation, with part 3 celebrating Adam and Eve's idyllic life in the Garden of Eden before the Fall. Each of the six days of creation is announced by one of the three soloists representing the three archangels, Raphael, Uriel, and Gabriel. The angels also sing as a trio, sometimes with the chorus, most notably at the end of part 1 ("The heavens are telling") and in the fugal chorus at the end of part 2 ("Achieved is the glorious work"). Adam and Eve sing two duets, including a tender love duet in contra danse style ("Graceful consort! At thy side"), and the work concludes with the chorus and soloists singing together ("Sing the Lord, ye voices all").

CREATION'S HYMN. (*Die ehre Gottes aus der Natur*). The fourth of six sacred songs (*Sechs Geistliche Lieder*, op. 48) by Beethoven to words by Christian Furchtegott Gellert (1715–1769). Possibly inspired by Ps. 8, this majestic hymn of praise celebrates the wonder of God's creation. Translated into English by J. Troutbeck, it has been variously arranged for choir and ensemble and as an instrumental solo.

CREEPING DEATH. Song from the album *Ride the Lightning* (1984) by the heavy metal band Metallica. Inspired by the Cecil B. DeMille epic film *The Ten Commandments* (1956) and narrated in the first person by the Angel of Death, known as "Creeping Death," it tells how he was given permission by the chosen one, Moses, to inflict death on the Pharaoh's son. Specific references to Exod. 1–12 include Israel's slavery for over 400 years (Exod. 12:40–41); the burning bush (Exod. 3:2); God's command "Let my people go" (Exod. 5:1; 7:16, etc.); the plagues of blood, darkness, hail, and the death of the firstborn (Exod. 7–12); and the night of the Passover (Exod. 13). In live performances, audiences traditionally chant the Angel of Death's words "Die by my hand."

CROWN HIM WITH MANY CROWNS. Hymn by Matthew Bridges (1851) with additional verses by Godfrey Thring, usually sung to the tune *Diademata* by George J. Elvey (1868). It celebrates Christ's victory over sin and death in a series of biblical allusions (Rev. 19:12; Isa. 2:4; Ps. 46:9).

CROWN OF ROSES, THE. One of Tchaikovsky's "Sixteen Songs for Children" (op. 54, 1883), known also by the title "Legend." Hauntingly beautiful in E minor, its lilting meter in 2/4 time tells the story of Jesus' boyhood in a garden tending roses whose thorns became the crown of thorns in his passion. The Russian lyric by Alekséy Pleshchéyev (1877) was translated into German by Hans Schmidt and into English by Geoffrey Dearmer, published in the *Oxford Book of Carols* (1928). Originally scored for high voice, it was subsequently transcribed by Tchaikovsky for voice and orchestra (1884) and later for mixed a cappella choir (1889).

CRUCIFIXION, THE: A MEDITATION ON THE SACRED PASSION OF THE HOLY REDEEMER. Oratorio for tenor and bass soloists, mixed chorus (SATB), and organ, including five hymns for chorus and congregation, by John Stainer (1887). It is dedicated to Stainer's pupil and friend William

Hodge. The libretto by Rev. J. Sparrow-Simpson is based on texts from the Gospel narrative of Christ's passion, supplemented by meditative choruses and hymns written for the oratorio and representing Victorian Christianity. Christ's words are sometimes sung by a bass and at other times by a male chorus, while the narrator's are sung by a tenor. It includes many well-known numbers, such as "Processional to Calvary" (no. 3), an instrumental for organ, followed by "Fling Wide the Gates," with "my God and my friend, to suffer, endure and die" in unison. The sublime quartet/chorus "God so loved the world" (Jn. 3:7–8), sung a cappella, is often performed as an anthem in its own right, and the hymn "Cross of Jesus" has become a standard in modern hymnbooks. The work is punctuated by settings of the **Seven Last Words** of Christ, and after Jesus' final word, a solo tenor sings a cappella, "And he bowed his head and gave up the ghost" (Jn. 19:30). The chorus and congregation conclude with a final hymn, "For the love of Jesus," and an **Amen**. An orchestrated version of the work by Barry Rose was commissioned by the Guildford Philharmonic Orchestra for a performance on 31 March 2001, the centenary of Stainer's death.

CRUCIFIXUS À 8. ("The Crucifixion for Eight Voices"). Motet in C minor for unaccompanied eight-part choir (SSAATTBB) and the most famous of Antonio Lotti's settings of the *Crucifixus* (1717–1719), from the Credo in F of his *Missa Sancti Christophori*. A setting of the words of the Nicene Creed, derived from the New Testament (Mt. 27:22–26, 50; Mk. 15:22–47; 1 Cor. 15:3–4; Phil. 2:5–8), dissonances, suspensions, and plaintive intervallic leaps illustrate musically the pain felt by Christ during his crucifixion, while long, sustained notes toward the end reflect the somber mood surrounding Christ's death and burial. A modulation to C major in the final measures points to his resurrection.

CURE OF SAUL, THE. Sacred ode in three parts by Samuel Arnold to a libretto by John Brown (1767). The music is lost, but the libretto tells the story of Saul's affliction by the fiend of melancholy because of his disobedience to God's command (1 Sam. 16:14–23). David, accompanied by a choir of shepherds, is sent to cure Saul with his music. Singing of the happiness of Adam and Eve in paradise before the Fall, the music has the opposite effect on Saul and evokes in him a resentment as to why others are happy when he is miserable.

• D •

DANIEL. Oratorio for eight soloists, SATB chorus, orchestra, and organ by American composer George Frederick Bristow (op. 42, 1866). The libretto, by W. A. Hardenbrook, is based on the biblical story of Daniel's refusal to worship the golden statue of Nebuchadnezzar (Dan. 3), with solo parts scored for two angels (SA), Azariah (T), Meshach (T), Daniel (B), Nebuchadnezzar (B), and two extrabiblical characters, Arioch (B) and a Herald (B). It opens with an overture, "The Captivity of Israel," followed by a choral movement based on Ps. 137:1–6. *See also* BY THE WATERS OF BABYLON.

DANIEL IN THE LION'S DEN. Cantata in one act for soloists, SATB chorus, narrator, two pianos, percussion, and electronic tape by Daniel Pinkham (1972), first performed by the Handel and Haydn Society, Boston, on 27 April 1973. The biblical story (Dan. 6), supplemented by the apocryphal Bel and the Dragon (Dan. 14), Ps. 116, and the hymn "The Creatures in the Lord's Hands" by John Newton (**Olney Hymns**, Book 2, 97), is scored for Daniel (Bar), Habakkuk (B-Bar), an Angel (T), and a spoken part for the Narrator. The electronic tape includes the distant sound of lions' growling and roaring.

DANZE DEL RE DAVID, LE. ("The Dances of King David"). Suite in seven movements for piano by Mario Castelnuovo-Tedesco (op., 37, 1925), inspired by the discovery of a notebook belonging to his late grandfather that contained prayers in three-part harmony based on Jewish liturgical melodies. Based on the biblical account of David's dance before the Ark (2 Sam. 6:14), the seven dances are energetic, tumultuous, and lyrical: *vivo e tumultuoso, ieratico, rapido e selvaggio, lento ed estatico, rude e ben ritmato, malinconico e supplichevole, allegro guerriero–alla chiusa, chiaro e solenne.*

DARK I AM BUT LOVELY. Song by Sinead O'Connor from the album *Theology* (2007). Inspired by verses from the Song of **Solomon** (Cant. 1:5–6; 3:1; 6:1; 5:16; 3:7; 8:7), it is written in first-person narration from the perspective of the woman and sung to the accompaniment of a lone guitar. Highly expressive, it tells of the woman's hardship in the vineyards and of the loss of her lover, whose lips, fragrances, and flavors she longs for. She appeals to the women of Jerusalem to find him and tell him that their love affair is far from over. *See also* NIGRA SUM.

DAS BUCH MIT SIEBEN SIEGELN. ("The Book with Seven Seals"). Oratorio for soloists, chorus, orchestra, and organ by Franz Schmidt based on the Book of Revelation, premiered in the Goldener Saal of the Musik-verein, Vienna, on 15 June 1938. Scored for John (Heldentenor) and the Voice of the Lord (B-Bar), it is in three parts: (1) Prologue in Heaven (Rev. 1–5, 20), (2) the opening of the six seals (Rev. 6–7), and (3) the opening of the seventh seal, the Last Judgment and Song of Praise (Rev. 8–22). The work abounds in symbolism, such as the sevenfold repetition of motifs and a timpani tremolo over seven measures. Memorable moments include the battle between Michael and the dragon and the fall of the dragon into the pit, illustrated musically by descending demisemiquaver runs played by the entire orchestra. The work concludes with John's farewell ("It is John who heard all this"), recalling the setting of his salutation at the beginning ("Grace be to you and peace").

DAS LIEBESMAHL DER APOSTEL. ("The Love Feast of the Apostles"). Work in three parts for male chorus and orchestra by Richard Wagner (WWV 69, 1843), inspired by Acts 2:1–13 and described by the composer as "a type of morality play." Originally written for a choral festival in Dresden's Frauen-kirche, the Church of Our Lady, it involved over 1,200 singers and large or-chestral forces and was performed without any pauses. The work depicts "the first feast of Pentecost and the outpouring of the Holy Spirit," and the descent of the Holy Spirit was represented by placing 40 singers in the Frauenkirche's cupola. The piece was arranged for brass band by M. Pohle for a performance by the U.S. Marine Band.

DAUGHTER OF JAIRUS, THE. Cantata for soprano, tenor and bass solo-ists, mixed chorus, and orchestra by John Stainer (1878), first performed at the closing service of the Worcester Festival (1878). The libretto is inspired by the story of the raising of Jairus's daughter (Mt. 9:18–25) combined with other biblical references (Isa. 25:8; 32:2, 30; Bar. 4:22, 23; Wisd. 2:1, 2, 6, 7, 8, 13, 17; Eph. 5:14; Rom. 6:11, 12). A chorus of women sings a section entitled "The Wailing," atmospherically prefaced by an interlude for oboe solo, and the work concludes with a series of jubilant **Amens** and **Hallelujahs** sung by the chorus and soloists.

DAVID AND BATHSHEBA. Opera in one act by David Thompson (1997) inspired by the story of David and Bathsheba (2 Sam. 11–12) and a Cornish play about the Legend of the Rood. The work portrays Uriah as an upright man, devoted to his wife, and Bathsheba as a woman seduced by David. It in-cludes an instrumental, "Funeral March," for Uriah, and Bathsheba's lament sung in recitative ("Alas that ever I was born; I shall faint for sorrow"). A short scherzo depicts the Israelites' "Building of the Temple," halted by God's voice offstage and followed by the death of David, whose body is carried off to a short instrumental.

DAVID AND BATHSHEBA. Opera/oratorio in two acts by Ståle Kleiberg (2007) to a libretto by Jessica Gordon. Based on 2 Sam. 11–12 and Pss. 8 and 51, it features four monologues set as arias. The first, sung by David (Bar), "Who is this that looks like the dawn?" includes a harp in the accompaniment and describes Bathsheba's beauty with allusions to the **Song of Songs** ("Her hair like a flock of goats streaming down the mountainside; her teeth like a flock of ewes come fresh from the dipping.") (Cant. 4:1–2; 6:10). His second, "Have mercy on me O God," is a setting of Ps. 51, ending with a plea to God to save his little son. In her first aria, Bathsheba (Mez) laments the loss of her husband Uriah while speaking of her love affair with **King David**; in the second, "Why has the fruit of my orchard failed?" laments the loss of her child. In a dialogue at the end, David tries to persuade his wife to leave aside her grief, but her reply is, "I cannot. My son is dead."

DAVID IN SPELUNCA ENGADDI. ("David in the Cave of Engedi"). Oratorio in two parts for soloists, chorus, and orchestra by Simon Mayr (1795), written for the Girls' Choir of S. Lazari Dei Mendicanti, Venice. The libretto, by Giuseppe Maria Foppa, based loosely on 1 Sam. 24, tells the story of **King Saul**'s jealousy and desire to kill David and how David spares Saul at Engedi, cutting off part of his robe while he is asleep. When Saul (S) awakes, he sings the aria "What do I hear! . . . I am deluded! . . . A harp!," followed by an ethereal solo for harp. Jonathan (S) and David (Mez) speak of their love for each other in several recitatives, although much of the plot focuses on David's betrothal and marriage with Michal, and the work ends with Michal's aria ("If you deny me my bridegroom, I shall die") and a chorus announcing the reconciliation of all in peace and love ("O joyful happy day!").

DAVID OF THE WHITE ROCK. (Welsh *Dafydd y Garreg Wen*). One of the most popular traditional Welsh songs, first published in the "Relics of the Welsh Bards" (1794). It tells the story of the blind harper and composer David Owen (1709–1739), who, on his deathbed, longed to play his harp one last time, like **King David**. The hauntingly beautiful melody with its heart-wrenching wide leaps and plaintive minor tonality was later arranged by Joseph Haydn (1732–1809) and Benjamin Britten (1913–1976) and performed by the renowned Welsh singer Katharine Jenkins and harpist Catrin Finch on the album *Living a Dream* (2005).

DAVIDE PENITENTE. ("Penitent David"). Cantata for SST soloists, chorus, and orchestra by Mozart (K. 469), commissioned by the Wiener Tonkünstler-Societät (Viennese Society of Musicians) for a Lenten benefit concert and first performed on 13 March 1785. The text, attributed to Saverio Mattei (1742–1795/1796), is an Italian paraphrase of the penitential Psalms (Pss. 6, 32, 38, 51, 102, 130, 145), traditionally associated with David's grief following his illicit union with Bathsheba and the death of their firstborn (2 Sam. 11–12; cf. Ps. 51:1). The music derives from the Kyrie and Gloria of the C Minor Mass (K. 427, 1782–1783), with two newly composed arias; a tenor aria in B-flat major, *A te, fra tanti affanni* ("From you, amid such troubles"); and a soprano aria in C minor, *Tra l'oscure ombre funeste* ("Amid the dark grievous shadows") in addition to a joyful cadenza for the soloists in the last movement.

DAVIDIS PUGNA ET VICTORIA. ("The Fight of David and His Victory"). *Dramma sacrum*/oratorio for soloists (SSAB) and five-part string orchestra by Alessandro Scarlatti (ca. 1679–1682), inspired by the story of David and Goliath (1 Sam. 17). The mournful arioso *Heu perii* ("Alas, I die"), sung by Saul (Ct), comprises suspensions and descending melodic lines to depict Saul's despair before the battle, and the relationship of Jonathan (S) and David (S) is explored in two duets, *O Jonathae spes una David* and *Sic et mortis orrore labente*, and the aria *In flore labente*. The work concludes with David killing Goliath and the double chorus *Heu sodales*, in which the laments of the Philistines are juxtaposed with the rejoicing of the Israelites.

DAVID'S DANCE. The first six orchestral dance movements from "Heritage Symphonic Dances" (2000) by Irish American John Duffy, based on the original sound track of a television series. It tells the story of the Jewish diaspora by evoking the sound of traditional dance music from Eastern Europe ("The Rabbi's Dance"), Italy ("Renaissance Dance"), Moorish Spain ("Spanish Dance"), and America ("America") and concludes with an uplifting "dance of affirmation" ("Waltz"). The first movement begins with the majestic sound of the Heritage theme, based on the notes of the shofar, and quickly moves to a contrasting section set in a fast 6/8 meter to replicate in sound David's frantic swirling movements as he "danced before the Lord" (2 Sam. 6:14). *See* HERITAGE SUITE

DAVID'S LAMENTATION. Anthem for four voices (SATB) sung a cappella in A minor, by American colonial composer William Billings (1778), performed today at Sacred Harp conventions in the American South and in Ireland, among other places. Based on 2 Sam. 18:33, it begins in four-part homophony ("David the King was grieving") followed by the announcement of David's cry sung by basses, "Then as he went, he wept and said," and then homophony, "O my Son, O my son." This leads to a climax on "Would to God I had died for thee, O Absalom, my son, my son," followed by a reprise from the basses and chorus. It has been recorded by many choirs, including the Mormon Tabernacle Choir on the album *The Lord's Prayer*, by the Watersons on the album *Sound, Sound Your Instruments of Joy* (1977), and by Chanticleer on the album *American Journey* (2002). An evocative arrangement by Joshua Shank is performed by high school choirs. *See also* PLANCTUS DAVID SUPER SAUL ET JONATHAN.

DAVID'S LAMENTATION OVER SAUL AND JONATHAN. Cantata for soloists, chorus, and orchestra by William Boyce (1736), revised for performances in Dublin in 1744. After a melancholic overture in G minor, the work recounts David's lament for Saul and Jonathan (2 Sam. 1:17–27) and includes many poignant numbers, including the chorus "For Saul, for Jonathan, they fast, they weep" and the recitative at the end, "How are the mighty fallen." Other settings of this text include a motet cycle for four voices entitled *Planxit autem David*, attributed to Josquin des Prez (before 1521). *See also* PLANCTUS DAVID SUPER SAUL ET JONATHAN.

DE BLIND MAN STOOD ON THE ROAD AND CRIED. African American spiritual inspired by the story of blind Bartimaeus (Mk. 10:46–52). In the spiritual, the man does not receive his sight as he does in the biblical story, and the song closes as it opens—with a cry for help. Arranged by H. T. Burleigh and Moses Hogan, it enjoys performances by choral groups and youth choirs.

DE PROFUNDIS. ("Out of the Depths"). Work in Hebrew for six-part mixed a cappella chorus (SSATBB) by Schoenberg (op. 50b, 1950). The last completed work by the composer before his death in 1951, it is dedicated to the newly formed state of Israel. It is a highly dramatic setting of Ps. 130 based on complex serial techniques. Other musical settings of *De Profundis* include most notably Arvo Pärt's work for four male voices (CtTBarB), percussion (ad lib.), and organ (1980). The slow, meditative tempo, which becomes more animated before dying away at the end, describes the penitent's endless period of waiting and his desperate prayer of supplication to the Lord, while the sound of a singular tubular bell captures the atmosphere of prevailing doom.

DEAD. Song by the Pixies from the album *Doolittle* (1989), inspired by the story of David's adulterous affair with Bathsheba and the premeditated killing of her husband Uriah (2 Sam. 11:2–17). David's overwhelming sexual desire for "Shebe" and his murderous intentions are represented by a pulsating drumbeat accompanied by electric guitar and the repeated shouting of the song's title.

DEAR LORD AND FATHER OF MANKIND. Hymn by the Quaker John Greenleaf Whittier (1807–1892) from his poem "The Brewing of Soma" (1872), in which a Christian's quiet spiritual communion is contrasted to the effects of drinking soma. Biblical allusions include Jesus' "Follow me" on the shores of Galilee (Mt. 4:19), "drop thy still dews of quietness" (cf. Isa. 45:8, NAB), and the "still small voice" from the Elijah story (1 Kgs. 19:12). It is sung to a variety of tunes, notably Repton, from Parry's oratorio *Judith* (1888), published in *The Repton School Hymn Book* (1924).

DEATH OF ABEL. Oratorio by Thomas Arne, first performed at the Theatre Royal, Smock Alley, Dublin, on 18 February 1744 and later at Drury Lane, London, on 12 March 1755. The only existing fragment is the popular Siciliana *The Hymn of Eve*, the tune of which was set as a hymn, "Away with our Sorrows and Fear," by Charles Wesley in *A Collection of Hymns for the People called Methodists* (1780). It features in the album *Sing Lustily and With Good Courage* by Maddy Prior and the Carnival Band (1994).

DEBORAH. Oratorio by Handel with a libretto by Samuel Humphreys, premiered at the King's Theatre, London, on 17 March 1733 (HWV 51). Described as a pastiche based on the biblical story (Judg. 4–5), it incorporates extracts from **Brockes' Passion**, two coronation anthems, and three **Chandos anthems** as well as the vespers Psalm setting *Dixit Dominus* (Ps. 110) and other works. The action takes place in a single day, and the music for the finales of all three acts, sung by the chorus, is borrowed from the coronation anthems, **Let Thy Hand Be Strengthened**, **The King Shall Rejoice**, and "O Celebrate . . . **Alleluia**." The most dramatic use of the chorus is found in act 2, "All your boast will end in woe," where, in an ensemble of soloists, Deborah (S) and Barak (A) are in conflict with Sisera (A) and Baal's Priest (B), climaxing in the entrance of a double chorus (SSAA-TTBB) representing the Priests of the Israelites and the Priests of Baal. Among the most popular pieces are two arias by Barak, "How Lovely is the Blooming Fair" and "In the Battle fame pursuing," and one by Abinoam (B), "Tears, such as tender fathers shed."

DEEP RIVER. African American spiritual popularly arranged for voice and piano (1917) by Harry T. Burleigh (1866–1949) and famously performed by bass-baritone Paul Robeson, baritone Rodney Clarke, contralto Marian Anderson, and mezzo-soprano Jessye Norman, among others. It features as the final spiritual in the oratorio **A Child of Our Time** by Michael Tippett. References to biblical imagery include the Promised Land, the Gospel Feast, and the River Jordan and point to a new life of freedom on earth and in heaven.

DÉLUGE, LE: POËME BIBLIQUE. ("The Flood: A Biblical Poem"). Innovative for its time, this work encapsulates three genres—oratorio, *poème lyrique*, and *cantate biblique*—as its subtitle indicates. It was composed by Saint-Saëns (op. 45, 1875) to a paraphrase of Gen. 6–9 by the librettist Louis Gallet for one character, God, and a narrator. The overarching theme, based on "God's grieving heart" (Gen. 6:6), is found also in two Mesopotamian myths: the epics of Atrahasis (3:5, 36–6:40) and Gilgamesh (11:164–206). Highly programmatic, the work is in three parts, preceded by a prelude that captures the mood of the entire work by introducing two subjects from which later motifs are derived. The first of these, played by solo viola, features a melancholic melody in E minor representing God's disappointment at his creation, while the second, played by a solo violin, represents "God's grieving heart" (Gen. 6:5–6). Part 1, opening with a tenor recitative to harp accompaniment, recounts the mythological story of the illicit union of the sons of God and the daughters of men (Gen. 6:1–4). Part 2 is a dramatic, musical depiction of the raging tempest with its cataclysmic thunder and lightning and swirling floodwaters (Gen. 7:11, 17–24). The mood of part 3 (based on Gen. 8:1–9:17) reflects the calm of the abated storm. Here, Saint-Saëns sound paints the text with musical motifs illustrating the gentle breeze, the flights of the raven and dove, the rainbow, and God's benediction ordaining the multiplication and spread of people all over the world. In the very last section, flutes and violins sound the motif of "God's grieving heart" for one last time to emphasize that God's grief continues for all eternity. *See also* LE DÉLUGE; NOYE'S FLUDDE.

DEM DRY BONES. African American spiritual composed by James Weldon Johnson (1871–1938), inspired by the story of the prophet Ezekiel's vision of the valley of dry bones brought back to life by the word of the Lord (Ezek. 37:1–14). Ascending semitones in the melody suggest the bones connecting together, "bone to its bone" (v. 7). An all-time favorite, it was especially popular in the 1930s–1950s, performed by southern gospel groups such as the Mills Brothers (1928), the Delta Rhythm Boys (1934), the Deep River Boys (1935), and the Plainsmen Quartet with Rusty Goodman (1954). *See also* OSSA ARIDA.

DER FALL BABYLONS. *See* THE FALL OF BABYLON.

DER FÜR DIE SÜNDE DER WELT GEMARTERTE UND STER-BENDE JESUS. ("The Story of Jesus, Suffering and Dying for the Sins of the World"). *See* BROCKES' PASSION.

DER STERN VON BETHLEHEM. ("The Star of Bethlehem"). Cantata in seven movements for soprano and bass soloists, chorus, and orchestra by Josef Rheinberger (op. 164, 1901). The title is an allusion to the Star Prophecy (Num. 24:17), and the libretto written by his wife was inspired by the Nativity story from Matthew and Luke's Gospels, in particular the adoration of the Christ child by the Shepherds and the Three Wise Men. In movement 6, the soprano soloist narrates the blissful scene of the Madonna's adoration of the Christ child in expressive harmonies and soaring melodies.

DER TOD JESU. ("The Death of Jesus"). Well-known 18th-century oratorio by Karl Heinrich Graun (1755) to a libretto by Carl Wilhelm Ramler, premiered on 26 March 1755 in Berlin. Without dialogues or dramatic personages, it is made up of solo recitatives and reflective arias and chorales sung by the chorus and audience. Characterized by upbeat music to reflect a joyful human response to Christ's passion and resurrection, the oratorio disappeared from concert repertoires in the 19th century, to be replaced by performances of Bach's more somber passions. Other works based on the same libretto include Telemann's passion oratorio composed in the same year (TWV 5:6, 1755) for a performance in Hamburg prior to Graun's premiere in Berlin.

DER TURM ZU BABEL. *See* TOWER OF BABEL, THE.

DES HEILANDS LETZTE STUNDEN. ("The Saviour's Last Hours," also known as "Calvary" or "The Crucifixion"). Oratorio in two parts for soloists, chorus, and orchestra by Louis Spohr (WoO 62, 1834–1835) based on the passion of Christ from the Gospels and Isaiah 53, first performed at Kassel on Good Friday 1835. Translated into English by Edward Taylor, it was performed at the Festival of Norwich under the direction of the composer himself in 1839. Most memorable are a tortured air for Peter ("Tears of sorrow, shame and anguish") in part 1 and Mary's melancholic air ("When this scene of trouble closes") in part 2.

DESTRUCTION OF SENNACHERIB. Interlude by American thrash/death metal band Ares Kingdom on the album *Incendiary* (2010). Fast riffs, raspy vocals, and throaty shrieks describe the killing of 185,000 Assyrians by the Angel of Death (2 Kgs. 19:35).

DESTRUCTION OF SENNACHERIB, THE (*Porazheniye Senna-kheriba*). Cantata for mixed chorus and orchestra (1866–1867; rev. 1874) by Mussorgsky with words from Lord Byron's poem **Sennacherib** (1815), it tells the story of Assyrian King Sennacherib's siege of Jerusalem and subsequent slaughter of the Assyrian army by the Angel of Death (2 Kgs. 18:13–19:37). Reputed to have been the last work the composer heard performed before he died in 1881, it was later arranged by Rimsky-Korsakov as a symphonic chorus (1894).

DEUS PASSUS. ("St. Luke's Passion" [*Passions-Stücke nach Lukas*]). Passion oratorio in 27 movements (lasting variously from one minute to nine minutes) for five soloists (SMezATBar), mixed chamber choir, chamber orchestra, harp, and organ by Wolfgang Rihm (2000), commissioned by the Internationale Bachakademie in Stuttgart to commemorate the 250th anniversary of the death of J. S. Bach. Inspired by the story of Christ's passion in Luke's Gospel and memories of the Holocaust, it also includes texts from the Good Friday **Reproaches**, the *Stabat Mater*, Isaiah 53, the sixth-century Latin hymn *Pange lingua* ("Of the Glorious Body telling"), and the poem *Tenebrae* ("Shadows/Darkness") by Paul Celan (Paul Antschel), a Holocaust survivor who committed suicide in 1970. The composer chose Luke's account of the Passion as the least anti-Semitic of the Gospels.

DIALOGO DEL GIGANTE GOLIA. ("Dialogue of the Giant Goliath"). Dialogue motet for two soloists, chorus, orchestra, and continuo by Carissimi. Inspired by the biblical story of conversations between Goliath (B), the young David (S), and the Israelites (1 Sam. 17), the work begins with a chorus of frightened Israelites (*Fugiamus* ["let us flee"]) in imitative counterpoint and concludes with the victory song sung first by a chorus of women then by the full chorus ("Saul has slain a thousand and David has slain ten thousand") (1 Sam. 18:7). There is another setting of this text by Giovanni Francesco Anerio.

DIARY OF ADAM AND EVE, THE. The first of three acts from the musical *The Apple Tree*, which opened on Broadway in 1966 and was revived in 2006 based on Mark Twain's book *The Diary of Adam and Eve*, it was composed by Jerry Bock with lyrics by Sheldon Harnick. In perhaps the most memorable song, "The Apple Tree (Forbidden Fruit)," inspired by Gen. 3:1–4 and performed by Larry Blyden in the original production, the devil tempts Eve with the promise that her newfound knowledge not only would surpass that of her husband's, including his knowledge of "plumbing and philosophy," but also would make him dependent on her for the rest of his life.

DIDN'T MY LORD DELIVER DANIEL. African American spiritual first published in *Jubilee Songs As Sung by the Jubilee Singers of Fisk University* by Theodore F. Seward (1872). It argues that if God delivered Daniel from the lion's den (Dan. 3), Jonah from the belly of a whale, and the three children from the fiery furnace, "Why not every man? . . . Yes Freedom shall be mine." Arranged by Moses Hogan for SATB a cappella chorus, it has also been performed by many soloists, including Paul Robeson, Barbara Hendricks with the Moses Hogan Singers, and Willard White.

DIE JAKOBSLEITER. ("Jacob's Ladder"). Unfinished oratorio by Schoenberg scored for SATTTBarB soloists, chorus, speaking chorus, and orchestra based on a libretto by the composer, completed by Winifred Zillig (no opus number) and first performed in Vienna in 1961. It was inspired by the story of Jacob at Bethel (Gen. 28:10–22).

DIE KINDHEIT JESU. ("The Childhood of Jesus"). Popular oratorio by J. C. F. Bach (HW14/2, 1773) to a libretto by Johann Gottfried Herder, subtitled *Ein biblisches Gemälde* ("A Biblical Picture"). Scored for SATBB soloists, SATB chorus, two flutes, two horns, strings, and continuo, it is a lyrical drama, in 12 movements, telling the story of the salvation of humanity through the thoughts and words of characters present at the birth of Jesus. Notable features of the work are an aria by the archangel Gabriel, a lullaby by Mary, and the well-known shepherds' chorus *Holde, hohe Wundernacht* ("Beautiful Night of Great Wonder").

DIE LETZTEN DINGE. ("The Last Things" or "The Last Judgment"). Oratorio in two parts for soloists (SMezTB), SATB chorus, and orchestra by Louis Spohr (1826) to a libretto by Friedrich Rochlitz (1769–1842), regarded as one of the most popular Apocalypse oratorios of the 19th century. After a sinfonia, it opens with the chorus "Glory and honour unto him, who is, who was, and who is to come" (Rev.1:4). Part 1 (based on Rev. 1:4, 5; 5:13; 1:17–18; 2:10; 4:15, 18; 5:5; 8, 9, 12, 13; 7:9–11, 14–15, 17) closes with the number "Hail! To the one who has mercy on us!" (Rev. 21:4, 7) for SATB soloists and chorus. Part 2 is built on texts from Jer. 29:13–14 and 37:27 and verses from Rev. 14, 20, 21, and 22 and concludes with the chorus "Great and Glorious are thy works, Lord God Almighty" (Rev. 15:3–4).

DIE WEIHNACHTSHISTORIEN. ("The Christmas Story"). Work for soloists, SSATTB chorus, and orchestra by Heinrich Schütz (SWV 435, ca. 1660). It is one of the earliest existing works to include recitatives by a narrator, the Evangelist. It also features eight intermediaries, most notably "The angel to the shepherds in the fields," accompanied by the pastoral tones of recorders and dulcian; "the Heavenly Host," represented by a six-part choir; and the high priests and scribes, accompanied by trombones. The work concludes with a joyful chorus, "Thank we all our God."

DIES IRAE. ("Day of Wrath"). Latin hymn attributed either to Thomas Celano or to Latino Malabranca Orsini describing the Day of Judgment and the sounding of the last trumpet to summon the souls of the dead before the throne of God. Perhaps inspired by Zeph. 1:15–16 and Rev. 20:11–15, it has been set to music by numerous composers, including Mozart, Verdi, Berlioz, Fauré, and Britten. The Gregorian melody appears as a musical quotation in many works, such as the *Symphonie Fantastique* by Berlioz, *Faust* by Gounod, *Totentanz* by Liszt, and six works by Rachmaninoff, including his symphonies, the Symphonic Dances (op. 45), and his Rhapsody on a Theme by Paganini (op. 43). It also features in the Star Wars movie *The Empire Strikes Back* (arr. John Williams) (1980) and as the basis of the oratorio *Dies Irae: Auschwitz Oratorium* by Penderecki (1967).

DIES SIND DIE HEIL'GEN ZEHN GEBOT. ("These Are the Holy Ten Commandments"). Inspired by Luther's hymn with the same title (Erfurt, 1524), Bach treated the subject of the Ten Commandments (Exod. 20; Deut. 5) in many of his works, highlighting the number 10. These include a cantata (BWV 77) in which the opening chorus has 10 imitative expositions and 10 trumpet entries in the accompaniment based on a chorale tune (BWV 298). There are also three pieces for organ (BWV 635, BWV 678, and BWV 679) and a chorale (BWV 298/BC F46).

DIG, LAZARUS, DIG!!! Song and title of an album by Australian alternative rock band Nick Cave and the Bad Seeds (2008). Inspired by the story of Lazarus (Jn. 11), it tells of the resurrection in New York City of a 21st-century Lazarus, called Larry, who does not know the reason for his resurrection and, having lost all sense of his identity, leads a wayward life that ends in homelessness and incarceration before he returns to the grave for a second time. The lyrics point out that nobody asked "poor Larry" if he wanted to be resurrected, that he was happier in death than in life, and that he spent his newly resurrected life digging himself back into the grave, hence the chant-like phrase, repeated periodically, "Dig, Lazarus, Dig."

DILUVIO UNIVERSALE, IL. ("The Universal Flood"). *Azione tragico-sacra* by Donizetti (1830), written in collaboration with the librettist Domenico Girlardoni and based on Francesco Ringhieri's tragedy *Il Diluvio* (1788) and

Lord Byron's mystery play *Heaven and Earth* (1821). For his interpretation of the biblical flood story, with allusions to Gen. 1, Daniel, and a variety of other texts (Mt. 24:38–39; Lk. 7:38; 1 Pet. 3:20–21; 2 Pet. 2:5; Heb. 11:7), Donizetti consulted Auguste Calmet's famous commentary (1718) and de Sacy's popular French Bible translation (1696). Highlighting the theme of wickedness from Gen. 6:5, Donizetti juxtaposes the biblical story with an imaginary story involving the Babylonians whose solo coloratura singing illustrates their lavish, decadent oriental lifestyles in contrast to Noah's sons-and daughters-in-law who sing lyrical melodies in ensembles to depict their steadfast faith in God.

DILUVIO UNIVERSALE, IL. ("The Universal Flood"). Oratorio for soloists, chorus, orchestra, and continuo by Michelangelo Falvetti (1682) with a libretto by Sicilian poet Vincenzo Giattini (1630–1697). Written in Messina, a region renowned for its tidal waves and earthquakes, it is inspired by the story of Noah and the Flood (Gen. 6–9). When Divine Justice (A) calls on the elements to destroy the earth for its sinfulness, Noé (T) and his wife (S), along with the chorus, sing together in a black sea (semiquavers) of contrapuntal writing, calling for its destruction. As the waters rise, various voices do not pronounce the final syllable of words to illustrate the death of individuals by drowning. Falvetti also depicted those who were drowning by scoring various voice parts to sing "O perfidious destiny" as a macabre death scream. The rainbow is illustrated by three sopranos whose voices and characters represent different colors in the spectrum, but the final number, sung by Death (Ct), is a tarantella, a merry dance of death accompanied by tambourines.

DIVES AND LAZARUS. Folk song and Christmas carol based on the parable of the rich man (Dives) and Lazarus (Lk. 16:19–31), published in *The English and Scottish Popular Ballads* (1902). Known by various names, including "The Fighting 69th" (United States), "The Star of County Down" (Ireland), "Gilderoy" (Scotland), and "Dilwyn" (Herefordshire), the melody was arranged by Vaughan Williams in a work entitled *Five Variants of Dives and Lazarus* for harp and string orchestra. It was also arranged as a hymn tune, "Kingsfold," for **I heard the Voice of Jesus Say** and "O Sing a Song of Bethlehem."

DIVINE HYMNS OR SPIRITUAL SONGS FOR USE OF RELIGIOUS ASSEMBLIES AND PRIVATE CHRISTIANS. A collection of hymns by Joshua Smith and others, first published in Norwich, Connecticut, in 1784 or 1797 and then in many subsequent editions. Reproductions of the 1803 edition are still readily available as a paperback. Hymns in this early collection that are still popular today include "Jesus, lover of my soul," "All hail the power of Jesus' name," and **Jesus Christ the apple tree**.

DIXIT MARIA. ("Mary Said"). Motet in imitative polyphony for SATB a cappella by Hans Leo Hassler from *Cantiones sacrae* (Augsburg, 1591). In a musical interpretation of Lk. 1:38, a dance-like tempo evokes the joy of Mary's response to the Angel on *Dixit Maria ad Angelum*, while the sanctity of Mary's words, *Ecce ancilla Domini* ("Behold the handmaiden of the Lord"), is expressed in homophony and longer note values. Melismas on *Angelorum* and *fiat mihi* ("let it be done unto me") suggest both the Angel's movement and the Incarnation.

DO NOT BE AFRAID. ("When You Walk through the Waters"). Popular hymn based on Isa. 43:1–4 with words and music by Gerald Markland. The words also inspired a choral arrangement by Philip Stopford on the album *Do Not Be Afraid* (2012). *See also* BE NOT AFRAID.

DO NOT LAMENT ME, O MOTHER. Hymn from the Orthodox Church from the Znamenny chant tradition sung during the Paschal Nocturne Service on Holy Saturday, it is an exchange between the crucified Christ and his mother in which Mary laments her son's death and Christ seeks to reassure her of his resurrection, at the same time promising to exalt those who magnify her. *See also* STABAT MATER DOLOROSA.

DO YOU SEE WHAT I SEE. Christian rock album by American contemporary Christian singer/songwriter Todd Agnew, comprising 11 songs sung by well-known artists (2006). It tells the Christmas story from the perspective of different characters in the story, such as the innkeeper ("No Room"), who is sick and tired of people knocking at his door, and Joseph, who tells of his dreams for his son ("This is all I have to give"). Mary sings a lyrical **Magnificat** accompanied by strings and Elizabeth a lullaby to John the Baptist accompanied by piano and strings. The song of the Three Wise Men ("God with us") incorporates a few measures of the carol **We Three kings**, and the Shepherds song ("Bethlehem Dawn") ends with the opening measures of the carol **Silent Night**.

DODI LI. ("My Beloved Is Mine"). Popular Hebrew song based on texts from the **Song of Songs**. *Dodi li* (Song 2:16) is the refrain, sung twice, and the three verses begin *Mi zot olah* ("Who is this, rising up?") (Song 3:6), *Libbavtini ahoti* ("You have ravished my heart") (Song 4:9), and *Uri tzafon* ("Arise, north wind") (Song 4:16).

DON OÍCHE ÚD I MBEITHIL. ("That Night in Bethlehem"). Traditional Irish Christmas carol. The lyrics and haunting melody tell of the birth of the Word (*Don Oíche úd i mBeithil go dtainig an Bhreithir slan* ["That night in Bethlehem when the Word was born"]) (Jn. 1:14), and the angels' song of glory (*Céad glóire anois don Athair i bhFlaitheasa thuas go hard! is feasta fós ar talamh d'fheara dea-mhéin siocháin!* ["Glory be to the Father in his Kingdom on high, And peace and goodwill to all men on earth henceforth!"]) (Lk. 2:14). There is a memorable arrangement performed by Celtic Woman on the album *A Christmas Celebration* (2006).

DONA NOBIS PACEM. ("Grant Us Peace"). Cantata in six continuous movements for chorus, orchestra, soprano, and baritone soloists by Ralph Vaughan Williams, commissioned for the centenary of the Huddersfield Choral Society and written as a plea for peace in 1936. The work opens with **Agnus Dei**, a prayer for peace from the Latin Mass, sung repeatedly by the soprano soloist and chorus, followed without a break by "Beat Drum, Beat, Beat!," a dramatic setting with drums and trumpet of the first of three poems by Walt Whitman (1819–1892) describing the devastation of the American Civil War. This is followed by a serene setting of his "Reconciliation," opening with a violin obbligato and sung by the baritone soloist and chorus, and "Dirge for Two Veteran Soldiers," a poignant description of the futility of war focusing on the solemn burial procession for a father and son killed in action. Next, the ominous baritone solo "The Angel of Death" who will spare no one, unlike the "Destroyer" in the Passover story (Exod. 12:23), was inspired by a speech made by the English politician John Bright during the Crimean War. After another prayer for peace from the Mass, *Dona Nobis Pacem*, sung by chorus and soprano, the terrors of war are again depicted in a canon based on a biblical text about the Babylonian destruction of Judah (Jer. 8:15–22). The final movement reflects a change in mood with an emphasis on peace taken from a variety of biblical texts, beginning with the angel's words of comfort to Daniel sung by the baritone and leading to a jubilant setting of "Glory to God in the highest" (Dan. 10:19; Hag. 2:9; Mic. 4:3; Lev. 26:6; Pss. 85:10; 118:19; Isa. 43:9; 66:18–22; Lk. 2:13). The work ends with a repetition of *Dona Nobis Pacem* in a hauntingly beautiful soprano solo accompanied by chorus.

DREAM OF GERONTIUS, THE. Oratorio by Elgar (op. 38), considered by many to be his greatest work, first performed at the Birmingham Music Festival in 1900. The work is scored for three soloists, a double chorus, and a large orchestra. Based on Cardinal Newman's famous poem, it follows the journey of Gerontius, a man of faith (T), through his last days with friends

(Assistants) on earth (part 1) to his awakening in the presence of angels and demons before the throne of judgment and his peaceful entry into the soothing lake of Purgatory. There he will rest, supported by "Masses on the earth and prayers in heaven," until his guardian angel (Mez) comes to wake him "on the morrow" (part 2). Gerontius's long aria near the end of part 1 contains allusions to the Latin Psalms (**De Profundis** [Ps. 130] and *Miserere* [Ps. 51]) and Christ's words on the cross (Lk. 23:46), and the chorus of Assistants recalls the rescue of Noah, Job, Moses, and David from distress and sings, "Go forth upon thy journey, O Christian soul" (*Proficiscere*), from the litany for the dead. In part 2, after arias by the Soul of Gerontius and his Guardian Angel, a chorus of raging demons, their words punctuated by derisive laughter, is followed by a choir of Angelicals and a poignant intercession by the Angel of the Agony (B). Newman's best-known hymn, "Praise to the holiest in the heights," features as a refrain and brings the work to a close. Under pressure from the Anglican establishment in England, Elgar removed references to explicitly Catholic doctrine in later editions.

DREI PSALMEN. ("Three Psalms"). Three works for a cappella chorus by Mendelssohn (op. 78, 1848), written while he was Generalmusikdirektor to King Frederick William IV in 1843–1844. Of the three works inspired by Pss. 2, 43, and 22, the third, scored for soloists and eight-part chorus, is especially effective. It opens in E minor with a lone tenor voice singing in chant-like recitation, "My God, My God why have you forsaken me?," answered by the chorus in homophony (v. 1). The second section, *Aber du, Herr, sei nicht ferne* ("But be not thou far from me, O Lord: O my strength, haste thee to help me") (v. 11), opens in the hopeful tonality of E major and employs a double chorus on *Dich will ich preisen in der grossen Gemeinde* ("My praise shall be of thee in the great congregation") (v. 25) and *und vor ihm anbeten alle Geschlechter der Heiden* ("and all the kindreds of the nations shall worship before him") (v. 27) at the end.

DROP DROP SLOW TEARS. Hymn from *The Hymnes and Songs of the Church* (1623) by the English poet Phineas Fletcher (1582–1650), inspired by the account of Mary Magdalene washing the feet of Christ with her tears (Lk. 7:38). There is a musical setting attributed to Orlando Gibbons, who also composed a five-part setting (SAATB) to the music of his madrigal "The Silver Swan." It has since been arranged for a cappella chorus, entitled "A Litany" (1916), by the 15-year-old William Walton; as a cantata by Kenneth Leighton in his *Crucifixus pro nobis* (op. 38, 1961); and as a chorale prelude for organ (op. 104) by American composer Vincent Ludwig Persichetti (1966).

DUM ESSET REX. ("While the King Was Reposing"). Gregorian antiphon based on verses from the Song of Solomon (Cant. 1:12; 2:18) and set as a motet for SAATB by Francisco Guerrero for the Feast of St. Mary Magdalene on 22 July 1589. Marcel Dupré's majestic setting for organ, in the first of his 15 *Versets sur les Vêpres du Commun des Fêtes de la Sainte Vierge* (op. 18, 1919), features the plainchant in the pedals.

DURCH ADAMS FALL IST GANZ VERDERBT. ("Through Adam's Fall All Was Corrupted"). Chorale Prelude in D Minor for organ by J. S. Bach (BWV 651–668) from the *Orgel-Büchlein* ("Little Organ Book") (BWV 599–644), part 2, *Glaubenslieder* ("Songs of Faith"). The theme's descending melodic motion and falling diminished sevenths in the pedals symbolize Adam's Fall, while the chromatic middle section represents the snake and the growth of evil in the world (Gen. 3:1–20), and the sense of anguish evoked represents humanity's suffering brought about by original sin. Bach used the chorale, which was written by the poet Lazarus Spengler (1479–1534) to a melody by an unknown composer, in other works, such as the chorale preludes for organ (BWV 705 and BWV 1101) and cantatas (BWV 18 and BWV 109). There are numerous settings by other composers, including Buxtehude, Pachelbel, Telemann, and Raphael.

• E •

EASTER ORATORIO. (*Kommt, eilet und laufet* ["Come, Hasten and Run"]). Large-scale work in 11 movements by J. S. Bach to a text most likely written by Picander (BWV 249, 1725; rev. ca. 1730). A reworking of his Shepherds' Cantata (BWV 249a), it was first performed in Leipzig on Easter Sunday, 1 April 1725, for the birthday of Duke Christian von Sachsen-Weissenfels. In place of a narrator, the characters Mary Magdalene (A), Mary the mother of James (S), John (B), and Peter (T) present the dramatic narrative events surrounding Christ's empty tomb in a series of recitatives, arias, and duets, followed at the end by a triumphant chorus celebrating Christ's victory over death (*Preis und Dank Bleibe, Herr, dein Lobgesang* ["Praise and thanks remain Lord, your hymn of praise"]). Memorable arias include Peter's *Sanfte soll mein Todeskummer* ("Gentle shall my death-throes be"), sung as a tender, rocking lullaby, accompanied by recorders, suggesting that death is no more painful than sleep, and the plangent alto aria of Mary Magdalene, *Saget, saget mir geschwinde* ("Tell me, Tell me quickly"), with oboe obbligato, alluding to the Song of Songs (Song 1:7; 2:6). Mary Magdalene tells of her search for her beloved and of her desolation without him: *Denn mein Hertz ist ohne dich ganz verweiset und betrübt* ("For my heart is without you, quite orphaned and distressed").

ECCE, QUOMODO MORITUR JUSTUS. ("Behold How the Righteous Man Dies"). Sacred motet for four voices, in the style of a madrigal, by Jacob Handl (Gallus) based on Isa. 57:1–2. In Leipzig, it was performed at the Good Friday Vespers Service immediately following a performance of the Passion. German versions of the motet appear in hymnals from Leipzig (1618) and Dresden (1725), and it is quoted in the funeral anthem for Queen Caroline, **"The Ways of Zion do Mourn"** (HWV 264), and in the opening chorus of the oratorio **Israel in Egypt**, both composed by G. F. Handel.

ECCOMI. ("Here I Am"). Popular modern Italian setting of Ps. 40 (Vulg. 39) in which the response, reminiscent of that of Abraham (Gen. 22:1), Isaiah (Isa. 6:8), and the Virgin Mary (Lk. 1:38), is derived from verses 7–8 (Vulg. vv. 8–9).

EDEN. Dramatic oratorio in three acts written by Robert Bridges (1844–1930), set to music by Charles Villiers Stanford, and first performed at the

Birmingham Festival of Music in October 1891. Act 1, set in heaven, opens with a Prelude incorporating the plainsong melody *Sanctorum meritis* from the Sarum missal and recounts the dialogues and songs of the angels in praise of God, culminating in a "chorus on man's free will and envy." In act 2, set in hell and characterized by discords, Satan dreams of the Fall and tells of his plan for humanity while the devils sing his praises as "King of death, King of hate, King of night." The final act, set on earth, describes the Fall (Gen. 2–3), Adam's vision of Christ, and other traditions taken from the postbiblical books of Adam and Eve and concludes with their return to paradise. The final chorus of praise by all the angels represents their return to heaven with ascending arpeggios in the orchestral accompaniment.

E'EN SO, LORD JESUS, QUICKLY COME. Anthem for SATB a cappella chorus by American composer Paul Manz (1953) to lyrics written by the composer's wife, Ruth Manz. Inspired by verses from the Book of Revelation (Rev. 1:4; 4:8; 22:20, 5), it was composed by the couple as a prayer for their three-year-old son, who was dying from an illness. After their appeal to the "Lord Jesus" to "quickly come" to their aid, the child made a miraculous recovery.

EGO FLOS CAMPI. ("I Am a Flower of the Field"). Motet for alto and basso continuo by Monteverdi (SV 301), based on verses from the Latin version of the Song of **Solomon** (Cant. 2:1–3). It makes copious use of melisma on words such as *campi* ("field"), *convallium* ("valleys"), *silvarum* ("trees"), and *sub umbra illius* ("under his shadow") and repeats the phrase *fructus eius dulcis gutturi meo* ("his fruit was sweet to my palate") for emphasis. Two motets by the 16th-century Dutch composer Clemens non Papa, one for three and one for seven voices, are settings of the same text. In the latter, the phrase *sicut lilium inter spinas* ("as a lily among the thorns"), repeated no fewer than seven times, is a reference to the Virgin Mary.

EHEU! SUSTULERUNT DOMINUM MEUM. ("Alas, They Have Taken Away My Lord"). Motet for SATB by Thomas Morley (1557–1603) inspired by Mary Magdalene's words to the angels in the empty tomb (Jn. 20:13). Set in a minor tonality to express Mary's grief, the opening measures paint her sobbing *Eheu* ("Alas!"), and melismas on *meum* ("my") in *Dominum meum* ("my Lord") highlight her personal loss. Dissonances within the final section, "And put him, I know not where" (*et posuerent eum, nescio ubi*), illustrate her frustration at not being able to see and touch Christ's body one last time, though a *tierce de Picardie* (Picardy third) at the end points to the Resurrection.

EIN FEST' BURG IST UNSER GOTT. ("A Mighty Fortress Is Our God"). Hymn written by Martin Luther, probably in 1529, translated into English by Miles Coverdale (1835), Thomas Carlyle (1831), Frederick Henry Hedge (1852), Catherine Winkworth, and many others. A paraphrase of Ps. 46, it was entitled "Hymn of Comfort" by Luther and renowned as "The Battle hymn of the Reformation," sung on many historic occasions as a majestic proclamation of faith in God. Among the many composers who have used it are Bach in his chorale cantata (BWV 80) and chorale prelude (BWV 720), Mendelssohn in his *Reformation Symphony* (1830), Meyebeer in *Les Huguenots* (1836), and Wagner in his "Kaisermarsch," as well as Max Reger (op. 27 and op. 67, no. 2) and Flor Peeters (op. 69) in works for organ.

EL SHADDAI. ("God Almighty"). Song by American singer/songwriter Michael Card on the album *Scribbling in the Sand: The Best of Michael Card* (2002). The song is a hymn of praise based on Hebrew names for God, *El Shaddai* (Gen. 17:1; Exod. 6:3) and *El Elyon* (Gen. 14:19), and *erhamkha* ("I love thee") (Ps. 18:1; Heb. 18:2). Verse 1 gives examples of God's saving grace from the Old Testament, the sacrifice of Isaac (Gen. 22), the crossing of the Red Sea (Exod. 14:21; Ps. 66.6), Hagar in the wilderness (Gen. 21), and the Exodus, while verse 2 focuses on God's saving work through his son Jesus Christ in the New Testament. Popularized by Amy Grant on the albums *Age to Age* (1982), *Behind the Eyes* (1997), and *Rock of Ages: Hymns of Faith* (2005) and on the single "Takes Little Time" (1997), it won the Gospel Music Association Dove Award for Songwriter of the Year and Song of the Year in 1983. In 2001, it was designated one of 365 Songs of the Century by the Recording Industry Association of America and the National Endowment for the Arts.

ELI. Oratorio in two parts by Michael Costa, first performed at the Birmingham Music Festival on 29 August 1855. The libretto by William Bartholomew is based on the biblical story of the priest Eli (1 Sam. 1–4) with references to many other texts, including Deuteronomy, Psalms, and the Gospels. Part 1 highlights Hannah's grief in a recitative and prayer (Ps. 25:16–17) and subsequent joy in a song of praise with melismas on "rejoice," dotted rhythms and staccato markings on "dancing," and falling intervals on "mourning" (Ps. 30:11; cf. 1 Sam. 1). The work also focuses on the grief of Eli (B) over the activities of his sons Hophni (T) and Phineas (B) ("For Everything there is a Season") (Eccl. 3:1). The Man of God (B), accompanied by tremolo strings, foretells the death of his sons, and Eli cries, "Woe is me now, my heart within me is desolate," answered by God's words, "Thou honorest thy sons above me." When Israel is defeated by the Philistines (1 Sam. 4), the chorus sings a

"Lament with doleful lamentation," highlighting the verbs "howl" and "cry," and when Eli dies at the news of the death of his sons, they sing, "The glory is departed from Israel" (1 Sam. 4:21–22). The work ends with a chorus of joyful **Hallelujahs** and **Amens**.

ELIJAH. Oratorio by Mendelssohn (op. 70), first performed in an English version at the Birmingham Music Festival in 1846, conducted by the composer. The first performance in the original German was in Leipzig in 1848, four months after his death. The libretto by Karl Klingemann retells the biblical story of Elijah (1 Kgs. 17–21; 2 Kgs. 2), expanded with numerous other biblical texts, especially from Psalms and Isaiah. The work begins with a short solo by Elijah (B) predicting a drought (1 Kgs. 17:1) and an instrumental overture followed by a cry for help from the chorus (Jer. 8:20; Lam. 1:17). The rest of part 1 is devoted to the stories of Elijah in the desert (1 Kgs. 17), the raising of the widow's son from the dead (Ps. 88:10), and the contest between Elijah and the priests of Baal on Mount Carmel (1 Kgs. 18), ending with a triumphant choral setting of Ps. 93:3–4. As well as Elijah's servant, Obadiah (T), and the Widow (S), there are a double quartet and a quartet of angels who sing passages from the Psalms (Pss. 91:11–12; 55:22; 108:5; 25:3). After the chorus "**Be not afraid**" (Isa. 41:10; Ps. 91:7), part 2 focuses on Elijah's conflict with Queen Jezebel (A) and his despair and wish to die, expressed in the aria "It is enough" (1 Kgs. 19:4; Job 7:16). Encouraged by the angels, represented by a *terzetto* for female voices (Ps. 121:1, 3) and SATB chorus (Pss. 121:4; 138:7), Elijah flees to Horeb, where he meets the Lord. A long chorus, "Behold God the Lord passed by" (1 Kgs. 19:11–12), is followed by "**Holy, holy, holy**" (Isa. 6:2–3), sung by a quartet for female voices and chorus. The work ends with Elijah's ascension to heaven in a fiery chariot (2 Kgs. 2:11; Sir. 48:1–16) accompanied by a soprano recitative (Mal. 4:5–6) and a quartet (Isa. 55:1, 3) between two great choruses, "But the Lord from the north" (Isa. 41:25; 42:1; 11:2) and "And then shall your light break forth" (Isa. 58:8; Ps. 8:1).

ELIJAH ROCK. African American spiritual celebrating the prophet Elijah's ascent into heaven (2 Kgs. 2:11–13) and praying that others can come up too. The rock is a metaphor for the Lord (Pss. 18:2; 19:14, etc.), but it is also a verb and a call to dance. The verses allude to Satan's wiles, the triumph of Moses, and the visions of Ezekiel and St. John. A popular arrangement by Moses Hogan (2001) describes Elijah's ascent into heaven from earth through the gradual entry of vocal parts, beginning with the lowest voices (B) and rising to the highest (S), to signify the prophet's joyful journey and arrival into heaven. This rendition is regularly performed at concerts.

ELISHA. Chancel opera for soloists and piano/organ accompaniment with optional violin by Susan Hulsman Bingham based on the story of the raising of the Shunammite woman's son by Elisha (2 Kgs. 4:8–37). The woman (Mez) is overcome with emotion when she sees her son alive again, and the opera ends with a song of consolation sung to her by her husband (Bar), her son (Tr), the prophet Elisha (Bar), and his servant Gehazi (Bar).

ELIYAHU HANAVI. ("Elijah the Prophet"). Hebrew song traditionally sung during the Maggid part of the Passover Haggadah, it is sung at the opening of the door for Elijah on pouring the fourth cup. The refrain names Elijah as a prophet, the Tishbite, and the Gileadite (1 Kgs. 17:1), and the verse beckons him to return with the Messiah son of David (cf. Malachi 3:1; 4:1).

EMENDEMUS IN MELIUS. ("Let Us Amend"). Motet for five voices by William Byrd, published in *Cantiones sacrae* (1575) and based on texts from the Psalms and Baruch 3:2. The last part, from Ps. 79:9 (Vulg. 78:9), is sung as a matins response in the Roman rite for the first Sunday of Lent and later at the imposition of ashes in the Ash Wednesday liturgy. Reserved in mood with a highly expressive choral declamation, it is largely homophonic in texture. The bipartite structure highlights the sinfulness of the people and God's forgiveness. Spanish composer Cristóbal de Morales (ca. 1500–1553) composed a piece with the same title, renowned as his most famous work, in recent times featuring in the horror movie *The Pit and the Pendulum* (1991), based on the short story by Edgar Allan Poe.

ENFANCE DU CHRIST, L'. ("The Childhood of Christ"). Oratorio in three parts or sacred trilogy by Berlioz (op. 25/H. 130, 1850–1854) based on the Massacre of the Holy Innocents (*Le songe d'Hérode*) (Mt. 2:16–18), the flight into Egypt (*La Fuite en Egypte*) (Mt. 2:13–15), and the apocryphal "Arrival at Sais" (*L'arrivée à Saïs*). It was premiered at the Salle Herz, Paris, on 10 December 1854. It is scored for a narrator (T), the Virgin Mary (Mez), Joseph (Bar), Herod (B), the father of a family of Ishmaelites (B), a Centurion (B), and a nonbiblical character, Polydorus, a commander who watches over Herod, and a chorus that sings various parts, such as Herod's soothsayers (TTBB), a chorus of Angels (SSAA), Shepherds (SATB), Romans (unison basses), Egyptians (BB), and Ishmaelites (SATB). Instrumental numbers include the *Marche nocturne* ("Nocturnal March") in part 1, describing musically the movement of the Roman soldiers in "A street in Jerusalem." Scene 2 includes Herod's well-known aria *Toujours ce rêve!* ("Always this dream!") and the chorus of soothsayers, who, after their wild dance to "invoke the spirits," confirm that he must kill every newborn child. Part 2 opens with an overture, followed by the popular *L'adieu des bergers* ("The Shepherds' Farewell") and the idyllic *Repose de la sainte famille* ("The Repose of the Holy Family"), which tells of the choirs of angels worshipping the Christ child as he rested with Mary and Joseph in the shade of a tree. Part 3, scene 2, includes the sublime extended trio for two flutes and harp, depicting the music making of the Ishmaelite children with whom the Holy Family stayed in Egypt for 10 years, and the work ends with a contemplative chorus for tenor and chorus, "O my Soul."

ENGLISH HYMNAL, THE. A collection of hymns in English edited by Percy Dearmer and Ralph Vaughan Williams and published in 1907 as a companion to the Book of Common Prayer in the Church of England. It aimed to include the best of the church's hymns, ranging from translations from Latin of "Jesus the very thought of thee" by Bernard of Clairvaux and **Ein fest' Burg** by Luther from German to English, compositions by George Herbert ("Teach me my God and king"), Milton (**Let us with a gladsome mind**), Addison (**The spacious firmament on high**), and a good number of 19th-century writers, including Scott, Tennyson, Wordsworth, Kingsley, Gladstone, and Kipling. For the music, the editors drew on English, French, and Italian traditional melodies as well as works by Gibbons, Tallis, Praetorius, Purcell, Bach, Haydn, Mendelssohn, Schumann, Wagner, and others. A number of settings by modern composers were included for the first time, such as those by Sullivan, Holst, and Vaughan Williams, whose "Down Ampney" remains the most popular setting for the hymn "Come down, O Love divine." A new edition was published in 1933 and the *New English Hymnal* in 1986 with the addition of many new compositions, such as Sydney Carter's "I danced in the morning," a modern version of the *Magnificat* beginning, "Tell out, my soul, the greatness of the Lord" and "Now the green blade riseth." A supplement with the title *New English Praise* was published in 2006, containing popular new hymns, such as "Be still" and "Lift high the Cross."

ENTRE AV' E EVA. ("Between Ave and Eva"). Song no. 60 from *Cantigas de Santa Maria* (1260–1280), a notable collection of medieval Spanish songs in praise of the Virgin Mary commissioned by King Alfonso X El Sabio ("The Wise"). Based on a variety of genres, including chant and popular troubadour melodies, they were written in the form of a virelay and scored in square notation. A pun on the Latin *Ave* (Maria), "Hail" (Mary) (Lk. 1:28), and "Eva" (Eve) (Gen. 3) symbolizes God's plan to reverse the sinfulness of Eve (*Eva*) through the Blessed Virgin Mary (*Ave*). Each verse of four lines is divided in two and sung by two singers, one highlighting the sinfulness of Eve and the other the purity of Mary.

ESHET CHAYIL. ("Woman of Valor"). Traditional Hebrew song, still sung or recited in some Jewish households by the husband on Sabbath Eve. Derived from the acrostic poem at the end of the Book of Proverbs (Prov. 31:10–31), it is a paean to the woman of the house, outlining the qualities of a virtuous wife. The text has been set to music by many composers, including Judith Lang Zaimont, Michael Isaacson in his *Jewish Wedding Suite*, and Israeli soul singer/songwriter Nomi Teplow. *See also* WOMEN OF VALOR.

ESTHER. Oratorio by Handel (HWV 50a, 1718; rev. 1820, HWV 50b, 1732) based on the biblical story and a play by Racine (1689), translated into English by Thomas Brereton. The libretto is thought to have been written by John Arbuthnot with revisions by Alexander Pope (1718) and later additions by Samuel Humphrey (1732). The earlier version (1718) was a masque for chamber orchestra in one continuous movement divided into six scenes. The later version (1732) was heavily revised and divided into three parts with larger orchestral forces and soloists. Esther enters in scene 4 with a recitative, "Why sits that sorrow on thy brow?," answered by Mordecai in a recitative and aria, "Dread not righteous Queen, the danger." Popular excerpts include the Israelites' chorus, "Save us, O Lord," and the finale recounting the death of Haman, "The Lord our Enemy has Slain," as well as the coronation anthem **My Heart is Inditing** (Ps. 45; Isa. 49) and **"The King shall Rejoice"** (Ps. 21) from the "Ode for the Birthday of Queen Anne."

ESTHER, THE BEAUTIFUL QUEEN. Cantata in two parts by the American William Batchelder Bradbury (1856) to a libretto by Chauncey Marvin Cady (1824–1889). Noted for its light, popular style and performances by amateur singers, it was one of the most popular large-scale choral works in the 19th century. The published score, written over five days, included an appended essay, "Concerning Esther and Mordecai and Haman," from Josephus's *Antiquities of the Jews* and features spoken narration of selected passages from the Book of Esther (Esth. 2:16–18; 3:1–2; 3:12–15; 5:1–3; 6:1–2), to be read by a "clergy man from the pulpit" or by "the best reader" available. The words are taken from the Book of Esther as well as Psalms (Pss. 28, 124, 126, 130, 141, 142, 150), Lamentations, Jeremiah, and Isaiah (Isa. 26:2–5; 25:4). Despite the prohibition on dances in religious compositions at the time, the work includes a number of dances, most notably in the instrumental "At the Banquet," marked "Waltz movement—Allegro." Other musical interpretations of Esther include works by Carissimi, Handel, and Aaron Avshalomov. *See also* ESTHER.

ETERNAL ROAD, THE. (*Der Weg der Verheissung*/"The Path of the Promise"). Biblical pageant/opera by Kurt Weill to a libretto by Franz Werfel, translated into English by Ludwig Lewisohn. Conceived to alert the public to Hitler's persecution of the Jews, it was premiered at the Manhattan Opera House on 7 January 1937 in a spectacular six-hour production, directed by Max Reinhardt with over 245 actors and singers and 1,772 costumes on a newly constructed five-tiered stage. Set in an unnamed synagogue amid a raging pogrom outside, a terrified Jewish community comes together in an all-night vigil where a Rabbi (T) recalls biblical stories of faith and courage beginning with the covenant with Abraham (Gen. 12–15) and concluding with Jeremiah and the destruction of the Temple (Jer. 52). In four acts ("The Patriarchs," "Moses," "Kings," and "Prophets"), it draws on traditional Ashkenazi liturgical music, such as the *Mi-sinai* ("From Sinai") melody for the Festival of Sukkot in act 3 and the setting of Ps. 144 for the Sabbath, which appears in acts 1, 2, and 4. Popular numbers include "Dance around the Golden Calf," "David's Psalm," "The March to Zion," "The Promise," and **"The Song of Miriam."** A version of the work was performed in Chemnitz, Germany, in November 1999, followed by performances in New York, Tel Aviv, and Poland.

EUROCLYDON. Anthem for a cappella SATB chorus by William Billings, published in *The Psalm-Singer's Amusement* (1781). It is based on Ps. 107:23–30 and the story of Paul's shipwreck off the island of Malta (Acts 27). The title is the name of a "tempestuous wind" (Acts 27:14, AV), and the words of the Psalm ("And he lifted up the waves . . . they reel and stagger") are vividly illustrated in the music. The stillness after the storm is reflected by longer note values on "So that the waves are still" (v. 29), and the work concludes with a rousing finale and extrabiblical words of welcome, "And all huzza. Welcome here again, welcome home."

ÈVE. Oratorio in three parts by Jules Massenet, with a libretto by Louis Gallet, premiered at the Cirque d'Eté, Paris, on 18 March 1875. Despite its reputation as one of the most sensuous oratorios in the history of the genre, it never quite achieved the same success as **Marie-Magdeleine.** Part 1 tells of the birth of Eve (S) and her first encounter with Adam (Bar) in the Garden of Eden. It contains their first dialogue, in which Adam extols Eve's beauty, "*Ton visage est brillant comme la fraîche aurore, tes yeux bleus sont pareils à l'azur de la mer*" ("Your face shines like the fresh dawn, your eyes are blue like the azure blue sea"), and the sumptuous duet, "*Autour de nous respire une éternelle paix*" ("Around us breathes eternal peace!"), as well as Adam's romantic recitative, "*Va, ton sang est mon sang et ma vie est ta vie*" ("Go, your blood is my blood and my life is your life"), and his naming of Eve, "*Ève sera ton nom comme Adam est le mien!*" ("Eve will be your name as Adam is mine") (cf. Gen. 2:23). Part 2 tells of Eve's walk in the fragrant forest, "*Ève dans la solitude*" ("Eve alone"), tempted by the seductive Voices of the Night, "*Viens! Nous te montrerons l'arbre de science dont l'amour est le fruit. Viens!*" ("Come! We will show you the Tree of Knowledge of which love is the fruit. Come!"), and the Spirits of the Abyss, "*Viens! C'est l'arbre de science! Veux-tu posséder la puissance humaine? L'amour te la donnera!*" ("Come! Here is the Tree of Knowledge! Do you want to possess human power? Love will give it to you"). In part 3, Eve gives in to temptation and seduces Adam. Eve: "*Aimons-nous! Aimer c'est vivre!*" ("Let us love! To love is to live"). Adam: "*Ève, qu'as-tu fait?*" ("Eve, what have you done?"). Fragments of the **Dies Irae** can be heard in the Epilogue, and the Spirits of Nature communicate details of God's curse, "*La douleur et la mort*" ("Sorrow and death"). In a final duet, Adam and Eve express neither guilt nor remorse and pray never to be separated, never to be free from the intoxication of love ("*Ne nous separe pas! Laisse-nous notre ivresse!*"). The work concludes with God's curse sung by the chorus, "*Soyez maudits!*" ("You are cursed!").

EVERY GOLIATH HAS ITS DAVID. Indie rock song by lead singer Jof Owen and instrumentalist/backup vocalist Peter Hobbs from the duo band The Boy Least Likely To (2009) on the album *The Law of the Playground* (2009). The lyrics tell the story of David and Goliath (1 Sam. 17) from the perspective of a child; for example, "I've got a little bag of marbles and a catapult wound around my fingers and I feel very small but I could make myself big if I wanted to," and the chorus, "And I know kung fu and I'm not afraid of you." The music evokes this child-like atmosphere with brushed drum strokes, tingling strings, rhythmic guitar chords, synthesizer, violin, clapping, and foot stamping.

EVE'S LAMENTATION. Song for soprano and piano taken from the oratorio *The Intercession* by Matthew Peter King (1864) with a libretto based on Milton's *Paradise Lost*. The Angel's recitative announcing the couple's eviction from the garden is followed by Eve's lament, "Must I leave thee, Paradise."

EXODUS. Reggae song from the album *Exodus* by Rastafarian Bob Marley, performed by Marley and the Wailers (1977). It draws on the biblical image of a new Exodus from Babylon (Isa. 48:20–21) and prays for "another brother **Moses**" to come and "set the captives free" (Isa. 45:13).

EXODUS. Concept album by progressive rock group Nathan Mahl (2008). Includes songs loosely based on biblical themes, such as "Burning Bush" (Exod. 3:2), "Let My People Go" (Exod. 5:1; 8:1; 9:1), "The Plagues" (Exod. 7:14–11:10), "Down from the Mountain" (Exod. 34:29–35), "40 Years" (Exod. 16:35; Num. 14:33–34), and "Zipporah's Farewell" (Exod. 18:2).

EXPECTANS EXPECTAVI. ("I Waited Patiently"). Anthem by Charles Wood, published in 1919. The Latin title derives from Ps. 40:1, while the English words are by the British war poet Charles Hampton Sorley (1895–1915). The piece poignantly describes a humble servant standing before God waiting to do service. In the context of World War I, it fittingly describes the situation of millions of young men across Europe waiting to do military service. *See also* SYMPHONY OF PSALMS.

EXULTATE JUBILATE. ("Rejoice, Be Glad"). Motet in three movements for soprano soloist and orchestra by the 16-year-old Mozart (K. 165, 1773). Written for the Italian castrato Venanzio Rauzzini, today it appears in concert repertoires of many well-known sopranos. Inspired by Ps. 81 and other texts, it is often associated with the Nativity. Regarded as a miniature vocal concerto, it is in three movements ("Allegro," "Andante," and "Presto"), with a recitative bridge, *Fulget amica* ("The friendly day glows"), between the first and second, followed by the delightful song to the Virgin, *Tu virginum corona* ("Thou O crown of virgins"). The third movement is an exuberant virtuosic finale based on the **Alleluia**.

EZECHIA. Dialogue motet for five soloists, chorus, strings, and continuo by Giacomo Carissimi, based on the story of King Hezekiah's illness, his prayer to God, and his miraculous recovery (Isa. 38). Two angels (SS) introduce the dialogue between God (B), Isaiah (A), and Hezekiah (T), and Hezekiah's plaintive petition to God, *Parce mihi, Domine, et miserere* ("Spare me, Lord, and have mercy"), which is the centerpiece of the motet. God promises to add 15 years to the king's life, the angels recount how the shadow on the sundial turns back 10 degrees, and the work concludes with a joyful polyphonic chorus praising the Lord God for all eternity.

EZEKIEL SAW DE WHEEL. African American spiritual popularly arranged for chorus by H. T. Burleigh, Gerre Hancock, William Dawson, Norman Luboff, and Moses Hogan, among others. It recounts, in a call-and-response form, Ezekiel's vision of the mysterious wheels (Ezek. 1:15–21). It has been sung by the Charioteers, Louis Armstrong, Woodie Guthrie, and many more.

• F •

FALL AND RESURRECTION. Work in three parts for soloists (SCtB), chorus, and orchestra, including organ, guitar, and a ram's horn, by John Tavener (1999) to a text by Mother Thekla, dedicated to HRH the Prince of Wales and in loving memory of the composer's father. Part 1, "Silence, Darkness," opens in complete silence to mark the time before creation, followed by the "Representation of Chaos," based on the Byzantine chant "Thy Cross We Adore." Here the music begins with hushed tones and then spirals dissonantly and loudly for about five minutes "into a colossal storm" with each note symbolic of the potential for good and evil. Movement 3, "Paradise," is a monody in which Adam (B) and Eve (S) sing to each other and to God, while movements 4 to 7 recount the Fall. A saxophone represents the presence of Satan, replicated by the voices of Adam and Eve to depict their encounter and likeness to Satan. "The implications of the Fall" and the sounding of the ram's horn with Satan's words "Fallen. Fallen. Fallen. Out. Out. Out" are followed by Adam's lament (movt. 6) and the lament of humanity (movt. 7). Part 2, "Prediction," features the voice of God (B) ("I planted you a vine . . . I will send you Elijah the prophet"). Accompanied on a type of flute used by shepherds in the Balkans and Anatolia known as a *kaval*, the countertenor sings of humanity's redemption in texts from Exodus, the Prophets, and Psalms amid a periodic cacophony of sound from the chorus to depict the chaos of earthly life. Part 3 opens with the ram's horn and the grand organ announcing the Incarnation of the Word and Mary's words to the Angel, "Be it unto me according to thy word" (Lk. 1:38), and concludes, after the shouts of the crowd "Crucify him, Crucify him, Crucify!," accompanied by the "thunderous cacophony of the uncreated chaos," with Mary Magdalene's "Rabboni" (Jn. 20:16) and prostration before the risen Christ and "The Cosmic Dance of the Resurrection."

FALL OF BABYLON, THE. (*Der Fall Babylons*). Oratorio in two parts for soloists, chorus, and orchestra by Louis Spohr (WoO 63, 1839–1840), composed for the Festival of Norwich and premiered in 1842. The English text by Edward Taylor was later translated into German by Friedrich Oetker. Modeled on Charles Jennens's libretto for Handel's **Belshazzar** (1744), it is inspired by biblical texts about the Babylonian exile and the fall of Babylon (e.g., Ps. 137; Isa. 46–47; Dan. 5). It is scored for Daniel (T), Cyrus (B), Belshazzar (B), and other solo parts, including Nicotris; the Queen Mother

(Mez), referred to by Herodotus but not in the Bible; a chorus of Jews; a chorus of Persian Priests; and a chorus of Priests of Bel. Act 1 ends with a mighty chorus calling on Babylon to "Come down and in the dust be humbled" (Isa. 47:1), and act 2 is set in the palace where Belshazzar's Feast is interrupted by the march of the approaching Persian army, and a solo recitative and aria sung by an Israelite woman (S) beginning "The ransom'd of the Lord shall return" (Isa. 35:10, 2) leads into the final chorus, "Give thanks unto God."

FILS PRODIGUE, LE. ("The Prodigal Son"). Ballet in three scenes by Sergei Prokofiev (op. 46, 1928–1929) with music by Boris Kochno, choreographed by George Balanchine, and premiered at the Théatre Sarah Bernhardt, Paris, on 21 May 1929, the last production by the impresario Serge Diaghilev for the Ballet Russes. Inspired by the parable of the prodigal son (Lk. 15:11–32), it opens with his departure from home and a feast with 12 comrades when he arrives at the city. After choreographic interpretations of his dance with a seductress, his drunkenness, and robbery at the hands his comrades, seductress, and servants, he awakens, scatters his comrades, and returns to his father. *See also* PRODIGAL SON, THE.

FIVE MYSTICAL SONGS. A cycle of five songs for baritone soloist, chorus, and piano by Vaughan Williams based on poems by George Herbert, first published in *The Temple: Sacred Poems and Private Ejaculations* (1633). The poems consider various biblical themes, including Christ's resurrection in "Easter" and "I got me flowers"; the Fall; Christ's passion; Paul's teaching on love (1 Cor. 13:1–13) in "Love Bade me Welcome"; and one of the seven "I am" sayings from John's Gospel (Jn. 14:6) in "The Call." The final song, "Antiphon," beginning "Let all the world in every corner sing," is often sung as an independent work.

FLEURY PLAYBOOK. (*Livre de Jeux de Fleury*). A medieval collection of 10 Latin plays, set to music in the style of plainchant (ca. 1200) and most likely performed by the monks of Fleury Abbey in St.-Benoît-sur-Loire. The manuscript is now held in the Municipal Library of Orléans (MS 201). The plays include the *Play of Herod*, the *Massacre of the Innocents* (**Ordo Rachelis**), the *Resurrection of Christ* (*Visitatio Sepulcri*), the *Supper at Emmaus* (*Peregrinus*), the *Conversion of St. Paul*, and the *Raising of Lazarus*. *See also* ORDO RACHELIS.

FLIGHT INTO EGYPT: SACRED RICERCAR. Cantata for soprano and baritone soloists, four-part mixed chorus, two oboes, English horn, bassoon, three trombones, chamber organ, and strings by John Harbison (1986), awarded the Pulitzer Prize for Music in 1987. Inspired by Mt. 2:13–23, the baritone acts as narrator, and the soprano sings the angel's words to Joseph in a dream (Mt. 2:13, 20). The chorus sings the three prophetic texts: "Out of Egypt have I called my son" (Hos. 11:1), sung as a canon in 2/4 meter; Rachel weeping for her children (Jer. 31:15) in imitative counterpoint with angular melodic lines and dissonant leaps; and "He shall be called a Nazarene" (Isa. 11:1–3, 53:2–3; Ps. 22:6) in imitative counterpoint. Violins accompany the angel's announcement to Joseph in imitation at the tritone; trombones introduce Herod, who orders the slaughter of the Holy Innocents; and a dissonant solo organ announces the news of his death.

FLOOD, THE. A musical play for tenor solo (Lucifer), two bass soloists (God), chorus (SAT), and orchestra, with speaking parts for Noah's wife, Noah's sons, a Narrator, and a Caller, by Igor Stravinsky. Partly inspired by the York and Chester mystery plays, it was first performed by CBS Television on 14 June 1962, featuring choreography by George Balanchine with principal dancers from the New York City Ballet. It opens with a Prelude and a choral **Te Deum** and closes with a **Sanctus** sung by the chorus. *See also* DÉLUGE, LE; NOYE'S FLUDDE.

FLOS CAMPI. ("Flower of the Field"). Suite in six continuous movements for solo viola, small SATB chorus, and orchestra by Vaughan Williams (1925). The work is a wordless musical interpretation of six texts from the Song of Songs (Cant. 2:2, 5, 11, 12; 3:1; 5:8; 6:1; 3:7–8; 6:13; 7:1; 8:6). It opens with the voice of the languishing lover, depicted musically by a bitonal duet for oboe and violin, and the oriental flavor of the melody played by the flute and viola sets the scene for the drama to follow.

FOR ALL THE SAINTS. Hymn by the bishop of Wakefield, William Walsham How, first printed in Earl Nelson's *Hymns for Saint's Days and Other Hymns* (1864) to the tune "Sarum" by Joseph Barnby and later to Vaughan Williams's "Sine Nomine," published in the *English Hymnal* (1906). Traditionally performed on the Feast of All Saints, it was inspired by a variety of biblical texts (Rev. 14:13; Heb. 12:1–2; Rev. 2:10; Jn. 17: 22; Prov. 4:18; 7:9–17). Each verse ends with a triumphant **Alleluia**.

FOR LO, I RAISE UP. Anthem for SATB and organ accompaniment composed by Charles Villiers Stanford (op. 145) composed in 1914 as a call for hope during World War I. Inspired by words from Hab. 1:6–12; 2:1–3, 14, and 20, it opens in F minor, with the voice of God, sung by alto, tenor, and bass voices combined, summoning the enemy to afflict his chosen people.

Trebles, followed by altos, tenors, and basses, describe the approaching Babylonians ("quicker than leopards . . . fiercer than wolves"), dividing into seven parts on ("their faces are) set as the East wind, and they gather captives as the sand" to highlight the magnitude of the threat. Nebuchadnezzar's contempt for God's chosen people ("yea, he scoffeth at kings") is depicted by word painting and unison singing, while a semiquaver figure in the organ played for three measures over a pedal E-flat describes the simile of the swirling wind, which gathers up the sand. In the next section, the voice of Habakkuk is scored for choir, sung in the major tonality, and God's reply (Hab. 3:2) is sung by the tenors and basses echoed by the sopranos and altos. The organ paints the movement of "the waters covering the sea" (Hab. 2:14). In the final section, marked "adagio" and "pianissimo," the phrase "Let all the earth keep silence before him" is sung in unison, followed by three measures of silence by the choir against the sound of the organ playing a unison F for the last two measures.

FORTY-SIXTH PSALM, THE: GOD IS OUR REFUGE. Cantata for four soloists, chorus, orchestra, and organ by 19th-century American composer Dudley Buck, first performed by the Handel and Haydn Society of Boston (op. 57, 1872). Bearing similarities to Mendelssohn's **Elijah**, the work is in seven movements, three sung by the choir, three by soloists, and movement 6, "Be still, then, and know that he is God" (Ps. 46:10) by a quartet.

FOUR BIBLICAL DANCES. Work for organ by Petr Eben based on four biblical episodes: the dance of David before the ark (2 Sam. 6:14–15), the dance of the Shulammite (Song of Songs 6:13), the dance of Jephthah's daughter (Judg. 11:34), and the wedding in Cana (Jn. 2:1–11).

FOUR BIBLICAL SETTINGS. Four biblical works for organ by Emma Lou Diemer, commissioned by the Ventura, California, chapter of the American Guild of Organists and premiered in 1933 by Sandra Soderlund in Santa Barbara, California. The use of the crescendo pedal in movement 1 expresses the sentiments of God's wrath in Ps. 90:7–11, and movement 3, based on Isa. 11, incorporates elements of Bach's motet *Jesu meine Freude* ("Jesus, my Joy") (BWV 227). The other two are musical interpretations of Ps. 121 and Isa. 35.

FOUR BIBLICAL TABLEAUX. Orchestral suite in four movements by Aaron Avshalomov (1928), each one lasting under four minutes, with the titles "Queen Esther's Prayer" (Esth. 14), "Rebecca by the Well" (Gen. 24), "Ruth and Naomi," and "Processional." It was commissioned by Rabbi Henry J. Berkovitz for the dedication of Temple Beth Israel in Portland, Oregon.

FOUR HORSEMEN, THE. Song by Jimmy Webb based on the Apocalypse (Rev. 6) and performed by Glen Campbell on the album *Show Me the Way* (1991). The opening instrumental conjures up an image of galloping horses followed by three strophic verses describing the color of each horse and the purpose of its journey (Rev. 6:1–8) and an account of the cosmic disturbances that ensued (Rev. 6:12–14). The chorus, which represents the great and lowly who hid themselves in caves and rocks, calls on the mountains to fall on them to hide their faces from the Lord (Rev. 6:16).

FOUR HORSEMEN, THE. Song from the album *Kill 'em All* (1983) by the heavy metal band Metallica. It sold over 3 million copies in the United States alone, an all-time favorite for Metallica fans. Based loosely on Rev. 6:1–8, the song represents the horsemen as the Angel of Death, whose approaching presence poses a threat to a world scourged by the ravages of time, famine, pestilence, and death. The chorus outlines the way in which humanity can escape death by choosing to ride with the horsemen rather than face death by engaging in a futile battle with the Evil One. In this striking reversal of Christian interpretations of the text, it is the Angel of Death who offers hope and salvation to the world.

FOUR MOTETS. A collection of four motets for a cappella mixed chorus by Aaron Copland, written while he was a student under the direction of Nadia Boulanger (1921; published 1979). They are loosely based on texts from Psalms and Lamentations: "Help Us O Lord" (Ps. 36:9; Lam. 3:40), "Thou O Jehovah, dost-abide forever" (Lam. 5:19–21), "Have Mercy on Us, O Lord" (Ps. 51), and "Sing Ye Praises to Our King" (Ps. 47:6; 46:9; 47:1).

FOUR PSALMS. Work for SATB soloists, SATB chorus, and orchestra by John Harbison, commissioned by the Israeli Consulate of Chicago to celebrate the 50th anniversary of the founding of the state of Israel (1999). It is a setting in Hebrew of four of the most popular Psalms (Pss. 114, 126, 137, 133), ending with **Hinne ma tov**.

FROM DEPTHS OF WOE I CRY TO THEE. Hymn by Martin Luther based on the penitential Ps. 130, first published in the *Gesangbüchlein* by Johann Walter (1524). It was sung at the funeral of his friend and patron Frederick the Wise, elector of Saxony, in 1525 and at Luther's own funeral in Wittenburg in 1546. *See also DE PROFUNDIS.*

FROM GENESIS TO REVELATION. First studio album by the British rock band Genesis, produced by Jonathan King and performed by band members and schoolmates Peter Gabriel (lead vocals), Tony Banks (Hammond organ), Mike Rutherford (bass guitar), Anthony Phillips (guitar), and John Silver (drums), who replaced Chris Stewart (1969). Designed as a concept album, songs such "The Serpent," which segues into "Am I Very Wrong?" (Gen. 1–3) and "In the Wilderness" (Numbers), were based loosely on the Bible, but to the annoyance of the group, King added a string arrangement to make the album sound like a "Bee Gees pastiche," and it sold only 649 copies.

FROM THE GOSPEL OF JOHN. (*Iz evangeliya ot Ioanna*). Song in A minor for voice and piano by Rachmaninoff (TNii/57, 1915). Based on Christ's words about men laying down their lives for their friends (Jn. 15:13), it was written as a comment on the unspeakable loss of life during World War I.

FUNERAL SENTENCES. Six biblical texts from the funeral service in the 1662 Book of Common Prayer, set to music by Thomas Morley, Thomas Tomkins, Henry Purcell, William Croft, William Boyce, John Goss, Charles V. Stanford, and Hugh Blair. William Croft's popular setting has been performed at every British state funeral since it was published in *Musica Sacra* in 1724, in modern times most notably at the funerals of Sir Winston Churchill (1965); Diana, Princess of Wales (1998); and Queen Elizabeth, the Queen Mother (2002). Sung a cappella as the coffin is carried in procession toward the high altar, the sentences begin with Christ's own words, "I am the Resurrection and the Life" (Jn. 11:25–26), and, after words from Job (19:25–27; 1:21, and 14:1–2) and 1 Tim. 6:7, conclude with **"I heard a Voice from Heaven"** from the Book of Revelation (Rev. 14:13). Croft incorporated into his setting Purcell's fourth sentence composed for the burial service of Queen Mary II (1695).

FÜRCHTE DICH NICHT. ("Fear Thou Not"). Motet for double chorus (SSAATTBB) in two movements by Johann Sebastian Bach (BWV 228) based on two verses from Isaiah and two verses from Paul Gerhardt's 1656 chorale *Warum sollt' ich mich denn grämen?* ("Why should I myself then grieve?"). It is thought to have been composed for the funeral service of Stadthauptmann Winkler (1726). It opens with a polychoral setting of Isa. 41:10, followed by Isa. 43:1 sung by the lower voices of the two choruses in a three-part chromatic fugue and accompanied by the chorale sung by the upper voices as a cantus firmus. *See also* BE NOT AFRAID; DO NOT BE AFRAID.

• G •

GABRIEL'S MESSAGE. *See* THE ANGEL GABRIEL.

GALLIA GALLIA: LAMENTATION. Motet by Gounod for soprano solo, chorus, orchestra, and organ, based on Lamentations, it was written for the opening of the London International Exhibition in 1871 as a lament for the people of France (Latin *Gallia*) after their defeat in the Franco-Prussian War. The first three movements, *Quomodo sedet sola* ("How lonely she sits") (Lam. 1:1–2), *Viae Sion lugent* ("The roads to Zion mourn") (Lam. 1:4), and *O vos omnes* ("All you who pass by") (Lam. 1:12), are characterized by descending melodic lines, chromaticism, and dissonances to evoke the sorrow of people lamenting the destruction of Jerusalem. The final movement for soprano solo and chorus, *Vide, Domine, afflictionem meam* ("O Lord, behold my affliction") (Lam. 1:9), rises to a climax with ascending melodies and a high tessitura in all vocal parts in a plea for Jerusalem to return to the Lord.

GANGSTA'S PARADISE. Rap song by Coolio released on the album *Gangsta's Paradise* (1995) and the sound track of the film *Dangerous Minds* (1995), sampling the chorus and melody of Stevie Wonder's "Pastime Paradise" (1976). The opening, based on Ps. 23:4, sets the mood through the first person of a young African American who reflects on his life of crime only to realize that he has nothing left. With over 5.7 million copies sold worldwide, it features as one of the best-selling singles of all time.

GAUDETE. ("Rejoice"). Traditional Christmas carol in Latin, first published in the Finnish/Swedish songbook *Piae Cantiones Ecclesiasticae et Scholasticae Veterum Episcoporum* (1582). It achieved popularity in the 1970s following its a cappella performance and recording by the electric folk group Steeleye Span.

GEISTLICHES WIEGENLIED. ("Sacred Songs"). Art song for alto, viola, and piano by Johannes Brahms (op. 91, no. 2/2, ca. 1878). The German text is by Emanuel von Geibel after the Spanish Renaissance poet Lope de Vega. The poem is a lullaby sung by the Virgin Mary to the Christ child, foretelling Christ's passion and death on the cross. In the third stanza, there is a change of mood signaled by dissonant harmonies, a change in tonality from F major to F minor, and a change in meter from compound duple to simple triple. The words of the poem are juxtaposed against a melody in the accompaniment, played by the viola obbligato, from the Christmas carol *Josef Lieber, Josef Mein*.

GENESIS. Cantata for chorus and orchestra by American maximalist composer Charles Wuorinen, commissioned by the San Francisco, Minnesota, and Honolulu state orchestras and first performed in 1989. It is a hymn in praise of God's creation using verses from the Latin version of Gen. 1: 1–26, 30, 31; 2:1–2; Pss. 32:6; 99:3; 33:6; and Rev. 19, with seven incipits from the Latin Mass. It comprises three choral movements separated by two orchestral interludes. In the first movement, described as "a series of celebratory starbursts," seven chant melodies and incipits sung in a maximalist idiom represent the seven days of creation. The first orchestral interlude, reflective in mood, is characterized by meter changes for the first seven bars, pointing once more to the symbolism of seven days, and punctuated with chant melodies from the first movement. The second choral movement, "Creation History," based on Gen. 1–2, opens with brass, percussion, and low strings to suggest uncreation, and God's voice is represented by a chorus of women's voices in three parts to suggest the Trinity. After the second orchestral interlude, "Cosmology," which opens with a "Big Bang" from the brass and percussion, the final movement, "Doxology," consists of a chorus of **Alleluias** framing each proclamation of God's lordship over creation (Pss. 32:6; 99:3). The work concludes with a setting of Ps. 98:1a, *cantate domino canticum novum quia mirabilia fecit Dominus, Alleluia* ("Sing unto the Lord a new song, for the Lord has done marvellous things, Alleluia").

GENESIS PRELUDE. Work for wordless chorus and orchestra by Arnold Schoenberg , the first composition in **Genesis Suite** (op. 44, 1945). It depicts "the opening words of Gen. 1:1–2, when the world was void and without form." God's act of creation is defined by order, illustrated by the twelve-tone row and a double fugue. The voiceless chorus, which ends with a single voice, points to the creation of humanity in its prelinguistic state. The atonality resolves to C major at the end and calls to mind the first movement of Haydn's **Creation**.

GENESIS SUITE. Work for narrator, chorus, and orchestra commissioned by Nathaniel Shilkret (1945). It consists of seven pieces, composed by seven composers, based on seven events in the primeval history (Gen. 1–11): **Genesis Prelude** by Schoenberg, *Creation* by Nathaniel Shilkret (Gen. 1–2), *Adam and Eve* (Gen. 2–3) by Alexandre Tansman, *Cain and Abel* (Gen. 4) by Milhaud, *Noah's Ark* by Castelnuovo-Tedesco (Gen. 6–8), *The Covenant* (Gen. 9:1–17) by Ernst Toch, and **Babel** (Gen. 11:1–9) by Stravinsky.

GERMAN REQUIEM, A. (*Ein Deutsches Requiem*). Work for soprano and baritone soloists, chorus, and orchestra by Brahms (op. 45), composed in the years following the death of his mother in 1865 and first performed in Leipzig in 1869. The libretto is a selection of biblical texts in Luther's German, bearing no resemblance to the Latin Mass and almost devoid of explicit references to Christian theology. It is in seven movements, the first a chorus beginning "Blessed are they that mourn" (Mt. 5:4) and the last "Blessed are the dead" (Rev. 14:13), with a third "beatitude" at the end of the exquisite middle movement beginning "How lovely are thy dwellings" (Ps. 84:1–2, 4). Between these three pivotal points in major tonalities, the intractable tragedy of death is explored in mournful choruses, such as "For all flesh is as grass" (Isa. 40:6–7) and "For here we have no lasting home" (Heb. 13:14), in minor tonalities, each followed by joyful outbursts in major tonalities, such as "But the Word of God stands for ever" (Isa. 40:8; 1 Pet. 1:25), "The ransomed of the Lord shall return" (Isa. 35:10), and "Death is swallowed up in victory" (1 Cor. 15:54–55), in major tonalities. The soul-searching of Ps. 39 ("Lord, teach me") is similarly answered in a choral setting of a verse from the apocryphal Wisdom of Solomon (Wisd. 3:1), and the fifth movement is a dialogue between an ethereal tessitura solo, "You now have sadness" (Jn. 16:22; Sir. 51:27), and the choral refrain, "I will comfort you," one of the few verses in the Bible where God is compared to a mother (Isa. 66:13).

GESANG DER JÜNGLINGE. ("Song of the Youths"). Work by Stockhausen (1956), synthesizing recordings of electronic and vocal sounds performed by a treble. Based on the apocryphal song of the three children sung in the fiery furnace (Dan. 3), the opening words, *Preiset den Herrn* ("Praise ye the Lord"), recur throughout as a type of refrain, while words, syllables, and phonemes taken from the text are varied sequentially to produce different word orders and different syllable and phoneme sequences. Consisting of six sections or structures based on serial techniques distributed among four or five loudspeakers, it is organized around 12 types of elements, ranging from sine-wave complexes (SW) to white noise (NO). Premiered in the large auditorium of Cologne's West German Radio, it is regarded as the first masterpiece of electronic music.

GEYSTLICHES GESANGK BUCHLEYN. ("Little Spiritual Song Book"). A collection of 43 polyphonic arrangements, 38 settings in German and five in Latin, based on Lutheran chorale tunes scored for three to five voice parts arranged by Johann Walter (Wittenburg, 1524) in collaboration with Martin Luther, who wrote the preface. It was perhaps sung in alternating style, with the choir singing one verse in polyphony and the congregation singing the next in unison. The collection contained 24 hymns by Luther, four of which were included in the **Achtliederbuch**. Other well-known chorale tunes include **Ein fest' Burg** ("A Mighty Fortress"), *Vom Himmel hoch* ("From Heaven High"), *Komm Heiliger Geist* ("Come Holy Spirit"), *In Dulci Jubilo* ("In sweet rejoicing"), and *Joseph Lieber Joseph Mein* ("Joseph, my beloved Joseph") as well as Martin Luther's metrical setting of Ps. 14, *Es Spricht der Unweisen Mund Wohl* ("The Mouth of fools must say indeed"). The *Geystliches Gesangk Buchleyn* appears in the painting *The Ambassadors* by Hans Holbein the Younger (1533).

GIDEON. Posthumous oratorio pastiche for soloists, chorus, and orchestra by John Christopher Smith Jr. (1769), student and assistant of Handel. It combines music by Smith from his oratorio *The Feast of Darius* (1762) with works by Handel, including *Dixit Dominus* (HWV 232) ("The Lord said") (Ps. 110) and *Laudate pueri dominum* ("Praise the Lord, ye servants") (Ps. 113) (HWV 237). The libretto by Thomas Morell is based on the story of Gideon, his destruction of Baal, the defeat of the Midianites, and the miracle of the fleece (Judg. 6–8). Other works based on this theme include an oratorio by John Stainer (1865), written as an exercise for his doctorate of music, and an oratorio by Israeli composer Marc Lavry (op. 277, 1962).

GIRL IN THE WAR. Protest song from the album *The Animal Years* by Josh Ritter (2006). Based loosely on the "Incident at Antioch" (Gal. 2:11–14), it tells of a conversation between St. Peter, representing Americans worrying about their loved ones in war-torn regions, and St. Paul. With references to the Keys of Heaven (Mt. 16:19), the Rock (Mt. 16:18), and the Dove (Mt. 3:16; Mk. 1:10; Jn. 1:32; Acts 2), Ritter vocalizes the anger felt by Americans about the war in Iraq and suggests that politicians indifferent to suffering "can go to Hell" (Mt. 25:45–46).

GIVE THANKS AND PRAISES. Reggae song by Rastafarian Bob Marley, performed by Marley and the Wailers and released posthumously on the album *Confrontation* (1983). It alludes to biblical verses about giving "thanks and praises to the Most-I (Jah!) . . . thanks and praises so high (so high) (cf. Pss. 92:1; 136:1), removing "that veil from off of your eyes" (2 Cor. 3:16), and rehabilitating the prophet Ham, father of black Africans (Gen. 6–9).

GIVE THANKS UNTO THE LORD. Anthem for four-part (SATB) a cappella chorus by the American composer Kirke Mechem inspired by Ps. 136:1–5. It won the triannual SAI Inter-American Vocal Music Award (1959), which brought the composer's work into greater prominence.

GIVE UNTO THE LORD. Anthem for chorus, organ, and orchestra ad lib. by Elgar (op. 74, 1914) based on Ps. 29. First performed in April 1914, the concluding words, "the Lord shall give his people the blessing of peace" (Ps. 29:11, BCP), were to be all the more poignant at the start of World War I later that year.

GLORIA IN EXCELSIS. ("Glory to God in the Highest"). Motet for SATB chorus by Claude Goudimel (ca. 1514–1520) inspired by the angel's proclamation announcing Jesus' birth (Lk. 2:14). There are many other settings, including Vivaldi's well-known *Gloria in D major* (RV 589, 1713); a setting for soprano solo, mixed chorus, and orchestra by Poulenc (FP 177, 1959–1960); and John Rutter's exuberant concert *Gloria* for brass ensemble, timpani, percussion, and organ (1974), scored in three movements, commissioned by the Voices of Mel Olson in Omaha, Nebraska. There are also some notable settings in Bach's *Mass in B Minor*, Beethoven's *Missa Solemnis* in D major (op. 123), and Britten's *Missa Brevis* in D (op. 63, 1959). The Gloria also features as a chorus in several Christmas carols, such as "Ding Dong Merrily on High," "Hark the Herald Angels Sing," and "Angels We Have Heard on High."

GLORIOUS THINGS OF THEE ARE SPOKEN. Hymn by John Newton inspired by Ps. 87:3 and other biblical verses, including Ps. 46:4 and Isa. 4:5–6 and 26:1, first published in *Olney Hymns* (1779). The tune "Austria" by Haydn was originally set to the prayer *Gott erhalte Franz den Kaiser* ("God save Francis the Kaiser") by Lorenz Leopold Haschka (1749–1827) and used by Haydn in his Emperor String Quartet (op. 76, no. 3, 1797). The tune is now the German national anthem.

GO DOWN MOSES. African American spiritual, published in *Jubilee Songs as Sung by the Jubilee Singers of Fisk University* by Theodore F. Seward (1872). Beginning "When Israel was in Egypt's land," a lead singer recounts details of the biblical story of Israel's captivity in Egypt (Exod. 1:8–14; 5:1–22; 6:10; 7:1–12:50), and the chorus responds with God's words of deliverance, "Let my people go." It has been performed by Paul Robeson, Louis Armstrong, Roland Hayes, Big Mama Thornton, Willard White, and many others. It features in Michael Tippett's oratorio **A Child of Our Time** (1939–1941).

GO TELL IT ON THE MOUNTAIN. African American spiritual based on Lk. 2:8–14. It was arranged by African American composer John Wesley Work and appeared in *Folk Songs of the American Negro* (1907) and *Religious Folk Songs of the Negro* (1927), published by R. Nathaniel Dett. The undulating melody of the chorus calls to mind the hills and mountains in Isa. 40:9 and 52:7 and Nah. 1:15. It has been popularly performed by numerous artists, including Mahalia Jackson, James Taylor, Garth Brooks, Bing Crosby, Frank Sinatra, Simon and Garfunkel, and many more.

GOD IS DEAD? Song written in 2013 by Geezer Butler and performed by heavy metal band Black Sabbath, it is inspired by accounts of Christ's death on the cross and Friedrich Nietzsche's famous statement "God is dead" (1882). The lyrics comment on humanity's skepticism and nihilism, with atmospheric wailing vocals by the "Godfather of Heavy Metal," Ozzy Osbourne, and mounting tension-filled riffs and solos by Tony Iommi, and end with the statement "I don't believe God is dead." An image of Nietzsche in front of an atomic explosion features in the artwork for the cover of the single.

GOD IS GONE UP. Ascension anthem for SATB (*divisi*) and organ or SATB (*divisi*), organ, and string orchestra by Gerald Finzi, composed for the feast day of St. Cecilia (op. 27, no. 2, 1951). Set to a poetic text, "Meditation Twenty," by American poet Edward Taylor, inspired by Ps. 47:5–7, it imagines the celebratory scene following Christ's ascension. Set in three sections, the first and third describe the power of God with dramatic fanfares on the organ and word painting on "God is gone up with a triumphant shout," including ascending melodic lines and a fortissimo on "shout," while the serene middle section describes the scene of the heavenly hosts encircling God's chariot as it ascends into heaven. There are many other settings of this text, including anthems by William Croft and Herbert Howells and a hymn by Gottfried W. Sacer (*Gott fähret auf den Himmel*, 1661), translated from German to English by Frances E. Cox in *Sacred Hymns from the German* (1841) entitled "Lo, God to Heav'n ascendeth!"

GODSPELL. Christian rock musical written and composed by Stephen Lawrence Schwartz, first staged in New York in 1971, based on biblical texts (mostly Matthew and Luke), and interspersed with hymns from the *Episcopal Hymnal* (1940). It begins with the Tower of Babel (Gen. 11:1–9) and then tells the story of Christ's life from his baptism to the Crucifixion, focusing particularly on the parables, the **Beatitudes**, and his dealings with the Pharisees, the woman taken in adultery, and Judas. One of its most memorable lyrics is "Prepare ye the way of the Lord" (Isa. 40:3; Mt. 3:3), which is sung in the wilderness at the beginning and again in the finale as Christ's body is taken down from the cross. Others include "Save the People" (*Hymnal* 496), "Day by Day" (*Hymnal* 429), and "Bless the Lord" (*Hymnal* 293). "Tomorrow will take care of itself" (Mt. 6:34) follows the **Beatitudes**, and a mournful setting of part of Ps. 137, beginning "On the Willows," accompanies an account of the Passion (Mt. 26–27).

GOLGOTHA. Passion oratorio for soloists, mixed chorus, orchestra, and organ by Frank Martin (1945–1948). Inspired by *The Three Crosses*, an engraving by Rembrandt (1653), it is in two parts, each divided into five movements. Biblical verses from the four Gospels (Mt. 21:2–9; 23:1–4, 13, 27–39; Mk. 11:8–10; 14:32–43, 45–46, 48–50; Lk. 22:14–16, 19, 20, 39, 53; Jn. 12:12–13, 27–32) and elsewhere (1 Cor. 15:55; Ps. 121; Job 12:27–32) are juxtaposed with a text based on St. Augustine's *Confessions*.

GOMORRAH. Song by the Jerry Garcia Band on the album *How Sweet It Is* (1975), based on the story of the burning of Gomorrah (Gen. 19:15–26). Asked who gave him "orders" to get out of Gomorrah, Mr. Lot replies that it was "the same voice" he always believes. Lot is regarded as a "righteous" man whose obedience contrasts with his wife's disobedience and subsequent death.

GOSPEL ACCORDING TO LUKE, THE. Song by American country music artists Skip Ewing and Don Sampson on the breakthrough album *The Coast of Colorado* (1989). Inspired by a homeless man called Luke whom Skip Ewing saw while in Nashville, there are echoes of Luke's Gospel (e.g., the widow's mite in v. 4; cf. Lk. 21:1–4), and "There's treasure in heaven for the generous few" in the chorus comes from Lk. 12:32–34. It reached the top 10 in the Billboard Hot Country Singles and Tracks.

GOSPEL PRELUDES. A set of gospel preludes for organ by William Bolcom, based on well-known hymns, commissioned for the 60th anniversary of the Dallas Chapter of the American Guild of Organists (1979). They incorporate a variety idioms from jazz, gospel, and cabaret. The hymns covered by the piece include **Rock of Ages**, **Jesus Loves Me**, **Amazing Grace**, **Blessed Assurance**, and **Nearer My God to Thee**.

GRADUALE ROMANUM. ("The Roman Gradual"). The official liturgical book (1974) of the Roman rite, from the Novo Ordo and revised Roman calendar, compiled by the Benedictine monks of St. Peter's Abbey, Solesmes, France, to replace the **Liber Usualis**, used for the Tridentine Mass.

GREAT EIGHTEEN CHORALE PRELUDES, THE. A work for organ by J. S. Bach (BWV 651–668) based on biblical texts, including *An Wasserflüssen Babylon* ("**By the Waters of Babylon**") (Ps. 137), *O Lamm Gottes unschuldig* ("O Lamb of God innocently slaughtered") (1 Pet. 1:19), *Nun Danket Alle Gott* ("**Now Thank we All Our God**") (Sir. 50:22–24), and *Nun komm der Heiden Heiland* ("Come Now Saviour of the Heathen"), based on the readings for the first Sunday of Advent (Mt. 21:1–9; Rom. 13:11–14; Rev. 3:20), and *Vor deinen Thron tret ich hiermit* ("Before your Throne I now Appear") (Rev. 4:1–11), thought to have been written on Bach's deathbed.

GREAT IS THE LORD. Anthem for bass solo, SSAAB chorus, and organ by Elgar (op. 67), written for the foundation or commemoration of a church and first performed in Westminster Abbey in 1912. Based on Ps. 48, it opens with unison altos, tenors, and basses singing of God's greatness followed by the delightful scoring for sopranos and altos *divisi* telling of the beauty of Mount Zion (Ps. 48:1–3). A contrasting section in common time with syncopation (*ma molto marcato*) depicts the assembly of kings "as they hasted away" (vv. 4–8). The text "We have thought on thy loving kindness, O God" for bass solo forms the centerpiece (vv. 9–10), and the work concludes with the joyful chorus "Let Mount Zion be glad . . . for this God is our God" (vv. 11–14).

GREATER LOVE HATH NO MAN. Anthem for chorus, treble and baritone soloists, and organ or orchestra by John Ireland (1912), commissioned for Passiontide by Charles Macpherson, the suborganist of St. Paul's Cathedral, London. The text, expressing frequent changes in mood, is based on verses from the Song of Solomon, John, Romans, 1 Corinthians, and 1 Peter. "Greater love hath no man than this" (Jn. 15:13) and "Who has called you out of darkness?" (1 Pet. 2:9) are a cappella, with the words "for his friends" sung in unison (Jn. 15:13). The sublime treble solo "Who his own self bore our sins" (1 Pet. 2:24) highlights Christ's innocence, while the baritone solo "that we being dead to sins should live unto righteousness" expresses faith in the power of Christ's resurrection and fellowship in his suffering. The work then rises to a climax with unison singing followed by a quieter concluding section, reflecting the mood of Rom. 12:1. The anthem became all the more poignant, given the context of World War I two years later.

GREATEST STORY EVER TOLD, THE. Film produced and directed by George Stevens (1965) retelling the life of Christ from the Nativity to his resurrection. The music, composed by Alfred Newman, includes the opening chorus of Verdi's *Requiem* for the **Via Dolorosa** sequence and the "**Hallelujah** Chorus" from Handel's **Messiah** for the resurrection of Lazarus.

• H •

HAEC DIES. ("This Is the Day"). Motet for six voices by William Byrd, published in *Cantiones Sacrae* (1589), it is one of four six-part works based on Ps. 118:24 and perhaps immortalized in the tradition that the same words were spoken by the Jesuit priest Edmund Campion when he was sentenced to death in 1581. Sung at Eastertide, the jubilant music in triple meter is suggestive of the priest's triumphant arrival in heaven amid a choir of heavenly hosts singing joyful **Alleluias**.

HAGAR IN THE WILDERNESS. One-act chamber opera in four scenes for soprano, bass-baritone, and tenor soloists by Sally Beamish to a libretto by Clara Glynn, produced in association with the Presteigne Festival, the Canterbury Festival and Music at Oxford supported by the Ralph Vaughan Williams Trust. Based on Gen. 21, it focuses on the themes of betrayal, jealousy, and motherhood. The American composer William Henry Fry's Sacred Symphony no. 3 is another musical interpretation of the "Hagar in the Wilderness" story (1854).

HAGAR'S LAMENT. (*Hagars Klage*). Song for soprano solo and piano by Franz Schubert (D.5, 1811), closely modeled on Johann Rudolf Zumsteeg's setting of the same text (1797), it is one of the earliest surviving completed works by the composer written when he was 14 years old. Based on a moving poem by Clemens August Schücking after Gen. 21:14–16 and scored in C minor to reflect the text's somber mood, this cantata-like song recounts Hagar's despair on seeing her baby Ishmael dying of thirst. Descending bass octaves in the piano accompaniment at "And then death will come" feature as a death motif in later works as well.

HAIL GLADDENING LIGHT. Well-known anthem for double chorus (SATBSATB) by Charles Wood, first published in 1919. The text comes from John Keble's translation of the third-century Greek hymn *Phos Hilaron*. Possibly inpsired by Jn. 8:12, it was originally sung at the lighting of the evening lamp, later incorporated into the Orthodox liturgy of the All-Night Vigil, and subsequently set by many composers, including Tchaikovsky in the *All Night Vigil* (op. 52, 1881–1882) and Alexander Grechaninov (op. 58, 1911). The luscious double chorus sound paints the radiating light of Christ, with antiphonal singing on "Holiest of Holies," homophony on "Jesus Christ our

Lord," and a rising climax at the end: "Therefore in all the world thy glories, Lord, they own." *See also* LIGHT OF THE WORLD, THE; LUMEN; NUNC DIMITTIS; O NATA LUX.

HAIL, MARY. *See* AVE MARIA.

HAIR. Song by PJ Harvey from the album *Dry* (1992). It is an imaginative dialogue between Samson and Delilah, loosely based, perhaps, on Judg. 16:4–7. A change in the dynamics contrasts the mood of Delilah's seductive words before the act of deception with Samson's when he realizes what has happened to him.

HALLELUJAH. Ballad by Leonard Cohen originally published in *Book of Mercy* (1984) with other poems inspired by the Bible and the Jewish liturgy and first released on the studio album *Various Positions* (1984). Over 100 cover versions of the song now exist, with popular renditions by Jeff Buckley, Bob Dylan, k.d. lang, Justin Timberlake, Regina Spektor, and, more recently, the 2008 UK X Factor winner Alexander Burke, whose single became the fastest-selling European digital download in history, selling over 105,000 copies in 24 hours. John Cale's version appeared in the movie *Shrek* (2001). The Christian rock band Cloverton added new lyrics that focus on the Nativity story (vv. 1–4) and Christ's crucifixion (v. 5), released as a single on *A Hallelujah Christmas* in 2011. The song's title derives from the Hebrew word *hallelu-yah*, "Praise the Lord," particularly in the Hallel Psalms sung at Jewish festivals (Ps. 113–118). With dramatic irony, this modern-day Psalm contrasts the adoration of the Lord in the Psalms of David with the narrator's adoration of his lover since, unlike David, whose mystical harp playing pleased the Lord (1 Sam. 16:26), he could never please his lover. He is like David captivated by Bathsheba's beauty when he saw her bathing (2 Sam. 11:2) but then is disempowered like Samson by Delilah (Judg. 16). Love led him along a path of sorrow and brokenness despite moments of intimacy, and in a final verse alluding to the killing of Uriah (2 Sam. 11:6–17), he tells us he learned nothing from love except how to ward off potential rivals. The original version in C major is in compound quadruple meter to create a lilting effect, and Cohen's performance, accompanied by theater organ, electric guitars, drums, saxophone, and backing chorus, evokes the sound of gospel music.

HAMAL'ACH HA-GO'EL OTI. ("The Angel Who Redeems Me"). Jewish nighttime prayer for children taken from Jacob's blessing of his grandchildren, the twins Ephraim and Manasseh (Gen. 48:16). It is sung to a variety of tunes, including Brahms's *Wiegenlied* ("Cradle Song") (op. 49) and, more recently, a melody by Stephen Levey, arranged by Motti Cohen and sung by chorister Eli Baigel on Shimon Craimer's album *Nashir Beyachad* ("Let's sing together") (2010). Canadian Orthodox Jewish composer Abie Rottenberg and American Hasidic singer/songwriter Mordechai Ben David, known as the "King of Jewish Music," composed another moving version, performed at a Hebrew Academy for Special Children concert in 1995 at the Lincoln Center, New York.

HANEROT HALALU. ("We Kindle These Lights in Remembrance"). Hymn sung at Hanukkah after the recitation of the Hanukhah blessings and during the lighting of the new light for the night, it commemorates the eight-day rededication of the Temple following the Maccabean victory (1 Macc. 4:36). There are numerous settings for choirs, including one by Jewish composer Hugo Adler, an arrangement for cello by Louis Lewandowski (1821–1894), and a modern rendition by Mike Boer performed by the Jewish group Six13.

HARK! THE HERALD ANGELS SING. Strophic hymn for Christmas Day written by English hymnist Charles Wesley and first published in *Hymns and Sacred Poems* (1739). The lyrics were later set to music by English composer William Hayman Cummings to a melody from the second movement of Mendelssohn's cantata *Festgesang* ("Festival Song") (1840) and published in 1856. In recent times, it has been arranged by David Willcocks for brass ensemble and organ with an added descant for the third verse (1961). It was sung at the end of the films *It's a Wonderful Life* (1946) and *A Christmas Carol* (1951).

HASHIRIM ASHER LISH'LOMO. ("Songs of Solomon"). A collection of 33 polyphonic settings of various Psalms, hymns, prayers, and synagogue songs by the Italian baroque musician Salomone Rossi (1623), edited and published by his pupil Leo da Modena. Scored for three to eight voices, it is one of the first collections of polyphonic music in Hebrew. The title has nothing to do with the biblical "Song of Solomon" (Hebrew *shir ha-shirim*, "Song of Songs") and appears to have been a play on the composer's first name.

HAVA NAGILA. ("Eve Let Us Rejoice"). Originally a folk song and instrumental, it was brought to Jerusalem from Ukraine and published by Jewish musicologist Abraham Zevi Idelsohn in his *Thesaurus of Hebrew-Oriental Melodies* (1914). The words, inspired by Ps. 118:24 and Prov. 15:13 or 17:22, are attributed to Idelsohn amid claims that they had been written by his student Cantor Moshe Nathanson (1899–1981). The Psalm's references to God are omitted, and the emphasis is on solidarity among friends and relations, the melody and words evoking the joy and hopefulness of the original Psalm. Played and sung to the Hora dance, it is popular at celebrations of various kinds, Jewish and non-Jewish. It has been performed by many artists and features in several films, including *Fiddler on the Roof* (1971), *The Jazz Singer* (1980), and the movie documentary *Hava Nigila: The Movie* (2012), which features Harry Belafonte, Regina Spektor, Glen Campbell, and Connie Francis.

HE TOUCHED ME. Grammy-winning gospel music album recorded by Elvis Presley (1972). The praise chorus *He Touched Me* (1963) by American singer/songwriter Bill Gaither refers to Jesus' act of touching people, physically and psychologically, in various New Testament references as well as in contemporary Christian life. Other well-known songs on the album include **Amazing Grace** by John Newton and the spiritual **Bosom of Abraham** (Lk. 16:22) by William Johnson, George McFadden, and Philip Brooks.

HEAR MY PRAYER. (*Hör' mein Bitten*). Anthem for treble soloist, chorus and organ, or orchestra by Mendelssohn (1944) to a libretto by William Bartholomew. Inspired by Ps. 55:1–7, it comprises the well-known "O for the Wings of a Dove" (*O könnt' ich fliegen*) (Ps. 55:6–8), sung by a treble and often performed as a solo work in its own right. After the plaintive "Hear My Prayer," sung first by the treble solo and then by the chorus, an urgent call-and-response passage depicts the soul surrounded by its enemies, followed by a solo prayer of supplication echoed briefly by the chorus. In the final section, the sublime "O for the Wings of a Dove" illustrates the flight of a dove with a soaring melody and concludes with the chorus and soloist singing, pianissimo, "and remain there for ever at rest."

HEAR MY PRAYER O LORD. Anthem for eight-part chorus (SSAA-TTBB) by Henry Purcell (Z. 15), performed at the funeral service of Charles II in 1685 and, more recently, at the funeral service of Margaret Thatcher in 2013. Based on Ps. 102:1, it opens with one voice (A) and gradually builds in texture to include all eight voices. The penitent's chant-like supplication is built around two notes. Chromaticism on "crying" expresses sorrow and remorse, while bare fifths at the end on "thee" ("let me crying come unto thee") paints the penitent's desolation. Purcell composed another anthem with the same title (Z. 14) but based on Ps. 55. There is also a setting of Ps. 55 by Mendelssohn for soprano solo, SATB chorus, and organ (1844) and another by Jacque Berthier as a Taizé chant in ostinato form (1982).

HERE I AM LORD. ("I the Lord of Sea and Sky"). Well-known hymn (1981) written by the Jesuit Dan Schutte and sung in Catholic and Protestant liturgies. The refrain beginning "Here I am Lord" refers to God's call to Abraham (Gen. 22:1), Samuel (1 Sam. 3:3–10), and Isaiah (Isa. 6:8), and the three verses contain numerous other biblical allusions, including God hearing the cries of his people (Exod. 3:7) and Christ tending the weak and the lame (Lk. 13:10–17). *See* ECCOMI.

HERITAGE SUITE FOR ORCHESTRA. Orchestral music in six movements inspired by biblical characters and events in Jewish history, it was composed by Irish American John Duffy for the nine-part television series *Heritage: Civilisation and the Jews* (1984). After an overture, the second movement, inspired by the Song of **Solomon** ("David and Bathsheba"), describes the sensuous union of David and Bathsheba through lyrical writing. The third movement, "Dance before the Golden Calf," based on Exod. 32:19, recalls **Moses**' sight of the Children of Israel and their frenzied dance before the idol. It is illustrated musically by a fast, rhythmic pulse and colorful orchestration. Following movement 4 ("Destruction before the Temple") and movement 5 ("Diaspora"), the work concludes with a finale ("Prophecy") inspired by Isa. 11:6 ("the wolf shall dwell with the lamb"), describing the return of the Children of Israel to the Promised Land.

HERZ UND MUND UND TAT UND LEBEN. ("Heart and Mouth and Deed and Life"). Cantata for SATB soloists, SATB chorus, orchestra, and continuo by J. S. Bach for the Feast of the Visitation of the Virgin Mary, first performed in Leipzig on 2 July 1723 (BWV 147). The libretto, inspired by the Epistle and Gospel readings for the day (Isa. 11:1–5; Lk. 1:39–56), is based on an earlier version of the cantata from Bach's Weimar years, composed for the fourth Sunday of Advent (BWV 147a, 1716). It is in 10 movements, of which the most famous is the last, *Jesu, meiner Seelen Wonne* ("Jesus, delight of my soul") by Martin Jahn (1661), sung to a melody, *Werde munter, mein Gemüte* ("Be alert, my soul") by Johann Schop (1642), and popularly known in Bach's arrangement as "Jesu Joy of Man's Desiring," with English words composed by Robert Bridges.

HERZLICH TUT MICH VERLANGEN. ("I Yearn from My Heart"). Passion chorale known also as *Ach Herr, mich armen Sünder* ("O Lord, poor sinner that I am") and *O Haupt, voll Blut und Wunden* ("O Head, full of blood and wounds"). The music was composed by Hans Leo Hassler for the secular love song *Mein G'mut ist mir verwirret* ("My mind, thou art confusing") and later adapted in 1656 by Johann Crüger for the hymn *O Haupt voll Blut und Wunden* by Paul Gerhardt. *See also* O SACRED HEAD SORE WOUNDED.

HE'S GOT THE WHOLE WORLD IN HIS HANDS. Folk song and African American spiritual first published in the hymnal *Spirituals Triumphant, Old and New* in 1927, it is thought to have been inspired by Job 12:10 and the "Kingship Psalms," such as Ps. 47, 93, and 97. Although there are several variations in existence, each one is similarly repetitive and joyful in mood as expressed by the syncopated rhythm in the lyric "He's got the whole world in his hands." With many performances by well-known artists, it has been included in the movies *Tootsie* (1982), *Roxanne* (1987), *Con Air* (1997), and *Rocket Man* (1997).

HEZEKIAH. Oratorio in two parts by John Truman Wolcott (op. 11, 1908) with text compiled by Rev. Howard Duffield. Based on the stories of the miraculous destruction of the Assyrian army (Isa. 36–37) and the recovery of Hezekiah from illness (Isa. 38), it is scored for soprano (Words of God/Isaiah/ Narrator), alto (Narrator), tenor (Hezekiah), baritone (Words of God/King of Assyria/Isaiah/Narrator), chorus, and orchestra. Memorable numbers include the instrumental "March of Sennacherib's Army upon Jerusalem" (Isa. 36:1), Hezekiah's prayers for deliverance from the Assyrians (Isa. 37:16–20) and from sickness (Isa. 38:3), the female quartet "Be Still and Know that I am God" (Ps. 46:10), and the chorus **"Thou Wilt Keep him in Perfect Peace"** (Isa. 26:3). It concludes with the joyful chorus "Great and Marvellous are thy Works" (Rev. 15:3).

HEZEKIAH: A SHORT ORATORIO. Work for soloists (SATB), chorus (SATB), and orchestra by Philip Armes (1878), based on the biblical story of Jerusalem's deliverance from the Assyrian army (Isa. 36–37) and King Hezekiah's deliverance from sickness (Isa. 38). The introduction opens with the instrumental "March of Sennacherib's Army upon Jerusalem" followed by the threatening words of Rabshakeh (B) and the prayer of Hezekiah (T), "O Lord of Hosts, God of Israel." The chorus responds with a reflective chorus, "Thou wilt keep him in perfect peace" (Isa. 26:3–4) , and the defeat of Sennacherib is foretold in a prophecy spoken by God (B) and a duet by Isaiah (S) and the Narrator (A) beginning "The Virgin the Daughter of Zion" (Isa. 37:22–29). The chorus sings of a sign that will be given to Hezekiah (Isa. 37:31–32), and a bass recitative marked "*allegro vivace*" and scored in semiquaver movement in the eight-bar instrumental introduction describes how the angel destroyed 185,000 in the Assyrian camp (Isa. 37:36). Hezekiah's prayer for deliverance from sickness (Isa. 38:3) is sung as a tenor solo, "Remember now O Lord, I beseech thee." God's promise of a miraculous 15-year extension to Hezekiah's life is told by Isaiah to Hezekiah in a bass recitative (Isa. 38:4–5), and the work concludes with a joyful chorus, "Sing unto the Lord" (Isa. 12:5–6).

HIDE NOT THY FACE FROM US, O LORD. Anthem for SATB chorus a cappella by Richard Farrant based on Ps. 27:10. Scored in homophony, repetitions on "for thy mercy sake, deliver us from all our sins" alternate between major and minor tonalities to illustrate the disquiet felt by the penitent, while the final chord concludes in a more hopeful key of D major, pointing perhaps to God's mercy.

HIGHWAY 61 REVISITED. Title track from the album *Highway 61 Revisited* (1965) by former Orthodox Jew Bob Dylan. Arguably one of the most important singles of the 1960s, combining garage rock, blues, and epic folk, it was performed by Bruce Springsteen, PJ Harvey, Dave Allen, and many others. The first stanza is a dialogue based on Gen. 22 in which Abraham (Abe) at first resists God's command but then agrees to kill his son not on a sacred mountain but on Highway 61, the "Blues Highway," which ran from Duluth, Minnesota, where Dylan was born, and Minneapolis, where he went to college, to Memphis, Tennessee, and New Orleans in the Mississippi Delta. Here it is seen as a place where natural law and order have been turned upside down and where neither a loving God nor a loving father exists, a possible allusion to Dylan's own father, who was called Abram (Abe) Zimmerman.

HINNE MA TOV. ("Behold How Good"). Popular Hebrew song based on the first verse of Ps. 133. Sung all over the world to a variety of tunes, it featured on the album *Harry Belafonte Returns to Carnegie Hall* (1960) and in the film *Raid on Entebbe* (1977). It was also popularized by the Miami Boys Choir in an arrangement by Moshe Jacobson (2000) and performed to a modern folk dance choreographed by Silvio Berlfein. *See also* AFRICA UNITE.

HODIE CHRISTUS NATUS EST. ("Today Christ Is Born"). Gregorian chant sung as the antiphon before and after the **Magnificat** for vespers on Christmas Day. The motet by Sweelinck for five-part chorus a cappella is perhaps one of his most well known works. Each verse begins with the tenor's announcement *Hodie, Hodie*, sung in joyful triple meter, reminiscent of a dance, and concludes with a series of joyful **Alleluias** interspersed with "Noel." Among numerous other settings are those of Byrd, Monteverdi, Palestrina, and Schütz.

HOLY, HOLY, HOLY. Hymn written for Trinity Sunday by Reginald Heber to the tune *Nicaea* (1861) by John Bacchus Dykes. Each of the four verses opens with the thrice-repeated "Holy" from the song of the Seraphim in Isaiah's vision (Isa. 6:3), and verse 3 picks up the theme of "sinful man" from the same passage (v. 6). The hymn features in the movie *Titanic* (1953), where it is sung by the passengers as they approach one of the icebergs. *See also* SANCTUS.

HOSANNA FILIO DAVID. ("**Hosanna to the Son of David**"). Entrance antiphon sung to a traditional Gregorian melody in mode VII celebrating Christ's triumphant entry into Jerusalem on Palm Sunday (Mt. 21:9), performed during the procession of palms. Well-known settings are by Victoria in Latin and by Gibbons and Weelkes in English.

HOSANNA TO THE SON OF DAVID. Full anthem for seven-part a cappella chorus (SSAATTB) by Orlando Gibbons composed during the reign of King James I. Based on Mt. 21:9, it is performed in liturgical contexts on Palm Sunday. Imitative polyphony describes the cries of the people as they hailed Christ's triumphant entry into Jerusalem, scattering their garments before him and waving palms and olive branches. There are also settings by Thomas Weelkes and, more recently, by American composer Dan Schutte (1995).

HOSEA'S WIFE. Song by New Zealand singer/songwriter Brooke Fraser from the album *Albertine* (2006) based on the account of Gomer's adulterous marriage to Hosea (Hos. 1–3). Introspective in style, Fraser presents Gomer as a symbol of humanity in search of an answer to the question "What do I live for?" The soaring, animated chorus invites listeners to look and listen for God's saving word in their "hearts and mouths." *See* THE SONG OF GOMER.

HYMN OF JESUS, THE. A choral work by Gustav Holst (op. 37) composed during World War I and first performed in London in 1920. Written for three choirs and orchestra, with percussion, celesta, piano, and organ, it begins with a rather otherworldly Prelude, featuring the Latin plainchant *Vexilla regis prodeunt* played by lone French horns and trombones, then with orchestral accompaniment, followed by a choir of distant female voices (*Vexilla regis prodeunt . . .*) and a choir of tenors and basses (*Pange lingua* ["Of the Glorious Body telling . . ."]) who sing the plainchant in free rhythm independently of the orchestra. This is followed by a choral setting of the Hymn, a passage from the apocryphal Acts of John, translated from the Greek by Holst himself. Two choirs, representing the Master and his students, engage in a ritual dialogue leading into an ecstatic dance ("Divine grace is dancing"). The work ends with the three choirs singing with a united voice against orchestral sounds of pain and suffering until the triumphant chorus picks up the plainchant melody *Vexilla regis* from the prelude, and "Learn how to suffer and ye shall overcome" leads finally to a chorus of peaceful **Amens**. The work seeks consolation for the horrors of World War I in the occult philosophy of an ancient gnostic hymn.

HYMN TO ST. PETER. Anthem for SATB, treble/soprano solo or semi-chorus, and organ by Benjamin Britten (op. 56a, 1955), written for the Quincentenary of the Church of St. Peter Mancroft, Norwich. It is based on the plainchant *Tu es Petrus* ("Thou are Peter"), first heard in unison on the organ. The biblical text (Mt. 16:18–19), with an **Alleluia** at the end, is taken from the Gradual Feast of St. Peter and St. Paul.

HYMN TO THE CREATOR OF LIGHT. Anthem in three sections for double a cappella chorus (SATB/SATB) by John Rutter, first performed in 1992 at the dedication of the Herbert Howells memorial window in Gloucester Cathedral. Inspired by Gen. 1:3, the words beginning "Glory to thee, O Lord . . . Creator of the visible light" come from a prayer by Bishop Lancelot Andrewes (1555–1626), combined with verses from a well-known hymn by Johann Franck (1618–1677) (EH 306), ending with "Sun, who all my life dost brighten . . . As thy guest in heaven receive us." All three sections encapsulate the image of the creation of light beginning with the medieval sound of chant sung in unison by choir 1 to suggest God's mysterious creative act, followed by choir 2 singing chromaticisms and dissonances to suggest the birth of the first rays of light, which culminate in a dense sonorous texture to suggest the bright sunlight of the first day of creation. The serene closing section is suggestive of the fading light at dusk and of the soul's journey and entry into heaven.

HYMNES AND SONGS OF THE CHURCH. The earliest hymnal of the English Church published by George Wither in 1623, containing many hymn tunes ascribed to Orlando Gibbons. Part 1 comprises compositions based on the songs of biblical characters, such as "The First Song of **Moses**" (Song 1: Exod. 15), "The Lamentation of David" (Song 5: 2 Sam. 1:17), "The Second Song of Isaiah" (Song 20: Isa. 12), "The Song of the Three Children" (Dan. 13:29–68), and "The Song of the Angels" (Lk. 2:13–14). Part 2 consists of spiritual songs organized according to the church's liturgical calendar, such as **"This is the day the Lord hath made"** (Ps. 118:24) for Easter and "Those, Oh thrice Holy Three-in One, Who seek thy nature to explain" for Trinity

Sunday. Many of the songs from this hymnal appear on the album *Gibbons: Hymns and Songs of the Church* performed by Tonus Peregrinus, conducted by Anthony Pitts (2006), who also arranged many of the songs on the album.

HYMNS ANCIENT AND MODERN. A hymnbook for use in the Church of England, first published in 1861 under the direction of the musician William Henry Monk. The first edition contained 273 hymns, most of them translations from Latin, supplemented by a relatively small number of English hymns by Charles Wesley, John Keble, Isaac Watts, and others. The melodies were mainly arrangements of traditional Latin, German, English, and other tunes with a few new compositions, such as "St. Ethelwald," by William H. Monk, for Wesley's hymn "Soldiers of Christ, arise" (Eph. 6:11) and "Nicaea," by John Bacchus Dykes, for **"Holy Holy Holy"** (Rev. 4:8–11). An early edition (1867) prints a biblical verse as a heading for every hymn as well as copious scriptural allusions. It was revised in 1887, 1904, and 1950 and in a "New Standard Edition" in 1983, containing many recent compositions. In 2000, the Canterbury Press, a subsidiary of Hymns Ancient and Modern Ltd, published a hymnal entitled *Common Praise* and in 2013 brought out a completely new edition, containing 847 hymns, with the title *Ancient and Modern: Hymns and Songs for Refreshing Worship*.

HYMNS FOR LITTLE CHILDREN. A collection of hymns based on the *Church Catechism*, published by Cecil Frances Alexander (née Humphreys) in 1848. Among the most popular are **Once in Royal David's City, All things Bright and Beautiful**, and "There is a green hill far away."

HYMNS FOUNDED ON VARIOUS TEXTS IN THE HOLY SCRIPTURES. A large collection of hymns by Philip Doddridge, published posthumously in 1755. They are a mixture of quite close paraphrases and more loosely worded verse compositions inspired by 361 passages of Scripture, arranged in order from Gen. 5:24 (with Heb. 11:5) to Rev. 22:20. The work is thus in effect a verse-by-verse poetic commentary on the Bible reflecting the beliefs of an influential 18th-century nonconformist leader and preacher.

HYMNS ON VARIOUS PASSAGES OF SCRIPTURE. Written by Thomas Kelly and first published in 1804, the 10th edition of 1853 contained 765 hymns, focusing on Christ's passion, death, resurrection, and ascension. They include **"The Head that Once was Crowned with Thorns"** (Heb. 2:9–10), "The Lord is risen indeed" (Mt. 28:6), and "Hark Ten Thousand Voices" (Rev. 5:11).

I AM THE BREAD OF LIFE. Hymn based on Jn. 6:35–59 written by Sr. Suzanne Toolan for the Roman Catholic Archdiocese of San Francisco (1966) and regularly sung as a Eucharistic hymn at funerals.

I AM THE ROSE OF SHARON. Well-known anthem for SATB a cappella chorus by William Billings published in *The Singing Master's Assistant* (1778). A setting of the Song of Solomon 2:1–11 (AV), it opens with the woman's words, sung by the soprano line, "I am the rose of Sharon and the lily of the valleys" (v. 1), followed by the chorus, and then a few measures later the basses sing the words of the woman's lover, "As the lily among the thorns so is my love among the daughters" (v. 2). Sopranos and basses, representing the lovers, sing together, "And his fruit was sweet to my taste" (v. 3), after which the meter changes to a lilting dance as the basses sing, "He brought me to the banqueting house, his banner over me is love!" (v. 4), and again at the end when the chorus sings, "For, lo, the winter is past; the rain is over and gone!" (v. 11). Other settings of the same text figures in a wedding anthem by the English composer Geoff Allen, first performed in 2010, and in a work for a male-voice quintet by Gabriel Jackson (2001).

I AM THE TRUE VINE. Work for four-part a cappella mixed choir (SATB) based on Jn. 15:1–14 by Arvo Pärt, composed for the 900th anniversary of the foundation of Norwich Cathedral (1996). Written in G major, the work illustrates the intertwining nature of a vine, depicted musically through the melody and text passing from one voice to another and voices entering or leaving in the middle of a word or a phrase, while other voices pick up where previous voices leave off and are stacked in ascending and descending motion. The work concludes with an E minor chord on "command" ("if ye do whatever I command"), pointing perhaps to humanity's propensity for sin.

I BEHELD HER AS A BEAUTIFUL DOVE. Anthem for a cappella chorus (SATB) by Healey Willan (HWC 312, no. 1, 1928), based on an eighth-century responsory text inspired by the Song of **Solomon** (Cant. 1:15; 3:6). An ethereal, undulating melody describes the dove's flight.

I HEARD A VOICE FROM HEAVEN. Anthem for SATB chorus a cappella by Thomas Tomkins, composed for the Burial Service of the Dead in the Book of Common Prayer. Based on Rev. 13:14, it is characterized by descending melismas on "blessed" ("blessed are the dead") and "labors" ("for they rest from their labors") with expressive longer note values on "blessed" and "rest."

I HEARD THE VOICE OF JESUS SAY. One of the best-known hymns of Horatius Bonar (1808–1889), published in *Hymns Original and Selected* (1846) and inspired by Jn. 1:16 ("Of his fullness have we all received") with allusions to Mt. 22:28, Jn. 4:4–15, and Jn. 8:12. The tune "Kingsfold" in the *English Hymnal* (1906) is derived from the folk song "The Red Barn," arranged by Vaughan Williams.

I SAT DOWN UNDER HIS SHADOW. Well-known anthem for a cappella SATB chorus by English organist and composer Sir Edward Cuthbert Bairstow. A blissful setting of verses from the Song of Solomon (Cant. 2:3–4), the slow compound duple meter reflects the woman's joy and the leap of a perfect fourth on her "great delight," while slow, reflective homophony on "his fruit was sweet to my taste" along with elongated notes on "sweet" and "taste" signify her sensual longing. The lover's "banner" of love is illustrated by the swell and climax of the melody and by the tied notes on "love." There is also a setting for SATB chorus by Aaron Copland (1972).

I, THE LORD OF SEA AND SKY. *See* HERE I AM LORD.

I WAS GLAD. Introit and coronation anthem based on Ps. 122, a Psalm of Pilgrimage or Song of Ascents, from the 1662 Book of Common Prayer. It was set to music by several composers, including Henry Purcell (1685) and William Boyce (1761), but best known is the setting by Hubert Parry (op. 51, 1902), which was performed as the processional anthem at coronations, royal weddings, and the Service of Thanksgiving on the occasion of the Queen's Golden Jubilee in 2012. After a majestic introduction played by the organ/orchestra representing the procession of the monarch, the choir enters with a jubilant six-part chorus ("I was glad"), followed by an imitative setting of "Our feet shall stand . . ." (v. 2) evoking the power and majesty of Jerusalem and a two-choir antiphonal exchange, "Jerusalem is builded as a city . . . ," (v. 3), concluding on a tonic chord to signify the unity and solidity of Jerusalem. The *vivat*, for example, *Vivat Regina Elizabetha* ("Long Live Queen Elizabeth"), sung on royal occasions, is nonbiblical. The work concludes with a solemn, meditative setting of **O Pray for the Peace of Jerusalem** (v. 6), sung by a semichorus with a magnificent climax rising to high B-flat in the sopranos on "Peace be within thy walls" (v. 7). *See also* BLEST PAIR OF SIRENS; JERUSALEM; LAETATUS SUM.

I WILL FOLLOW. Song by rock band U2 on the album *Boy* (1980). The lyrics, perhaps inspired by Ruth 1:16, were written by Bono as a tribute to his mother when she died in 1974. *See also* I WILL GO WHERE YOU WILL GO; RUTH; WHITHER THOU GOEST.

I WILL GO WHERE YOU WILL GO. The first of three songs from the song cycle "Bridges of Love" for soprano/tenor soloist, viola, clarinet, and piano (2009) by the Los Angeles–based Israeli American composer Sharon Farber. The only song of the three based on a biblical text (Ruth 1:16–17), it tells how Ruth pledges never to leave her mother-in-law after her husband died along with his brother and father (Ruth 1:1–5). After a dialogue between viola and clarinet, representing the conversation between Ruth and Naomi (Ruth 1:8–17), Ruth sings her dramatic words of devotion to Naomi in Hebrew, ending on a high A in the final measure. *See also* I WILL FOLLOW; RUTH; WHITHER THOU GOEST.

I WILL LIFT UP MINE EYES. Setting of Ps. 121 for voice and organ by Leo Sowerby (H.147, 1919), on the album *I Will Lift Up Mine Eyes* (1997). In a lyrical 7/4 meter setting, the Psalm also forms part of John Rutter's **Psalmfest** (1993).

IF KING MANASSES. Anthem for six voices and organ by Thomas Weelkes. The text, from "St. Peter's Complaint" by the poet and Catholic martyr Robert Southwell, is inspired by Peter's remorse over his betrayal of Christ (Lk. 22:61–62) and likens him to the evil King Manasses, whose prayer for repentance is in the Old Testament Apocrypha (cf. 2 Chron. 33:10–20).

IF YE LOVE ME. Well-known anthem for four voices (originally AATB, alternatively SATB and TTBB) a cappella by Thomas Tallis (ca. 1547–1548) based on Jn. 14:15–17. It demonstrated the new style of English music with its largely homophonic texture and ABB form.

IF YOU HAD A VINEYARD. Song by Sinead O'Connor from the album *Theology* with words adapted from Isa. 5. Hauntingly beautiful, it highlights the depth of God's sorrow at the wicked behavior of his people.

IL EST NÉ. ("He Is Born"). French traditional carol, first published by R. Grosjean in *Airs des Noëls lorrains* (1862), performed by professional and amateur choirs all the over the world as well as by Plácido Domingo, Édith Piaf, Annie Lennox, Siouxsie and the Banshees, the Chieftains, and many others. It was arranged by Gounod (1888) for children's chorus, oboe, cello, double bass, and organ; as a set of variations on a theme for organ by Dupré (1922); and, more recently, in choral arrangements by David Willcocks (1978) and John Rutter (1988).

ILLUMINARE JERUSALEM. ("Jerusalem Rejoice for Joy"). Carol for eight-part a cappella choir by British composer Judith Weir (1985), suitable also for the Feast of Christ the King and the Feast of the Epiphany, it was commissioned by King's College, Cambridge, for the annual Festival of Nine Lessons and Carols. The anonymous 15th-century text in medieval Scots is a setting of a verse poem from the Bannatyne MS with the refrain based on Isa. 60:1 ("Arise, Shine"). The final iteration of the verse, marked "Suddenly mysterious and urgent," is sung quietly to the accompaniment of low organ notes in the pedal for a mystical effect.

I'M GONNA SING TIL THE SPIRIT MOVES IN MY HEART. African American spiritual inspired by numerous biblical references (Exod. 15:1; Ps. 13:6; Acts 2:1–21; Gal. 5:13–22; 1 Cor. 11:26; 14:15; Col. 3:16). It is arranged by Moses Hogan for a cappella chorus (SATB *divisi*) and soloist (1995). Combining a call-and-response pattern found in traditional spirituals along with a complex polyphonic texture and fast, repetitive rhythms, this arrangement produces an invigorating whirlwind of sound that conjures up in the imagination the movement of God's Spirit. Published in *This Far by Faith*, the new African American hymnal (1999), it is regularly performed in churches and at concerts.

IN CHRIST THERE IS NO EAST OR WEST. Hymn by the English writer William Arthur Dunkerley inspired by various biblical texts (Isa. 49:12; Lk. 13:29; Acts 17:26; Col. 3:11). It was set to the tune "McKee" by Harry T. Burleigh, after Elmer M. McKee, rector of St. George's Episcopal Church, New York. The tune, according to Charles V. Stanford, was of Irish origin, adapted as an African American spiritual entitled "I Know the Angels Done Changed My Name."

IN DULCI JUBILO. ("In Sweet Rejoicing"). One of the oldest macaronic Christmas carols, originally written in Latin and German. The melody is a 16th-century dance song in either 3/4 or 6/8 meter for which John Mason Neale wrote "Good Christian Men Rejoice," published in *Carols for Christmastide* (1854). The melody has been set by numerous composers, including Praetorius, Scheidt, Bach, Dupré, Rutter, and Mike Oldfield (1975), whose arrangement featured in the opening ceremony of the 2012 Olympic Games in London.

IN EXITU ISRAEL DE AEGYPTO. ("When Israel Went Out"). Gregorian chant and antiphon for Sunday vespers based on Ps. 114. It exalts God's dominion over the earth and recalls the exodus of the Israelite people from slavery in Egypt. Sung in a call-and-response pattern, the choir responds with "**Alleluia**" after the cantor's recitation of each verse. It was also set to music by Josquin, Vivaldi, Martinez, and Mendelssohn. *See also* BE-TZET YISRAEL.

IN GUILTY NIGHT. Dramatic dialogue for three soloists and basso continuo by Henry Purcell, published in John Playford's *Harmonia Sacra: Second Book* (Z. 134, 1693). Lasting just under 12 minutes, it tells the story of Saul's visit to the Witch of Endor (1 Sam. 28:8–19) in arioso style with Italianate features, such as bursts of semiquavers on "powerful (arts)" and "raise (the ghost)." The distressed conversation of Saul (Ct), who is frequently compared to Cromwell in 17th- and 18th-century literature, is marked by the inclusion of syncopation and dissonances and punctuated by musical rests to suggest sobbing and speech sung on the weak beat of the measure. The work also emphasizes through repetition words that characterize him as "guilty," "false" (disguise), and "forsaken." In an extrabiblical "farewell scene" at the end, Samuel (B) and the melodic lines of the Witch (S) sandwich Saul's in the manner of a mother and father supporting a sobbing child where Saul sings "Oh!" in ascending semitones. Other settings include an oratorio (H. 403, 1681–1682) and an opera (H. 490, 1688) by Charpentier and **Le Roi David** by Honegger (H.37, 1921).

IN JEJUNIO ET FLETU. ("In Fasting and Weeping"). Motet for five voices by Thomas Tallis published in *Cantiones sacrae* (1575). Based on Joel 2:12 and 17, it is sung as a response for matins from the Roman rite for the first Sunday of Lent. Descending melodic lines and cross relations describe the fasting and weeping of priests as they plead with God to spare the people's heritage. Toward the end and at the higher range of each vocal register, all five voices cry out for mercy in descending melodic sequences.

IN MANUS TUAS. ("Into Your Hands"). Respond at compline on Passion Sunday, set as a motet for five-part chorus (SATTB) by Tallis and published in *Cantiones quae ab argumento sacrae vocantur* (1575). Based on Christ's last words (Lk. 23:46) together with Ps. 31:5, it is characterized by imitative polyphony for much of the work with chordal homophony on *redemisti me* ("redeemed me") to emphasize God's saving grace. There is a well-known setting by 16th-century composer John Shepherd and a modern Taizé chant in ostinato form that was performed at the funeral of Brother Roger in 2005.

IN TERRA PAX. ("On Earth Peace"). Short oratorio for five soloists (SMez TBarB), two mixed choruses, and orchestra by Frank Martin (1944), commissioned by Radio Geneva and premiered in May 1945 to mark the end of World War II. Inspired by texts from Isaiah, the Gospels, and Revelation, it focuses on the evils of war, earthly peace, forgiveness, and divine peace. Part 3 includes a sublime setting of **The Lord's Prayer** (Mt. 6:5–13), sung by the chorus in unison, and the work ends with a magnificent setting of Rev. 21:1.

IN THE BEGINNING. Through-composed work for mezzo-soprano and four-part mixed chorus (SATB) a cappella by Aaron Copland, commissioned for the 1947 Harvard Symposium on Music Criticism, and premiered in the Harvard Memorial Church, Cambridge, Massachusetts, on 2 May 1947. Based on the story of the six days of creation in Gen. 1–2, the soloist, who acts as a narrator, recites God's pronouncements while the chorus describes their execution, concluding each time, "And the evening and the morning were the . . . day." There are numerous instances of word painting, including the division of the waters colorfully illustrated through a variety of key changes (Gen. 1:6–7) and the creation of the great creatures of the sea recited by the basses to a gentle, moving melody line that paints the whales' movement, while the upper voices sing of the creation of the birds of the air (Gen. 1:21–2). The work reaches a climax at the end, building to a quadruple forte, when man becomes "a living soul" (Gen. 2:7). Fellow American composer Daniel Pinkham also composed a work entitled *In the Beginning of Creation* for mixed chorus and tape (1970).

IN THE GARDEN. Gospel song by Austin Miles first published in 1912 and performed by many great artists, including Perry Como (1958), Doris Day (1962), Elvis Presley (1967), and Johnny Cash (2003). It alludes to the two gardens where the risen Christ appears in the New Testament, the Garden Tomb (Jn. 19:41) and the Garden of the Glory of God (Rev. 2:2), and also to the Garden of Eden (Gen. 2–3) and the Garden of Gethsemane (Mt. 26:36–56; Mk. 14:32–42; Lk. 22:39–46; Jn. 18:1).

IN THE UPPER ROOM. Ballet in nine movements for soprano soloist, strings, woodwind, trumpets, horns in F, and keyboard by Philip Glass (1986); commissioned by the Twyla Tharp Dance Foundation Inc.; and choreographed by Twyla Tharp. Inspired by the biblical account of events in the Upper Room, the ballet includes the Last Supper, Jesus' washing of the disciples' feet, the prophecies of Jesus concerning Judas and Peter, the New Commandment, the gathering of the disciples after the Ascension (Acts 1:12–14);

the election of Matthias as an apostle (Acts 1:21–26); and the descent of the Holy Spirit at Pentecost (Acts 2:1–13). Another notable work on this theme is the American spiritual "The Upper Room," popularized by Mahalia Jackson and featured as a single in 1952 and later on the albums *Gospels, Spirituals & Hymns* (1991) and *The Essential Mahalia Jackson* (2004).

INCIPIT LAMENTATIO. ("Here Begins the Lamentation"). There are many settings of this text from Lam. 1:1–3 by composers of the 16th and 17th centuries, including two by Gregorio Allegri for four voices for performance on Maundy Thursday and Holy Saturday. The first words are articulated in a simple, dignified manner, reflecting the text's somber mood, while suspensions on *Plorans ploravit in nocte* ("she wept bitterly in the night") suggest sobbing and weeping (Lam. 1:2).

ISACCO, FIGURA DEL REDENTORE. ("Isaac, a Figure of the Redeemer"). Oratorio libretto by Habsburg court poet Pietro Metastasio (1740), based on Gen. 22 and other biblical references, with copious footnote references to the church fathers and notable 17th- and 18th-century biblical scholars. Written in the spirit of the Counter-Reformation, it equated the Holy Roman emperor Charles VI with Abraham, "the friend of God" (Isa. 41:8). At least 27 composers set it to music in the period 1740–1812, including Nicolo Jommelli (1714–1774), Josef Mysliveček, Francesco Morlacchi (1817), and Metastasio's goddaughter Marianne Martinez (1781). The 15-year-old Franz Schubert also composed settings of two arias (*Quell' innocente figlio* ["That innocent Son"] and *Entra l'uomo allor che nasce* ["From the moment man is born"]) for different combinations of voice as composition assignments for his teacher Salieri. *See also* ABRAMO ED ISACCO.

ISAIAH. Oratorio in two parts by William Patten scored for the prophet Isaiah (Bar), SAT soloists, SATB chorus, orchestra, and harp or piano. After an orchestral introduction, part 1, *The Prophecies*, opens with the chilling baritone recitative "Behold! The name of the Lord cometh from afar" (Isa. 30:27–28), followed by a chorus beginning "Hear the word of the Lord, Ye Rulers" (Isa. 1:10) and a baritone aria, "Bring no more vain oblations" (Isa. 1:13). Other verses cited in part 1 from Isaiah's ferocious attacks on his people's sins include Isa. 9:8, 10:3, 58:1, 3:16, and 63:1–3, interspersed with occasional glimmers of hope (Isa. 26:3–4; 58:8) and concluding with a more optimistic chorus based on Isa. 30:30 and 31:6. The intermezzi, between Parts 1 and 2, are an orchestral lament expressing the deep sorrow and penitence of the people and a contralto solo, "The Lord will comfort Zion" (Isa. 51:3). Part 2, *The Promises*, begins with an introduction and chorus, "The earth mourneth and languisheth" (Isa. 33:9–10), and then turns to prophecies of hope taken mainly from Isa. 35, including "the desert shall rejoice and blossom as the rose" (Isa. 35:1) and "Strengthen ye the weak hands" (Isa. 35:3), set for tenor solo, and the final chorus, "They shall obtain joy and gladness and sorrow and sighing shall flee away" (Isa. 35:10), starting maestoso and ending allegretto.

ISAIAH 6. Song by American contemporary Christian singer/songwriter Todd Agnew from the album *Reflection of Something* (2005), based on Isaiah's vision (Isa. 6). Scored for soloist, electric guitar, bass guitar, drums, strings, Wurlitzer organ, and background vocals, three verses are sung by Isaiah (Isa. 6:1–2, 5, 6), each followed by a chorus with backing vocals representing the seraphim singing their song of praise (Isa. 6:3).

ISAIAH 6. Song from the album *Smash* by Christian metal and thrash crossover band One Bad Pig with Kosher Womack as lead screamer accompanied by Paul Q-Pek (guitar and vocals), Phillip Owens (drums and vocals), Daniel Tucek (bass and vocals), and Lee Hanley (guitar and vocals). Inspired by Isa. 6, the verses, which represent the voice of Isaiah, are sung unaccompanied, and the chorus "Here I am, send me" (Isa. 6:8) is sung first unaccompanied by the lead singer ("Here I am") and then by the band, joining in on "send me." *See also* HERE I AM, LORD.

ISAIAH'S PROPHECY. Christmas oratorio for six soloists, chorus, and orchestra by Paul Creston (Giuseppe Guttoveggio) (1962), premiered at the University of Florida, Tampa, on 12 December 1962. Cast for the prophet Isaiah (Bar), Mary the Mother of Christ (Mez), the Evangelist (T), and the three Magi, Caspar (T), Melchior (Bar), and Balthazar (B), it tells of the fulfillment of Isaiah's prophecy (Isa. 11:1) in the Nativity story, sung in a recitative by the Evangelist, and includes a setting of the **Magnificat** and the hymns **O Come, O Come Emmanuel, While Shepherds Watched their Flocks by Night**, Sleep Holy Babe, and **We Three Kings of Orient Are**, concluding with the chorus "**Alleluia**, Alleluia, Earth to Heaven Replies." Other works include the symphonic oratorio *Isaïe, le prophète* for SATB chorus and orchestra by Alexandre Tansman (1949–1950). *See* ARIEL.

ISRAEL IN EGYPT. Oratorio in three parts by Handel (HWV 54, 1738) for SSATBB solos, double chorus, orchestra, and continuo, with texts taken directly from the Bible (Exod. 15:1–21; Pss. 78, 105, 106), to a libretto perhaps assembled by Handel himself. While there is no dramatic plot or any part for individual characters, much of the story is recounted by the chorus, with a handful of arias and duets sung by the soloists. Part 1, which is rarely performed today, is entitled "The Lamentation of the Israelites for the Death of Joseph" and is taken from Handel's funeral anthem for Queen Caroline, **"The Ways of Zion Do Mourn"** (1737). The 1756 revision of the work, which is the more familiar version to audiences today, does not include part 1. Part 2, "The Exodus," begins with the announcement of the new king of Egypt, a depiction of the plagues, and the passage through the Red Sea. Of interest is the inclusion of the first phrase of the Lutheran chorale tune **Christ lag in Todesbanden** in the first chorus, "And the Children of Israel Sighed by Reason of the bondage" (Exod. 2:23), which makes a comparison between the bondage of the Children of Israel and that of Christ in his passion and death. Colorful writing describes the hopping movement of the frogs through a dotted rhythmic pattern (alto aria no. 5) and a series of fast ascending and descending notes in the violins to depict the flight of buzzing flies ("He spake the Word," no. 6). There are many other dramatic effects, especially in the chorus, "But the waters overwhelmed their enemies" (no. 14), based on Ps. 106:11, where the orchestration underscoring the text depicts the furious waves covering the enemy through timpani rumbles, triplet figures in the strings, and melodic leaps in the violins, violas, and oboes.

Part 3, "The Song of Moses," celebrates the Israelites' crossing of the Red Sea and could be classified as an extended anthem. The momentous Handelian chorus "I will sing unto the Lord" (Exod. 15:1–18, 21) appears at the beginning and end. *See also* MIRIAM'S SONG; MIRJAMS SIEGESGESANG.

ISRAELSBRÜNNLEIN. ("Fountain of Israel"). Sacred madrigals for five voices and continuo by Johann Hermann Schein (1586–1630), first performed in 1623. Renowned as masterworks of German choral music, they comprise 27 four-minute settings of Psalms and other lyrical passages taken mostly from the Old Testament. Each motet combines word painting from the early madrigalists, especially Monteverdi, with German musical rhetorical devices to illuminate the affective content of the text. They include "Rejoice in the Wife of your Youth" (Prov. 5:18), "The Lord has forsaken me" (Isa. 49:14–16), and, the most moving of all, "When Jacob had finished the instructions" (Gen. 49:33, 50:1). Melodic lines scored in parallel sixths depict Joseph's poignant lament as he wept and kissed his father's remains.

IST NICHT EPHRAIM MEIN TEURER SOHN. ("Is Not Ephraim My Dear Son?"). Johann Hermann Schein composed two pieces inspired by Jer. 31:20, the first a motet (no. 20) for eight voices (*Cymbalum Sionium sive Cantiones sacrae*, 1615) and the second a sacred madrigal (no. 12) for five voices and basso continuo (SWV 040) in **Israelsbrünnlein** (1623). The earlier of the two for two mixed choirs (SAAT/ATBB) is characterized by a dramatic echo effect, and at the climactic point for two measures, only the choirs sing in homophony, "I will surely have mercy on him" (*das ich mich seiner erbarmen muss*). The interjection "said the Lord" (*spricht der Herr*) is distributed among all eight voices to reinforce the Lord's offer of mercy to his people. Two further settings of the text survive, one by Heinrich Schütz in **Psalmen Davids** (op. 2, SWV 22–47, 1619) and the other by Samuel Scheidt (*Cantiones Sacrae*, 1620).

IT AIN'T NECESSARILY SO. Well-known song from the folk opera *Porgy and Bess* (1935) composed by George Gershwin with lyrics by Ira Gershwin. Sung in a call-and-response pattern, the character of Sportin' Life, a drug dealer, questions the truth of David's slaying of Goliath (1 Sam. 17), Jonah's ability to survive in the belly of the whale (Jonah 2), the story of Moses in the bulrushes (Exod. 2:1–11), and Methuselah's longevity (Gen. 5:27). It has been performed by numerous artists, including Aretha Franklin and Bobby Darin (1959), Cher and Jamie Cullum (2002), Brian Wilson (2010), and Hugh Laurie (2011).

IT CAME UPON A MIDNIGHT CLEAR. Christmas hymn written by Edmund Sears and sung to the tune "Carol" by Richard Storrs Willis (1850) or "Noel" by Sir Arthur Sullivan (1874). It is inspired by the story of the host of angels that appeared to the shepherds in the Nativity story (Lk. 2:13) and a verse from the Wisdom of **Solomon** about "midnight" and "the world in solemn stillness" (Wisd. 18:14). In the 1940s and 1950s, arrangements of this carol in a slow, melancholic style were performed by Judy Garland, Frank Sinatra, Bing Crosby, and Perry Como, among many others.

IT IS MY WELL BELOVED'S VOICE. Anthem for six voices a cappella (SSATBB/SSATTB) by Thomas Tomkins based on a verse from the Song of Solomon (Cant. 2:8). Ascending melodies at a high tessitura paint the scene of the mountaintop, and intervallic leaps describe the lover's delight on seeing her beloved "skipping over the hills" (AV).

• J •

JACOB'S DREAMS. (*Les Rêves de Jacob*). Dance suite for oboe, string trio, and double bass by Darius Milhaud (op. 294,1948), commissioned by Elizabeth Sprague Coolidge for the Jacob's Pillow Dance Festival in Tanglewood, Massachusetts, where it was premiered in 1949. Based on the biblical story, it is in five movements: "Jacob's Pillow" (Gen. 28:11, 18–22) (*Animé*), "First Dream: The Angels' Ladder" (Gen. 28:12) (*Mystérieux*), "Prophecy" (Gen. 28:13–15) (*Modéré*), "Second Dream: Fight with the Dark Angel and Benediction" (Gen. 32:24–25) (*Modérément animé*), and "Israel" (Gen. 32:26–28) (*Modérément animé Solenne*). The voice of God is represented by the oboe, which plays a significant role in the work. Other musical interpretations of the same theme include works by Samuel Adler (1981) and Anthony Davis (1997) and Judith Bingham's *Parable for organ and strings* (2007).

JACOB'S LADDER: BLAKE'S PICTURE CYCLE II. Ballet music for 16 players (strings, wind, percussion, harp, and celesta) by Dmitri Smirnov (op. 58, 1990) from a cycle of four instrumental pieces based on watercolors by William Blake entitled *The Moonlight Story* (1988), *Jacob's Ladder* (1990), *Abel* (1991), and the *River of Life* (1992). Inspired by the biblical story (Gen. 28:10–17), the piece represents the figure of Jacob by a solo bassoon; the ladder with scales based on the overtone series; the stars by bell-like metal percussion, harp, and celesta; the movement of the angels by strings and wind; and God's words by a bass drum. Other musical interpretations of this theme include *Jacob's Ladder* for mixed chorus and organ by Samuel Adler (1981) and Judith Bingham's mini-concert for organ and strings entitled *Jacob's Ladder: Parable* (2009).

JAUCHZET GOTT IN ALLEN LANDEN. ("Praise God in All Lands"). Cantata by J. S. Bach (BWV 51) composed for the 15th Sunday after Trinity and "for any occasion." The libretto, inspired by the Epistle and Gospel readings for the day (Gal. 5:25–6:10; Mt. 6:24–34), is by Johann Gramann (movt. 4) and possibly by Bach himself (movts. 1–3) and contains allusions to other biblical texts (Pss. 26:8; 138:2; Lam. 3:22–23). Scored for soprano soloist, orchestra, and continuo, the final movement features the chorale melody *Sei Lob und Preis mit Ehren* ("Now Laud and Praise with Honor") followed without interruption by a final virtuoso **Alleluia**.

JEHOVA QUAM MULTI SUNT HOSTES MEI. ("Lord, How Are They Increased That Trouble Me"). Motet for chorus, soloists, and continuo by Purcell (Z. 135), based on Ps. 3. It opens with a chorus representing the tens of thousands of people (Ps. 3:6) who, because of their lack of faith, have become the Psalmist's enemies (vv. 1–2). Emotive solos for tenor and baritone represent the Psalmist singing of his faith in God's great power (v. 3), and the phrase *Respondit mihi* ("he responded to me") is repeated several times in polyphony to emphasize God's faithful response. The sopranos sing in parallel thirds on *quia Jehova sustentat me* ("for the Lord sustains me") to signify the Psalmist's unbreakable relationship with God, and the piece ends with the chorus proclaiming God's power and glory.

JEPHTA: RHAPSODIC POEM FOR ORCHESTRA. (Symphony 5). Tone poem in one movement by Ernst Toch (op. 89, 1963) inspired by Lion Feuchtwanger's novel *Jefta und seine Tochter* ("Jephthah and his Daughter") (1957), which is a modern retelling of the biblical story (Judg. 11:29–40).

JEPHTE. ("Jephthah"). Oratorio by Carissimi, one of the most famous Latin oratorios of the 17th century. Based on an anonymous paraphrase of the biblical story (Judg. 11:28–40), it employs mostly recitative for the narrative and dialogue, with arioso for more animated sections. Jephte's famous arioso *Heu, heu mihi* is noted for its word painting and audible sobs, and the daughter's sorrowful lament *Plorate, colles, dolete, montes* ("Lament, lament, O hills; Mourn, mourn, O mountains") includes the dramatic use of echo sung by the chorus of virgins; single, double, and triple suspensions; and descending chromaticisms, which constitute the climax of the work.

JEPHTHAH. Handel's last oratorio (HWV 70, 1751) with a libretto by Thomas Morell based loosely on Judg. 11 and George Buchanan's *Jephthes sive votum* ("Jepthah or the Vow") (1554), first performed at the Theatre Royal in Covent Garden, London, on 26 February 1752. It is scored for Jephthah (T); his daughter Iphis (S); his wife, Storgè (Mez); his brother Zebul (B); Hamor, the lover of Iphis (A); an Angel (S); and a chorus of Israelites, Priests, and Virgins. Unlike the biblical story, an angel intervenes to save the life of Iphis, who then dedicates her life to the Lord. Two well-known numbers include the *accompagnato* from act 2, "Deeper, and deeper still, O Lord are thy decrees," and the air from act 3, "Waft her angels, thro' the skies," both sung by Jephthah and sometimes performed together on their own. *See also* JEPHTA: RHAPSODIC POEM FOR ORCHESTRA; JEPHTE.

JEPHTHAH'S VOW. (*Jephtas Gelübde*). *Songspiel* in three acts with ballet by Jacob Meyerbeer based on a libretto by Alois Wilhelm Schreiber, premiered at the Hoftheater in Munich on 23 December 1812. Loosely based on the biblical story of Jephthah (Judg. 10:6–12:7), it adds a love triangle between Jephthah's daughter Sulima, her suitor Asmaweth, and the tribal leader Abdon, illustrated in a tender love duet (*Deine Liebe ist mein Leben* ["Your love is my life"]) and the aria (*Dich soll die Hölle fassen!* ["May you burn in Hell!"]). In another change to the biblical story, Jephthah's daughter is saved through the intervention of the high priest, who alludes to Isaac's redemption in Gen. 22 ("Obedience is an offering more pleasing to me than the sweet smell of incense"). The work concludes with a chorus ("The Lord is wise and good, Our blood shall not be shed to him as a sacrifice"). The full orchestral score and piano reduction were never published.

JEREMIAH SYMPHONY. Symphony no. 1 for mezzo-soprano solo, orchestra, and piano by Leonard Bernstein (1942). Inspired by the biblical story of Jeremiah and texts from the Book of Lamentations, it is in three movements: "Prophecy," "Profanation," and "Lamentation." The first movement, drawing on themes derived from Jewish daily prayer, is emotive and captures Jeremiah's pleas to the people to repent (Jer. 3:11–14). The second movement opens with a theme derived from Ashkenazi cantillation of the prophets, distorted into violent, dance-like rhythms to illustrate the mocking priests (Jer. 26:1–9). The work concludes with a setting of verses from Lamentations mourning the city's fate (Lam. 1:1–3, 8; 4:14–15; 5:20–21), sung in Hebrew by the mezzo-soprano and incorporating musical allusions to the Jewish prayers of supplication (*selichot*) recited at New Year and Yom Kippur.

JERICHO ROAD. Song by American alternative country singer/songwriter Steve Earle on the album *Washington Square Serenade* (2007). The dangerous road from Jerusalem to Jericho provided the setting for the parable of the good Samaritan (Lk. 10:25–37). Set at a walking pace in common time, with a continuous riff on guitar and a harmonica for atmospheric effect, the song lists the people the singer met on Jericho Road, including his father, mother, sister, and brother, and the troubles that have afflicted them. He includes a reference to *Joshua Fight the Battle of Jericho* and draws a parallel between his sister and Mary the mother of Christ. It features as the last number on Joan Baez's album *Day after Tomorrow* (2008). *See also* ON THE JERICHO ROAD.

JERUSALEM. Setting by Hubert Parry (1916) of Blake's poem "And did those feet in ancient times" (1808). Inspired by the apocryphal story of Jesus' visit to Glastonbury, accompanied by his uncle Joseph of Arimathea, the text, based on Rev. 3:12 and 21:2, describes the Second Coming of Christ and the establishment of the New Jerusalem and implies that, for a brief time, heaven existed in England. The hymn was written as part of the suffragette campaign and performed at a celebratory concert conducted by Parry himself. Known popularly as England's unofficial anthem, it is sung every year at the London Proms to Elgar's orchestration (1822). In 2008, it was banned by the dean of Southwark for its overly nationalistic tone and failure to praise the glory of God.

JERUSALEM. Well-known sacred song by British composer Michael Maybrick, alias Stephen Adams (1841–1931), with words by Frederick E. Weatherly (1892), based on John's vision of the New Jerusalem in the Book of Revelation (Rev. 21:2) and popularized in the blockbuster movie *San Francisco* (1936). A favorite of James Joyce, it figures in his novels *Stephen Hero* (1944) and *Ulysses* (1922), where he equates celestial Jerusalem with "Bloomusalem," the new city of Dublin. Dramatic in tone with copious word painting, it is scored in C major to reflect the celestial status of the New Jerusalem. Other notable songs by Maybrick and Weatherly include "The **Star of Bethlehem**," based on Mt. 2:2 and 9.

JESU MEINE FREUDE. ("Jesus My Joy"). Funeral motet for five voices in 11 movements (BWV 227, 1723) and chorale prelude (BWV 610) by J. S. Bach. One of the composer's longest motets, it is based on a German hymn by Johann Franck (1650) with a melody by Johann Crüger. The six verses of the hymn alternate with verses from Paul's Letter to the Romans (Rom. 8:1–2, 9–11). Translated into English as "Jesu, priceless treasure" by Catherine Winkworth (1869), it was arranged as a chorale cantata in four movements for chorus and strings by Mendelssohn in 1828.

JESUS CHRIST SUPERSTAR. Rock opera in two acts composed by Andrew Lloyd Webber with lyrics written by Tim Rice. It was first released as a concept album (1970) before opening on Broadway in 1971 and then in London in 1972. Inspired by the Gospel of St. John, the story is based around events from the last week of Jesus' life, beginning with the arrival of Jesus and his disciples in Jerusalem and concluding with the Crucifixion. Focusing particularly on Christ's humanity, it adds details not recorded in the biblical text, such as Judas's concern over Jesus' rise to power and Jesus' relationship with Mary Magdalene, who is presented as a prostitute. The musical features the hit numbers "Jesus Christ Superstar," sung by Judas, and "I don't know how to love him," sung first by Mary Magdalene, who professes her great love for Jesus, and later by Judas when he accuses God for his untimely death. Other memorable numbers include "Heaven on Their Minds," "What's the Buzz," "**Hosanna**," "The Temple," and "King Herod's Song." The final number, "John Nineteen Forty One," is a meditative setting for orchestra that is performed as Christ's body is taken from the cross and laid to rest in the tomb (Jn. 19:41–42). It was adapted for film in 1973, shot in Israel and other Middle Eastern locations, and adapted for the stage in 2000.

JESUS CHRIST THE APPLE TREE. Folk carol based on an anonymous New Hampshire text first published in Joshua Smith's *Divine Hymns or Spiritual Songs* (1784) and best known in a setting by Elizabeth Poston (1967). Hauntingly beautiful, this five-stanza strophic carol, opening and closing with unison trebles, portrays Christ as an apple tree, source of life, happiness, and rest (Cant. 2:3; cf. Gen. 2:9; Lk. 13:19; Rev. 22:2).

JESUS DER DU MEINE SEELE. ("Jesus, You Who My Soul"). Cantata by J. S. Bach composed for the 14th Sunday after Trinity on 10 September 1724 (BWV 78). The libretto, inspired by the Epistle and Gospel readings for the day (Gal. 5:16–24; Lk. 17:11–19), is based on the chorale *Jesu Der Du Meine Seele* ("Jesus you have rent my soul") by Johann Rist (1641). Scored for SATB soloists, SATB chorus, orchestra, and continuo, the work is in seven contrasting movements, beginning with a chorale fantasia in the form of a passacaglia in G minor, a tonality traditionally associated with lamentation, and concluding also in G minor with a setting of the chorale for SATB chorus (*Herr, ich glaube, hilf mir Schwachen* ["Lord, I believe, help my weakness"]).

JESUS LOVES ME. One of the most popular Christian hymns of all time, written by Anna Bartlett Warner (1819–1885), perhaps with Mt. 19:14 and Rev. 1:5 in mind. It was set to music in 1862 by William Batchelder Bradbury (1816–1868), who added the chorus "Yes, Jesus loves me." Performances by contemporary artists include those by Whitney Houston, Destiny's Child, Hillsong Kids, the Gaither Vocal Band, and Dolly Parton.

JESUS LOVES THE LITTLE CHILDREN. Well-known children's hymn inspired by Mt. 19:14. It was written by Clare Herbert Woolston (1856–1927) and sung to the American Civil War tune "Tramp! Tramp! Tramp!" (1864) by George Fredrick Root. The song was originally composed to give hope to Union prisoners of war, giving poignant relevance to the reference to the children's skin color, "red and yellow, black and white."

JESUS REMEMBER ME. Taizé chant by Jacques Berthier (1978) in ostinato form, based on the words of the thief crucified beside Christ (Lk. 23:42).

JESUS WALKING ON THE WATER. Song by American alternative rock band Violent Femmes from their second album, *Hallowed Ground* (1984), the title derives from the story of Jesus walking on the water in Mt. 14:22–33, Mk. 6:45–52, and Jn. 6:16–21. The upbeat folk sound of acoustic guitar, fiddle, mariachi bass, drums, autoharp, and vocals evokes a pastoral scene, and the lyrics ask if it is true that Christ died on the cross, drawing a parallel between rising from the dead and walking on the water.

JESUS WAS AN ONLY SON. Song by Bruce Springsteen from his 13th studio album, *Devils and Dust* (2005), sung to the accompaniment of piano and harmonica. It explores the loving relationship between Mary and her son Jesus as she accompanies him on the road to Calvary and as she stood at the foot of the cross.

JESUS WEPT. Strophic song in 15 verses by English folk song writer and performer Ralph McTell from the album *Travelling Man* (1999). Inspired by Jn. 11:35 and set in Jerusalem on Palm Sunday, the song suggests reasons as to why Jesus wept—the Crusades, the Inquisition, and Hiroshima—as well as Peter's denial, Judas's kiss (Ps. 55:12–14), the suicide of Judas (Acts 1:18–19), the cleansing of the Temple, the agony in the Garden (Mt. 26:36–46; Mk. 14:32–42; Lk. 22:39–46), the Crucifixion (Ps. 22; Isa. 53), and, finally, childhood memories of Mary and Joseph.

JEZEBEL. Song by singer/songwriter Sam Beam/Iron and Wine (1974) on the album *Woman King* (2005). Inspired by the story of the violent death of Jezebel (2 Kgs. 9:30–37), foretold by the prophet Elisha (2 Kgs. 9:10), it asks six times "Who's seen Jezebel?" and suggests that the beautiful non-Israelite queen and her polytheistic practices were misunderstood. She was "born to be the woman we could blame."

JEZEBEL. Well-known popular song by Wayne Shanklin (1951), first recorded by Frankie Laine with the Norman Luboff Choir and Mitch Miller and His Orchestra (1951) and covered extensively by numerous artists, including Édith Piaf (in French, 1951), Shakin' Stevens (1988), and Tom Jones (2012). It portrays Jezebel (2 Kgs. 9) as a type of devil without horns whose mission it was "to torment man . . . night an' day, every way."

JEZUS ES A KUFAROK. ("Jesus and the Traders"). Choral work for mixed voices (SATB) a cappella by Zoltán Kodály (1927) inspired by the story of the cleansing of the Temple (Jn. 2:15–22; Mk. 11:15–18). It opens with the sopranos and altos in unison, joined by the tenors and basses, singing "As the feast approached Jesus went up," followed by homophony on "and entered into the Temple" with "Jerusalem" sung pianissimo and in longer note values. Jesus' angry discovery of the traders in the Temple is sung in animated polyphony, and extended melismas depict him driving them out. A reflective passage follows, led by the basses, reaching a climax on "What have ye made of it? A den of robbers?," and the work concludes with the comments of the Scribes and Pharisees.

JOB. Oratorio for soloists (TrTBarB), SATB choir, and orchestra by Parry, premiered at the Three Choirs Festival in Gloucester in 1892 to great public acclaim. The 42 chapters of the Book of Job are condensed into four scenes beginning with the dialogue between God (T and B chorus) and Satan (Job 1:1–12), sung mostly in recitative. Scene 2 first depicts a pastoral scene with an aria by the shepherd boy (Tr) ("The flocks of my master are blessed of God") in strophic form and based on a pentatonic melody played on solo clarinet. This is abruptly followed by the destruction of Job's family and wealth by the Sabeans, described in another solo by the Shepherd Boy; a solo by Satan (T), "Arise O wind of the Sea" (cf. Job 1:18–19); and a choral number ("See the Clouds that sweep o'er the heavens, the earth is hid as with a veil"). In scene 3, Job's friends remain silent not only when they arrive (Job 2:11–13) but also throughout the oratorio while Job (B) recites a long soliloquy consisting of verses from the dialogue (Job 3:3–22; 9:2–11; 10:1–22; 14:1–12; 29:2–25; 30:16–23). Scene 4 is an extended symphonic chorus that represents God in the whirlwind (Job 38:1) and concludes with Job's repentance (Job 42:1–3, 5–6). The work is noted for its use of leitmotifs illustrating musically the characters of Job, Satan, and God.

JOB: A MASQUE FOR DANCING. Ballet by Walton inspired by the Book of Job after William Blake's 21 famous illustrations (1820–1826), the work is in one act and scored for orchestra with choreography by Ninette de Valois, orchestrations by Constant Lambert, and set designs by Gwendolen Raverat. It was premiered at the Cambridge Theatre, London, on 5 July 1931, and two months later, it was staged at the Old Vic Theatre, London, on 22 September 1931. The designation *masque* is not strictly applicable to this work and was applied only because the composer disliked the word *ballet*. Each of the nine scenes is constructed around a dance form and prefaced by a quotation from the Book of Job. Satan's Dance of Triumph in scene 2 is based on Job 2:7, and the "Dance of Job's sons and their wives" is a minuet performed during a lavish feast and interrupted by a great wind that destroys the family home and kills Job's children (Job 1:13–19). In "Job's Dream" (Job 4:14), Satan evokes a vision of plague, pestilence, famine, battle, murder, and sudden death, including a funeral cortege for Job's sons and their wives, and the Dance of Job's Three Comforters in Job 5:17 begins with an air of sympathy and then becomes progressively more animated until Job curses God and invokes a vision of Satan sitting on God's throne. The "Sons of the Morning" dance a galliard in scene 8 (Job 38:7) and drive Satan away, and the work concludes with an epilogue (Job 42:12) showing Job blessed by God and surrounded by his family. Other works based on the Book of Job include *Job: Una Sacra Rappresentazione* by Luigi Dallapiccola (1950) and an oratorio by Maxwell Davies (J. 286, 1997) that was also inspired by William Blake's illustrations.

JOB FOR ORGAN. Cycle for organ in eight movements with optional narrator by Petr Eben, commissioned by the Harrogate International Festival and first performed in Ripon Cathedral in 1987. Each movement expresses a theme based on a quotation from the Book of Job: destiny (Job 1:1–3, 6–21), faith (Job 2:1–10), acceptance of suffering (Job 3:1–2, 11–13, 20–23), longing for death (Job 7:16–21), mystery of creation (Job 38:1–12, 33, 35:1–2), penitence (Job 42:1–6), and God's reward (Job 42:10, 12–13, 15–17). The first movement, scored in two parts, includes a motif representing Job's destiny and becomes more turbulent in the toccata-like section, and the final movement, scored also in two parts, describes Job's penitence and his resignation, illustrated by the quiet sound of **Veni Creator Spiritus**. The work contains musical quotations from other well-known plainchants, including the *Exsultet* and **Gloria in Excelsis Deo** and the chorale tune *Wer nun den lieben Gott lässt walten* ("If thou but suffer God to guide thee"), and throughout contrasts Job's restlessness (forte) with his quiet submission (pianissimo), concluding with chorale-like variations on the Czech melody *Kristus priklad pokory* ("Christ the Model of Humility") to represent Christ as the ultimate Suffering Servant.

JOB'S WIFE. Chamber opera in three acts by Elizabeth Hoffman with a libretto by James Labe, commissioned by the Seattle Arts Commission and premiered in Seattle in 1995. Set in Penuel with allusions to Jacob's ladder (Gen. 28:12) and Jacob wrestling with an angel (Gen. 32:22–31), it tells how Job's wife returns from the dead to attend the wedding of her daughter. When the time comes for her to return to the land of the dead, she puts up a fight with the angel, which she wins, and remains among the living.

JOHN 3:16. Rap by DJ Muggs, performed by Wyclef Jean and DJ Muggs on the album *Soul Assassins* (1997), featuring the pop song "It's Me That You Need" (1969) by Elton John. Each verse tells a story of the rise of evil in the world, most notably in verse 3, which tells of a drug dealer who had his dreadlocks cut off by a sinner like Mary Magdalene named Delilah. The chorus, which is based on Jn. 3:16, questions how God could love a world full of evil. This verse, which forms the title of songs by other artists, has been set to music by Method Man on the album *Mathematics: The Problem* and by the duo Ruby Throat on the alternative folk album *The Ventriloquist* (2007).

JONAH. Chamber cantata in four movements for soloists, mixed chorus, and instrumental ensemble by John Beckwith (1963), commissioned by the Festival Singers of Toronto. In addition to allusions to the biblical story of Jonah, it includes the hymn *Laudate nomen Domini* (Ps. 135) and newly written verses by Jay Macpherson. It is scored for a narrator (A), Shipmaster (T), Jonah (Bar), and God (B-Bar). Jonah's prayer to God in movement 4, accompanied by cellos and violins, is marked "angry" (forte) and sarcastic" to express Jonah's anger and resentment with God for sending him to Nineveh. But the concluding chorale, sung a cappella, leaves vengefulness and pride to man: "The Lord who made both sea and shore. . . . Hates nothing he has made, his mercy is our shade." Other works based on the story of Jonah and the Whale include **The Whale: A Biblical Fantasy** by John Tavener (1965–1966), **Jonah and the Whale** by Dominick Argento (1973), *Jonah: A Musical Morality* by William Mathias (1989), and *Jonah: A Cantata* by Samuel Adler (2004). *See also* BELLY OF THE WHALE.

JONAH AND THE WHALE. Oratorio by Dominick Argento commissioned for Vocal Essence by the Plymouth Congregational Church and the Cathedral Church of St. Mark in Minneapolis, Minnesota, and first performed in 1973. It is scored for narrator, Jonah (T), God (B), chorus, chamber orchestra of three trombones, three percussionists, piano, harp, and organ. In addition to the Book of Jonah and allusions to *Kyrie eleison*, Ps. 130 (*De profundis*), and other biblical texts, the libretto is based on a 14th-century English poem, "Patience" (known also as "Jonah and the Whale"), and a sea shanty, *Greenland Whale Fisheries*, first published in 1725. *See also* BELLY OF THE WHALE.

JONAH–MAN JAZZ. Pastiche jazz cantata incorporating blues and rock and roll for children's voices, narrator, and orchestra to music and words by Michael Hurd (1966). It is a child-friendly version of the story of Jonah and features popular numbers like "Nineveh city was a city of sin," "Go Down, Jonah, deep in the Ocean" (chorus), and the upbeat chorus "We had a wonderful Party and Jonah had a whale of a time."

JOSEPH AND THE AMAZING TECHNICOLOR DREAMCOAT • 125

JOSEPH. Oratorio for five soloists, chorus, and orchestra by George Alexander Macfarren (1887) to a libretto by E. G. Monk, commissioned for the Leeds Musical Festival, where it was performed in September 1877. Based on the biblical story of Joseph (Gen. 37–45), the work is in two parts, the first set in Canaan, the second in Egypt, both beginning and ending with a chorus. The nine dialogues include "Our Father loveth Joseph," sung by Reuben (T), Joseph (Bar), and Jacob (B); a semichorus, "My sons tell me all," a trio sung by Benjamin (S), Reuben, and Jacob; and the sextet "Forgive" (SSATBarB). As well as frequent references to Genesis, the libretto draws extensively on texts from the Psalms (e.g., Pss. 65:9–13; 77:2–8; 105:1, 2, 8, 11, 16, 17, 19, 34), the Song of Solomon (Cant. 8:6), Jeremiah (Jer. 14:2–5, 18; 31:15–16), Lamentations (Lam. 3:52, 55, 57–59), Ecclesiasticus (Sir. 9:2, 3, 7; 34:14, 16; 37:24; 49:14–15), 2 Esdras (2 Esdr. 3:3; 16:65–67), Hebrews (Heb. 1:1; 11:9–10; 12:1, 2; 13:1), and elsewhere (Jn. 7:5; 1 Jn. 4:7–8), as well as from the *Te Deum*. Other works on the same subject include an opera by Méhul and an oratorio by Handel. *See also* JOSEPH AND HIS BRETHREN.

JOSEPH AND HIS BRETHREN. Oratorio by Handel with a libretto by James Miller based on Gen. 38–45 and Apostolo Zeno's Italian oratorio *Giuseppe* (Joseph) (1722), premiered at the Theatre Royal in Covent Garden, London, on 2 March 1744 (HWV 59). Opening with Joseph in prison (Gen. 39:19–23), act 1 tells of his interpretation of Pharaoh's dreams; his love affair and marriage to Asenath, daughter of the high priest Potiphar; and the encounter with his brothers who fail to recognize him, along with Simeon's incarceration in jail (Gen. 39–42). Act 2 tells of the brothers' return to Egypt a year later (Gen. 43–44), and act 3 tells of Benjamin's near incarceration and Joseph's revelation of his identity (Gen. 45). It is scored for Pharaoh, king of Egypt (B); Joseph/Zaphnath (A); Reuben (B); Simeon (T); Judah (T); Benjamin (S); Potiphera, high priest of On (A); Asenath (S); Phanor, chief butler to Pharaoh (A); a chorus of Egyptians; a chorus of Brethren, and a chorus of Hebrews. Popular numbers include Joseph's aria "Come divine inspirer, come" from act 1 and Asenath's recitative "Art thou not Zaphnath?" from act 3. *See also* ISRAELSBRÜNNLEIN; JOSEPH; JOSEPH AND THE AMAZING TECHNICOLOR DREAMCOAT; JOSEPHSLEGENDE.

JOSEPH AND THE AMAZING TECHNICOLOR DREAMCOAT. Musical also known as a pop oratorio or pop opera, composed by Andrew Lloyd Webber and lyricist Tim Rice. Originating as a 15-minute pop cantata (1968) composed for Colet Court School in London, it was recorded as a concept album in 1969, and with some additional songs, it was staged in the West

End in 1973 and on Broadway in 1982. After revivals in the West End (1991, 2003), Toronto (1992), Australia (1993), and Broadway (1993), as well as successful tours of North America (1998, 2005, and 2007), it was adapted as a movie (1999) starring Donny Osmond in the title role, Richard Attenborough as Jacob, Joan Collins as Mrs. Potiphar, Robert Torti as Pharaoh, and Maria Friedman as the Narrator. The musical brings the saga of Joseph from Gen. 37–46 alive through an array of dazzling costumes, state-of-the-art lighting, imaginative choreography, and an eclectic range of musical styles in "Any Dream Will Do" (ballad), "Close Every Door" (ballad), "One More Angel in Heaven" (country and western), "Those Canaan Days" (Apache dance), "Potiphar" (Charleston), "Go, Go, Go Joseph" (disco), "Song of the King" (rock and roll), and "Benjamin Calypso" (reggae), among others. Joseph's "dazzling coat of many colours" (Gen. 37:3, LXX, AV) appears as a lavish multicolored costume during the song "Jacob and Sons/Joseph's Coat" and in a book for children written by Lloyd Webber and Rice with humorous illustrations by Quentin Blake. On tour in the United Kingdom since 2010, the musical continues to be a popular choice for school productions and amateur and professional theater groups.

JOSEPHSLEGENDE. ("The Legend of Joseph"). One-act ballet by Richard Strauss (op. 63, 1912–1914) based on a libretto by Harry Kessler and Hugo von Hofmannsthal, commissioned by Sergei Diaghilev, and premiered by the Ballets Russes in the summer of 1914. A filmed production of the ballet from the Wiener Staatsoper was choreographed and directed by John Neumeier in 1977. Inspired by Gen. 37–39, Joseph is depicted as a virtuous shepherd, a dancer, and a dreamer who rejects the seductive advances of Potiphar's wife. Falsely accused of rape, he is chained and sentenced to death. His rescue by an archangel is followed by the death of Potiphar's wife. Notable dances include "Sulamith's Dance: The Most Ardent Desire" (no. 7), the "Dance of Joseph: The Shepherd Boy's Innocence" (no. 11), and "An Archangel Clad in Gold" (no. 27). Strauss used a third of this work in "Sinfonisches Fragment aus 'Josephs Legende'" (op. 63, AV 148/TrV 231a, 1947).

JOSHUA. Oratorio by Handel (HWV 64, 1747; rev. 1752) with a libretto by Thomas Morell based on the Book of **Joshua**, written against the backdrop of the Jacobite rising of 1745 and premiered at the Theatre Royal in Covent Garden, London, on 9 March 1748. Retelling the story of Israel's conquest of the Land of Canaan under Joshua's leadership, it highlights the love story between Caleb's daughter Achsah and Othniel (Josh. 15:16–19). Scored for Joshua (T), Othniel (A), Caleb (B), Achsah (S), Angel (Tr), a chorus of Israelites, the Tribe of Judah, Youths, and Virgins, it is noted for its choruses, including "Glory to God" for chorus and tenor soloist, recounting the Battle of Jericho, and the march "See, the conqu'ering hero comes," which achieved popularity when Handel later incorporated it into a revision of **Judas Maccabaeus**. The soprano aria "Oh had I Jubal's lyre/Miriam's Tuneful Voice," sung by Achsah in act 3, is also performed on its own.

JOSHUA FIGHT (FIT) THE BATTLE OF JERICHO. African American spiritual based on Josh. 6. The refrain, with syncopated rhythms and downward melodic movement, suggests the tumbling walls of Jericho. An arrangement by John Rutter entitled "A Cycle of Spirituals for mezzo soprano, choir and orchestra" on the album *Feel the Spirit* (2001) depicts the blowing of the "rams' horns" and "trumpets" with brass instruments, horns, and trumpets, while the women's voices, accompanied by percussive instruments, evoke other joyful occasions when women danced with tambourines and drums (Exod. 15:20; Jer. 31:4; 1 Sam. 18:6). The song was first recorded in 1922 by the Harrod Jubilee Singers and has been performed by Mahalia Jackson, Elvis Presley, and Bing Crosby, among many others.

JOURNEY OF THE MAGI, THE. Canticle for three soloists (CtT Bar) and piano accompaniment by Benjamin Britten (op. 86, no. 4, 1971). A setting of T. S. Eliot's poem (1927) and dedicated to the performers James Bowman, Peter Pears, and John Shirley-Quirk, it is inspired by the Magi's journey to Bethlehem (Mt. 2:1–12). The mundane aspects of the journey are told by one of the Magi, sung by all three voices together, with the piano accompaniment illustrating the camels' lumbering footsteps. The inclusion of the plainsong antiphon *Magi videntes stellam* ("The Magi saw a star") in the piano accompaniment toward the end is a reminder to the Magi of the true purpose of their journey.

JOY TO THE WORLD. Popular Christmas hymn by Isaac Watts inspired by Ps. 98, celebrating the Second Coming of Christ. First published in the *The Psalms of David* (1719) and later arranged to the tune "Antioch" by Lowell Mason, it is thought that the first four notes were inspired by the chorus "Glory to God" from Handel's Messiah and the refrain "Heaven and nature sing" by the orchestral accompaniment of "Comfort ye my people." The opening notes, based on the descending scale, are intended to evoke the sound of pealing bells.

JUDAS. Electro house song and dance by Lady Gaga from her second studio album *Born This Way* (2011). Inspired by Mary Magdalene, the song tells the story of a woman in love with the man who betrayed her. The song is accompanied by a video full of biblical allusions, including the 12 disciples in leather-studded jackets, riding motorbikes on a freeway, with Jesus wearing a golden crown of thorns and Mary Magdalene riding pillion behind him. They arrive in the bikers' club called Electric Chapel, where a brawl breaks out with Judas at the center. When she attempts to protect Jesus from the brawl and to warn him of his betrayal by Judas, she falls in love with Judas. There are numerous other allusions, including Peter as the rock of the Church ("Build a house"), Jesus' entry into Jerusalem, the washing of Jesus' feet associated with Mary Magdalene (Lk. 7:38), and the kiss of Judas. The video concludes with the death of the woman by stoning, a reversal of the story of the woman taken into adultery (Jn. 8:1–11).

JUDAS. Song from the fourth and final studio album *Forth* (2008) by the Verve. Psychedelic in sound, it was written after Richard Ashcroft ordered a "double-shot" latte on Columbus Circle in New York City and, when asked for his name, carried out a social experiment by calling himself "Judas" to see the reactions of those in the shop. The song urges humanity to let go of negative feelings.

JUDAS AND MARY. (or "Said Judas to Mary"). Song/hymn by folksinger/songwriter Sydney Carter (1964), performed at the First International Festival of Music in Seville, Spain, in 1967. The tune "Judas and Mary" is a beautiful lilting melody in compound duple time. Inspired by Jn. 12:1–8, it is based on two imaginary dialogues in which Judas asks Mary why "the ointment so rich and so rare" was used to anoint Jesus' feet and not sold to buy blankets and bread for the poor, and Jesus tells her that his body represents "the poor of the world." In the final verse, he tells her that she and her sister will find him again and "wash all the sorrows away," an allusion to their participation at the cross and the Holy Sepulchre. *See also* LORD OF THE DANCE.

JUDAS KISS, THE. Song from the album *Death Magnetic Death* (2008) by the heavy metal band Metallica. As in *Creeping Death*, the narrator of the "The Judas Kiss" is the Angel of Death, who lures his listeners with a kiss and a promise of eternal life into selling their souls. As proof of his faithfulness, he tells them that Judas, the faithful disciple, lives for all eternity and, in a dark inversion of the parable of the sower (Mt. 13:1–23), invites them to plant the evil seeds of Satan's plan in the hearts of the feeble.

JUDAS MACCABAEUS. Oratorio by Handel (HWV 63, 1746), one of the most popular oratorios during his own lifetime, with a libretto by Thomas Morell based on 1 Maccabees and Josephus's *Antiquities of the Jews*. Written against the backdrop of the Jacobite rebellion (1745–1746) and first performed at the Theatre Royal in Covent Garden, London, in 1747, it was intended as a compliment to Prince William, duke of Cumberland, on his victory at Culloden on 16 April 1746 by comparing the victory of Judas Maccabaeus over the Seleucids to Prince William's victory over the Jacobites. Part 3, which opens with a Festival of Thanksgiving, includes the well-known chorus "See, the conqu'ring hero comes," sung by the Israelites in praise of their hero Judas Maccabaeus. Originally composed for **Joshua** (1748), it was inserted into a 1757 revision of *Judas Maccabaeus* and later inspired Beethoven to compose 12 variations on the chorus for piano and cello (WoO 45, 1796).

JUDGE NOT. Song and first single written by the then 16-year-old Bob Marley and released in Jamaica without much success (1962) and later rereleased on the album *Songs of Freedom* (1992). Inspired by a verse from the Sermon on the Mount (Mt. 7:1), the song begins "Don't you look at me so smug" and ends with "Someone else is judging you" repeated over and over again. Backing music was performed by Lloyd Brevett on bass; Jerome "Jah Jerry" on guitar; Roland Alphonso on tenor sax, who also played solo; and Arkland "Drumbago" Parks. It also includes a pennywhistle, which is rarely (if ever) used in ska. It was covered by Sublime on the album *Everything under the Sun* (2006).

JUDITH: CHOREOGRAPHIC POEM FOR ORCHESTRA. Ballet by William Schuman (1949), written at the request of Martha Graham and premiered on 4 January 1950 by the Louisville Orchestra. Scored in five sections, each one represents a part of the story of Judith, beginning with a mournful adagio to represent the city of Bethulia under threat by the Assyrian general Holofernes (Jud. 1–7:32). It is followed by Judith's preparation and journey to Holofernes' camp (*Moderato con moto*) (Jud. 8:1–10:10); her encampment in the tent of Holofernes (*tranquillo*); the beheading of Holofernes (*presto*), marked by frenzied staccato brass chords; and Judith's solemn procession homeward with the head of Holofernes (*andante*) (Jud. 13:19). Other musical interpretations of the Judith story include oratorios by Arne (1764), Parry (1888), and Honegger (1927). *See also* BETHULIA LIBERATA, LA.

JUDITHA TRIUMPHANS DEVICTA HOLFERNIS BARBARIE. ("Judith Triumphant Conqueror of the Barbaric Holofernes"). A sacred military oratorio for female soloists, female chorus and string orchestra, timpani, trumpets, theorbos, recorders, *chalumeaux*, oboes, and organ by Vivaldi (RV 644), commissioned to celebrate the victory of the Republic of Venice over the Turks and premiered in the Ospedale della Pietà, a girls' orphanage, in

Venice in 1716. It is the only existing oratorio by the composer. In the poetic libretto by Iacopo Cassetti, based on the Book of Judith, allegorical parallels are drawn between Holofernes (Mez) and the Turkish King, Judith (A) and the Adriatic, Abra, Judith's maidservant (S); the Faith (Bethulia) and the Church; and Ozias, priest of Bethulia (A) and the Supreme Pontiff. The opening chorus announces the arrival of the Assyrian army, *Arma, caedes, vindictae, furores* ("Arms, slaughter, vengeance, fury"), and the work ends with a choral celebration of their dramatic defeat by Judith (A), who is hailed as the savior of the Bethulians, *Adria vivat et regnet in pace* ("Let the Adriatic live and reign in peace"). Memorable arias include Judith's lyrical lullaby *Vivat in pace* ("Live in peace"), in which she lulls Holofernes to sleep before killing him, and her aria *Veni, veni me sequere fida* ("Come, follow me"), accompanied by a *chalumeau*, in which she asks her beloved, widowed companion Abra to follow her into the camp of Holofernes. *See also* JUDITH: CHOREOGRAPHIC POEM FOR ORCHESTRA.

JUST ANOTHER POOR BOY. Song by Chris de Burgh on the album *Spanish Train and Other Stories* (1975). It tells the story of Jesus of Nazareth from the perspective of his mother, Mary. The verses and chorus in particular emphasize that up until his crucifixion, he was "just another poor boy."

JUSTORUM ANIMAE. ("The Souls of the Righteous"). One of Stanford's three Latin motets for a cappella chorus (SATB *divisi*) (op. 38. no. 1, 1905). Inspired by verses from the Wisdom of Solomon (Wisd. 3:1–3), it is in three sections, mainly meditative in character with a more animated middle section that includes imitative polyphony and unison singing. Other settings of this passage include those of Orlando de Lassus (1582), Palestrina (1593), and William Byrd (1605) in Latin and those of Walford Davies (vv. 1, 3; published 1918), Geraint Lewis (vv. 1–2; 1992), Vaughan Williams (vv. 1–5; op. 38, 1947), Gabriel Jackson (2010), and Matthew Curtis (2014) in English.

• K •

KING DAVID. Musical/pop oratorio in two acts by Tim Rice, scored for soloists, large mixed chorus, and orchestra, originally written to commemorate the 3,000th anniversary of David's capture of the city of Jerusalem (2 Sam. 5:6–10) and staged in a concert version in Disney's New Amsterdam Theatre in 1997. Based on the books of Samuel, Chronicles, and Psalms, act 1 opens with a prologue (David, Bathsheba, Solomon, Joab, and a chorus) and recounts the stories of the anointing of David as king, Saul's Madness ("The Enemy Within") (1 Sam. 18–19), David's slaying of Goliath ("Saul has slain his Thousands") (1 Sam. 18:7), David's flight to the hills ("Hunted Partridge on the Hill") (1 Sam. 26:20), and the death of Saul ("The Death of Saul"; "How the Mighty are Fallen") (2 Sam. 1:19–26). Act 2 opens with "This New Jerusalem" celebrating David's kingship, "The Ark Brought to Jerusalem," David's separation from Michal ("Never Again"), and David's love affair ("Warm Spring Night") with Bathsheba ("When in Love") (2 Sam. 11–12) and includes the death of Uriah and Absalom and the birth of Solomon. It concludes with the death of David ("David's Final Hours"; "The Long Long Day") and the new reign of Solomon ("This New Jerusalem") (1 Kgs. 1–2).

KING DAVID. Oratorio in two parts by George Alexander Macfarren (1883), set to a libretto by Edwin George Monk and written for the Leeds Musical Festival of 1883. Part 1 opens in the tonality of B-flat major with a programmatic overture (no. 1) representing David's early life with a "shepherd-boy" theme played by horns, trumpets to signify the call to battle, the harp to represent David's music making before Saul, a rhythmic figure to signify Saul's unrest, and sharp tonalities to represent Saul's jealousy and death. David's account of the procession of the Ark into Jerusalem, (1 Chron. 16:8–9, 32–34) is based on the melody of the Old 100th (no. 3), while a narration of David's sin (2 Sam. 11) is sung a cappella by the chorus to the words "Spare us, Good Lord" taken from the litany of the English Church (no. 10). The prophet Nathan (1 Chron. 17; 2 Sam. 12; Ps. 51) figures in three of the numbers (nos. 6, 11, 12), and part 1 concludes with an account of God's vengeance (Heb. 10:30; Pss. 31:9; 73:18). Poignant numbers in part 2 include a scene of battle (2 Sam. 18; Isa. 63:8–11; Deut. 32:10–11; Pss. 103:11; 7:6) where David repeatedly asks his servants, "Is the young man Absalom safe?" (no. 27), his lament following Absalom's death, "O Absalom, my son" (2 Sam. 18–19), sung to harp and string accompaniment (no. 28), and the choral number in F minor, "The king weepeth," with a plaintive melody, sung by David, "O Absalom, my son," scored above the chorus (no. 29). Christological references abound, including David's song "Who am I Lord?" (1 Chron. 17:16, 18, 19) with harp and string accompaniment (no. 7), followed by a choral fugue, "The Seed of David is great and is called the Son of the Highest" (Lk. 1:32–33), with an organ accompaniment in B-flat major (no. 8). The work concludes with David's song of repentance scored in E-flat major, followed by a joyful chorus in B, "For the Son of Man has come in glory," to recount heaven's joy at the repentance of a sinner (Lk. 15:7, 10), the promise of salvation (Lk. 19:10), and the lesser doxology "Glory be to the Father."

KING DAVID. Poem by Walter de la Mare set to music by several composers, including Herbert Howells, whose arrangement for voice and piano was published in *A Garland for de la Mare* (1923). Hauntingly beautiful and intensely expressive, this melancholic song in E-flat minor tells of David's great sorrow, the cause of which was unknown to David but which recalls his grief at the death of Absalom (2 Sam. 18) and the death of Bathsheba's first child (2 Sam. 12:14–31) if not also Ps. 51. A "hundred harps" failed to ease his melancholy; only a nightingale's sorrow brought consolation.

KING DAVID'S DANCE. ("And David Danced before God with All His Might"). Work for wind ensemble by American composer Stephen Shewan from the album *Parables of God and Man* (2006). An infusion of jazz rhythms and pop idioms describes David's exhilarating dance before the Lord (2 Sam. 6:14).

KING DAVID SONATA. Instrumental solo for harp by Canadian composer Srul Irving Glick from the album *Illuminations* (1998). It is in three parts, each calling to mind a setting for David's harp playing: when he was a shepherd boy watching over his father's sheep (1 Sam. 16:11), when he soothed King Saul with his harp playing (1 Sam. 16:14–23), and when he was king and accompanied himself singing the Psalms.

KING DAVID: THE MUSICAL. Musical by Canadian composer Eyal Bitton (1970). Based on episodes in the life of King David (Samuel and Chronicles), it includes an account of David's slaying of Goliath ("Save us"), the fall of Jonathan and Saul in battle ("Fire, Fire"), the union of David and Bathsheba ("Secret Encounter"), and the death of their firstborn ("Sleep Little Child"). It also contains a setting of Ps. 23 ("The Lord is My Shepherd").

KING HEROD AND THE COCK. Traditional ballad/carol arranged by Vaughan Williams and performed at the annual Service of Nine Lessons and Carols in Kings College, Cambridge, on Christmas Eve 1977. Based on a legend of St. Stephen, it tells how the birth of Christ was proved to Herod through the miracle of a roasted chicken that rose up out of a pie and proclaimed *Christus natus est* ("Christ is born").

KING OF KINGS, THE. Silent black-and-white epic film, with Technicolor inserts, written by Jeanie Macpherson and directed and produced by Cecil B. DeMille (1927), telling the story of the passion, death, and resurrection of Christ. The score by Hugo Riesenfeld was composed for the rerelease in 1928 with added sound effects, including a crash of thunder and the roar of crowds. Nicholas Ray's 1961 version with Orson Wells as narrator begins with the Nativity. The music was by Miklós Rózsa, who also arranged choruses from the King of Kings and Ben-Hur for choral performance and organ on the album *The Twelve Choruses* recorded by Winchester Cathedral Chamber Choir (2014).

KING SAUL. Oratorio in four acts for SATB soloists, chorus, and orchestra by Hubert Parry (1894), premiered in Birmingham on 3 October 1894. Based on events in the life of Saul (Bar) (1 Sam. 9–33), it highlights David's love affair with Michal (S) (Song 2:8, 10–12, 16; 3:2, 20; 5:10–12; 6:3, 5, 10–12, 15; 7:5, 13; 8:6–8; Rev. 3:20) and her song of Triumph ("Arise and Sing ye Daughters of Israel"). Act 2 describes Saul's visit to the Witch of Endor (S) and his death on the battlefield, followed by David's lament (2 Sam. 1), accompanied by Michal and the chorus. Parry excluded Jonathan from the oratorio but scored a vocal part for the evil spirit (A) (1 Sam. 16–18, 19), who appears in every act, taunting him, inciting him to jealous outbursts over David's slaying of Goliath ("Saul! art thou King indeed? Say the night of thee but thousands?") and David's relationship with Michal ("Doth thy power decline even in thine own house?"), and instructing him to go to the Witch of Endor since God had forsaken him ("Thou enquirest of him but he giveth thee no answer"). Parry contrasts the person of Saul at the beginning of the oratorio when his spirit soared "on wings of delight" with the man at the end who was enslaved by the taunts of an evil spirit unto death. The oratorio concludes with the chorus "Weep ye for the Slain, Weep ye for Saul."

KING SOLOMON. Work in three movements for chorus, narrator, and orchestra by Sir Granville Bantock composed for the coronation of George VI in 1937. It opens with a Processional (Ps. 21), featuring a fanfare and an extended orchestral march, followed by King Solomon's Request for Wisdom

(2 Chron. 1) and the stately choral hymn "Praise Ye the Lord" (Ps. 148). Thirteen years earlier, Arthur Bliss composed incidental music with the same title for a play by Ira Remsen (F. 86, 1924).

KINGDOM, THE. Oratorio in five scenes for SATB soloists, mixed chorus, and orchestra by Elgar (op. 51), premiered at the Birmingham Festival in 1906. Based on a compilation of biblical texts and the Didache and reusing themes from Elgar's Apostles, the work is set in Jerusalem and describes the activities of the Apostles and the "Holy Women" following Jesus' ascension (Acts 1). After an orchestral prelude depicting Jerusalem, scene 1, "In the Upper Room," opens with Peter (B), John (T), the two "Holy Women," the Blessed Virgin (S), and Mary Magdalene (A) quoting Jesus' words from the Gospels and other texts (1 Chron. 12:18; Isa. 63:8; Wisd. 18:15; Ps. 107:2; Sir. 25:2; Ps. 113:1; Joel 2:26; Acts 1:16, 20, 24, 26; 2 Chron. 29:11; Mal. 2:1; 3:1). Scene 2 takes place on "The Morn of Pentecost," with the two Marys reminiscing on Jesus' healing miracles (Sir. 47:9, 10; Acts 3:2; Job 6:14; Ps. 102:19; 2 Chron. 35:16; Ps. 122:1) and the narrator (T) describing the descent of the Holy Spirit and the speaking in tongues (Acts 2; Sir. 39:6; Isa. 12:2; Ps. 104:3, 4; Jer. 1:9; Amos 3:8; Prov. 31:5; Isa. 28:11; Jer. 23:29, 9; Zech. 12:10; 13:1; Jas. 1:18; Acts 3:13). Scene 4, "The Sign of Healing," set "At the Beautiful Gate," opens with an interlude, the healing of the lame man by Peter, and "The Arrest" of the two apostles (Acts 3; Mal. 4:2) and concludes with a beautiful nocturnal interlude, "The Sun Goeth Down," sung by Mary as a reflection on everything she has witnessed (Ps. 104:19, 20; 77:6; 63:6; Dan. 4:3; Isa. 4:2; 45:7; Ps. 42:8). Scene 5, "In Fellowship," returns to "The Upper Room," where Peter and John recount their arrest and interrogation and together receive Holy Communion (Didache; Ps. 118:15; Acts 4; Joel 2:26; Mt. 6:9–13; Rom. 8:15; Isa. 63:16).

KOL NIDRE. ("All Vows"). A piece for solo cello and orchestra by Max Bruch (op. 47), composed in Liverpool and published in Berlin in 1881. Entitled "Adagio on Two Hebrew Melodies for Cello and Orchestra with Harp," it begins with a setting of the Aramaic prayer known as *Kol Nidre*, which is chanted on the eve of Yom Kippur ("Day of Atonement") (cf. Num. 14:20; 15:26). The other melody comes from a setting by Isaac Nathan of Byron's paraphrase of Ps. 137 in *Hebrew Melodies* (1815). The work consists of a series of variations in which the cello imitates the voice of the Jewish cantor. There is a choral setting of the *Kol Nidre* prayer by Arnold Schoenberg (op. 39 1938), arranged for organ solo by Leonard Stein (1992), and it also featured in film versions of *The Jazz Singer*, where it was sung by Al Jolson (1927), Jerry Lewis (1959), and Neil Diamond (1980), as well as on the album *Release of an Oath* by the American rock band Electric Prunes (1968).

• L •

LA DANSE DE LA MORT. Oratorio in seven parts without interruption for soloists (SAB), narrator, mixed chorus, orchestra, and organ by Honegger (H. 131, 1938). The libretto by Paul Claudel was inspired by Holbein's woodcuts *Danse Macabre* (1526). It opens with an orchestral introduction depicting a thunderclap announcing the dialogue between the prophet Ezekiel (narrator) and God (Chorus) (Ezek. 37:1–10), in which each verse is spoken by the narrator and answered by a choral commentary. After an exhortation by a small chorus, "Remember man that thou art spirit" (cf. Job 7:7), section 2 evokes the frenzied medieval *Danse des Morts* ("The Dance of the Dead") with well-known popular songs, such as "Sur le pont d'Avignon on y danse," sung by the large chorus, and the children's song *Nous n'irons plus au bois* ("we'll go to the woods no more") with the Gregorian melody from the **Dies Irae**, played on organ and trumpet. A lament for solo baritone based on allusions to Genesis (Gen. 3:19) and Job (Job 10:19; 19:20–21; 7:7–19; 14:12; 14:3–6) culminates in the words "I know that my Redeemer Liveth" (Job 19:25–26). The fourth section, *Sanglots* ("sobbing"), a setting of a Latin text inspired by Job 10:21, includes the laughter of the people who are unaware of their fate and is followed by *La Réponse de Dieu* ("God's answer") based on Ezek. 37:11–14. The sixth section, *Espérance dans la Croix* ("Faith in the Cross"), sung by each soloist in turn and then by the chorus, foretells the coming of the Savior and the arrival in the Promised Land of the Children of Israel (Jn. 20:20, 25, 27; 17:21; Mt. 11:29; Isa. 49:15; Ezek. 37:16, 22, 28). The final movement, *Affirmation*, sung by the chorus, is based on Mt. 16:18 (*Souviens-toi, homme, que tu es Pierre et sur cette pierre je bâtirai mon église* ["Remember man, you are Peter and on this rock I will build my church"]).

LA PASIÓN SEGÚN SAN MARCOS. ("The Passion according to St. Mark"). Oratorio passion in Spanish, Latin, Galician, and Aramaic by Osvaldo Golijov, commissioned by the Internationale Bachakademie Stuttgart to commemorate the 250th anniversary of the death of J. S. Bach. Composed in Afro-Cuban style, it is scored for soloists, mixed chorus, *berimbau*, accordion, guitar, piano, two trumpets, two trombones, six violins, six cellos, a double bass, 37 percussion instruments, and a capoeira dancer. In addition to Mark's Gospel, the libretto draws on other texts, including Lamentations (Lam. 1:12), Psalms (Ps. 113–118), and a Galician poem by Rosalia de Castro, *Lúa descolorida* ("Colorless Moon"). The narrator is a guitarist who plays

135

three different types of guitar—the *tres*, the *quatro*, and the *cavaquinho*—and the work is three divisions marked by three capoeira dances, accompanied by berimbau: the "Dance of Sacrifice" representing Jesus' last moments on earth, the "Dance of the White Sheet" depicting the mysterious man who ran away naked (Mk. 14:51), and the "Dance of the Purple Veil" symbolizing the soldiers' mocking of Christ (Mk. 15:17). The work ends with a recitation of the Kaddish following the death of Christ.

LA PASSIONE DI GESÙ CRISTO. ("The Passion of Jesus Christ"). Oratorio libretto in two parts for four soloists and chorus by Pietro Metastasio (1730), first set to music by Antonio Caldara in the Hofburgkapelle, Vienna, for a performance during Holy Week (1730). Loosely based on the story of Christ's passion, it begins with the words of Peter (A) after his denial of Christ and answers by John (S), Mary of Magdalene (S), and Joseph of Arimathea (B). In typical Metastasian style, Christ's passion is treated offstage, and the series of reflections, provided by the four protagonists, sought to move 18th-century audiences to live a Christian life in the light of Christ's passion and death, as in Mary Magdalene's words, "From this tree shall every soul draw salvation." It was set as an oratorio as well as an opera seria by numerous 18th-century composers, including Niccolò Conti (1743), Niccolò Jommelli (1749), Josef Mysliveček (1773), Antonio Salieri (1776), Giovanni Paisiello (1783), and Johann Simon Mayr (1794), as well as by Francesco Morlacchi (1812).

LA RÉDEMPTION. ("The Redemption"). A sacred trilogy of oratorios for soloists, chorus, and orchestra by Gounod (1868–1869; 1882) with a libretto by the composer, translated into English by the Rev. John Troutbeck, premiered at the Festival of Birmingham on 30 August and 1 September 1882, and performed in New York on 6 December 1882. Part 1 begins at creation with an orchestral prologue depicting primeval chaos with chromaticism and tells the story of our salvation down to the Annunciation and Christ's passion and death. Part 2 is devoted to the Resurrection and part 3 to Pentecost. Other programmatic orchestral numbers include the "March to Calvary," the "Darkness" at the Crucifixion, and the lyrical passage "Apostles at Prayer" following the descent of the Holy Spirit at Pentecost. A "Christ the Redeemer" leitmotif in the orchestra appears in nine places, including creation, the promise to the Penitent Thief, Christ's appearance to the women at the Sepulchre, and the Ascension. The lamentation for female voices in part 1 comes from the plainchant hymn for vespers on Passion Sunday **Vexilla Regis proderunt** ("Forth the Royal Banners go"), and the **Reproaches** is a paraphrase of the liturgical text sung during the Adoration of the Cross on Good Friday. Mary's solo "While my watch I am keeping" is accompanied by the **Stabat Mater** chant from the Catholic liturgy. The work ends with the longest segment of the oratorio, "The Hymn of the Apostles," beginning "The Word is Flesh become." Samuel Arnold previously composed a work with the same title in 1786, and Gounod composed the symphonic poem (FWV 52) for narrator, women's chorus, mixed chorus, and orchestra in 1871 (rev. 1874).

LA RESURREZIONE DI NOSTRO SIGNOR GESÙ. ("The Resurrection of Our Lord Jesus"). Italian oratorio in two parts for soloists, chorus, orchestra, and continuo by Handel (HWV 47, 1708) to a libretto by Carlo Sigismondo Capece, commissioned by one of Handel's patrons, Marquis Francesco Maria Ruspoli, and first performed at his residence, the Bonelli Palace in Rome, on Easter Sunday 1708. Act 1 opens in hell with a fiery theatrical exchange between the Angel (S) and Lucifer (B), just before Christ's triumphant descent into hell, while on earth Mary Magdalene (S) and Mary Cleopas (A) lament his death on the cross in the poignant aria *Dolci chiodi, amate spine* ("Sweet nails, beloved thorns"). John (T) reflects on the grief of Christ's mother in his tender aria *Così la tortorella talor piange e si lagna* ("Thus may the turtle dove weep and lament") and beckons to them to return to the tomb to await the arrival of the risen Christ. Act 2 tells of the women's arrival at the empty tomb, the angel's announcement of Christ's resurrection, and Magdalene's encounter with the risen Christ and concludes with a joyful chorus, *Diasi lode in cielo, in terra* ("Let praises sound in heaven and earth to the King of Earth and Heaven!").

LA TRAGÉDIE DE SALOMÉ. ("The Tragedy of Salome"). Ballet in eight movements for chamber orchestra, dedicated to Stravinsky, by Florent Schmitt (op. 50, 1907), later revised as a symphonic suite in five movements scored for a larger orchestra (1911). Based on an evocative poem by Robert d'Humières, inspired by the biblical story (Mt. 14:6–11; Mk. 6:21–28), it comprises five dances, beginning with a prelude, *Danse des perles* ("Dance of the Pearls") and *Les Enchantements sur la mer* ("Sorcery at sea"). The frenetic *Danse des éclairs* ("Dance of Lightning") is a spectacular dance in which Herod tears the veils from Salomé's body and John the Baptist appears and covers her naked body with his cloak. Following his execution, his head is carried on a large platter and seized by Salomé, who hurls it into the sea. In the final *Danse de l'Effroi* ("The Dance of Fear"), the severed head multiplies in number and follows Salomé with its gaze from every direction. *See also* SALOME.

LA TRANSFIGURATION DE NOTRE SEIGNEUR JÉSUS-CHRIST. ("The Transfiguration of Our Lord Jesus Christ"). Large-scale oratorio for mixed chorus, seven instrumental soloists, and large orchestra by Messiaen (1965–1969). Inspired by the mystery of Christ's transfiguration, the libretto is made up of texts in Latin from Matthew's Gospel (Mt. 17:1–9), Genesis (Gen. 28:17), Psalms (Pss. 77:19; 84:1–3; 104:2; 43:3; 26:8), the Wisdom of Solomon (Wisd. 7:26), and Paul's Letters (Phil. 3:20–21; Heb. 1:3) as well as from the liturgy for the Feast of the Transfiguration (6 August) and Thomas Aquinas's *Summa theologica* (1265–1274) (q. 45, art. 4, conclusion; q. 45, art. 2, solution 3; q. 45, art. 4, solution 2). It is divided into two parts, each alternating Gospel narrative with meditative commentary and ending with a chorale (Pss. 48:2; 26:8). A complex work, it features the text of the Gospel as an accompanied recitative with vocalizations on the words "Transfiguration" and "*Terribilis*" and the characteristic sounds of Messiaen's birdcalls, including starling, Baltimore oriole, barred owl, rock thrush, and nightingale, awakened by the supernatural light, while multicolored harmonies, trilled chords, and a variety of percussion instruments paint the range of colors.

LABORAVI IN GEMITU MEO. ("I Am Weary of My Groaning"). One of two motets by Thomas Weelkes scored for six-part a cappella chorus (SSAATB). Based on Ps. 6:6, the Psalmist's grief is expressed in the polyphonic texture, melismas on *laboravi* ("I am weary"), *lavabo* ("I will wash"), and *rigabo* ("I will moisten") and dissonances on *lacrymis meis* ("my tears").

LAETATUS SUM. ("I Was Glad"). Motet for triple chorus (SATB, SATB, and SSABar) by Victoria (1583). Inspired by Ps. 122, the work's magnificent polychoral structure reflects the Psalm's joyful mood. It inspired a Mass setting for 12 voices and organ also composed by Victoria and numerous settings by 17th- and 18th-century composers, including Monteverdi, Vivaldi (RV 607), Charpentier (H. 161), Alessandro Scarlatti, Domenico Scarlatti, and Johann Michael Haydn, among others. *See also* I WAS GLAD.

LAGRIME DI SAN PIETRO. ("The Tears of St. Peter"). A cycle of 20 spiritual madrigals in Italian (*madrigali spirituali*) and a concluding motet in Latin (*Vide homo* ["Behold, man"]) (1594) by Orlando de Lassus, the work is a meditation on St. Peter's denial of Christ (Lk. 22:61–62). Based on poetic texts by the Italian poet Luigi Tansillo (1610–1668), it was the last work composed before the composer died. Divided into three sequences of seven compositions, it is scored for seven voices and based on seven of the eight church modes (Madrigals 1–4 in mode I, 5–8 in mode II, 9–12 in modes III and IV, 13–15 in mode V, 16–18 in mode VI, and 19–20 in mode VII), with the last motet based on the *tonus peregrinus*. Madrigals 1 to 6 depict St. Peter as an old man awaiting death and describe his painful recollections of the moment when after his betrayal of Christ in the garden of Gethsemane, Jesus turned and looked at him (Lk. 22:61–62). The cycle imagines the rebuke in Christ's gaze (nos. 7–8); St. Peter's attempt to escape it, after which his eyes filled with tears (nos. 9–14); and his subsequent despair regarding his own salvation (nos. 15–20). In the final motet, an anguished Christ speaks to listeners from his cross, urging them to look on his suffering, which is less painful than humanity's ingratitude.

LAMB, THE. Well-known anthem for four-part a cappella chorus (SATB) by Taverner (1982). It is a setting of William Blake's poem from *Songs of Innocence* (1789), in which the title is a reference to Christ the "little lamb" born in Bethlehem as well as Christ the sacrificial Lamb of God (Jn. 1:29). Sung syllabically in free rhythm guided by the words to a largely homophonic texture, the opening notes of the soprano's melodic line, based around the tonality of G major, make up the motivic material for the entire work, featuring later in inversion, retrograde, and augmentation. There is another setting by Vaughan Williams for tenor and oboe in *Ten Blake Songs* (no. 5, 1957).

LAMB OF GOD, THE. Passion oratorio in two parts for soloists (SATB), reader, chorus (SATB), orchestra, and organ by William Wallace Gilchrist (Schleifer 115, 1909). The work contains long segments of narrated text from the Gospels (Mt. 26–27) alongside sung sections both from the Gospels (Mt. 27:33–44; Lk. 23:28, 34, 30, 38) and the prophets (Isa. 53:7, 8, 11; 50:6; Jer. 9:1). It also includes the lyrics of three well-known hymns: "Go to Dark Gethsemane" by James Montgomery, "Christian! Dost thou see them" with words by J. M. Neale from the Greek of St. Andrew of Crete, and "Behold the Lamb of God! O Thou for sinners slain" by Matthew Bridges (1848).

LAMENTABATUR JACOB. ("Jacob Lamented"). Motet in two parts for five voices (SATTB) by Cristóbal de Morales (published 1543). The text is not biblical but is inspired by the story of Jacob's grief when he thought he might never see his sons Joseph and Benjamin again (Gen. 43:14). It makes poignant use of descending melodic lines on *Lamentabatur* ("Jacob was lamenting") and *heu me, dolens sum* ("woe is me, I am distraught"). Other settings include those of Jacob Regnart (1540–1599) and Alonso de Tejeda (1540–1628).

LAMENTATIONS OF JEREMIAH, THE. Since medieval times, extracts from the Book of Lamentations have been chanted during Holy Week and in the 16th century intoned to the *tonus lamentationum* as directed by the Council of Trent. The nighttime service, comprising three Psalms (Pss. 68–70) and three lessons, recount Jeremiah's lamentations over the destruction of Jerusalem and point to Christ's passion and death on the cross. Following the Hebrew text, each Lamentation is prefaced by a successive letter of the Hebrew alphabet (aleph, beth, gimel, daleth, etc.) that is decorated with a melisma and framed by a nonbiblical announcement, such as *Incipit Lamentatio Ieremiae Prophetae* ("Here begins the Lamentation of Jeremiah the Prophet"), and a concluding refrain from Hos. 14:1, *Jerusalem convertere ad Dominum Duem tuum* ("Jerusalem, return unto the Lord your God"). From the Renaissance, many composers, including Ockeghem, Arcadelt, Sermisy, Morales, Tallis, Byrd, White, Palestrina, Victoria, Allegri, and Lasso, composed polyphonic settings of parts of Lamentations for a cappella chorus. There were settings for chorus, soloists, and instrumental accompaniment in the 17th and 18th centuries by Scarlatti, Jomelli, Zelenka, Couperin, Charpentier, Gilles, and others. While there were very few settings in the 19th century, there are some notable 20th-century settings, including Ernst Křenek, *Lamentatio Jeremiae Prophetae* (1941/1942); Leonard Bernstein, **Jeremiah** Symphony (1943); Alberto Ginastera, *Hieremiae prophetae Lamentationes* (1946); Edmund Rubbra, *Tenebrae-9 Lamentations* (1951); Igor Stravinsky, **Threni, id est Lamentationes Jeremiae Prophetae** (1958); and, more recently, Z. Randall Stoope, *Lamentations of Jeremiah* (1999).

LAST JUDGMENT, THE. Oratorio by Elgar intended as the third part of a trilogy with *The Apostles* (1903) and *The Kingdom* (1906) but never completed.

LAST WORDS OF DAVID, THE. Anthem by Randall Thompson written in 1949 for four-part chorus of mixed voices with piano, band, or orchestral accompaniment. Commissioned by the Boston Symphony Orchestra for the 25th anniversary of Serge Koussevitzky as music director, it is a majestic setting of David's last words (2 Sam. 23:3–4). The opening, which portrays David as a just and powerful king (v. 3), is sung fortissimo and subito forzando with vertical accents and tenuto markings to the accompaniment of ascending scale-like passages of demisemiquavers arranged in septuplets. The description of David as the morning light, the rising sun, the clear sky, and a new blade of grass (v. 4) is illustrated with a gentle melody in ascending stepwise movement, sung pianissimo, with word painting on "riseth," "springing," and "shining" against a block chordal accompaniment. The **Alleluia** at the end, sung in imitative counterpoint and a cappella for three and a half measures, floats above the accompaniment as if to represent the departure of David's soul, and the work concludes with an **Amen** in block chords against the accompaniment of an ascending scale-like passage, now set in crotchets, to represent his ascent into heaven.

LAUDATE JEHOVAM OMNES GENTES. ("Praise the Lord, All Ye Nations"). Epiphany cantata in three movements for SATB chorus, two violins, and basso continuo by Telemann (TVW 7–25, 1758), based on Ps. 117, the shortest Psalm in the Psalter. The work concludes with a festive **Alleluia**.

LAZARUS. Song from the album *Meds* (2006) by British alternative rock band Placebo. Written by Brian Molko, Stefan Olsdal, and Steven Hewitt, it tells how Lazarus (Jn. 11) is bored with his resurrected life, "full of apathy," and "caught in a trap [he] cannot escape."

LAZARUS COME FORTH. Gospel song by contemporary Christian music artist and evangelist Carman (Carmelo Domenic Licciardello). Inspired by the story of the raising of Lazarus (Jn. 11), it tells of his encounter with various Old Testament characters, including "Elijah, Moses, Samuel, even Ruth / And all the others jammed up in a room." At a meeting convened by Moses, they testify to their encounter with Christ: Solomon credits Christ with making him "smart," and Ezekiel testifies to knowing him as a "wheel within a wheel" (Ezek. 1:16). It opens with a narrator speaking Christ's words, "I am the resurrection and the Life/He that believeth in me/though he were dead/Yet shall he live," and closes with his dramatic call, "Lazarus come forth" (Jn. 11:43). It was rereleased on the album *Carman: Anthems of a Champion* (2013).

LAZARUS, OR THE CELEBRATION OF THE RESURRECTION. (*Lazarus, oder die Feier der Auferstehung*). Unfinished cantata scored for soloists (SSSTTTBar), chorus (SSAATTBB), and orchestra by Franz Schubert, begun in 1820 (D. 689, 1866). The libretto by theologian and poet August Hermann Niemeyer (1754–1828), based on the story of the miracle of the raising of Lazarus (Jn. 11:1–14), includes a reference to the daughter of Jairus named Jemina (S), who visits Lazarus as he approaches death and assures him of an afterlife by describing her entrance into heaven following her death (Mk. 5:21–43). Act 1 and a fragment of act 2 were set by Schubert with a prominent focus on the illness and death of Lazarus with no setting of his resurrection (act 3). Niemeyer's libretto was also set to music by Johann Heinrich Rolle in 1778.

LAZARUS REQUIEM, THE. Work for SATB chorus, SSTBar soloists, and orchestra by Patrick Hawes (2005) to a libretto by the composer's brother, Andrew Hawes. Inspired by the story of Christ raising Lazarus from the dead (Jn. 11), it combines a setting of the Requiem in Latin, sung by chorus and orchestra, with six tableaux sung mostly in English by a semichorus accompanied by muted strings, harp, and baritone saxophone. The two exceptions are the **Benedictus** sung by Mary (S) and the climax of the work, when Christ (T) addresses death with the words "Unbind him! Loose him! Let him go!," accompanied by full orchestra with unmuted strings. The work concludes with a magical setting of Lux Aeterna for chorus, soloists, and orchestra.

LE CHEMIN DE LA CROIX. ("The Way of the Cross"). Tone poem for organ by Marcel Dupré (op. 29, 1931). It originated at a concert in Brussels as an improvisation between the reading of 14 poems by Paul Claudel, ambassador to the United States at the time, entitled "Le Chemin de la Croix" (*The Way of the Cross*, 1911). It was later written down and performed annually during Lent at Saint-Sulpice in Paris. The work is a somber meditation on the suffering and agony of Christ's passion and death.

L'ENFANT PRODIGUE. ("The Prodigal Son"). One-act cantata for soloists (STBar) and orchestra by Debussy (L. 57, 1884; rev. 1908), to a libretto by Edouard Guinand, awarded the Prix de Rome in 1884. Set near Lake Gennesaret (Sea of Galilee), it begins just before the prodigal son Azaël (T) arrives home and focuses on his mother Lia (S), who is weeping inconsolably over her son's long absence. When he returns, she urges her husband Symeon (B) to forgive their son, and the work concludes with the family's song of praise to God. *See also* PRODIGAL SON, THE.

LE RENIEMENT DE SAINT PIERRE. ("The Denial of St. Peter"). Oratorio/dramatic motet by Charpentier (H. 424), regarded as a masterpiece. It opens with an account of the Last Supper (*Cum caenisset Jesus et dedisset discipulis*), where Christ predicts Peter's three acts of denial, and concludes with Christ's gaze and Peter's bitter tears of remorse (*Et egressus foras, flevit amare* ["He went out and wept bitterly"]) (Lk. 22:62), the words *flevit amare* scored with tortured dissonances and agitated suspensions over 30 measures.

LE ROI DAVID. ("King David"). Symphonic Psalm (*Psaume symphonique*) in three parts for narrator, three soloists (SAT), two choruses, and orchestra by Honegger (H. 37, 1923), originally performed as incidental music to *Le Roi David*, a play by René Morax (1921). The libretto, based on the biblical story of David, combines spoken narrative with texts from the Psalms, **Job** (Job 14:1–2), Isaiah (Isa. 11:1), and a nonbiblical Psalm by the Renaissance poet Clément Marot. Part 1 recounts the story of David's youth and focuses on. Saul's jealousy, culminating in his defeat and death at Gilboa (1 Sam. 16–31). Part 2 celebrates David's coronation, his dance before the ark (2 Sam. 6), and the prediction by an angel of Solomon's birth (cf. 2 Sam. 7), concluding with a chorus of angels singing "**Alleluia**." Part 3 tells the tragic stories of David and Bathsheba (2 Sam. 11–12) and the death of Absalom (2 Sam. 18–19) but ends with David's repentance (Ps. 51), prayerfulness (Ps. 121), loyalty (Ps. 18), and peaceful death (1 Kgs. 2), followed by a chorus of serene Alleluias suggesting the ascent of David's spirit into heaven. There are many notable numbers, including "The Song of David the Shepherd" inspired by Ps. 23, the soprano lament "Oh had I Wings like a Dove" (Ps. 55:6), and the dramatic incantation of the Witch of Endor (1 Sam. 28), where the witch calls up Samuel, first in a whisper that crescendos to a loud roar. In this number, percussion instruments (snare drum, bass drum, cymbals, tambourines, tam-tams, celesta, harp, and timpani) lend a supernatural atmosphere. There are some memorable instrumentals, including the "March of the Hebrews," the "March of the Philistines," and the "Coronation of Solomon."

LEAD KINDLY LIGHT. Hymn by Cardinal John Henry Newman, inspired by 2 Cor. 4:6, written when he was critically ill and "becalmed in the Straits of Bonifacio," and set to music by John Bacchus Dykes to the tune *Lux Benigna* ("Kindly Light") in 1865 and in the 1920s to the tune "Alberta" by William H. Harris. It was set as an anthem for SATB and soprano/tenor solo by John Stainer (1868) and, more recently, by Howard Goodall in "Eternal Light: A Requiem" (2008).

LEAD ME LORD. Well-known short anthem for SATB chorus and organ, with optional choral alto or soprano solo by Samuel Sebastian Wesley. Part of the anthem *Praise the Lord, O My Soul*, meditative in character, and often sung at funerals, it is a setting of two verses from the Psalms (Pss. 5:8; 4:9), the second ("For it is thou Lord only that makes me dwell in safety") sung twice like a refrain.

LEGEND OF JUDITH, THE. Ballet in one act with music by Mordecai Seter (1962), choreography by Martha Graham, premiered at the Martha Graham Dance Company Theatre in Tel Aviv on 25 October 1962. Drawing on the biblical story of Judith and Holofernes (Jud. 8–16), the action is played out in Judith's mind as she remembers herself as a young woman, her bridegroom, the tyrant Nebuchadnezzar, and her seduction of the enemy Holofernes. It was reworked as a symphonic chaconne for orchestra in 1963.

LEKHA DODI. ("Come My Beloved"). Jewish liturgical song recited on Friday evenings to welcome the Sabbath: during the singing of the last verse, the congregation turns to the open door "to greet the bride" (*liqrat kala*). The eight stanzas contain many allusions to biblical language and imagery, especially the Song of Songs (Cant. 7:11) and Isaiah (Isa. 51:17; 52:2; 40:5; 62:5; 54:3). Composed by the 16th-century kabbalist Alqabetz of Safed, it is sung to a variety of melodies, including an old Moorish tune and a Polish folk song. It has been arranged for choir and organ by several composers, including Berlinski (1953).

LET ALL MORTAL FLESH KEEP SILENCE. Fourth-century Greek hymn from the Litany of St. James, published in an English translation by Gerard Moultrie in *Lyra Eucharistica* (1864) and the *English Hymnal* (1906) and sung to the traditional French carol tune "Picardy," arranged by Vaughan Williams. Inspired by Hab. 2:20 and texts from the Nativity story, it was set as an anthem for mixed chorus a cappella by Sir Edward Bairstow (1925) and arranged by Gustav Holst for soprano and bass soloists, mixed chorus (SATB), and orchestra (op. 36a, no. 1, 1916). More recently, it was performed by American gospel singer Cynthia Clawson on the album *Hymnsinger* (2012) and by Red Mountain Music on the album *Silent Night* (2011).

LET ALL THE WORLD IN EVERY CORNER SING. Well-known hymn by George Herbert from *The Temple* (1633), commonly called "Antiphon," inspired by Ps. 95 and sung to the tune "Luckington." Well-known settings include anthems by Vaughan Williams (no. 5, 1911) in the cycle **Five Mystical Songs**, Kenneth Leighton (1965), Thomas Dunn (1971), Herbert Howells (1976), and William Matthias (op. 96, no. 2, 1987).

LET ME IN. Work for mixed chorus by Roxanna Panufnik with text by Jessica Duchen (2010). Based on the apocryphal Infancy Gospel of Thomas 15:1–2, it opens with a segment of the Mourner's Kaddish (*Yitgadal v'yitkadash sh'mé rabba, Amén* ["Magnify and sanctify his Great name, **Amen**"]), which is chanted in Aramaic over the death of a little girl and alluded to throughout the work. The title is a reference to Jesus' words to the mother who has locked the door of her house out of grief. The work tells how the boy Jesus also fashioned sparrows out of clay as well as raising the girl from the dead. It appears on the album *The Boy Whose Father Was God* (Chanticleer, 2010).

LET MINE EYES RUN DOWN WITH TEARS. Choral setting of verses from Jer. (13:17–22) by Purcell, regarded as one of his finest masterpieces (Z. 24, ca. 1682), employing a sophisticated use of antiphonal exchange between soloists and choir. Downward melodic movement on "let mine eyes run down with tears night and day" depicts Jeremiah's flowing tears, false relations on "great breach" paint the desolation of Jerusalem, and the final chorus, "therefore will we wait upon thee, for thou hast made all these things," ends in a mood of hopeful resignation. *See also* PLORANS PLORABIT.

LET THE NIGHT PERISH. ("Job's Curse"). Song in C minor for voice, organ, or harpischord and basso continuo by Purcell (Z. 191) to a text by Jeremy Taylor inspired by Job 3:3–10. Characterized by a gloomy minor tonality, word painting abounds with depressive descending intervals on words like "perish," "cursed," "give a groan and die," "no sun," "gloomy darkness," "poor," and "the slave" and upbeat ascending melodies and intervals on "the Lord," "joy," "palaces of State," "rulers," "the rich," and "the monarch." The song concludes on a descending melody, "the silent chambers of the grave," to its final resting place on a vacant unison C.

LET THE PEOPLE PRAISE THEE O GOD. Anthem for chorus and organ by William Mathias (op. 87, 1981) inspired by Ps. 67. It was composed for the wedding of Prince Charles to Lady Diana Spencer at St. Paul's Cathedral, London.

LET THY HAND BE STRENGHTENED. Coronation anthem for mixed chorus and orchestra by Handel (HWV 259, no. 2, 1727), composed for the "Recognition" part of the coronation service, that is, when King George II was presented to the people. Based on Ps. 89:13–14, it begins and ends in G major with a joyful section, "Let thy hand be strengthened," and a triumphant **Alleluia**, with a melancholy setting of verse 14 in the middle.

LET US WITH A GLADSOME MIND. Hymn based on a selection of stanzas from a paraphrase of Ps. 136 (vv. 4–9, 25) written by John Milton when he was a schoolboy at St. Paul's, London, at age 15 (1616). It is normally sung either to the tune "Harts" (1769) or to the tune "Melling" (1830).

LET'S MISBEHAVE. Duet by Cole Porter that was originally written for the musical *Paris*, which premiered on Broadway in 1929 but was cut and replaced by the song "Let's Do It, Let's Fall in Love." It was later included in the 1962 revival of the musical *Anything Goes*. Alluding to the marriage of Adam and Eve in Gen. 2–3, the main character, Reno Sweeney, beckons

Lord Evelyn Oakleigh "to misbehave" before his marriage to American heiress Hope Harcourt with the suggestion that he would become like Adam, who after his marriage to Eve, "wouldn't stand for teasin'." A hit for Irving Aaronson and His Commanders in 1928, it appeared in a number of movies, including the opening sequence of Woody Allen's *Everything You Always Wanted to Know about Sex* *But Were Afraid to Ask* (1971); *The Great Gatsby* (2013), which featured the original 1928 recording by Aaronson; and *De-Lovely* (2004), where it is sung by Elvis Costello.

LIBER USUALIS. ("The Usual/Common Book"). A collection of Gregorian chants in Latin compiled by the Benedictine monks of the Abbey of Solesmes, France, in 1896, used extensively until the Second Vatican Council (Vatican II; 1962–1965). The *Liber Usualis* contains chants for the Mass, Ordinary and Proper, Hours of the Divine Office (matins, vespers, and so on), Psalms, canticles, introits, responsories, antiphons, sequences, graduals, alleluias and tracts, hymns, and chants for every liturgical occasion, including feast days, baptisms, weddings, funerals, and ordinations. While still in use, it has officially been replaced by the *Graduale Romanum* (chant book of the Roman rite) (Solesmes 1961; rev. 1970, 1974), which follows the post–Vatican II *Novus Ordo* Mass and calendar.

LIFT UP YOUR HEADS, O YE GATES. Anthem for SATB chorus and organ by William Mathias (op. 44, no. 2, 1969), commissioned for the 1973 collection of *Anthems for Choirs I* edited by Francis Jackson. Based on Ps. 24:7–10, it is an exuberant work with jazzy syncopations reflecting the Psalm's joyful mood. Earlier settings of the same text include a chorus for SSATB in Handel's **Messiah** and a cantata, *Machet die Tore weit* ("Open wide your gates"), by Telemann, written for the first Sunday of Advent (1719).

LIGHT IN THE WILDERNESS, THE: AN ORATORIO FOR TODAY. Oratorio in two parts for chorus, baritone soloist, orchestra, and organ by jazz composer and pianist Dave Brubeck (1968) with text adapted from the New Testament by Iola and Dave Brubeck. For the temptations of Christ in the wilderness (Mk. 1:12–13), intervals of a perfect fifth represent the barrenness of the desert and bitonalites its hostile environment, while the teachings of Christ, most notably the Sermon on the Mount (Mt. 5), are sung by baritone solo and chorus with improvisations. Inspired by the composer's military service in World War II, the heart of the oratorio is in two numbers for baritone solo and chorus: "The Great Commandment" and "Love your Enemies." Part 2 deals with matters of faith in numbers, such as the baritone solo "Where is God?" and the choral interlude "We seek Him," with a focus on Christ's promise of peace in "Peace I Leave you" (Jn. 14:27). The solo "Let not your heart be troubled" (Jn. 14:1) was written for the composer's brother following the death of his 16-year-old son from a brain tumor. It is characterized by contrasting meters, such as 5/4 in the "Temptations" and a pastoral 6/8 in the **Beatitudes**. In the words of the composer, the work is characterized by "quick jumps from modern to modal, Middle Eastern to country hoe-down, jazz, rock n'roll and martial drums." It was performed by the Masterworks Chorale at Harvard University in 2014.

LIGHT OF LIFE, THE. Oratorio for four soloists, chorus, and orchestra by Edward Elgar to a libretto by the Rev. Edward Capel Cure (op. 29, 1896). Originally entitled *Lux Christi*, it was premiered at the Three Choirs Festival in Worcester Cathedral in 1895–1896. Based on the story of Christ restoring sight to the blind man (Jn. 9), the solos are scored for the mother of the blind man (S), the narrator (A), the blind man (T), and Jesus (B), while the chorus is scored for the Levites of the Temple, the Pharisees, and a chorus of women. The prelude, called a "Meditation," contains the work's leitmotif, in which a G major third represents Christ as the light of the world, as it does in the oratorio **The Apostles**. The work concludes with a dialogue between Christ and the man who was blind (Jn. 9:35–38), Jesus' aria "I am the Good Shepherd" (Jn. 10:11–18) accompanied by solo violin, and a choral fugue proclaiming Christ as the light of the world (Jn. 8:12).

LIGHT OF THE WORLD, THE. Oratorio in two parts for SSATBarB, chorus (SATB), and orchestra by Arthur Sullivan, dedicated to Grand Duchess Marie Alexandrovna of Russia and first performed at the Birmingham Festival in 1873. After a prologue (Isa. 11:1; Lk. 4:18), part 1 is in four sections, set in Bethlehem, the Synagogue in Nazareth (Lk. 4:16–20), the house of Lazarus, and the Way to Jerusalem, and includes two soprano airs, "My soul doth magnify the Lord" (Lk. 1:46–55) and "In Rama there was a voice heard" (Jer. 31:15; Mt. 2:18) for soprano solo and chorus, and the well-known choral number "I will pour out my spirit" (Joel 2:28). Part 1 also includes two settings of "**Hosanna to the Son of David**," the first for a chorus of children and the second for mixed voices. Part 2, divided into two sections, set in Jerusalem and at the Holy Sepulchre (Jn. 20), concludes with the joyful final chorus "Him hath God exalted" (Acts 5:31).

LIKE A SEA WITHOUT A SHORE. Advent folk hymn by Estelle White first published in the *20th Century Folk Hymnal* (1976) and a year later in *Hymns Old and New: A Hymnal for the Irish Church* (1977). It includes the Aramaic phrase *Maranatha* ("Our Lord, come") (1 Cor. 16:22) in the chorus. Other hymns with this phrase include *Maranatha* by Gerard Chiusano, "Prepare the Way of the Lord" by Jacques Berthier, "*Maranatha* Come" by Francis Patrick O'Brien, and "*Maranatha*, Come Lord Jesus" by Janèt Sullivan Whitaker.

LIKE AS THE HART. Best known of four anthems for chorus and organ by Herbert Howells (1941). The beautiful blues-inspired, languid melodic lines of this work, inspired by Ps. 42:1–3, evoke an air of eroticism in the deer's search for water and the soul's longing for God. Other settings of this text include the anthem *As pants the hart* by Handel, first composed for the Chapel Royal in 1713 and modified several times over the next 25 years, and *Wie der Hirsch schreit* by Mendelssohn (1837/1838). *See also* O PRAY FOR THE PEACE OF JERUSALEM; SICUT CERVUS.

LITTLE DAVID PLAY ON YOUR HARP. African American spiritual inspired by the story of David, the young shepherd boy who played the harp (1 Sam. 16). The verses tell of David's triumph over Goliath (1 Sam. 18) and the persistence of **Joshua**, son of Nun (Josh. 1:5–7), while the refrain adds "*Hallelu, Hallelu*" to the title. Arranged for chorus and piano by Rollo Dilworth, it is a popular choice for youth choirs.

LITTLE DRUMMER BOY, THE. ("Carol of the Drum"). Popular Christmas song by American composer Katherine Kennicott Davis (1941). Possibly based on a Czech carol, it is inspired by the story of the Three Wise Men bearing gifts. It tells how the drummer boy, who has no gift other than his music, plays his drum for the Christ child with the Virgin Mary's approval. The words of the lyrics "Pa rum pum pum pum" mimic the sound of the drum, while orchestral versions include drumrolls as part of the accompaniment. First recorded in 1951, it was later recorded by the Trapp Family Singers (1955) and numerous well-known artists worldwide, including Johnny Cash (1963), Marlene Dietrich (*Der Trommelmann*, 1964), Nana Mouskouri (*L'enfant au tambour*, 1965), Stevie Wonder (1970), the Brady Bunch (1977), Bing Crosby (1962) with David Bowie (1977), Ringo Starr (2007), Josh Groban (2011), Justin Bieber (2011), and the punk rock band Bad Religion (2013).

LIVERPOOL NATIVITY, THE. A modern musical version of the Christmas story acted out on the streets of Liverpool and broadcast live on British television in 2007. Popular songs drawn from artists and bands originating in Liverpool, such as the Beatles, the Zutons, and Echo and the Bunneymen, capture the mood of the biblical story (Lk. 1–2). Mary, who works in a café, is approached by Gabriel, director of the city's closed-circuit television system, and with the help of Joseph, an asylum seeker, her baby is eventually born among the barrels of a local pub and laid in a shopping trolley. The action is accompanied by contemporary music, including John Lennon's "Imagine" and "Beautiful Boy" and the Beatles' "All You Need Is Love," "Let It Be," "Here Comes the Sun," and "Lady Madonna."

LO, HOW A ROSE E'ER BLOOMING. (*Es ist ein' Ros entsprungen*). German Christmas carol and Marian hymn based on Lk. 1–2 and Isa. 11:1–10, thought to have originated in the 14th or 15th century and later harmonized by Michael Praetorius in his *Musae Sioniae* VI (1609). It was translated into English by Theodore Baker (1894) and subsequently adapted as a hymn, "The Spotless Rose," by Catherine Winkworth. In an exquisite setting for a cappella SATB chorus and baritone soloist by Herbert Howells (1919), the second verse, sung by the soloist and repeated by the chorus, is narrated by Isaiah, who explains that the "Rose," sprung from its tender root in Mary, is the "blessed Babe," Jesus Christ. It also inspired a carol by Philip Ledger (2002) for the Choir of King's College for the Festival of Nine Lessons and Carols.

LO THE FULL, FINAL SACRIFICE. Anthem for SATB and organ by Gerald Finzi (op. 26, 1946). The English words are from a 17th-century hymn by Richard Crashaw based on two Latin hymns by Thomas Aquinas: *Adoro te* ("I adore thee") and *Lauda Sion salvatorem* ("Zion praise thy saviour"). It refers to Old Testament texts prefiguring the Eucharist, such as the sacrifice of Isaac (Gen. 22:1–19; Heb. 11:17), manna in the desert (Exod. 16; Jn. 6:31), the Paschal Lamb (Exod. 12:3–11; 1 Cor. 5:7), and the Good Shepherd (Isa. 40:11; Jn. 10:14). A soothing, meditative work with occasional short-lived climactic moments, it features a serene eight-part setting of the **Amen** and a dissonance in the final measure, pointing perhaps to Christ's death on the cross.

LORD LET ME KNOW MINE END. Full anthem for two trebles, chorus, and organ by Maurice Greene (1743). Inspired by verses from Ps. 39, it is a reflection on the brevity and uncertainty of life, most notably in the exquisite treble duet "For man walketh in a vain shadow" (v. 6). It concludes with an earnest prayer of supplication sung by the chorus, "And now, Lord, what is my hope?" (v. 7). Psalm 39 also provides the text for one of Hubert Parry's *Songs of Farewell* for double choir (1918).

LORD OF THE DANCE. Popular hymn written by the Quaker songwriter and folksinger Sydney Carter (1963), sung to the tune of a 19th-century Shaker song, "Simple Gifts" (1848). Composed in the tempo of a reel, it depicts Christ's role in God's plan of salvation as beginning "in the morning when the world was begun" (Prov. 8:30–31) and ending with his resurrection on Easter Sunday. Similar to the carol **Tomorrow shall be my dancing day,** it gives Jesus' own account of his life, each verse followed by a refrain inviting us to dance with him: "And I lead you all in the dance, said he." It has been performed numerous times, including an arrangement for mixed choir and orchestra by John Rutter (1999) and a musical and dance production by Irish American dancer Michael Flatley (1996), where it is danced as a treble reel. It also features in a well-known setting by Aaron Copland in his ballet *Appalachian Spring* (1943–1944).

LORD'S PRAYER, THE. Work for solo voice and orchestra by Albert Hay Malotte (1935), performed by many great opera singers, song artists, and groups, including Mario Lanza, José Carreras and Andrea Boccelli, Elvis Presley, Mahalia Jackson, Aretha Franklin, Perry Como, Doris Day, and the Beach Boys. Other settings in English include the Millennium Prayer sung to the tune "Auld Lang Syne" by Cliff Richards, a rock version by Arnold Strals (1972) performed by the Australian nun Sister Janet Mead, and a setting by Selah on the album *You Deliver Me* (2009). Other settings include a work by Rimsky-Korsakov for mixed chorus (1883) and a work by John Taverner for children's a cappella chorus (SSA), commissioned by Les Petit Chanteurs de Saint-André de Colmar (1966). *See also* PATER NOSTER; PSALMS FOR I; VATER UNSER.

LOT'S WIFE. Rasta-inspired song by roots reggae singer Prince Allah (1979). Written in the style of a Nyabinghi chant, it tells the story of Lot's wife, who turned into a "pillar of salt" on Judgment Day (cf. Gen. 19:24–29). The repetition at the end, "O woman don't look back now," followed by "Lot's wife turned a pillar of salt," contrasts the woman's disobedience with the obedience of her husband Lot.

LOVE CAME DOWN AT CHRISTMAS. Popular Christmas carol written by Christina Rossetti, inspired by Jn. 3:16 and first published in *Time Flies: A Reading Diary* (1885). It was set to a gentle Irish melody called "Gartan" (or "Garton") and more recently arranged by Moya Brennan on the album *An Irish Christmas* (2006).

LOVE FEAST OF THE APOSTLES, THE. *See* DAS LIEBESMAHL DER APOSTEL.

LUCIFERO, CAELESTIS OLIM. ("Lucifer's Fall from Grace"). Dialogue motet by Carissimi, scored for a bass (Devil), soprano (God), and continuo. Based on Isa. 14:12–15, Lucifer proclaims his intention to set himself above God, highlighted in the virtuosic coloratura of both characters.

LUGEBAT DAVID ABSALOM. ("David Mourned for Absalom"). Motet for eight voices by Nicholas Gombert, formerly attributed to Josquin des Prez, based on two chansons inspired by David's lament for his son Absalom (2 Sam. 18:33, 19:4). The first part tells how David mourned the death of his son and wished he could have died in his place. The second repeats that he covered his head and cried in a loud voice, *Fili mi Absalon, O fili mi* ("My son Absalom, O my son"), his heartrending words repeated over and over again.

LUMEN. ("Light"). Gregorian chant based on the Song of Simeon (Lk. 2:29–32). The verse beginning *Lumen ad revelationem gentium* ("A light to lighten the Gentiles") is repeated at the beginning and at the end after the lesser doxology and as an antiphon between verses. Sung at Candlemas as the candles are blessed and lit, it emphasizes the theme of Christ as the light of the world. *See also* NUNC DIMITTIS.

• M •

MAGDALENE: A CHANCEL OPERA ABOUT JESUS' CLOSE DIS-CIPLE. Chancel opera in six scenes for soloists and piano by Susan Hulsman Bingham based on Mary Magdalene's friendship with Jesus. It is inspired by a variety of texts from the Bible (e.g., Ps. 133; Cant. 1:2–3; Lam. 1:12; Zech. 12:10; Mk. 14:3–9; Rev. 5:6) and from nonbiblical sources, including the apocryphal Gospels of Peter (12:50; 13:57) and Mary (17:18–18:50) and the Gnostic *Pistis Sophia* (36:71). Scored for seven unclean spirits (sopranos/mezzo-sopranos)—the Magdalene (S); Mary of Bethany (S); the Angel (Tr/S); Martha (S); Joanna (Mez); Mary, mother of James (Mez); a Female Pharisee (Mez); Jesus (T); Simon (T); Andrew (T); John the beloved disciple (T); Judas (Bar); and Matthew (Bar)—it includes well-known biblical stories, such as the woman caught in adultery (Jn. 8:1–11), the anointing of Jesus' feet with oil (Lk. 7:36–50), the Crucifixion (Jn. 19), and the appearance of Jesus at the empty tomb (Jn. 20:11–18).

MAGDALENE AT THE FEET OF CHRIST. (*Maddalena ai piedi di Cristo*). Oratorio in two parts for six voices, scored for strings, lutes, organ, clavecin, and bassoons by Antonio Caldara (1670–1736) to a libretto by Lodovici Forni (Rome, ca. 1700). The main thrust of the oratorio focuses on a battle between Heavenly Love (Ct) and Earthly Love (A), representing the forces of Good and Evil, to win the soul of Mary Magdalene (S), traditionally identified with Mary the sister of Martha (S) (Lk. 7:36–50; Jn. 11–12). Part 2 recounts the scene of Mary washing the feet of Christ (T) in the house of the Pharisee (B) and concludes with a victory for Heavenly Love, sung as a recitative by Mary with her words of penitence renouncing all worldly pleasures.

MAGNIFICAT, THE. The Latin title of a hymn sung by Mary (Lk. 1:46–55) that was from early times an important part of morning worship in the Eastern Church and of vespers in the West. Its revolutionary tone (Lk. 1:51–53) made it popular with liberation theologians in Latin America, where in some countries it was banned for a time. Bach's famous extended setting for SSATB choir and orchestra (1723) is in 12 movements, mostly in E-flat major and F major, with minor tonalities for verses 48, 50, 52, and 54 and some additions, including Luther's hymn *Vom Himmel hoch* ("From Heaven High") after verse 47. Among other notable musical settings are those of Tallis, Schütz, Monteverdi, Purcell, Schubert (1816), Bruckner (1852), Rachmaninoff (1915), Vaughan Williams (1925), and Arvo Pärt (1989).

MAN FROM NAZARETH: THE LIFE OF CHRIST FROM BIRTH TO ASCENSION. A "spiritual musical" by Edward Hammond Boatner (1898–1981) for 40-part mixed chorus telling the life of Christ through the eyes of African American slaves. Twenty-one spirituals, arranged by the composer, many prefaced by narration, include all-time favorites, such as **Go Tell It on the Mountain, Wade in the Water**, and Rise and Shine, as well as lesser-known ones, such as "New Born," "Done Found My Lost Sheep," and "They Led My Lord Away." *See also* CHILD OF OUR TIME, A.

MANCHESTER PASSION, THE. A modern passion play staged on the streets of Manchester, England, and broadcast live on British television on Good Friday 2006. Popular songs drawn from artists and bands originating in Manchester, such as Oasis, Robbie Williams, and Elkie Brooks, capture the mood of the biblical story. The play begins with the singing of Robbie Williams's "Angels" in the gay and red-light district and then progresses past Chinatown and St. Peter's to Albert Square, where Jesus sang the Stone Roses lyric "I am the Resurrection" (Jn. 11:25) in the finale. Other memorable moments were Jesus' performance of the Joy Division hit "Love Will Tear Us Apart," Judas singing the Smiths' "Heaven Knows I'm Miserable Now" as he betrays Jesus, and a duet rendering of the New Order lyric "Blue Monday" by Jesus and Judas.

MANY AND GREAT, O GOD, ARE THY THINGS. Hymn based on verses from Jeremiah (Jer. 10:12–13), commonly known as the Dakota hymn, written by Joseph R. Renville to the Native American tune "Lac qui parle" and published in his edited hymnal *Dakota Odowan* (1842).

MARANATHA. *See* LIKE A SEA WITHOUT A SHORE.

MARGATE EXODUS, THE. A contemporary retelling of the Exodus story filmed on location for British television in Margate, Kent, in September 2007. Moses rejects his privileged background and leads the "undesirables" out of "Dreamland," the ghetto in which they have been imprisoned, while the authorities are plagued by 10 "terrorist attacks." Local songwriters were commissioned to compose music for each of the 10 plagues (Exod. 7–13), such as "Blood" by Klashnekoff, "The Meaning of Lice" by Stephin Merritt (the

Magnetic Fields), "Boils" by Cody Chesnutt, "Darkness" by Scott Walker, and "Katonah" ("Death of the Firstborn") by Rufus Wainwright.

MARIA MAGDELENA. ("Mary Magdalene"). One of two Eurovision songs with the same title. One was performed in German by Tony Wagas, representing Austria with music by Christian Kolonovits and Johann Berti and words by Thomas Spitzer (Jerusalem, 1999), and the other representing Croatia, by the Croatian "queen of pop," Doris Dragović, with music composed by Tonči Huljić and lyrics by Vjekoslava Huljić (County Cork, Ireland, 1993). In the latter, the words are spoken in first-person narration, with allusions to Christ ("Your love got me crucified and I've been lost but now I'm found") and a dramatic chorus repeating the Magdalene's name.

MARIE-MAGDALEINE. Popular oratorio for soloists (SATB), chorus, and orchestra by Jules Massenet (1871–1872) to a libretto by Louis Gallet, based on Ernest Renan's *La Vie de Jésus* (1863). Premiered at the Théatre National de l'Odéon, Paris (1873), it was one of Massenet's most popular oratorios among 19th-century Parisian audiences and critics. Inspired by the biblical story of Mary Magdalene, the reformed prostitute, it is in three acts: act 1: "Mary Magdalene at the Well"; act 2: "Jesus at the House of Mary Magdalene"; and act 3: "Golgotha, the Magdalene at the Cross, the Tomb of Jesus and the Resurrection." The air and chorus *"O mes soeurs,"* which features at the beginning of act 1, is one of the most memorable numbers in the oratorio and features on the album *Amoureuse: Sacred and Profane Arias by Jules Massenet* (2008), sung by the renowned Australian soprano Rosamund Illing.

MARY. Song by folksinger/songwriter Patty Griffin from the album *Flaming Red* (1998) telling of Mary's grief and loss after Jesus' violent death on the cross. *See also* STABAT MATER DOLOROSA.

MARY, DID YOU KNOW? Christmas song by Buddy Greene (1984) set to music by Mark Lowry and first performed by Michael English on the album *Michael English* (1992). It was later performed by country music singer Kathy Mattea on the album *Good News* (1993) and as a duet by Wynonna Judd and country music superstar Kenny Rogers on the albums *The Gift* (1996) and *The Bible: Music Inspired by the Epic Miniseries* (2013). Each line asks, "Mary, did you know that your baby boy would . . . walk on water . . . calm the storm . . . heal the blind" (Mt. 14), and the piece concludes by asking her if she knew that her sleeping child was "Lord of Creation," "Heaven's perfect Lamb" (Rev. 21:22), and "Great I am" (Exod. 3:14–15).

MARY MARY. Sound track for the supernatural thriller *Stigmata* (1999), written by Chumbawamba, a British alternative rock band. Sung in the first person, it opens with a spoken recitation of the "Hail Mary" (Lk. 1:28–35, 42–48), followed by a description of the narrator's wanton life, and concludes with an allusion to "Bloody Mary" and her reign of persecution through the opening lines of the nursery rhyme "Mary Mary quite contrary." Lyrics describe the possession and persecution of the protagonist's body by an evil spirit as it periodically etches the stigmata on her flesh (Gal. 6:17), and a repeated recitation of the "Hail Mary" implores Jesus' mother to save her persecuted soul. The film's third sound track, *O Sacrum Convivium*, is a musical setting by Thomas Tallis (published 1575) honoring the Eucharist as a banquet, memorial, and sacrifice, calling to mind the Last Supper (Mt. 26:17–30; Mk. 14:12–26; Lk. 22:7–39; Jn. 13:1–17:26).

MARY'S LAMENT. Song for soprano and orchestral accompaniment by Irish songwriter Brendan Graham, performed by Fionnuala Gill on the Secret Garden album *Winter Poem* (2011). Scored in compound duple time, it is both a gentle lullaby sung by Mary to the Christ child as he lies sleeping in the manger and a sorrowful lament for her son, whose passion and death she foresees (Lk. 2:35).

MAYIM BE-SASSON. ("Water with Joy"). Popular Hebrew song and dance tune originally composed in 1937 for a festival celebrating the discovery of water in the desert. Based on a verse from Isaiah, "Joyfully shall you draw water from the fountains of triumph" (Isa. 12:3, JPS), the refrain consists of the word *mayim mayim* ("water water") sung repeatedly, followed by *be-sason* ("in joy").

MEDITATIONS ON ECCLESIASTES. (Originally "Variations on a Theme"). Orchestral work by American composer Norman Dello Joio for string orchestra, derived from his dance work composition *There is a Time*, inspired by Eccl. 3:1–8. Divided into 12 sections, each one is marked with an appropriate tempo marking to capture the contrasting moods of the biblical text. Thus, section 3, *Solenne* ("Solemn") poignantly illustrates Eccl. 3:2, "a time to die," and section 9, *Spumante* ("Sparkling") represents the liveliness of Eccl. 3:4, "a time to dance" and "a time to laugh." The final section, *Adagio semplice*, based on Eccl. 3:8, concludes with a lush solo cello accompanied by strings depicting the spirit of love and peace. First performed at the Juilliard in New York on 20 April 1956, it won the Pulitzer Prize in 1957.

MEMBRA JESU NOSTRI. ("The Limbs of Our Jesus"). A cycle of seven cantatas for five voices (SSATB), two violins, viol consort (Cantata 6), and basso continuo by Dietrich Buxtehude, regarded as the first Lutheran oratorio (BuxWV75, 1689). Based on a medieval poem, attributed variously to Arnulf of Leuven and Bernard of Clairvaux, it is a mystical meditation, quoting biblical texts, on the seven wounds of Christ: on his feet (*Ad pedes*) (Nah. 1:15), knees (*Ad genua*) (Isa. 66:12), hands (*Ad manus*) (Zech. 13:6), side (*Ad latus*) (Cant. 2:13–14), breast (*Ad pectus*) (1 Pet. 2:2–3), heart (*Ad cor*) (Cant. 4:9), and face (*Ad faciem*) (Ps. 31:16). Each cantata is divided into six (Cantatas 2–7) or seven parts (adding Cantata 1), opening with an instrumental (sonata), followed by a choral setting of the poem with instrumental accompaniment (concerto) and arias scored for a soloist or various combinations of voices. All the cantatas conclude with a return to the opening choral movement (concerto) except the last one, which ends with an extended **Amen**. Cantata 6 ("the heart"), the only one scored in sharps and with a five-part viol consort in place of the violins for added poignancy, ends with the serene chorus (*vulnerasti cor meum* ["you have wounded my heart"]) in slow tempo, played in tremolo style to suggest the heartbeats of the dying Christ. The most famous adaptation is the hymn **O Sacred Head, sore Wounded** (*O Haupt voll Blut und Wunden*) taken from the final cantata ("the face").

MERCY SEAT, THE. Song by Nick Cave and Mick Harvey performed by Nick Cave and the Bad Seeds on the album *Tender Prey* (1988) and later by Johnny Cash on the album *American III: Solitary Man* (2000). Inspired by the biblical image of the mercy seat, or throne of God, in the Holy of Holies sanctuary (Heb. 9:5; cf. Exod. 25:17–22), it tells of an innocent man on death row facing execution. The refrain refers to the electric chair as the mercy seat ("And the mercy seat is waiting") and quotes the *lex talionis* ("law of retaliation"): "An eye for and eye and a tooth for a tooth" (Exod. 21:24).

MESSIAH. Handel's best-known work, first performed in Dublin in 1742 and subsequently by amateur and professional choirs worldwide, especially at Christmas, as the world's best-loved oratorio. The libretto by Charles Jennens makes brilliant use of Scripture, selected from the Anglican Prayer Book, to prove the truth of the Gospel against 18th-century rationalists. It inspired Handel to compose the music for it, much of it strikingly original, in a few weeks. After an orchestral overture that moves from a slow, sighing, mournful elegy (grave) to an allegro expressing the violent, fruitless, upward striving of the oppressed, part 1 announces the coming of the Messiah in words taken mostly from Isaiah (Isa. 40:1–5, 11; 7:14; 60:1–3; 9:2, 6; 35:5–6) and Luke (Lk. 2:8–13). Part 2 considers the suffering death and resurrection of Christ in words, again, mostly from Isaiah (Isa. 53:3–6, 8; 50:6) and Psalms (Pss. 22:7–8; 24:7–10; 2:1–4, 9), ending with the "**Hallelujah** chorus" from

Revelation (Rev. 19:6, 16; 11:15). Part 3 is a hymn of thanksgiving based on passages from the Burial Service (Job 19:25–26; 1 Cor. 15:20–22, 51–57), with a closing doxology from Revelation (Rev. 5:12–14). It is said that some of the most important arias were written for the celebrated contralto Mrs. Susanna Maria Cibber, including "O thou that tellest good tidings to Zion" (Isa. 40:9) and "He was despised and rejected" (Isa. 53:3), while the fact that the first performance in Dublin in 1742 was in aid of charity and that an important subsequent performance took place at the Foundlings' Hospital in London in 1750, highlights expressions of compassion for the poor evident in such arias as "He shall feed his flock' (Isa. 40:11) (A) and the chorus "Surely he hath borne our griefs" (Isa. 53:4–5).

MICHAEL ROW THE BOAT ASHORE. African American spiritual published in *Slave Songs of the United States* (1867), the first published collection of African American music, edited by Allen, Garrison, and Ware. Sung in a call-and-response pattern, it is a classic example of a traditional work song calling on the archangel Michael (Dan. 12:1; cf. Josh. 5:13–15) to assist in rowing the boat across the River Jordan and deliver the souls of the faithfully departed on their journey homeward to heaven. It has been performed by many artists, including Pete Seeger (1963), and by Rufus Wainwright and others as a tribute to Pete Seeger on his 90th birthday in a concert at Madison Square Garden (2009).

MINE EYES HAVE SEEN THE GLORY. *See* BATTLE HYMN OF THE REPUBLIC, THE.

MIRACLE MAKER, THE. Animated movie written by Murray Watts and directed by Derek Hayes and Stanislav Sokolov (2000) recounting the life of Christ through the eyes of the "terminally ill" daughter of Jairus (Mark 5:22–43), named Tamar in the movie. It features the voices of many well-known actors, including Ralph Fiennes (Jesus), William Hurt (Jairus), Ian Holm (Pilate), Julie Christie (Rachel), Richard E. Grant (John the Baptist), and Miranda Richardson (Mary Magdalene). The music was composed by Anne Dudley, and the movie ends with a sublime setting of the **Pie Jesu** for boy soprano and orchestra.

MIRIAM'S SONG. Song by Debbie Friedman, Jewish singer, songwriter, choral conductor, and educator. In the style of a folk song, Miriam's joyful song of praise after the crossing of the Red Sea (Exod. 15:20–21) is portrayed by strummed guitar, rhythmic piano, and percussive instruments in the refrain, together with a quaver melody line in the verses. It was recorded live at Carnegie Hall in 1999 and released in the year of her death on the album *Debbie Friedman: Live at Carnegie Hall* (2011). It calls to mind the Jewish Passover song *Miriam HaNevia* ("Miriam the Prophet"). Miriam's song (Exod. 15:21) has also been popularly set to music by Franz Schubert in **Mirjams Siegesgesang** and, more recently, by John Flaherty and Aaron Keyes.

MIRJAMS SIEGESGESANG. ("Miriam's Victory Song"). Cantata in 10 continuous movements for soprano soloist, SATB chorus, and piano by Franz Schubert (D. 942, Post. 136, 1828) based on a text by the poet Franz Grillparzer (1791–1872). Inspired by the "Song of the Sea" (Exod. 15:1–21), it is characterized by a variety of moods but opens and closes with the soprano's joyful song, reiterated by the chorus "Strike the cymbals, sound the strings." Memorable moments include movement 2 ("Out of Egypt before his people, like a shepherd with his staff for protection") in pastoral compound duple time and movement 6 ("It is the Lord in his wrath"), in which the musical texture gradually builds up to depict the "towers of water" caving in to drown "man and horse, steed and rider," and it concludes with the chorus singing in slow, somber homophony, "the drivers and teams are dead." In movement 7, the soprano solo at a low tessitura, "Will you resurface, Pharaoh? Down you go," is repeated by the chorus with descending melody lines depicting Pharaoh's body sinking to the bottom of the sea.

MISERERE MEI. ("Have Mercy on Me"). One of the ***Penitential Psalms*** (Ps. 51). The best-known setting is the last and most popular of 12 *falsobordone* settings by Gregorio Allegri (1614–1638). Written for two choirs of four and five voices, which alternated *falsobordone* with monophonic chant, up to the 1870s it was performed exclusively by the Papal Choir in the Sistine Chapel in complete darkness at the end of the Tenebrae Service in Holy Week. The ornamentations (*abbellimenti*) that were added to the *falsobordone* were never written down, and transcription was forbidden on pain of excommunication. It was supposedly copied from memory after a single hearing by the 14-year-old Mozart, who later gave it to Charles Burney, who had it published in 1771 without the elaborate ornamentation. It was later transcribed by Felix Mendelssohn (1831) and Franz Liszt (1862). Other popular settings include a canon (Z. 109) by Henry Purcell, a chorus for three mixed SATB a cappella choruses and boys' chorus (SSAA) by Penderecki as part of his **Passion According to St. Luke** (1965), a setting for eight-part chorus by Gorecki (1981), a cello solo by Rudi Tas (2003), and a setting for a cappella chorus by James MacMillan (2011).

MISS PERSIA. Musical comedy by Canadian composer Eyal Bitton based on the Book of Esther. The orphan Hadassah/Esther, raised by her cousin

Mordecai, wins a "Miss Persia Contest" and as her prize marries King Ahasuerus (Xerxes) and becomes queen of Persia. When the wicked Haman plotted to kill all the Jews in the Persian Empire following Mordecai's refusal to bow down to him, she intervenes to save the life of her people. A cross between *Aladdin* and *My Fair Lady*, this Disney-type musical was premiered in Toronto on 16 March 2008. *See also* ESTHER.

MOÏSE: BALLET SYMPHONIQUE FOR ORCHESTRA. Concert suite in nine movements, also known as *Opus Americanum* no. 2, by Darius Milhaud (op. 219, 1940), performed as a ballet in 1950 by the Rome Opera Ballet and later in 1957 by the ballet of La Scala with choreography by Aurel von Milloss. After an overture depicting the slavery of the Israelites in Egypt, it tells the biblical story of Moses from his birth and adoption by the Egyptian Princess (II. *Modéré*) to his death on Mount Nebo (Deut. 34) (IX. *Modéré*).

MORNING HAS BROKEN. Hymn written by Eleanor Farjeon and sung to the Gaelic folk tune "Bunessan," first published in *Lachlan Macbean's Songs and Hymns of the Gael* (1888) and popularized in 1970 by Yusuf Islam (Cat Stevens). Inspired by Gen. 2, the opening broken arpeggio paints the rising of the sun in the Garden of Eden, while the triple dance-like meter recounts Adam and Eve's delight in the sights and sounds of the first morning, including the dew on the grass and the blackbird's dawn chorus. The tune was associated with the Christmas carol "Christ in the manger, Infant of Mary" by Mary Macdonald and later with the hymn "Christ Be Beside Me," known also as "St. Patrick's Breastplate."

MORS ET VITA: A SACRED TRIOLOGY. ("Death and Life"). Oratorio in Latin for STB soloists, chorus, and orchestra by Gounod, written as a sequel to **The Redemption** (1882) and first performed at the Birmingham Festival on 26 August 1885. The prologue, "A fearful thing, to fall into the Hands of the living God" (Heb. 10:31), contains the "death motif," a sequence of three major seconds sung in unison by the chorus, and a baritone solo in C, "I am the Resurrection and the Life" (Jn. 11:25–26). The oratorio is then in three parts. Part 1, entitled "Death" (*Mors*), is a Requiem Mass, followed by part 2, entitled "Judgement" (*Judicium*), which opens with a gentle adagio played by the orchestra to reflect the movement's title, "The Sleep of the Dead," but in the second section, *molto moderato e maestoso*, the interval of the augmented fifth symbolizes the awakening of the dead (1 Cor. 15:52; 1 Thess. 4:16), and "The Trumpets at the Last Judgement" (Rev. 8:7–11:19) are represented by trumpets, trombones, and tubas. Part 2 contains settings of verses from Mt. 25:31–46 and Rev. 4, leading to an exquisite soprano solo, "The Righteous shall enter into Glory eternal" (Mt. 25:46), followed by a chorus, "In remembrance everlasting." Part 3 (*Vita*) is based on an apocalyptic vision of a "New Heaven, New Earth" (Rev. 21:1) and the "Celestial Jerusalem" (Rev. 21:10–27) and concludes with three magnificent choruses: "I am the Alpha and the Omega" (Rev. 22:13), "Lo, the Tabernacle of God is with men" (Rev. 21:3), and "Hosanna in Excelsis" (Mt. 21:9; Mk. 11:10).

MOSES. Musical by Canadian composer Eyal Bitton (2004). Based on the biblical account of the life of **Moses** (Exod. 2–15), it tells of his childhood in the Egyptian royal household, the murder of the Egyptian taskmaster, his flight to Midian, and his return to Egypt, where he unites with his family and frees the Israelites from slavery. Notable songs include "Worthless slave" and "Here I am." *See also* ECCOMI; HERE I AM LORD.

MOSES. Song by alternative rock band Coldplay (2003), inspired by the actress Gwyneth Paltrow, wife of lead singer Chris Martin. Telling of the power of falling in love with the most beautiful woman in the world, the title alludes to the name of the couple's second child and draws a parallel between the power of Moses over the sea (Exod. 13:17–14:29) and Paltrow's power over her husband.

MOSES: A BIBLICAL ORATORIO. Oratorio in four parts for soloists, chorus, orchestra, harp, and organ by Max Bruch (op. 67) to a libretto by Ludwig Spitta, premiered on 19 January 1895 in Bremen, Germany. Scored for Moses (B), Aaron (T), the Angel of the Lord (S), and the People of Israel (Chorus), it recounts four events from the life of Moses: *Am Sinai* ("At Sinai") (Exod. 19; 34:28); *Das goldene Kalb* ("The Golden Calf") (Exod. 32); *Die Rückkehr der Kundschafter aus Kanaan* ("The Return of the Spies from Canaan"), including the battle with the Amalekites (Deut. 25:12–19; Num. 13–14); and *Das Land der Verheissung* ("The Promised Land") (Deut. 34:4; Exod. 34; Jos. 4:1). Memorable numbers include the chorus (*Also starb Moses, der Knecht des Herrn* ["So died Moses the Man of God"]), followed by the people's lament and their journey onward to the Promised Land.

MOSES IN EGYPT. (*Mosè in Egitto*). A three-act bel canto opera by Rossini (op. 24, 1818), with an Italian libretto by Andrea Leone Tottola, premiered on 5 March 1818 at the Teatro San Carlos in Naples, Italy. It was revised in 1827 with a French libretto and the new title *Moïse et Pharaon, ou Le passage de la Mer Rouge* ("Moses and Pharaoh, or The Crossing of the Red Sea"). Based on the play *L'Osiride* by Francesco Ringhieri (1760) and the biblical story, it opens with the plague of darkness (Exod. 10:21–29) and closes with the parting of the Red Sea (Exod. 14–15). It introduces into the story a tragic romance between the Egyptian prince Osiride (T) and the Hebrew girl Elcia (S). The haunting Prayer of Moses (B), *Dal tuo stellato soglio* ("From thy starry throne"), with SATB chorus, is one of the most popular numbers in the opera, frequently performed on its own in Italy, and was arranged by Paganini for cello and piano in "Introduction and Variations on *Dal tuo stellato soglio*," "Mosè-Fantasia" (op. 24, MS 23) and as a fantasia for piano (op. 33).

MOSES UND ARON. ("Moses and Aaron"). Unfinished opera/oratorio in three acts by Schoenberg, regarded as a 20th-century masterpiece. The libretto, which was written by Schoenberg, was completed in 1928 and the music for acts 1 and 2 with sketched fragments for act 3 in 1932, but the first staged performance was at the Zurich Stadttheater on 6 June 1957, six years after the composer's death. A performing version of act 3 was more recently completed by Zoltán Kocsis (2010). The work, which calls for elaborate staging, including a procession of camels, asses, and horses, is scored for numerous soloists, including an ensemble of six (SMezATBarB) to sing the voice coming from the burning bush, 70 elders (basses), 12 tribal leaders (tenors and basses), dancers, and other naked people for the scene of the Golden Calf as well as three choruses and a large orchestra. The opposition between Moses and Aron is emphasized by scoring the part of Moses in *Sprechstimme*, with one optional phrase scored for him to sing and the fluid singing part for Aron for bel canto tenor, the only lead singing role in the opera. Structured according to the principles of twelve-tone serialism, the entire work is based on a single tone row. It has been suggested that Schoenberg also dropped the second "a" in "Aaron" to ensure that he had 12 rather than 13 letters in the title. Based on the biblical story of Moses, from his call by God (Exod. 3) (act 1) to the Golden Calf episode (Exod. 32) (act 2) and the death of Aron (Num. 33) (act 3), the work focuses on personality clashes between Moses (speaker), Aron (T), and the people; the inability of Moses to communicate; and the absence of Moses contrasted with the presence of Aron and the people's need for a visible God, Aaron's Golden Calf over the invisible God of Moses. Act 1, which comprises six scenes, opens with the scene of the burning bush (Exod. 3). It depicts Moses praying to God (*einziger, ewiger, allgegenwärtiger, unsichtbarer und unvorstellbarer* ["Only one, infinite, thou omnipresent one, unperceived and inconceivable God"]) and the voice of God (Die Stimme), scored in *Sprechstimme* for four and then six singers, echoed by six singers from the orchestra, speaking with and calling on Moses to become the leader of the Chosen People. Act 1 treats Moses' meeting with Aaron in the wilderness, the establishment of their relationship, and bringing God's word to the people, and in the final scene, it describes the miracles of the leprous hand, the rod that changes into a serpent, and the transformation of water into blood. The interlude between acts 1 and 2 describes the absence of Moses from the Chosen People, when he sojourned for 40 days on Mount Sinai, sung by the chorus as questions: *Wo ist Moses?* ("Where is Moses?") (whispered) and *Wo ist sein Gott?* ("Where is his God?"). Act 2 includes the magnificent scene of the Golden Calf (Aron: *Volk Israels! Deine Götter geb ich dir wieder und dich ihnen* ["O Israel! I return your gods to you and also give you to them"]), after which the orgies take place, including the Orgy of Drunkenness and Dancing, the Orgy of Destruction and Suicide with wild dancing, and the Erotic Orgy, in which a succession of naked people run past the altar. Moses descends from the mountain (scene 4), destroys the golden image (*Vergeh, du Abbild des Unvermögens, das Grenzenlose in ein Bild zu fassen!* ("Begone you image of powerlessness to enclose the boundless in a finite image"), and remonstrates with Aaron. It concludes with his words *O Wort, du Wort, das mir fehlt?* ("O word, thou word that I lack") as he sinks to the ground in despair.

MUSIC INSPIRED BY THE STORY. Eighteen songs by lyricist Nichole Nodeman to music by Bernie Herms written in first-person narration expressing the thoughts of various biblical characters, including Adam and Eve, Abraham and Sarah, Moses, Ruth, Esther, the Virgin Mary, Jesus, one of the thieves crucified with Jesus, Mary Magdalene, and Paul. The sequence begins with an overture ("I am") based on Gen. 1 and concludes with "The Great Day," announcing the Second Coming of Christ. Produced by World Vision, Zondervan, EMI Christian Music Group, Provident Label Group, Word Entertainment, Proper Management, and CAA (2011), the songs are performed by a host of well-known artists.

MUSIKALISCHE EXEQUIEN. ("Musical Obsequies" or "Funeral Music"). A collection of three motets for six singers and/or SATTBB chorus and continuo by Heinrich Schütz (SWV 279–281, op. 7, 1636) commissioned by Prince Heinrich von Reuss for a performance at his own funeral. Described as a "German Requiem," the first motet begins with a "Kyrie" made up of biblical passages about death sung by soloists (Job 1:21; Phil. 1:21; Jn. 1:29) alternating with paraphrases of the Kyrie sung by the chorus (SSATTB) and a "Gloria" made up biblical passages about the Resurrection (e.g., Jn. 3:16; Isa. 26:19; Job 19:25–26) alternating with hymns by Martin Luther and others. The second motet for double chorus is based on Ps. 73:25–26, and the final motet comprises two choruses, one sung by SATTB based on the **Song of Simeon** (Lk. 2:29–32) and the other sung by SSB based on "Blessed are the Dead" (Rev. 14:13; Wisd. 3:1).

MY BELOVED IS MINE. Canticle in four sections for tenor and piano by Benjamin Britten (op. 40, no. 1, 1947), written for the memorial concert of Dick Sheppard, founder of the Peace Pledge Union. It is a setting of the poem "A Divine Rapture" by Francis Quarles (1592–1644), which was inspired by a phrase from the Song of Songs (Cant. 2:16) and clearly alludes to Britten's relationship with Peter Pears. Modeled on Purcell's "Divine Hymns," it begins with a flowing Barcarolle ("Ev'n like two little band-dividing brooks"), followed by a short recitative ("If all those glitt'ring monarchs") and a canonic scherzo ("Nor time, nor place, nor chance, nor death"), and ends with a tender epilogue ("He is my Altar, I, his Holy Place"). Each section ends with a version of the phrase "I my best beloved's am." *See also* DODI LI; MY BELOVED SPAKE.

MY BELOVED SPAKE. Verse anthem in five movements for CtTBB chorus, strings, and continuo by Purcell (Z. 28, before 1678), one of the earliest existing works by the then 18-year-old composer. Based on verses from the Song of Solomon (Cant. 2:10–13,16), it depicts the end of winter and the beginning of spring with vivid word painting. After a symphony (an instrumental), the quartet "My beloved spake and said unto me: Rise my love, my fair one and come away" (Cant. 2:10) stresses the word "rise," distributed between the voices. In movement 2, the subdued minor tonality and dissonances of the beloved's words "For lo! The Winter is past, the rain is over and gone" contrasts with the major tonality of "The flowers appear on the earth," while in movement 3, "the singing of birds" figure is repeated and illustrated musically by a dotted quaver and semiquaver figure. An upbeat **Hallelujah** sung by the quartet is based on the "singing of birds" figure. Following another short symphony (instrumental), the winding motion of the violin obbligato accompanying the tenor in the fourth movement, "The fig tree putteth forth her green figs," imitates the shape of the fig tree, and the work concludes with "My beloved is mine and I am his" and another joyful **Hallelujah** sung by the soloists and repeated by the chorus. There is also a setting by Patrick Hadley (1939).

MY HEART IS INDITING. Coronation anthem in four parts for mixed chorus (SAATB) and orchestra (HWV 261, no. 4, 1727), by Handel, performed at the coronation service of King George II and Queen Caroline in Westminster Abbey (1727) and specifically at the coronation of the queen. Based on verses from Ps. 45 and Isaiah, it opens with an air of royal grace (Ps. 45:1) followed by two lyrical movements, "Kings' daughters" and "Upon thy right hand" (Ps. 45:9), and ends spectacularly with blazing ceremonial trumpets in "Kings shall be thy nursing fathers" (Isa. 49:23). An anthem by Purcell, composed for the coronation of King James II in 1685, is a setting of the same text but contains a verse from Psalm 147 (Ps. 147:2), missing from Handel's version.

MYSTERY SONATAS, THE. Fifteen short suites for violin and continuo composed by Heinrich Ignaz Franz von Biber (1644–1704). Also known as the *Rosary Sonatas* and the *Copper-Plate Engraving Sonatas*, as each sonata is prefaced by a small engraving, they are dedicated to Prince Archbishop Maximilian Gandolph von Kuenburg and were possibly written for the Salzburg Rosary devotions held during the month of October. Each "Mystery" forms a meditation on an aspect of the life of Jesus and his mother, Mary, arranged in three groups of five: the Joyful Mysteries (Annunciation, Lk. 1:26–38; Nativity, Lk. 2:1–21, etc.), the Sorrowful Mysteries (Agony in the Garden, Mt. 26:36–46 and Lk. 22:39; Crowning of Thorns, Mt. 27:27–30, Mk. 15:16–20, Jn. 19:2, etc.), and the Glorious Mysteries (Resurrection, Mt. 28:1–8, Mk. 16:1–18, Lk. 24:1–12, Jn. 20:1–29; Assumption). Biber used a variety of musical rhetorical devices to sound paint the content and mood of each mystery. In the first sonata, for example, the Annunciation, a fluttering semiquaver melody, announces the arrival of the angel Gabriel, and in the first movement of the Crucifixion (X), the rhythm of the continuo replicates the hammering of nails into Jesus' hands and feet. Major and minor tonalites are sometimes used to good effect, as in the Annunciation (I) and the Nativity (III), both of which, despite the joyous occasions, in a minor key, point forward to the suffering and death of Christ. For the same reason, the adagio from the Crucifixion (X) is present in both the Nativity (II) and the Presentation in the Temple (VI). Biber also uses the *scordatura* technique to suggest the strain Jesus felt as he carried the cross (IX) and the excruciating pain he suffered as the crown of thorns pierced his flesh (XIII). The extensive use of *anabasis* in Sonata V signifies the rising panic and ecstatic joy of Mary and Joseph on losing and finding Jesus in the Temple, while *katabasis* signifies blood falling from his brow in the Agony in the Garden (VI).

• N •

NAAMAN. Oratorio for soloists, chorus, and orchestra by Michael Costa (1864) with a libretto by William Bartholomew, dedicated to the memory of the Prince Consort and premiered in Birmingham in 1866. Based on the biblical story of the miracles performed by the prophet Elisha, part 1 begins with Elijah's ascension to heaven witnessed by Elisha (B) and the chorus of the sons of the prophets (2 Kgs. 2) and then tells of the widow (A) and her miraculous cruse of oil (2 Kgs. 4:1–7). Elisha comes to the house of the Shunammite Timna (A) and his wife (S) and in return for hospitality promises that she will have a child. The Syrian Naaman (T) arrives, suffering from leprosy, and Adah (S), a Jewish captive, suggests that he ask Elisha to heal him. Part 2 opens with the lament of the Shunammite woman over the death of her son and her appeal to Elisha for help. Elisha miraculously brings him back to life (2 Kgs. 4:32–37) and then instructs Naaman to wash seven times in the River Jordan to cure his leprosy (2 Kgs. 5:1–14). He reluctantly does this, and the work ends with a quintet and chorus of praise. *See* ELISHA.

NAAMAN THE LEPER. Chancel oratorio in costume by Susan Hulsman Bingham, premiered in the Episcopalian Church of the Mediator in Allentown, Pennsylvania, in 2012. Scored for adult soloists, treble chorus, piano, tambourine, and triangle or hand cymbals, it tells the story of Naaman (Bar), valiant commander of the army of the king of Aram, who contracts leprosy, seeks the help of the prophet Elisha (Bar), and reluctantly follows his instructions to immerse himself in the River Jordan. His miraculous return to health persuades him to believe in the Israelite God (2 Kgs. 5:1–19). *See* ELISHA.

NABUCCO. Opera in four acts by Verdi, first performed in Milan in 1842. Based loosely on the biblical story of Nabucco (Nebuchadnezzar), king of Babylon, it tells of the destruction of Jerusalem and exile of the Israelites in Babylon (Jer. 21:10), where Nabucco (Bar) goes mad for a time and then converts to Judaism (Dan. 4:28–37). The Babylonian idol crashes to the ground (Jer. 50:2), and the Israelites are free. Running through the opera is the story of the love between Fenena (S), younger daughter of Nabucco, and the Israelite prince Ismaele (T) and the jealousy of the elder daughter Abigaille (S), who tries to have the Israelite prisoners executed. Fenena converts to Judaism like her father, while Abigaille is defeated in the end and commits suicide. The chorus of the Hebrew slaves, "Va pensiero," from the end of act 3, which recalls Ps. 137 ("**By the waters of Babylon**"), was sung spontaneously by the crowds at Verdi's funeral in 1901 and has been popular ever since.

NATIVITY ACCORDING TO ST. LUKE, THE. A musical drama in seven scenes for SATB chorus, soloists, and small orchestra by Randall Thompson (1961). Movements include Zacharias and the Angel, the Annunciation, the Visitation, the Naming of John, the Apparition, and the Adoration, and memorable moments include the **Magnificat** sung by the soprano soloist in scene 3 and Mary's lullaby "Upon my lap my sov'reign sits" in scene 6. It is popularly performed by youth and adult groups at Christmas.

NAZARETH. Christmas song by Gounod known also by the title *Jésus de Nazareth* (1856). The original French text by A. Porte was translated into English by Henry F. Chorley. Scored in verse–chorus format, it recounts Christ's lowly birth (Lk. 2:6–7), the angelic birth announcement to the shepherds (Lk. 2:8–14), the arrival of the **Three Kings** (Mt. 2:1–12), and Christ's second coming (2 Pet. 1:19; Rev. 22:16). More recently, it has been performed by Plácido Domingo on the album *Our Favourite Things* (2001) to an arrangement by French songwriter Patrice Guirao.

NEARER MY GOD TO THEE. Hymn by Sarah Flower Adams (1805–1848) inspired by Jacob's dream at Bethel (Gen. 28:10–20). It was first published by William John Fox in *Hymns and Anthems* (1841) and later set to music by Sullivan (1872) and Routley (1938). It is reputed to have been the last piece of music played on the *Titanic* before it sank.

NEW 23RD PSALM, THE. Song by Ralph Carmichael (1969) popularized by the Billy Graham crusades in the 1970s. Rewritten in contemporary English, the musical phrasing aids reflection on various key words and phrases. It features in "His Land," a documentary of Cliff Richard's visit to the Holy Land, and on an album by the same name (1970). *See also* THE LORD'S MY SHEPHERD.

NEW VERSION OF THE PSALMS OF DAVID, A. An influential metrical version of the Psalms by Nicholas Brady and Nahum Tate, first published in 1696. Among their compositions still popular in churches today are "As pants the hart" (Ps. 42) and "While humble shepherds watch their flocks" (Lk. 2:8–14).

NIGRA SUM. ("I Am Black"). Antiphon inspired by words from the Song of Solomon (Cant. 1:5, 2:10–12), interpreted in the Middle Ages as referring to the Virgin Mary as the Black Madonna, and sung at vespers on the Feast of the Blessed Virgin. There are numerous settings by Praetorius, Palestrina, Victoria, Vivaldi, Monteverdi, and others. Palestrina's is a five-part parody mass, published in 1590, and Pablo Casals's well-known setting for women's two-part chorus (1966) enables the woman's sweet voice to tell her sensuous tale to the Daughters of Jerusalem. *See also* DARK I AM BUT LOVELY.

NIMROD. Variation no. 9 (adagio) from the *Enigma Variations* by English composer Edward Elgar, it is one of his most widely performed works. The 14 variations are portraits of Elgar's close friends, framed by the first, dedicated to his wife, and last to the composer himself. "Nimrod" refers to the mighty hunter and great-grandson of Noah (Gen. 10:8–10; 1 Chron. 1:10), referring to Augustus Jaeger (1860–1909), a music publisher whose surname means "hunter" in German. Celebrating their shared love of Beethoven, this poignant variation reflects the second movement of Piano Sonata no. 8, the *Pathétique*, and is frequently played at funerals as well as at the annual Remembrance Day Service held at the Cenotaph in Whitehall to commemorate those who died in World War I.

NINE PSALM TUNES FOR ARCHBISHOP PARKER'S PSALTER. Nine Psalm tunes by Thomas Tallis (1567) published in the metrical Psalter of Archbishop Matthew Parker (1504–1575). They include, among others, "Why Fum'th in Fight" (Ps. 2), used by Vaughan Williams as the basis for his *Fantasia on a Theme by Thomas Tallis* (1910; rev. 1913), and "God Grant with Grace" (Ps. 67), also known as Tallis's Canon, sung as a tune for the hymn "Come, Holy Ghost, Creator, Come." *See also* VENI CREATOR SPIRITUS.

NIÑO, EL. ("The Child"). Staged oratorio, with accompanying film, by the American composer John Adams (2000). It retells the story of the Nativity in three languages—English, Spanish, and Latin—from the perspective of Mary and Joseph. Adams based his libretto on a wide variety of texts drawn from the Gospels of Matthew and Luke in the King James Bible translation, the apocryphal Gospel of James, the Wakefield mystery play, and Martin Luther's Christmas Sermon, along with poetry by Nobel Prize winner Gabriela Mistral (1899–1957), Rosario Castellanos, Sor Juana Inés de la Cruz, and Rubén Dario and texts by librettist Peter Sellars, whose accompanying film, set in Los Angeles in the 1990s, was projected as a backdrop during the performance. One of the most poignant moments in the piece is the juxtaposition of Hildegard of Bingen's **O quam preciosa** with Castellanos's poem "The Christmas Star," evoking Mary's ecstasy and pain at Christ's birth (Lk. 2:35).

NISI DOMINUS. ("Unless the Lord"). Motet in G minor for countertenor, strings, and continuo by Vivaldi (RV 608, ca. 1710s), one of the composer's longest motets for solo voice. It is a setting of Ps. 127 in nine movements. The doxology *Gloria Patri* ("Glory be to the Father") is uncharacteristically dark and meditative, while *Sicut erat in principio* ("As it was in the beginning") is a musical pun, returning as it does to the music of the opening movement. The concluding **Amen** is gloriously joyous. Other notable settings of Ps. 127 include those of Charpentier (H. 150 and H. 160), Monteverdi in his *Vespers* (1610), and Handel (HWV 241, 1707).

NOBLE JOSEPH, THE. (*Blagoobraznyj Josif*). Troparion (hymn) sung in the Russian Orthodox Church at great vespers on Holy Friday during the veneration of the Epitaphios, a cloth icon depicting an image of Christ's body. The hymn's somber mood reflects the sorrow of Joseph of Arimathea when he removed the body from the cross, wrapped it in linen, and laid it in his own tomb (Mk. 15:46).

NOLO MORTEM PECCATORIS. ("I Do Not Want a Sinner's Death"). Anthem for a cappella mixed chorus (SAB), attributed to Thomas Morley although more likely composed by John Redford, whose name appears on the score (1540). Based on the words of a macaronic poem, the verses in English, in first-person narration, are the imagined words of Christ as he contemplates his death in the Garden of Gethsemane (Mt. 26:36–46). The Latin title is from Ezek. 33:11.

NOTHING THAT IS, THE. Work for baritone solo, two narrators, chorus, and chamber ensemble by Libby Larsen (2004). The text is adapted from the *Apollo 13* flight transcript; the writings of Ptolemy, John Donne, Charles Pierce, and John F. Kennedy; and some biblical verses (Jn. 1:1; Pss. 90, 13, 131). The four parts, entitled "Logos," "To Zero," "Pure Zero," and "*Ad Astra Per Aspera*," are a reflection on the number 0, which exists ad infinitum, and the role of faith in survival. Each of the vocal parts assumes a role: the baritone as a guide, the narrators as astronauts and ground crew, and the chorus as the Greek chorus who sing the countdown for the launch as well as settings of the three Psalm texts. The work concludes with a resolution based on Ps. 13:5.

NOTRE PÈRE. A setting of **The Lord's Prayer** (Mt. 6:9–13) for a cappella SATB chorus by Duruflé (1978), originally scored for unison male chorus and organ (op. 14, 1977). The last and shortest work by the composer, it was composed after a serious car crash and is dedicated to his wife.

NOW THANK WE ALL OUR GOD. (*Nun danket alles Gott*). Popular hymn (ca. 1636) inspired by the great hymn of praise sung by Simon the high priest (Sir. 50:22–24). Written by Martin Rinkart around 1630, it was translated into English by Catherine Winkworth in the 19th century. The tune, attributed to Johann Crüger, appears in two of Bach's cantatas (BWV 79 and BWV 192) and three of his chorale preludes (BWV 252, BWV 386, and BWV 657); in Mendelssohn's second symphony, known as *Lobgesang* ("Hymn of Praise") (1840); and in one of Karg-Elert's chorale improvisations for organ (op. 65, no. 59).

NOYE'S FLUDDE. One-act opera by Benjamin Britten (op. 59, 1957) based on the text of the Chester mystery play, premiered at the Aldeburgh Festival in June 1958 in Orford Church. It was written for amateur performers, especially children, with some adults performing the roles of the Voice of God (spoken), Noye (B-Bar), Mrs. Noye (A), and others, and the orchestral accompaniment includes strings, organ, piano, and timpani, supplemented by recorders, bugles, handbells, and other percussion instruments to enable children to participate. It includes hymns for audience participation, such as the opening "Lord Jesus think on me," sung to the tune "Southwell" from *Damon's Psalter* (1579), and "Eternal Father Strong to Save," sung to Dykes's "Melita" during the storm scene. At the end, God's voice is heard, to the accompaniment of handbells, with the promise that there will be no more floods, and when the rainbow appears, the bells ring out in joyful chimes. The final thanksgiving, based on Tallis's Canon, is Joseph Addison's hymn "The Spacious Firmament on High" (from Ps. 19:1–3), sung first in unison by Noye's children and their wives to the accompaniment of strings and bells, followed by Noye and Mrs. Noye in unison with the addition of bugles and various other arrangements until the final verse is sung in eight-part canon, accompanied by the full orchestra, bells, bugles, and percussion. Finally, God's voice is heard for the last time with a blessing bestowed on Noah, against clanging bells, and the music broadens to a climax with bugles and cymbals that fade away in the distance.

NUMBER OF THE BEAST, THE. Song from Iron Maiden's seventh album and second single of the same name, one of their greatest hits on the charts in both the United Kingdom and the United States. Written by band member Steve Harris after watching the movie *Damien: Omen II* and inspired by the narrative poem "Tam o' Shanter" by Robert Burns (1759–1796), the song opens with text from the Book of Revelation (Rev. 12:12; 13:18), read by the actor Barry Clayton, and is renowned for the high-pitched guttural wail of singer Martin Birch, signifying perhaps Satan's deathly call. Performances feature videos of monsters and a ballroom dance routine by a couple each bearing the number 6 on their back and a gyrating red devil holding the number 6 in his hand.

NUNC DIMITTIS. ("Now Let Your Servant Depart"). Latin title of the song sung by the aged Simeon when he held the baby Jesus in his arms in the Temple at Jerusalem (Lk. 2:28–35). It features in the evening liturgy of many Christian traditions, East and West. Among the most popular settings are a plainchant theme by Thomas Tallis, Rachmaninoff's setting in his *Vespers* (1915), and a beautiful arrangement for eight voices a cappella by Holst. There are others by Victoria, Byrd, Mendelssohn, Stanford (1879), and Arvo Pärt (2001). A setting by Geoffery Burgon provided the incidental music for the successful television adaptation of John Le Carré's novel *Tinker Tailor Soldier Spy* (1979). *See also* LUMEN; SONG OF SIMEON.

• O •

O ANTIPHONS. Seven eighth-century prayers from the *Liturgy of the Hours* of the Roman Catholic Breviary, chanted or recited at vespers at Advent. They are so called because each one begins by addressing an attribute of the Messiah drawn from the prophecies of Isaiah: *O Sapientia* ("Wisdom") (Isa. 11:2–3), *O Adonai* ("Lord") (Isa. 11:4–5), *O Radix Jesse* ("Root of Jesse") (Isa. 11:1), *O Clavis David* ("Key of David") (Isa. 22:22), *O Oriens* ("Radiant Dawn") (Isa. 9:2), *O Rex Gentium* ("King of Nations") (Isa. 9:6), and *O Emmanuel* ("God with us") (Isa. 7:14). The initials form an acrostic that, when read backward, means "I come (will be) tomorrow" (Latin *ero cras*). They have been set to music by Marc-Antoine Charpentier, Arvo Pärt, Peter Hallock, and Roderick Williams and are the basis of the hymn **Veni, Veni Emmanuel** ("O come, O come Emmanuel").

O CLAP YOUR HANDS. Ascension anthem for eight-voice double chorus by Orlando Gibbons (1622), possibly written as an exercise for Gibbons's admission to the degree of doctor of music in Oxford (1622). Based on Ps. 47 with the lesser doxology at the end, it is regarded as a contrapuntal masterpiece with dramatic exchanges between the vocal parts, most notably on "O sing praises." There are many instances of word painting, such as a quarter note on "clap" to depict clapping and leaps of perfect fourths and fifths on "(God is) gone up." Other settings of Ps. 47 include an arrangement for SATB chorus and orchestra by Vaughan Williams (1920) and another for SATB (1920) chorus and orchestra by John Rutter (1973). Grammy Award–winning Christian music artist Israel Houghton has also recorded a setting entitled "Resurrection Power."

O COME, O COME EMMANUEL. Advent hymn from the 12th century originally written in Latin, **Veni, Veni Emmanuel**, and translated into English by John M. Neale in *Mediaeval Hymns* (1851). Based on a 15th-century French processional hymn, it first appeared in the 18th century in the *Psalteriolum Cantionum Catholicarum* (1770). Although there are many existing versions with variations in the number of verses, the text encapsulates the seven **O Antiphons** sung before and after the **Magnificat** at vespers during the octave before Christmas. The first verse of the hymn, the last of the **O Antiphons** sung on 23 December, recalls the Babylonian exile, while other verses refer to titles of the Messiah, such as "Emmanuel" (Isa. 7:14; Mt.

171

1:23), "rod of Jesse" (Isa. 11:1, 4), and "key of David" (Isa. 22:22). There have been numerous other translations, most notably by Thomas Alexander Lacey and Henry Sloane Coffin.

O GOD BEYOND ALL PRAISING. Popular hymn written by Canon Michael Parry (1982) to the tune "Thaxted" from Holst's orchestral suite *The Planets* (1914–1916), inspired by verses from Psalms (Pss. 5, 8, 33, 91, 104, 135, 138), Isaiah (Isa. 55:8), and numerous New Testament texts, including John, Romans, 1 and 2 Corinthians, Hebrews, and Revelation. The tune is best known from Holst's setting of the popular secular song by Cecil Spring-Rice "I vow to thee my country" (1908).

O GOD OF BETHEL. Paraphrase of Gen. 28:20–22 by Philip Doddridge (1702–1751) written to accompany a sermon entitled "Jacob's Vow," published posthumously in *Hymns Founded on Various Texts in the Holy Scriptures* (1755). The original version was later altered by Michael Bruce and then by John Logan, who falsely claimed it under his own name in the publication *Poems* (1781). Sung to a variety of tunes, including "Burford" by Henry Purcell and "Salzburg" by John Michael Haydn, it is frequently performed at state occasions, including the funeral services of Scottish missionary and explorer David Livingston (1873) and Britain's oldest prime minister, William Ewart Gladstone (1898), and the Silver Jubilee service of Queen Elizabeth II in 1977.

O GOD OUR HELP IN AGES PAST. Paraphrase of Ps. 90 by Isaac Watts (1719), originally entitled "Man frail and God eternal." The tune "St. Anne" was composed by William Croft in 1708, named after the Church of St. Anne in Soho, where he was organist at the time. It is often sung at Remembrance Day services and features in Evelyn Waugh's novel *Decline and Fall* (1928) and the film *Tom Jones* (1963).

O HAPPY DAY. Traditional gospel song popularly arranged by Edwin Hawkins in 1967, it is based on the 18th-century hymn "Rejoicing in our Covenant Engagements to God," inspired by 2 Chron. 15:12 and 15. The words were written by Philip Doddridge (1702–1751) and the music by J. A. Freylinghausen. The refrain "Oh Happy Day, Oh Happy Day, when Jesus washed my sins away" (Acts 22:16) was added later by Edward Francis Rimbault along with a melody adapted from the secular song tune "The Happy Land" (1854). In the 20th century, the original hymn verses were omitted, leaving Rimbault's refrain as the basis for the song. The upbeat melody, which is sung in a call-and-response pattern, conveys the joyful news of the fulfillment of the Old Covenant in the New. As a forerunner of pop songs naming Jesus, its first appearance on the album *Let Us Go into the House of the Lord* (1969) has been followed in recordings by hundreds of artists. More recently, it appeared in the movie *Sister Act 2: Back in the Habit* (1993).

O HAUPT VOLL BLUT UND WUNDEN. *See* O SACRED HEAD, SORE WOUNDED.

O HEARKEN THOU. Offertory anthem for chorus, organ, and orchestra by Elgar (op. 64) composed for the coronation of King George V in Westminster Abbey on 22 June 1911. The words are taken from a Psalm (Ps. 5:2–3).

O HOW AMIABLE ARE THY DWELLINGS. Anthem based on Ps. 84:1–2 and 13 for SAATB chorus by Thomas Weelkes and numerous other composers, including Thomas Tomkins, Robert Croft, Maurice Greene, Sebastian Wesley, Hubert Parry, Ralph Vaughan Williams (Pss. 84, 90), and John Rutter in *PsalmFest* (1993). The Latin version (*Quam dilecta tabernacula tua*) was set for baritone chorus, choir, organ, and grand organ by Widor (op. 23, no. 1, 1875) and by Kenneth Leighton for soprano, SATB chorus, and organ (1967). Settings in German include those of Brahms in his *German Requiem* (1866–1869), Josef Rheinberger (op. 35), and Heinrich Schütz as one of his **Psalmen Davids** (SWV 29, op. 2, no. 8, 1619). *See also* GERMAN REQUIEM, A.

O JONATHAN. Sacred madrigal for six voices (SSATB) a cappella by Thomas Weelkes (published 1622) based on David's lamentation for Jonathan (2 Sam. 1:25–26) and written in first-person narration. It was written in 1612 as a tribute to Prince Henry, son of James I. *See also* THEN DAVID MOURNED.

O LORD, GRANT THE KING A LONG LIFE. Coronation anthem for SATB/SATB choruses and organ by William Child, thought to have been performed during the procession into Westminster Abbey for the coronation of Charles II (23 April 1661). Based on Pss. 61:6–7 and 132:18, it is largely homophonic, alternating between two choirs, and concludes with an exuberant **Hallelujah**. Other settings include an anthem for ATB chorus, two violins, and continuo by Purcell (Z. 38, 1685), written when Charles II was gravely ill, and an anthem for chorus and orchestra by Thomas Attwood for the coronation of William IV (8 September 1831). Thomas Tomkins and Thomas Weelkes also composed settings.

O LORD IN THY WRATH. Anthem for SSAATB chorus a cappella by Orlando Gibbons based on Ps. 6:1–4. Dissonances and false relations capture the penitential mood of the Psalm and the anguish of the penitent praying to God for mercy.

O LORD MY GOD. Anthem for SATB chorus and organ by Samuel Sebastian Wesley based on Solomon's prayer from 1 Kgs. 8:28 and 30. The meditative work reaches a climax toward the end with Solomon's plaintive request for God's forgiveness.

O LORD OUR GOVERNOR. Anthem by Healey Willan composed for the coronation of Queen Elizabeth II (1953). It is a setting of Ps. 8 in the 1552 *Book of Common Prayer* translation. Other settings of Ps. 8 include a verse anthem for three trebles and two bass soloists and chorus by Purcell (Z. 141), an Anglican chant by Henry Lawes (1596–1662), and a *fauxbourdon* setting by Gerre Hancock (1998).

O LORD THE MAKER OF ALL THINGS. Anthem by William Mundy (1548), a gentleman of Queen Elizabeth's Chapel Royal, to a text ascribed to King Henry VIII in the *King's Primer* (1545). It is an English translation of the office hymn for compline beginning *Te lucis ante terminum* ("To thee before the close of day") with a title inspired by Isa. 44:24. Other settings include those of Thomas Tallis and, more recently, John Joubert (1952).

O LORD THOU ART MY GOD. Verse anthem for SSAATTBB choir and organ by Samuel Sebastian Wesley, performed in Magdalen Chapel, Oxford, in 1839. His longest anthem, it begins with two choral settings of verses from Isa. 25, "O Lord thou art my God" (vv. 1, 4) and "He will swallow up death for ever" (v. 8), with a short bass solo from Psalms, "For our heart shall rejoice in him" (Ps. 33:21–22), in between. Verses from 1 Corinthians 15 (vv. 53, 34, 51–52) are then sung by a five-part choir (SSATB), and the work ends with a return to Isa. 25 and an elaborate chorus for eight parts, ending fortissimo, "This, this is the Lord, and he will save us" (v. 9).

O MAGNUM MYSTERIUM. ("O Great Mystery"). The fourth responsorial chant for matins on Christmas Day highlighting the mystery of Christ's incarnation among the lowly animals (Hab. 3:2 Lxx; Isa. 1:3) and the adoration of the Blessed Virgin Mary (Lk. 1:28). There are numerous settings, most notably in the 16th century by Cristóbal de Morales, Palestrina, Byrd, Victoria, and Giovanni Gabrieli and in the 20th century by Poulenc (1952), Pierre Villette (1983), John Harbison (1991–1992), Frank La Rocca (2003),

Judith Bingham (1995), and Morten Lauridsen (1994). Lauridsen's motet for unaccompanied SATB *divisi* choir was commissioned by Marshall Rutter in honor of his wife, Terry Knowles, and was premiered by the Los Angeles Master Chorale in 1994. Scored in D major to a largely homophonic texture, appoggiaturas, seconds, and ninths serenely evoke the opening of heaven's boundaries and the mystery of Christ's birth. A single G sharp appoggiatura sung by the altos on *virgo* injects a momentary stab of pain into the music as the Virgin foresees the Passion (Lk. 2:35) before resolving to the dominant to express her jubilation at the birth of her beloved son. There are two contrasting recitations of the **Alleluia**, the first sung fortissimo and the second sung piano and pianissimo at the very end, fading away as if to illustrate the return of the choirs of angels to heaven and the closure of heaven's boundaries.

O NATA LUX. ("O Light Born"). Anonymous 10th-century hymn in seven verses sung at the office of Lauds on the Feast of the Transfiguration. Thomas Tallis set the first two verses in a through-composed motet for SATTB a cappella chorus, published in *Cantiones sacrae* (1575). Based on the story of Christ's transfiguration (Mt. 17:2; Lk. 29:9; cf. Jn. 8:12), it expresses the believer's longing for union with Christ's mystical body (*beati corporis*), poignantly represented through false relations and dissonances at the final cadence. Morten Lauridsen's motet for a cappella SATB is an evocative setting of the same text, written for the Los Angeles Master Chorale in response to his mother's final illness.

O PRAISE THE LORD OF HEAVEN. Anthem for SATB a cappella chorus by William Billings entitled "Anthem for Thanksgiving" and published in *The Continental Harmony* (Boston, 1794). Inspired by Ps. 148, the music rises to a joyful climax in a final **Hallelujah**, "Praise the Lord."

O PRAY FOR THE PEACE OF JERUSALEM. Anthem based on verses from Ps. 122. There are numerous settings by English composers, including John Blow, Thomas Tomkins, John Goss (1854), and Herbert Howells (1933). The text has also inspired a setting by the American artist Paul Wilbur, "Shalom Shalom, Jerusalem" on the album *Shalom Jerusalem* (1995).

O QUAM GLORIOSUM. ("O How Glorious"). Antiphon for vespers on the Feast of All Saints, inspired by Rev. 7:12, set to music by many Renaissance composers, including Nicholas Gombert, Orlande de Lassus, Victoria, Jacob Clemens non Papa, Francisco Guerrero, Palestrina, and William Byrd. Victoria's motet for a cappella SATB chorus, published in Venice in 1572, was later recast as a parody Mass (1583). The opening measures, based on the dominant, evoke an atmosphere of mystique, while word painting on *gaudent* illustrates, in ascending passages, the sight and sound of the saints rejoicing with Christ, and imitative polyphony on *sequuntur Agnum* the procession of saints following the Lamb.

O QUAM PRETIOSA. ("O How Precious"). Responsory for the Virgin from *Symphonia Armonie Celestium Revelationum* (no. 22) by Hildegard of Bingen. Written for the Feast of the Epiphany, it is based on texts from Ezekiel and Luke depicting the Virgin's womb as the closed gate of the Temple (Ezek. 44:1–3), through which only the Holy Spirit entered once and for all (Lk. 1:31–35). Serenely beautiful, it captures the mystery of the Incarnation in all its glory.

O SACRED HEAD, SORE WOUNDED. Hymn based on a medieval poem, attributed variously to Arnulf of Leuven and Bernard of Clairvaux, in which each of seven stanzas forms a meditation on the wounds of Christ's crucified body (**Membra Jesu Nostri**). Translated into German by Paul Gerhardt (1656), the final stanza, beginning *O Haupt voll Blut und Wunden* ("O Sacred Head, sore wounded"), became a popular hymn, set to music by Leo Hassler and used by Bach in the **St. Matthew Passion** (1727). English translations include those of James Waddell Alexander (1830), Sir Henry Baker (1861), and the poet Robert Bridges (1899). American "queen of Christian pop," Amy Lee Grant, arranged her own version for her album *My Father's Eyes* (1979/2007).

O SANCTISSIMA. ("O, the Most Holy One"). Popular hymn inspired by the story of the Annunciation (Lk. 1:26–38) and sung on Marian feast days. Sung in Latin to a Sicilian tune that recalls the Christmas carol "O thou happy, O thou holy," the hymn calls on the Virgin Mary, who is both "holy" and "lowly," to "pray for us." An ethereal arrangement by Beethoven in *Stimmen der Völker in Liedern* (1807) evokes the dulcet sound of the heavenly choirs of angels, sung a cappella by female voices and then by male voices to string accompaniment.

O TASTE AND SEE. Short anthem for a cappella SATB chorus, with an optional organ introduction, composed by Vaughan Williams for performance during the taking of Communion at the coronation of Queen Elizabeth II (1953). A meditative work reflecting the sanctity of Holy Communion, the words "O taste and see how gracious the Lord is. Blessed is the man that trusteth in him" (Ps. 34:8) are first intoned by a solo treble and then repeated in polyphony by the chorus.

O VOS OMNES. ("O All You"). Responsory for Holy Week based on Lam. 1:12, it was set to music as a motet in the 16th and 17th centuries, most notably by Tomás Luis de Victoria, Hieronymus Praetorius, Carlo Gesualdo, Giovanni Gabrieli, and Robert Ramsey, and in the 19th and 20th centuries by Ralph Vaughan Williams (1922) and Pablo Casals (1932). Gesualdo, who was a manic-depressive and is renowned for murdering his wife and her lover, composed two settings of *O Vos Omnes* for five voices (1603) and six voices (1611). Tortured harmonies and expressive chromaticisms produce a melancholic introspective effect reflecting Jeremiah's grief.

OCTOBER. Second album by U2 (1981), which includes a number of tracks inspired by the Bible, including "Gloria" (Lk. 2:14) with its Latin chorus *Gloria in te domine* ("Tomorrow"), which includes allusions to the Resurrection ("Won't you be back tomorrow"), the suicide of Judas (Mt. 27:51–54) ("who tore the curtain"), the healing miracles (Mt. 8:2, 5, 14; 9:2, 20, 27–31; 12:10, 22; 15:32; 20:29), the Lamb of God (Jn. 1:29; 1 Pet. 1:19), and the Second Coming (Lk. 21:25–36; Rev. 1:7; 19:11–16).

OH, MARY, DON'T YOU WEEP. African American spiritual about Mary, who wept before Jesus following the death of her brother Lazarus (Jn. 11:32–33), or possibly Mary the mother of Jesus, who stood by the cross when he died (Jn. 19:25). "Pharaoh's army got drowned" (Exod. 15:4–5) in the refrain celebrates the promise of eternal life to those who believe. First recorded in 1915 by the Fisk Jubilee Singers, it has since been performed by numerous artists, including the Soul Stirrers with Sam Cooke, Jimmy Witterspoon, Aretha Franklin, Nat King Cole, and Bruce Springsteen. *See also* STABAT MATER DOLOROSA.

OH WHAT A BEAUTIFUL CITY. Traditional song based on Rev. 21:12–13 as arranged by Marion Hicks and performed by Pete Seeger to banjo accompaniment. It features on various albums, including *American Favourite Ballads* (vol. 2, 1958), *We Shall Overcome: The Complete Carnegie Hall Concert, June 8th, 1963*, and *The Essential Pete Seeger* (2005). Audiences generally join in the singing of the chorus. *See also* TWELVE GATES TO THE CITY.

OLD HUNDREDTH, THE. Well-known hymn tune attributed to Louis Bourgeois and published in the second edition of the Genevan Psalter, *Psaumes Octante Trois de David* (1551), set to a paraphrase of Ps. 134 by the Protestant theologian Theodore Beza. Today, it is best known set to a paraphrase of Ps. 100 ("All people that on earth do dwell") by William Kethe, first published in the Anglo-Genevan Psalter (1561). It appears in Bach's chorales BWV 326 and BWV 327 and his cantata BWV 130, Hubert Parry's *Three Chorale Fantasias*, Benjamin Britten's cantata *St. Nicholas*, and Mendelssohn's Piano Trio in C Minor (op. 66) and was featured at the coronation of Queen Elizabeth II in an arrangement by Vaughan Williams (1952).

OLD RUGGED CROSS, THE. Popular hymn composed by Methodist hymn writer and preacher George Bennard, sung for the first time in the First Methodist Episcopal Church, Pokagon, Michigan, in 1913 and later popularized by members of the Billy Sunday campaign. Inspired by Jn. 3:16 and written in a verse–chorus pattern in lilting compound duple time, it is a sentimental meditation on Christ's passion and death on the cross. It has been recorded by the Stoneman Family on the album *Old Rugged Cross* and by many popular artists, including Al Green, Brad Paisley, Elvis Presley, Chet Atkins, Jim Reeve, Johnny Cash, Mahalia Jackson, Patsy Cline, Harry Secombe, and Daniel O'Donnell.

OLNEY HYMNS. A collection of hymns by William Cowper (1731–1800) and John Newton (1725–1790), mostly the latter, published anonymously in 1779. In addition to many popular hymns, such as **Amazing Grace**, **Glorious things of thee are spoken** (Ps. 46), "Now may he who from the dead" (Heb. 13:20–22), and "O for a closer walk with God," it contains *Hymns on Select Texts of Scripture* arranged in the order of the books of the Old and New Testaments, ranging from "Adam" (Gen. 3), "Jacob's Ladder" (Gen. 28), "The Golden Calf" (Exod. 32), and the "Queen of Sheba" (1 Kgs. 10) to "The Leper" (Mt. 8), "The Sower" (Mt. 8), "Peter Walking on Water" (Mt. 14), "Paul's Voyage" (Acts 27), "Salvation Drawing Nearer" (Rom. 8), "Ephesus" (Rev. 2:1–7), and "The Little Book" (Rev. 10).

ON THE BIRTH OF CHRIST. Popular Byzantine hymn (*Kontakion*) by the sixth-century Greek hymnographer Romanos. Considered one of the poet's masterpieces, the text, inspired by Mt. 2:1–14, is a dialogue between Mary the mother of Christ and the Magi whose visit to the Christ child is celebrated in Eastern Orthodox tradition on the same day as the Nativity.

ON THE JERICHO ROAD. Country gospel song by Don and Marguerete McCrossan (1928), inspired by biblical references to the Jericho Road, known for violence and robberies (Lk. 10:25–37) and, in songs and hymns, a symbol of suffering in the world. It was performed by Elvis Presley, Johnny Cash, and the Hee Haw Gospel Quartet with Grandpa Jones, Roy Clarke, Buck Owens, and Kenny Price.

ON THE ROAD TO EMMAUS. Chancel opera for three soloists with piano/organ and flute accompaniment by Susan Hulsman Bingham, premiered at Trinity Church on the Green, New Haven, Connecticut, in 1980. It tells the story of the appearance of the Risen Jesus (T) on the Road to Emmaus to Cleopas (T) and an unnamed disciple (T/S) who may have been female (Lk. 24). Other works include the a cappella motet for SATTB chorus by Lassus, *Qui sunt hi sermones*, based on Lk. 24:17–19 and published in *Sacrae cantiones quinque vocum* (1582), and Carissimi's dialogue motet *Historia Dei Pellegrini di Emmaus* (date unknown) for three voices (SST). More recently, Judith Bingham composed a work for organ, *Missa Brevis, "The Road to Emmaus": Prelude and Voluntary* (2003) for Ascensiontide. The prelude illustrates musically the sunshine on the road to Emmaus, and the voluntary subtitled *Et cognoverunt eum* ("And they recognized him") is a depiction of Christ's ascension. John Harbison's cantata *The Supper at Emmaus* for four SATB soloists, SATB chorus, and orchestra, based on Lk. 24:5–8 and 13–35 and 1 Tim. 1:15–17, was composed in 2013.

ON WILLOWS AND BIRCHES. The first movement of John Williams's concerto for harp and orchestra written for the retirement of Anne Hobson-Pilot, harpist of the Boston Symphony Orchestra (2009). The quotation "We hanged our harps upon the willows" (Ps. 137:2) is written on the score. *See also* BY THE WATERS OF BABYLON.

ONCE FOR ALL. Hymn by Philip P. Bliss first published in *Sunshine for Sunday Schools* (1873). It was inspired by the phrase "Once for all" (Rom. 6:10; 1 Pet. 3:18) and other biblical texts (e.g., Rom. 10:4).

ONCE IN ROYAL DAVID'S CITY. Well-known Christmas hymn by Cecil Frances Alexander, first published in *Hymns for Little Children* (1848) to the tune "Irby" by Henry John Gauntlet and later in the United States in *Cantica Sacra, Hymns for the Children of the Catholic Church* (Boston, 1865). With Victorian children in mind, the hymn, based on Lk. 2:6–12, encourages children, like the Christ child, to seek salvation through the cultivation of humility and obedience. Since 1919, it has been sung as the processional hymn at the Christmas Eve Service of Nine Lessons and Carols at Kings College, Cambridge, the first verse sung a cappella by a lone chorister. There are popular descants by David Willcocks and Stephen Cleobury along with harmonizations by Henry John Gauntlett and Arthur Henry Mann.

ONE LOVE. Reggae song from the album *Exodus* by Rastafarian Bob Marley and Curtis Mayfield (1977), performed by Marley and the Wailers.

Named the "Song of the Millennium" by the BBC, it alludes to well-known biblical references to love (Jn. 13:34–35; Phil. 2:2; 1 Pet. 4:8) along with "thanks and praises to the Lord" (cf. Pss. 92:1, 136:1) and the Second Coming of Christ (Mt. 24:30).

OPELLA NOVA. ("A New Collection of Works"). Two collections of concertos for voices, instruments, and continuo by Johann Hermann Schein. Set in the new Italian style, they were based mainly on biblical texts and organized according to the liturgical year. The first collection, for three, four, and five voices (1618), comprises 31 works, including the chorales *Vom Himmel hoch* ("From Heaven High"), **Christ lag in Todesbanden** ("Christ lay in death's bonds"), *Komm heiliger Geist* ("Come Holy Ghost"), **Vater unser** ("Our Father"), *O Lamm Gottes* ("O Lamb of God"), and **Ein fest' Burg** ("A Mighty Fortress"). The second collection, for three, four, five, and six voices (1626), comprises 28 works, including *Hosanna dem Sohne David* ("**Hosanna to the Son of David**") and *Selig sind, die da geistlich arm sind* ("Blessed are the poor in spirit") as well as other settings of *Vater unser* ("Our Father") and *Komm heiliger Geist* ("Come Holy Spirit").

ORATORIO DE NOEL. ("Christmas Oratorio"). Oratorio in Latin for soloists (SMezATBar), chorus, strings, harp, and organ by Saint-Saëns (op. 12, 1858). Perhaps inspired by Bach's **Christmas Oratorio**, it is in 10 movements, opening with a prelude for organ and strings in the style of Bach and then comprising nine settings of biblical texts from Luke (Lk. 2:8–14), Psalms (Pss. 40:1; 118:26–28; 2:1; 110:3; 96:9–13), Isaiah (Isa. 49:13; 62:1), and elsewhere. Settings of the **Alleluia** and other texts from the Gradual of the Mass for Christmas at Midnight and Christmas Day also appear. Other musical interpretations of the story of the Nativity include works by Schütz (1664), Charpentier (1690), Gottfried Stölzel (1728), Vaughan Williams (1912), Messiaen (1935), Britten (1942), Honegger (1953), and Frank Martin (1959). *See also* UNE CANTATE DE NOËL.

ORDO RACHELIS. ("The Ceremony of Rachel"). Medieval liturgical play existing in four versions (Limoges, Laon, Freising, and Fleury), thought to have been performed as part of the Feast of the Holy Innocents or Childermas (28 December in the Western Church and 29 December in the Eastern Church). The title recalls Jeremiah's prophecy about Rachel weeping for her children (Jer. 31:15; cf. Mt. 2:18). The Fleury version contains an account of the Flight into Egypt and is also the only version to include the return journey of the Holy Family. *See also* VOX IN RAMA AUDITA EST.

OSSA ARIDA. ("Dry Bones"). Setting of Ezek. 37:4 for male chorus and organ four-hands accompaniment by Franz Liszt (1879). The eerie sight of the bones connecting together is suggested by a low B on the organ, gradually building a diminished seventh chord that is sustained while the right hand builds a seventh chord on C in the same manner until all the notes of the diatonic scale are played together. The dissonance increases further when the primo part enters in a similar manner and the secondo sustains a series of block chords while the chorus sings forte "Dry bones" in three languages: Latin, German, and French. At the words "Listen to the word of God," the chorus divides into six parts, and the primo and secondo play descending crotchets as if to represent the marching army, and the composition concludes with a unison chorus singing the "Word of God" accompanied by organ in A major, free of dissonance. *See also* DEM DRY BONES.

OUR TIME IN EDEN. Album by 10,000 Maniacs (1992), written and performed by Natalie Merchant. Inspired by a variety of biblical texts, the singer likens her beloved to a dove in "Noah's Dove," whose "time was set for leaving" (Gen. 8:12; cf. Cant. 2:14; 5:2). In "Eden," she laments that, like Adam and Eve, she and her beloved were not honest or close enough, while in the chorus "Jezebel," she regrets wanting to abandon the relationship in the same way that Jezebel persuaded her husband, King Ahab, to abandon Yahweh (1 Kgs. 16:31).

OUT OF THE DEPTHS. Song by Irish singer/songwriter Sinead O'Connor based on Ps. 130:1–4 from the album *Theology* released in 2007 and dedicated to the Irish biblical scholar Wilfred Harrington. The lyrics compare the sinner who cries out for mercy to God, who is also heartbroken ("nobody hears you crying all alone") and lonely ("you're like a ghost in your own home"). It is written in strophic form to emphasize the mutual suffering of God and those who cry out for his mercy. *See* DE PROFUNDIS.

• P •

PALESTINE. Oratorio in two parts by William Crotch (1811), premiered in London on 21 April 1812 and printed no fewer than six times during the 19th century. Based on a long poem by Reginald Heber that won the Newdigate Prize, Oxford, for the best composition in English verse, it tells the history of Palestine from the time of **Joshua** to the coming of Christ. Handelian influences are evident in the French Overture, the 17 SATB choruses, and the final choruses "**Hosanna**," "Worthy is the Lamb," **Hallelujah**, and **Amen**, fittingly scored in the triumphant tonality of D major. The many themes include the Battle of Jericho, the **Ten Commandments**, the slaying of Goliath, **King David**, Solomon's Temple, the Babylonian captivity, the Nativity, the Magi, Christ's passion and crucifixion, the destruction of the Second Temple, and St. John's visions from the Book of Revelation.

PARABLE: A TALE OF ABRAM AND ISAAC. Cantata by Judith Lang Zaimont in two versions, both composed in 1985, one scored for voices and organ and the other for voices, five strings, and harpsichord. In addition to the biblical text (Gen. 22:1–13), the libretto draws on other sources, including the 15th-century Brome mystery play *Abraham and Isaac*, Wilfred Owen's poem *The Parable of the Old Man and the Young* (1918), and the Jewish *Qaddish Yatom*, or Mourner's Kaddish. Commissioned by the Florilegium Chamber Choir, the conductor, JoAnn Rice, suggested the Brome mystery play to the composer, who expressed discomfort with the unmodulated grimness of Owen's poem on its own and needed words for all three principal characters to speak to one another and express emotion. As the mother of a two-year-old son at the time of writing, Zaimont grappled with the violence in this story, wondering how a loving father could ever consider killing his only son, and embellished the biblical story with extrabiblical details calling the loving father Abraham by his earlier name, Abram (Gen. 17:5), to signify a person less wise than his biblical counterpart and focusing less on the death of Isaac than on God's test of his unquestioning obedience.

PASSIO DOMINI NOSTRI JESU CHRISTI SECUNDUM MATTHEUM. ("The Passion of Our Lord Jesus Christ according to Matthew"). One of the earliest surviving polyphonic passions by a named composer. It was composed by the Renaissance composer Richard Davy and is found in the Eton Choirbook (1500–1505). Taken from Matthew's Gospel (Mt.

27:11–26), the words of Pilate, his wife, and the crowd are sung in polyphony, in contrast to Jesus' poignant words, which are sung by a bass soloist and the solemn narration, intoned in the manner of plainchant, by a tenor soloist.

PASSIO ET MORS DOMINI NOSTRI JESU CHRISTI SECUNDUM LUCAM. ("St. Luke Passion"/"The Passion and Death of Our Jesus Christ according to Luke"). Well-known oratorio in Latin by Penderecki (1966), commissioned by the Westdeutscher Rundfunk on the 700th anniversary of Münster Cathedral and dedicated to the composer's wife, Elizabeth. Scored for three soloists (SBarB), reciting voice, boys' chorus, three mixed choruses, and orchestra with a large percussion section, piano, and organ, it was modeled on the passions of J. S. Bach with spoken recitations by the Evangelist (Bar); arias sung by Christ (Bar), Pilate (B), Peter (B), a Servant (S) and others; and choruses representing the crowd (*turba*), who scream, shout, and whistle. As well as twelve-tone serialism and sonorism, the work incorporates quotations from Bach's four-note motif based on his name (B–A–C–H), Penderecki's **Stabat Mater** (1962), and Gregorian chant, including *O Crux ave* from the Palm Sunday vespers hymn **Vexilla Regis proderunt** and *Crux fidelis* from the Good Friday hymn *Pange lingua* ("Of the Gorious Body telling"). The work ends with *In Te Domine, speravi* (Ps. 31:1–5) as soloists and chorus call on God for deliverance. *See also* DEUS PASSUS.

PASSION ACCORDING TO MARY, THE. (Syriac title *Hachô dyôldat Alôhô*). Contemporary oratorio for soprano soloist, mixed chorus, and baroque instrumental ensemble (violas da gamba, *archlute*, mute cornet and cornet, and sackbuts), percussion, harpsichord, and organ by Zad Moultaka, commissioned by the Ambronay Festival and premiered in the Abbey Church of Ambronay, France, on 23 September 2011. Scored for Mary the mother of Christ (S) and choral soloists Mary Magdalene (A), Judas (Ct), John (T), and Peter (T), it recounts the story of Mary's passion at the foot of the cross, based on fragments from the canonical and apocryphal Gospels as well as from poems by Rainer Maria Rilke and Louis-Ferdinand Céline, a Japanese haiku, and an Italian folk lullaby.

PASSION: MUSIC FOR THE FILM THE LAST TEMPTATION OF CHRIST. Composed by Peter Gabriel as the original sound track for the Martin Scorsese film based on the novel by Nikos Kazantzakis (1953; English translation 1960), it was released as an album in 1989. To capture the mood and atmosphere of Christ's passion (Mt. 26–27; Mk. 14–15; Lk. 22–23; Jn. 12–19), Gabriel incorporates Eastern folk tunes played on modern and traditional instruments by musicians from the Middle East, Africa, and southern

Asia. The opening track, "The Feeling Begins," is a mournful melody played on the *duduk* depicting Christ's growing acceptance of his fate, while in "Passion," the haunting vocals of *qawwali* singer Nusrat Fateh Ali Khan and boy soprano Julian Wilkins movingly illustrate the intensity of Christ's suffering (Mt. 27; Mk. 15; Lk. 23; Jn. 19). This is followed by the sublime choral "With this Love," sung a cappella as a musical meditation on the image of Christ crucified (Mt. 27:35–44; Mk. 15:24–32; Lk. 23:33; Jn. 19:23–29).

PASSION OF MARY, THE. A dramatic oratorio for soloists, chorus, and orchestra by Howard Blake. Originally entitled **Stabat Mater** before its revision in 2006, it tells the story of Jesus' passion through the eyes and ears of his mother, Mary. The four movements recount (1) the Visitation (Lk. 1:39–56), the Nativity (Lk. 2:1–21), and the childhood of Jesus (Mt. 2:16–18; Lk. 2:42–51), with a setting of the **Magnificat** (Lk. 1:46–55); (2) the temptation in the wilderness (Mt. 4:1–11; Mk. 1:9–13), the Sermon on the Mount (Mt. 5:1–12), and the Crucifixion (Mt. 27:35–44; Mk. 15:24–32; Lk. 23:33; Jn. 19:23–29); (3) *Stabat Mater Dolorosa*; and (4) the Resurrection (Mt. 28; Mk. 16; Lk. 24; Jn. 20) and Salve Regina. Mary's exquisite music is set for a high tessitura to reflect her mixed emotions of ecstatic joy and intense grief, while Satan's temptation of Christ, scored for a bass voice a cappella, has an equally dramatic effect. At the end of the second movement, the violence of the crucifixion scene is vividly portrayed in a fast and furious programmatic instrumental section.

PASSION OF THE CHRIST, THE. Film music by John C. Debney for Mel Gibson's highly acclaimed but controversial movie starring James Caviezel as Jesus (2004). Despite historical inaccuracies and deviations from the biblical text, including an overemphasis on the brutality of Christ's passion, the plot is based on the Gospels, with an opening quotation from Isa. 53:5 and allusions to Gen. 3:15 and the Psalms. The script was translated into Aramaic and Latin and then screened with English subtitles. The orchestral score includes a variety of ethnic instruments, including the oud, *duduk*, bamboo flutes, and Chinese *erhu* (Karen Han) representing Satan, and the double violin (Gingger Shankar). Choral and solo singing, chanting, and wailing include a haunting performance by Lisbeth Scot and a chorus of the pièce de résistance, *Resurrection*. Debney expanded the score, which received an Academy Award nomination for Best Original Music Score, in a work entitled *The Passion of Christ Symphony* for chorus and orchestra, premiered in Rome in 2005 and comprising a prologue based on the Garden of Gethsemane scene, seven movements containing two of the stations of the cross per movement, and a "Resurrection" epilogue. The performance was accompanied by the projection of a series of paintings illustrating the Passion.

PASSION OF THE SADDUCEES. (*Kata Saddukaion*). Cantata in seven parts (Ast 251, 1982) for tenor, baritone, bass, speaker, choir, and orchestra by Greek composer Mikis Theodorakis, commissioned by the ninth Berlin Music Biennale. Based on a poem by the Greek poet Michalis Katsaros (1923–1998), the work draws a parallel between the Sadducees of the Gospels who failed to survive the destruction of the Temple in 70 CE and the mistakes of the Greek political left.

PATER NOSTER. ("Our Father"). There are many settings of **The Lord's Prayer** in Latin (Mt. 6:9–13; Lk. 11:2b–4), both as part of the Mass and as a work in their own right, beginning with a Gregorian chant and then as an a cappella motet by Renaissance composers, such as Josquin des Prez (SATTTB), whose setting, combined with **Ave Maria**, is regarded as one of his finest motets. Other settings include those of Jacob Handl for SSAATTBB, Palestrina for SSATB (1575), John Sheppard (1549–1550), Verdi for SSATB (in Italian), and Stravinsky (1926). *See also* LORD'S PRAYER, THE.

PEACE IN THE VALLEY. Gospel song written by Thomas Dorsey for Mahalia Jackson (1937), popularly sung at funerals. It is a vision of heaven based loosely on Isa. 11:6 and Rev. 21, with an allusion to Ps. 23:4, recorded by Elvis Presley and the Jordanaires (1957), Johnny Cash at a live concert to inmates of San Quentin State Prison (1969), and, more recently, Irish country music singer Daniel O'Donnell (2009).

PEACEABLE KINGDOM, THE. A cycle of eight sacred choruses for a cappella chorus by Randall Thompson, commissioned by the League of Composers for the Harvard Glee Club and Radcliffe Choral Society and premiered in Cambridge, Massachusetts, on 3 March 1936. Inspired by Edward Hick's paintings of Isaiah's prophecy (Isa. 11:6–9) (1823–1847), the libretto is made up of verses from the Book of Isaiah in the King James version. The first two movements focus on the separation of the righteous from the wicked (Isa. 3:10, 11; 65:14) and a series of threats ("Woe unto them") (Isa. 5:8, 11, 12, 18, 20, 22; 17:12) chanted first by the tenors, then altos, sopranos, and finally basses, while the chorus cries "Woe." "The Noise of the Multitude" (Isa. 13:4, 5, 7, 8, 15, 16, 18) describes the battle between the Lord of Hosts and the evildoers with the wailing, at a higher tessitura, of the defeated, immediately followed by "Howl Ye" for double chorus (Isa. 13:6; 14:31) and, in movement 5, "The Paper Reeds by the Brook" (Isa. 19:7), a lament by the survivors. Movement 6 celebrates the merits of the saved with staccato markings to paint the sound of clapping (Isa. 55:12). The work ends with a recitative for chorus (Isa. 40:21) and a joyful double chorus with dance-like passages celebrating the victory of good over evil (Isa. 30:29).

PENITENTIAL PSALMS, THE. *See* PSALMI DAVIDIS POENITEN-TIALES.

PIE JESU. ("Good Jesus"). The last couplet of the hymn **Dies Irae** in the Requiem Mass, set as an independent movement by many composers, including Cherubini, Gabriel Fauré, Duruflé, Rutter, Dudley, and Andrew Lloyd Webber. Of these, Fauré's ethereal setting in B-flat major for soprano solo (1888) is by far the best known. Lloyd Webber's *Pie Jesu*, which he combines with **Agnus Dei**, was a popular hit in 1985 and is still widely performed.

PILATE. Cantata for four soloists (MezBarTB), SATB chorus, and orchestra by Frank Martin (1964) inspired by the mystery play *Le Mystère de la Passion* by Arnoul Gréban (1450). The oratorio focuses on the person of Pilate in the Gospels and the conflict of good and evil.

PLANCTUS DAVID SUPER SAUL ET JONATHAN. ("The Lament of David over Saul and David"). The last of six biblical *planctus*, or laments, composed by the medieval French philosopher and theologian Peter Abelard. Narrated in the first person, each *planctus* retells the story of the protagonist's relationship with another character, now deceased (*Planctus* 1, 3–6) or held in captivity (*Planctus* 2), and clearly reflects Abelard's own grief following his forced separation from his beloved Héloise. While the whole sequence survives in a single manuscript held in the Vatican library (MS *Reginensis latinus*, 288), *Planctus* 6 exists also in two other manuscripts (Paris, Bib. Nat., MS NAL 3126; Oxford Univ. Lib., MS Bodl. 79). Inspired by 2 Sam. 1:17–27, it poignantly expresses David's unceasing love and unrelenting grief for his beloved soul mate, Jonathan. In the final stanza, David, weary from keening, lays his harp to rest. The other five, whose melodies are written in adiastematic or unheightened neumes without a staff and cannot be transcribed with any accuracy, tell of Dinah's grief over the murder of Shechem (Gen. 34) and how she forgave him for raping her (*Planctus* 1); Jacob's anxiety about his sons, Joseph, Simeon, and Benjamin, while they were in Egypt (Gen. 42:36; 43:14; 37:5–9; 35:18) (*Planctus* 2); the mourning of the virgins of Israel for the daughter of Jephthah (Judg. 11:29–40), who, in this imaginative rendition, relieves her father from the burden of his vow by taking her own life on the sacrificial altar (*Planctus* 3); Israel grieving for Samson (Ps. 35:7; Judg. 13–16); and David mourning for Abner (2 Sam. 3:26–39) (*Planctus* 5). *See also* DAVID'S LAMENTATION.

PLAY OF DANIEL, THE: A MEDIAEVAL DRAMA. (*Ludus Danielis*). Thirteenth-century liturgical drama for soloists (SSTTTTTBarBarB), chorus, and instruments (*vielle*, harps, flutes, organ, and bells), possibly a revised version of an earlier play by Hilarius, pupil of Peter Abelard. Possibly staged at the Feast of Fools on 1 January, its complexity and breadth of musical style set it apart from any other medieval play of this time. It tells the story of Belshazzar's Feast (Dan. 5) with the mysterious writing on the wall and Daniel in the lion's den (Dan. 6), where he sings *Kyrie Eleison* and later receives a meal from the prophet Habakkuk (Dan. 14:33). Daniel's part is accompanied by the harp to represent his nobility. Solos are unmeasured to allow for dramatic declamation, and the choruses are treated rhythmically. The work concludes with an angel's announcement of Christ's birth and a joyful **Te Deum**, suggesting that the work was performed during matins.

PLORANS PLORABIT. ("Weeping [My Eye] Shall Weep"). Penitential motet for five voices (ATTBB) by William Byrd published in *Gradualia, ac cantiones sacrae, Liber Primus* (1605). Regarded as a masterpiece in affective imitative style, it is Byrd's last political motet and a fitting tribute to his friend and teacher Thomas Tallis. Inspired by Jer. 13:17–18, expressive word painting on *plorans* ("weeping"), *plorabit* (["my soul] shall weep"), and *humiliamini, sedete* ("be humbled, sit down") depicts Jeremiah's prophesy about the Babylonian exile as well as lamenting the state of the Catholic Church in Elizabethan England. The same text was popularly set to music by Thomas Tallis, Niccolò Jommelli, Emilio De Cavalieri, and Francisco Valls in the 16th and 17th centuries and, more recently, by Andrew Smith for the Girl Choristers of Washington National Cathedral and by Hilary Campbell as part of the Boston New Music Initiative.

PONTIUS PILATE'S DECISION. Work for hard-bop trombone soloist and piano by Delfeayo Marsalis (1992). Rollicking repetitive rhythms point to Pilate's dilemma about setting an innocent man free and his fear of insurrection by the maddening crowd (Mt. 27:24; Jn. 19:13–14). Other works that deal with Pilate'a dilemma include Pilate's Dream from **Jesus Christ Superstar** and the song "Hands Bleeding Fear (Pontius Pilate)" by black metal group Nefarium on the album *Ad Discipulum* (2010). *See* PILATE.

PRAISE THE LORD, O JERUSALEM. Short anthem for SATB and organ by Jeremiah Clarke for the coronation of Queen Anne (1702). Based on verses from Psalms (Pss. 147:12; 48:8; 21:13) and Isaiah (Isa. 49:23), it is largely homophonic in texture and concludes with a joyful **Hallelujah**.

PRODIGAL DAUGHTER. Song by Michelle Shocked on the album *Arkansas Traveller* (1992), inspired by the complicated relationship of the songwriter's father and sister. Spoken in first-person narration, the daughter tells how, unlike the return of the prodigal son (Lk. 15:11–32), her homecoming, which brought shame to the family name, was marked with silence. A similar reinterpretation of the prodigal son theme features on the album *Careful What You Wish For* (2007) by the American folksinger Jonatha Brooke.

PRODIGAL SON. Delta blues song (ca. 1920) by Rev. Robert Wilkins inspired by the story of the prodigal son (Lk. 15:11–32), it was originally entitled "That's No Way to Get Along" and later named "Prodigal Son" by Wilkins when it was re-recorded in 1964. It was covered on the album *Beggar's Banquet* (1968), and, although later corrected, the lyrics were erroneously credited to Keith Richards and Mick Jagger with Wilkins credited only for the tune. The song features a walking low guitar line, jangly acoustic guitar, interior monologues, and speeches by the prodigal son, a swineherd, and the prodigal son's father.

PRODIGAL SON, THE. Oratorio in three parts by Samuel Arnold (1773) with a libretto by Thomas Hull. Based loosely on the parable (Lk. 15:11–32) and prefaced with Lk. 15:10, it expands the biblical story into a family affair by including the prodigal son's mother, sister, friends and neighbors, rustics, and a chorus of invisible spirits. A musical score no longer exists.

PRODIGAL SON, THE. Church parable by Benjamin Britten (op. 81, 1968) with a libretto by William Plomer, dedicated to Dmitri Shostakovich and premiered at the Aldeburgh Festival on 10 June 1968. Inspired by the parable of the prodigal son (Lk. 15:11–32), it opens with a procession of monks chanting a plainsong *Jam lucis ordo sidere* ("Now in the sun's new dawning ray"). The Tempter, played by the Abbot (T), confronts the Younger Son (T) ("Do not think I bid you kneel and pray. I bring you no sermon, what I bring you is evil"), and, on their journey into the city ("The world's all before you, yes before you"), it is noticeable that the two voices are strikingly similar. In the city, there are nine different choruses: first, the Parasites and Siren Voices welcome the prodigal son into the city and offer him wine ("Come and try") and "nights of ecstasy," gold, and pity, then, finally, the beggars sing "We are starving" to depict the loss of all his wealth. His return home is marked by a song and dance to the words of Ps. 98:1, "O Sing Unto the Lord a New Song," sung by a chorus of servants with the Father (B-Bar) and Elder Son (T). Other musical interpretations of the parable include works by Charpentier (1690), Camilla de Rossi (1709), Samuel Arnold (1773), Henri-Montan Berton (1812), Daniel Auber (1850), Arthur Sullivan (1869), Hugo Alfvén (R. 214, 1957), and Langston Hughes (1961). *See also* L'ENFANT PRODIGUE; FILS PRODIGUE, LE.

PROMISED LAND, THE. Song by Chuck Berry to the traditional folk melody "The Wabash Cannonball," featured on the album *St. Louis to Liverpool* (1965). Written when the songwriter was in prison, the lyrics refer to his deprived childhood when he traveled from Norfolk, Virginia, to the "Promised Land" of Los Angeles, California. It was covered by many well-known artists, including Elvis Presley (1973, 1974, 1975), Meatloaf (1983), W.A.S.P. (2009), and the Grateful Dead (1971–1995). Bruce Springsteen composed a song with the same title on his album *Darkness on the Edge of Town* (1978).

PROPHET SONG, THE. Song by Brian May from Queen on the album *A Night at the Opera* (1975) and performed by progressive rock artists Freddie Mercury, Rodger Taylor, and Brian May. Written by May after a dream while he was recovering from an illness, the reference to "the prophet" in the title is to Noah, regarded as a preacher of righteousness (Gen. 6:9; 2 Pet. 2:5). Opening and closing with the sound of the wind (Gen. 8:1), a lone acoustic guitar accompanied by a toy (i.e., miniature) koto, a traditional Japanese stringed instrument, paints the sound of God's presence. A chorus sung first by Mercury and then by Mercury, Taylor, and May urges "the people of the earth" to "listen to the wise man." God's voice appears in the final verse with the words "Love is the only answer" and then disappears as another voice, no doubt that of Satan, resounds with the words "Listen to the Madman!"

PROPHETIAE SIBYLLARUM. ("Prophecies of the Sibyls"). One of the most celebrated works of Lassus (ca. 1550) comprising a cycle of 13 highly chromatic movements for SATB chorus, including 12 polyphonic songs, preceded by a prologue entitled "Carmina chromatico." The songs are Latin translations of texts from the *Sibylline Oracles*, a Greek work containing prophecies made by women known as "Sibyls," later appropriated by Jews and Christians because they apparently foretell the coming of a messianic age. The title of each of the 12 songs identifies the prophet, beginning with

Sibylla Persica ("Persian Sibyl"), who foretells the virgin birth; *Sibylla Lybica* ("Lybian Sibyl") and *Sibylla Delphica*; and, finally, *Sibylla Agrippa*, whose prophecy tells of one who will judge our sins and whose "unchanging honor and certain glory will endure."

PSALM 25:15. Song from the album *Spirityouall* (2013) by Bobby McFerrin. It is a meditative blues setting of the words "My eyes are ever on the Lord, for only He will release my feet from the snare" repeated over and over again, every syllable soulfully enunciated. It was performed at the Kennedy Center for the Performing Arts Concert Hall in Washington, D.C., on 14 May 2013.

PSALM 126. Choral work by Philip Glass, commissioned by the American Symphony Orchestra for a concert at the Lincoln Center, New York, celebrating the 50th anniversary of the state of Israel in 1998. The words of the Psalm, seen as a Psalm of thanksgiving for the restoration of the fortunes of the Jewish people, are spoken by a narrator to wordless syllables by the chorus accompanied by the orchestra. It was released by Milken Archive Naxos on the album *Psalms of Sorrow and Joy* (2005).

PSALM 150. Short choral work for four-part children's chorus, two treble instruments, bass instrument, percussion, and keyboard by Benjamin Britten (op. 67, 1962), composed for the centenary of his old prep school, Buckenham Hall School, formerly South Lodge School, Lowestoft. Instruments are played when mentioned in the Psalm (Ps. 150:3–5), and the words "Praise him upon the loud cymbals" are shouted fortissimo. César Franck also composed a setting of Ps. 150 for the inauguration of the Cavaillé-Coll organ at the Institute for the Blind in Paris on 17 March 1883. It opens and closes with joyful **Hallelujahs**, set antiphonally at the beginning and chromatically at the end.

PSALM SETTINGS. A series of Psalm settings by Charles Ives. They were composed mostly in the 1890s, apart from Psalm 42, which was written in 1888, when he was only 14 years old, and the best known, Psalm 90, Ives's personal favorite, was not completed until 1924. They are set for a cappella chorus (Pss. 24, 67, 54); double-chorus a cappella (Pss. 14, 100); chorus and organ (Pss. 25, 150); solo voice, chorus, and organ (Ps. 42); and chorus, bells, and organ (Ps. 90).

PSALM XC. ("Psalm 90"). Choral work for mixed chorus, soprano and tenor soloists, organ, and bells by Charles Ives (1894/1901, rev. 1923/1924), characterized by polytonalities, chord clusters, musical palindromes, serialism, and unison singing. Based on Ps. 90, the organ introduces a number of signature harmonies at the beginning, and these reappear in the verses to represent the Eternities, the Creation, God's wrath against sin, prayer and humility, and rejoicing in beauty and work. A pedal C dominates throughout the work to represent God's omnipresence, most notably at the end as the choir sings in unison and then in harmony to the accompaniment of serene bells to represent humanity's rejoicing.

PSALMEN DAVIDS SAMPT ETLICHEN MOTETEN UND CONCERTEN. ("Psalms of David with Several Motets and Concertos"). A collection of 26 motets and concertos in German for voices and instruments by Heinrich Schütz, dedicated to his patron Johann Georg (SWV 22–47, op. 2, 1619). Twenty of the pieces are settings of Psalm texts (including Pss. 1, 2, 6, 8, 23, 84, 98, 100, 110, 111, 115, 121, 122, 130, 136, 137, 150), and two are settings of texts from the prophets (Isa. 49:14–16; Jer. 31:20). Written in the Venetian polychoral style after Giovanni Gabrieli, they are arranged for eight to 20 parts, the majority of settings in eight parts.

PSALMFEST. A collection of anthems for soprano and tenor soloists, SATB chorus, and orchestra by John Rutter, premiered at the Morton Meyerson Symphony Center in Dallas, Texas, in 1993. It consists of settings of nine well-known Psalms, including *O Be Joyful in the Lord* (Ps. 100), **I will lift up mine eyes** (Ps. 121), **The Lord is My Shepherd** (Ps. 23), and **O How Amiable are thy Dwellings** (Ps. 84). The others are Pss. 146, 97, 27, 47:1–7, and 148.

PSALMI DAVIDIS POENITENTIALES. ("The Penitential Psalms of David"). Motet cycle for five-part a cappella voices by Orlando de Lassus, commissioned by Duke Albrecht V of Bavaria in 1563 (first published 1584). Each one is a multimovement setting of one of the seven Penitential Psalms (Pss. 6, 32, 38, 51, 102, 130, 143), with duos, trios, and quartets interspersed. The Penitential Psalms are first mentioned as a group in the sixth-century *Expositio Psalmorum* by Cassiodorus and traditionally believed to have been written by **King David** after his adulterous affair with Bathsheba. Each motet is set in one of the church modes, beginning with mode I (Ps. 6), mode II (Ps. 32), and so on, and ends with the lesser doxology. A classic example of *musica reservata*, a term used by Samuel Quickelberg (1559) to characterize the work of Lassus, it illustrates the range of techniques used to achieve the high level of emotional expressivity found in this work.

PSALMS FOR I. Album (1975) by Jamaican reggae deejay, producer, and Rastafarian Prince Far I featuring nine tracks based on Pss. 49, 48, 24,87, 95, 53, 23, 2, and 1 with **The Lord's Prayer** placed at the heart of the album (track 5). It is dedicated to those who cannot read the Bible for themselves. Each Psalm is chanted in spoken style as a song of praise to God and a plea for Babylon to repent over heavy root rhythms played by the Aggrovators, with rhythms for Ps. 24 produced by Alton Ellis and for Ps. 53 voiced on Lee Scratch Perry's rhythm "Mighty Cloud of Joy." The album was reissued in 2002 with an additional dub track, "Record Smith and the All Stars: Psalm 48 Version after Psalm 48."

PSALMS, HYMNS, AND SPIRITUAL SONGS. A collection of hymns by Isaac Watts, published in 1851, combining his *Hymns and Spiritual Songs* (1707) and *Psalms of David. Imitated in the language of the New Testament* (1719).

PSALMUS HUNGARICUS. ("Hungarian Psalm"). Choral work for tenor soloist (David), SATB chorus, children's chorus, and orchestra by Zoltán Kodály (op. 13, 1923). Inspired by Ps. 55, it opens with an instrumental introduction followed by a unison chorus telling of David's sadness, followed by the tenor solo "Lord in thy mercy, hear. I cry to thee. Do not forsake me," punctuated by the chorus singing "Sad was King David." After a delightful musical interlude scored for David's instrument (the harp), with clarinet, violins, violas, and cellos, the mood changes, and David sings of the new courage that has now entered his sad soul, followed by his affirmation of faith in God: "God will protect me, save me, drive away all care" (Ps. 55:16–23). The piece ends with a moralizing chorus explaining the relevance of the story for Christians everywhere.

PSAUME XLVII. ("Psalm 47"). Work for orchestra, organ, soprano solo, and chorus by Florent Schmitt (op. 38, 1904). Regarded as a masterpiece, it was premiered in Paris in 1906 with Nadia Boulanger on organ. Inspired by a trip to Istanbul in 1903 when the composer witnessed the ceremonial acclamations of the Ottoman sultan, it is written in a pronounced exotic, oriental style. It opens and closes with the spirited invocation "**O Clap your hands all ye people**" (Ps. 47:1), accompanied by the full force of the orchestra, organ, and a colorful display of brass and percussion, the latter sounded most notably on "frappé" (clap). The emotional high point occurs during the sensuous and ravishingly beautiful middle movement in D-flat major, when the soprano soloist, preceded by a lush solo violin cantilena, sings "He hath chosen his inheritance, the beauty of Jacob whom he loved" (Ps. 47:4), accompanied by the low murmurs of the orchestra, chorus, harp, and solo violin. This section was extracted and performed at the baptismal ceremony of Prince Albert of Monaco in 1958.

PUER NOBIS NATUS EST. ("A Boy Is Born to Us"). Gregorian chant and introit for the Third Mass on Christmas Day based on Isa. 9:6 and Ps. 98:1. It was used as a cantus firmus by Thomas Tallis in his seven-part *Missa Puer Natus Est.*

PUERI HEBRAEORUM. ("The Children of the Hebrews"). Motet for four voices by Tomás Luis de Victoria, published in *Officium Hebdomadae Sanctae* (1585) and based on Mt. 21:9. Polyphonic in style, the opening phrase is reminiscent of the Gregorian melody of the same name. The proclamation **Hosanna** is set in homophony to represent the unity of thought among the crowd. Other notable settings include a motet for four voices by Palestrina and a motet for four voices by Schubert (published 1891).

PUT YOUR HAND IN THE HAND. Gospel pop song (1971) by Canadian songwriter Gene MacLellan, it was first performed by Anne Murray and then by the Canadian gospel rock band Ocean. Released as a single and then as the title track to the album *Put Your Hand in the Hand,* it sold over 1 million copies in the United States and Canada. The chorus, which is repeated several times, refers to Jesus as the "man from Galilee," the man who "stilled the waters . . . the man who calmed the sea" (Mt. 8:23–37; Mk. 4:35–41; Lk. 8:22–25).

• Q •

QUAERITE PRIMUM REGNUM DEI. ("Seek Ye First the Kingdom of God"). Twenty-two-measure antiphon for a cappella chorus composed by the 14-year-old Mozart as an academic exercise for entry to the Academia Filarmonica in Bologna (K. 86/73v., 1770). *See also* SEEK YE FIRST.

QUAM PULCRA ES. ("How Beautiful Thou Art"). Motet for three voices by John Dunstable. One of the most popular works of the 15th century, inspired by verses from the Song of Songs (Cant. 7:4–7, 11–12), it is renowned for the sonorous inclusion of thirds and sixths, known as the *la contenance angloise* ("English countenance"), over bare intervals of a fourth, a fifth, and an octave and graceful melismas on *deliciis* ("delight"), *turris eburnea* ("ivory tower"), *dilecte* ("beloved"), and *in agrum* ("into the fields"). It concludes with an **Alleluia**.

QUATRE MOTETS POUR LE TEMPS DE NOEL. ("Four Motets for the Christmas Season"). A choral work by François Poulenc (1950–1952) comprising **O Magnum mysterium** ("O great mystery," 1952), *Quem vidistis pastores* ("Whom did you see, shepherds?," 1951), *Videntes stellam* ("At the sight of the star," 1951), and *Hodie Christus natus est* ("Today Christ is born") and borrowing the jubilant text of the antiphon for the **Magnificat** of the Christmas evening vespers.

QUATUOR POUR LA FIN DU TEMPS. ("Quartet for the End of Time"). Chamber work by Olivier Messiaen for violin, clarinet, cello, and piano premiered on 15 January 1941 in Görlitz, Germany, where the composer was a prisoner of war. Inspired by the vision of the Angel of the Apocalypse announcing the end of time (Rev. 10:5–6), the eight movements are linked musically and thematically. Movements 1 and 3 represent the silence and timelessness of heaven through a theme symbolizing birdcalls played by the clarinet (blackbird) and violin (nightingale). Movements 2 and 7 portray the powerfulness of the angel (Rev. 10:6), with one foot on the earth and the other on the sea and crowned with a rainbow, illustrated musically by a cascade of colorful chords played on the piano (Rev. 10:1). Movements 5 and 8, in praise of the eternity and immortality of Jesus as the eternal word of God (Jn. 1:1), are scored in the tonality of E and portray the eternity of Christ in long solo passages on the cello and the soul's ascent toward God in a violin melody rising to the higher register of the instrument. Movement 6, in F-sharp, the most rhythmic of the eight, is characterized by use of extended note values, augmented and diminished rhythmic patterns, nonretrogradable rhythms, and instruments playing in octaves to represent the seven trumpets that announce six catastrophes (Rev. 8:6–11:14) and the final consummation of the mystery of God (Rev. 10:7, 11:15–19). *See also* COULEURS DE LA CITÉ CÉLESTE.

QUEEN OF SHEBA, THE. (*Die Königin von Saba*). Opera by Karl Goldmark, first performed in Vienna in 1875 and in New York in 1885. It is a romantic retelling of the biblical story (1 Kgs. 10:1–13) with the additional complication of a love affair between the Queen of Sheba (Mez) and Assad, one of Solomon's ambassadors (T), who is betrothed to Sulamit (S). Solomon (Bar) banishes Assad to the desert, where the queen tries to persuade him to return with her to her kingdom. When he refuses, he is caught up in a violent sandstorm from which he barely survives, then dies, pleading for forgiveness, in the arms of Sulamit. Written in the style of grand opera, the work contains some memorable moments, such as the bacchanal celebrating the arrival of the queen at the beginning of act 3 and the final duet. Goldmark achieves an oriental atmosphere in places, and the singing of the high priest (B) is reminiscent of traditional Jewish liturgical music.

QUO VADIS: DRAMATIC SCENES. ("Where Are You Going?"). Oratorio in one act for soloists, chorus, orchestra, and organ by Feliks Nowowiejski (op. 30, 1907) to a libretto by Antonie Jüngst (1843–1918) based on Henryk Sienkiewicz's historical novel (1895) and translated into English by Grace Hall. It was inspired by the story told in the apocryphal Acts of Peter of the encounter of Peter (Bar) with the risen Christ (B) outside the city of Rome and Christ's command to Peter to return to Rome to die as a martyr. The final scene features Peter's heartfelt solo, recalling his denial of Christ (Lk. 22:54–62), and the work concludes with the chorus "Glory crown thee, O Mighty One"; a double fugue, "Hail, Bless and Laud him, the Anointed"; and the lesser doxology.

• R •

RAISING OF LAZARUS. Chancel opera for soloists and small chorus of men and women for the purpose of acting and piano/organ accompaniment with optional flute by Susan Hulsman Bingham, designed for performance during a service in a church or a synagogue and premiered at Trinity Church on the Green, New Haven, Connecticut, in 1979. Based on the story of the raising of Lazarus (Jn. 11), it is scored for a Messenger (Tr), John (B-Bar), Jesus (Bar), James (T), John (B-Bar), Peter (Bar), Andrew (Bar), Martha (S), Mary (Mez), Lazarus (silent), Caiaphas (B), two unnamed men (BarB), and a chorus of male and female onlookers, mourners, and villagers (SATB). It includes some arias and declamatory recitatives based on traditional harmony with some chromaticism.

RAISING OF LAZARUS, THE. (*Voskresenije Lazarja*). Setting in F minor for alto or bass and piano by Rachmaninoff (op. 34, no. 6) of a poem by Russian Orthodox poet Aleksei Khomiakov. Inspired by the story of the raising of Lazarus (Jn. 11:38–53), it is dark in timbre and reaches a climax at the end on "Praise to You, the Radiance of our Father's glory," followed by a reverent pianissimo on "To You who died for us."

REDEMPTION, THE. *See* LA RÉDEMPTION.

REJOICE IN THE LAMB. Festival cantata in eight short sections for treble, alto, and tenor soloists and SATB chorus and organ by Benjamin Britten, commissioned by Rev. Canon Walter Hussey for the 50th anniversary of the consecration of St. Matthew's Church, Northampton (op. 30, 1943). A setting of Christopher Smart's poem *Jubilate Agno*, written while he was an inmate in an asylum, it celebrates the worship of God by human beings, living creatures, and inanimate objects. The slow and mysterious opening chorus, "Rejoice in God, O Ye Tongues," in unison moves into a lively dance-like section that names various biblical characters, such as Nimrod, Ishmael, Balaam, Daniel, Ithamar, Jakim, and David, and ends in a quiet **Hallelujah** fading away to nothing. Three solo pieces, sung by Jeffrey the Cat (S), the Mouse (A), and the Flowers (T), are followed by a chorus telling of Smart's mental and physical suffering compared to Christ's passion ("For I am under the same accusation with my Saviour"). A short bass recitative on the attributes of God based on four letters of the alphabet (H for [Holy] Spirit, K for King, L for Love, and M for Musick) leads into the final chorus on the rhymes of various musical instruments, ending peacefully ("For this time is perceptible to man by a remarkable stillness and serenity of soul") and a reprise of the **Hallelujah**.

REPROACHES. (*Improperia*). Twelve short texts adapted from the Old testament, in which Christ on the cross rebukes the Jews for sending him to his death. Beginning "My people, what did I do to you?" (*Popule meus, quid tibi feci?*), they contrast what God did for them with what they have done to Him, for example, "I led you out of Egypt (Exod. 20:2), you prepared a Cross for me; I opened the sea before you (Exod. 14:21), you opened my side with a spear; I gave you a royal sceptre (Gen. 49:10), you gave me a crown of thorns." Each verse is followed by a refrain in Latin and Greek: *Sanctus Deus, Hagios Ischyros . . . eleison hemas, miserere nobis* ("Holy God, have mercy on us"). Their origin is obscure, but they are known to have been popular in the Western Church from the 12th century. Traditionally sung during the veneration of the cross on Good Friday, they have been set to music by many composers, including Victoria and Palestrina, but are rarely performed today because of the risk of a blatantly anti-Semitic interpretation.

REQUIEM MASS. A Catholic service for the dead (*Missa pro defunctis*) made up of texts inspired by or derived from the Bible. The traditional Requiem text begins with the *Pange lingua* ("Of the Glorious Body telling"), *Requiem aeternam dona nobis* ("Grant us eternal rest") and, in addition to the Kyrie, Sanctus, **Benedictus**, and **Agnus Dei** from the Ordinary of the Mass, includes the **Dies Irae** ("Day of Wrath"), the offertory **Domine Jesu Christi** ("Lord Jesus Christ"), and Lux aeterna ("Everlasting light"). The earliest Requiem Masses were sung to Gregorian chants, with polyphonic settings by Catholic composers, such as Palestrina, de Lassus, and Victoria, emerging during the Renaissance. The earliest existing polyphonic setting is by Franco-Flemish composer Johannes Ockeghem (ca. 1461?). Mozart's unfinished setting in D minor (K. 626, 1791), which was completed by Franz Xavier Süssmayr (1792) after the composer's death, is by far the most famous setting of the 18th century. In the 19th century, Brahms, in his **German Requiem** (1869), moved away from the traditional Latin, while in the 20th century, Benjamin Britten, in his War Requiem (1962), juxtaposed the war poetry of Wilfred Owen with the traditional Latin text. Herbert Howells, in his a cappella *Requiem* (1936) in English, includes three new texts (Ps. 23, 121; Rev. 13:14). Other well-known settings include those by Jommelli (1756), Haydn (1771), Berlioz (1837), Liszt (1868), Verdi (1874), Dvořák (1890), Fauré (1877, 1889–1893), Duruflé (1947), Stravinsky (1966), and Andrew Lloyd Webber.

RESURRECTION: CONCERTO FOR PIANO AND ORCHESTRA. Piano concerto by Penderecki (2001; rev. 2007) scored in 10 continuous movements and dedicated to the victims of 9/11.

RISE UP LAZARUS. Country song by Patty Loveless from her 11th album, *Mountain Soul* (2001). Inspired by the story of Jesus raising Lazarus from the dead (Jn. 11), it provides hope of eternal life to those who believe in Jesus Christ. *See also* RAISING OF LAZARUS, THE.

RISE UP, MY LOVE, MY FAIR ONE. Anthem for six voices a cappella by Healey Willan from *Three Motets in Honour of Our Lady* (HWC 312, no. 3, 1928). Based on verses from the Song of Solomon (Cant. 2:10–12; 2:1), it was composed for performance at Easter. Word painting on "Rise up my love," depicted with an ascending melody line, together with the lush sound of sonorous chords and mingling melodies, describes the affectionate scene of the lover's request to his beloved.

RITORNO DI TOBIA, IL. ("The Return of Tobias"). Oratorio in two parts by Joseph Haydn with a libretto by Giovanni Gastone Boccherini, commissioned by the Vienna Tonkünstler Societät and premiered in Vienna on 2 April 1775 (Hob. XXI:I, rev. 1784). Inspired by the closing chapters of the Book of Tobit, it tells of the homecoming of Tobias with his new wife, Sara, and the angel Raphael, and the cure of his father's blindness. The work opens with a prayer sung by Tobias's parents, Anna (A) and Tobit (B), and a chorus of Hebrews (*Pietà* ["Have pity"]) and ends with a hymn of thanksgiving sung by the chorus and four soloists: Anna and Tobit, joined by Tobias (T) and Sara (S). There are several virtuosic arias, such as Tobias's love song *Quando mi dona un cenno* ("When your sweet lips"), Sara's exquisite aria *Non parmi esser fra gl'uomini* ("I appear not to be among mankind") with its *concertante* writing for wind and horns, and Anna's *Come in sogno* ("As in a dream"), in which she sings of her nightmare. Other works based on this story include oratorios by Johann Simon Mayr (1794) and Gounod (CG 31, 1854; published 1865). *See also* TOBIE.

RIVERS OF BABYLON. Rastafarian song (1970) written and performed by Brent Dowe and Trevor McNaughton of the Jamaican reggae group the Melodians, based on Pss. 137 and 19. It appeared in the movie *The Harder They Come* (1972) and was famously covered by disco band Boney M (1978) on the albums *Nightflight to Venus* (1978) and *The Magic of Boney M* (1980), among others. The song omits the Psalm's references to war and violence, including the slaughter of the infants (Ps. 137:9), and concludes with a lament and a prayer for help based on Ps. 19:4. Another popular setting includes "Babylon" by Don McClean on the album *American Pie* (1971), which is based on a four-part round by the 18th-century English composer Philip Hayes. *See also* BY THE WATERS OF BABYLON.

ROCK OF AGES. Popular hymn by the English Calvinist preacher Augustus Montague Toplady (1740–1778), first published in *The Gospel Magazine* (1776). It is said to have been inspired by 1 Cor. 10:1 and 4 and written while the author sought refuge from a raging storm. Sung to the tune "Toplady" by Thomas Hastings in the United States and "Petra" by Richard Redhead in the United Kingdom, it is also set to the tune "New City Fellowship" by James Ward. It was a favorite of Prince Albert, played on his deathbed in 1861, and performed at the funeral of William Ewart Gladstone in 1898.

ROCK: THE STORY OF SIMON PETER. Musical by Roger Jones (2008) based on the story of Simon Peter as told by the centurion Cornelius from the setting of his home in Caesarea (Acts 10). In a series of flashbacks, it tells the story of his call ("I will follow you") (Mt. 4:19), discipleship ("You are Messiah"; Mt. 16:13–20; "In this bread, in this wine"), and denial ("Surely you must have been with him" and "The look of love") (Mt. 26:69–75). Characters include Peter; Cornelius; Jesus of Nazareth; Peter's wife, Zillah (1 Cor. 9:5), and his mother-in-law, Miriam (Mt. 8:14; Mk. 1:29–31), who are not named in the biblical story; John, a fisherman and friend (Jn. 1:38–39; Mt. 4:21, 10:2, 17:1); James, the brother of John (Mt. 4:21–22; Mk. 1:19–20); Susannah, a maid at the high priest's house (nonbiblical); Andrew, the brother of Peter (Jn. 1:40); and the evangelist Philip and three of his four daughters, who remain nameless in the Bible but are named Rhoda, Dinah, and Lois in the musical (Acts 21:8–9).

ROMAN VESPERS. Choral work by Handel, also known as the Carmelite vespers and most likely written for the Festival of Our Lady of Mount Carmel while he was in Rome (1707). Part 1 consists of an overture, including motets, antiphons, and arias based on Marian texts. Part 2 includes settings of the Psalms for soloists and chorus: *Dixit Dominus* (Ps. 110), *Laudate Pueri* (Ps. 113), and **Nisi Dominus** (Ps. 127).

RORATE CAELI DESUPER. ("Drop Down Dew, Ye Heavens, from Above"). The Advent prose introit for the fourth Sunday of Advent based on Isa. 45:8 and Ps. 84:8, included in the *English Hymnal* and the *New English*

Hymnal. In addition to motets by Byrd and Palestrina, there are modern settings by John Joubert and Thea Musgrave, the latter a setting of words by the Scottish poet William Dunbar (1460–1520).

ROUND THE GLORY MANGER. African American spiritual arranged for a cappella SSATB and solo by K. Lee Scott. It is a joyful meditation on the humble birth of Jesus with the chorus representing angels singing "**Hallelujah**" and "Wasn't that a bright morning all around the glory manger."

RUN, SAMSON, RUN. Song by Jewish songwriters Neil Sedaka and Howard Greenfield. Released as a single in 1961, it appeared on the album *Neil Sedaka Sings Little Devil and His Other Hits* (1961) and as a combo re-release in 2010. This catchy song in B-flat major, modulating to B major for the final verse and chorus, tells the story of Samson's fatal seduction by Delilah (Judg. 16). Likening Delilah to the devil, the chorus, scored for banjo, drums, and backing vocals, with the addition of a French horn, urges Samson to run away from the lady barber before she approaches, and in the final verse, the narrator warns men against the seductive trait found in every woman. This was the second of two songs about Delilah; the first, a solo single, *Oh Delilah!* (1958), in first-person narration by Samson, failed to become a hit.

RUTH. Lyrical opera in one act for soloists, chorus (SATB), chamber orchestra, and piano by Lennox Berkeley (op. 50) to a libretto by Eric Crozier, premiered at the Scala Theatre, London, in 1956 with Anna Pollack as Ruth and Peter Pears as Boaz. Inspired by the Book of Ruth, scene 1 opens with Naomi (S) urging her two Moabite daughters-in-law, Ruth (Mez) and Orpah (S), to return to their homeland for fear of a hostile reception in Bethlehem, knowing that the Moabites were enemies of the Israelites. Orpah obeys, but Ruth stays by her mother-in-law and sings the aria **Whither thou goest** (Ruth 1:16–17). In scene 2, in a harvest field belonging to Boaz, a kinsman of Naomi, Ruth is shunned as "a foreign woman, the Moabite" and as a witch, but Boaz (T) intervenes and asks Ruth for her forgiveness. Scene 3 takes place at night in the vicinity of a threshing floor where, on Naomi's advice, Ruth offers herself as a wife to Boaz. The aria sung by Boaz to Ruth, "Thou comest in the stillness of night," is a type of passacaglia based on a recurring twelve-tone row, and the gentle love duet "Lo, my beloved, my soul's delight, to thee I give my hand" is a testimony to their love. Boaz presents his wife to his people, who laud her and predict that she will bring forth kings from her womb, and the work ends with a song of praise to God sung by Ruth and Boaz. Other musical interpretations of this narrative include works by César Franck (1847; rev. 1871) and Georg Schumann (1946), the latter combining texts from Ecclesiastes and Song of Songs with the Ruth narrative. *See also* I WILL FOLLOW; I WILL GO WHERE YOU WILL GO.

RUTH. A sacred pastoral in two parts by Otto Goldschmidt (op. 20, 1867) composed for the London Festival of Three Choirs and dedicated to Oscar Fredrik, prince of Sweden and Norway. It is based on the Book of Ruth and other biblical texts, including Isaiah (Isa. 12:1–2), Jeremiah (Jer. 23:5–40), Matthew (Mt. 5:4, 8), and many of the Psalms (Ps. 106, 34, 112, 121, 65, 107, 126, 30, 128, 4, 37, 82). The chorale, which features in the scene between Boaz and the reapers, "Ye powers that he in man hath planted," is drawn from two German hymns: *O dass ich tausend Zungen hätte* ("Oh that I had a thousand tongues") by Johann B. König (1738) and the harvest hymn *O Gott von dem wir alles haben* ("O God from whom we have everything") by Caspar Neumann. The choral cantilena "The Lord made her like Rachel and like Leah" (Ruth 4:11) is based on a Hebrew melody sourced in *Ancient Melodies of the Liturgy of the Spanish and Portuguese Jews* by David Aaron de Sola and Emmanuel Aguilar (1857). *See also* I WILL FOLLOW; I WILL GO WHERE YOU WILL GO; WHITHER THOU GOEST.

RUTH. Short song for soprano and piano by Penelope Smith (1850) based on Ruth 1:16–17, arranged for guitar by Madame Sidney Pratten, and dedicated to HRH Princess Louise, daughter of Queen Victoria.

SACRAE LECTIONES EX PROPHETA JOB. ("Sacred Readings from the Prophet Job"). A motet cycle for four voices by Orlando de Lassus (H. xix/3, 1560; published 1565). One of the earliest musical settings of readings for *Officium Defunctorum ad Matutinum* ("Matins of the Office of the Dead"), it opens with a plainchant introduction based on Ps. 94, after which each reading from the Book of Job is followed by a responsory. The cycle includes the following motets: *Parce mihi, Domine* ("Spare me, Lord") (Job 7:16–21), *Taedet animam meam vitae meae* ("My soul is weary of my life") (Job 10:1–2), *Manus tuae Domine fecerunt me* ("Thy hands have made me") (Job 10:8–12, 21), *Responde mihi* ("Answer me") (Job 13:22–28), *Homo natus de muliere* ("Man that is born of a woman") (Job 14:1–6), *Quis mihi hoc tribuat* ("If only you would hide me") (Job 14:13–15), *Spiritus meus attenuabitur* ("My spirit shall be wasted") (Job 17:1–3, 11–16), *Pelli meae* ("My bones cleave to my skin") (Job 19:20–27), and *Quare de vulva eduxisti me?* ("Why didst thou bring me forth out of the womb?") (Job 10:18–22). A second motet cycle by Lassus, *Lectiones sacrae novem ex libris Hiob. Excerptae II*, was published in Munich in 1582 and as a setting for SSATTB chorus by Victoria (1605).

SACRIFICE OF ISAAC: A LITURGICAL DRAMA. Cantata with lyrics in Hebrew and English by Judith Kaplan Eisenstein (1974), scored for five voices (unspecified), chorus, violin, cello, soprano recorder, small percussion, and shofar. It is a setting of the narrative poem *Et Sha'arey Ratzon* ("When the gates of mercy") written by Judah ibn Abbas (12th century), telling of the binding of Isaac and recited before the blowing at the shofar on Rosh Hashanah in the Sephardic ritual. Structured in the form of a medieval liturgical drama, the work is strictly monophonic in texture with unison instrumental accompaniment. Expanded to include a number of Sephardic *selihot*, or penitential songs, it includes "Sleepers Wake!," sung by the first voice or cantor, and "Little Sister" (*Ahot Ketannah*) (no. 3), scored as a duet for the second and third voices with chorus, violin, cello, and tambourines joining in for the repeat. "Little Sister," from the Song of Songs (Cant. 8:8), is an allusion to the Jewish people and perhaps to the sorrowful mother in the Akedah story. Other *selihot* include Isaac's song "Lord, Have Mercy" (no. 5), set to a melody from Aleppo in which each verse concludes with the phrase "The altar, the binder, and the bound," and "The Lord with the sound of the

Shofar" (no. 8), introducing the ceremony of the blowing of the shofar. *See also* ABRAHAM AND ISAAC.

SACRIFICIO DI IEFTE, IL. ("The Sacrifice of Jephtha"). Oratorio by Johann Simon Mayr (1795) to a libretto by Giuseppe Maria Foppa (1760–1845). Inspired by the biblical story (Judg. 11:29–40), it is scored for Jephtha (S); his daughter, named Seila (Mez) in the libretto; Abner, an extrabiblical character, who is a prince and betrothed to Seila (T); High Priest Jaddo (B); another extrabiblical character; a chorus of Gileadites; maidens of Seila; and orchestra. It brings together the dramatic events of a love affair between Seila and Abner and the revelation of Jephthah's vow at the end of act 1. In act 2, Seila refuses to run away, insisting instead on resolute obedience to God's will: *Se Dio l'impon, si faccia; io nò, non tremo* ("If God bids it, so be it; I do not tremble"). Abner threatens to take his life, *Pria con un ferro il seno mi passerò* ("Nor with a sword will I pierce my breast"). The priest Jaddo intervenes to tell the family that God does not want blood sacrifice and that Seila ought to dedicate her life to the service of God. Jephtha offers his daughter a choice: to pay some money or to offer up her life in service to God. In choosing the latter, Abner and not the daughter becomes the victim of the story and the one who is unable to reconcile himself to God's will, as expressed in the final chorus, *O giorno di terror!* ("O day of terror!").

SACRIFICIUM ABRAHAE. ("The Sacrifice of Abraham"). One of three *histoires sacrées* for soloists, chorus, strings, and continuo by Marc-Antoine Charpentier (1645–1704). The tonality of C major at the beginning and end points to a Christological interpretation of the biblical story (Gen. 22), and the use of melismas sound paints the flickering flame (Gen. 22:6), Isaac's descendants like stars and sand (v. 17), and the joy felt by Abraham and Isaac following the angel's intervention (v. 11). The suspense between verses 10 and 11 is expressed by a measure of complete silence, and the work concludes with a duet sung by Abraham and Isaac with melismas on *multiplicabit semen eorum* ("he will multiply their seed"), repeated by the chorus.

SACRIFIZIO DI ABRAMO, IL. ("The Sacrifice of Isaac"). Oratorio in two parts by Camilla de Rossi (1708) for a Lenten concert at the Viennese Court of the Emperor Joseph I (1705–1711). The libretto by Francesco Maria Dario is based on the Latin Vulgate translation of the text (Gen. 22), with an implied typological reference to Isaac as Christ. In a variation on the biblical story (Gen. 22:1–18), Sarah (S) is given a minor role to play at the beginning of parts 1 and 2. Portrayed as a sorrowful mother in her recitative *Discostatevi ormai* ("Begone at last") (part 2), she fears for the safety of Abraham and Isaac, and in the aria that follows, *Stráli, fulmini, tempeste* ("Darts, lightning, tempests"), she offers to sacrifice her own life in place of her spouse and son. While many of the arias and recitatives are scored in the minor tonality to reflect the story's somber mood, significant moments, such as the questions that Abraham (T) asks the Angel (S), *Uccidero mio figlio?* ("Shall I kill my son?") and *Io figlizidio?* ("I, killer of a son?"), and the jubilant song of praise sung by Abraham (T) and Isaac (A) at the end of the oratorio are set in major tonalities.

SAID JUDAS TO MARY. *See* JUDAS AND MARY.

ST. BARNABAS: THE CHRISTIAN GRACES ILLUSTRATED BY HIS LIFE. Cantata or church oratorio for soloists (STBarB), mixed chorus (SSAATTBB), and organ by Philip Armes (1891) to a libretto by Joseph Powell Metcalfe, dedicated to Rev. Vincent King Cooper, precentor at Durham Cathedral. Opening with a prologue based on verses from the Book of Job (Job 34:10, 11, 16), the work is divided into five parts, illustrating the five graces (Christian Communion, Example, Charity, Work, and Praise) as found in the life of St. Barnabas (Acts 11:21–30; 13:2–3; 15:1, 2, 6–9, 11–12) with a reflective commentary based on other biblical texts (Jer. 32:36–41; Isa. 58:6–10; Jer. 1:7–8; Ps. 145).

ST. JOHN PASSION. Passion oratorio in two parts by Johann Sebastian Bach, premiered in St. Nicholas Church, Leipzig, for the Good Friday Vespers Service on 7 April 1724 (BWV 245). Highlighting the Son of Man glorified on the cross (Jn. 12:23), the work juxtaposes the trial and death of Jesus with an account of Peter's remorse after his denial of Jesus. It departs from the narrative in John's Gospel (18–19) that emphasizes Christ's divinity and focuses on his humanity, incorporating texts from a passion poem by Barthold Heinrich Brockes, *Der für die Sünde der Welt gemarterte und sterbende Jesus* ("Jesus who Suffered and Died for the Sins of the World") (1712), and a passion libretto by Christian Heinrich Postel (ca. 1700) along with allusions to the Gospels of Matthew and Luke. The story is recounted by the Evangelist and other biblical characters in recitativo secco (speech-like narrative style accompanied by the continuo) with arioso recitatives and arias sung by soloists and the familiar tunes of the 11 chorales intended to evoke a reflective response in the audience to the unfolding drama of Christ's passion and death. The plangent opening chorus, *Herr unser Herrscher* ("Lord, our sovereign") (1), in G minor and full of dissonance, is addressed to Jesus. After a recitative (2a/2) in which the narrator recounts the betrayal in the Garden of Gethsemane, Jesus asks, "Whom do you seek?," and the chorus (2b/3 and 2d/5), representing the Pharisees and servants of the high priest, answer Jesus' question with the retort "Jesus of Nazareth." Memorable moments include the tenor recitative *Er leugnete aber* ("But he denied it") (12c/18), recounting Peter's denial of Jesus for the third time (Jn. 18:27), in which the 12 chromatic tones illustrate Peter's remorse, *und weinete bitterlich* ("and wept bitterly"), and the poignant aria *Ach, mein Sinn* (13/19) ("O, my spirit"), that follows. Part 1 concludes with the moving chorale (no. 14) *Petrus, der nicht denkt zurück* ("Peter, who does not think back") (Lk. 22:61–62). Part 2 deals with Jesus' interrogation by Pilate, the flogging, and the Crucifixion. The text of the chorale *Durch dein Gefängnis* (22/40) ("Through your captivity O Son of God"), between the interrogation of Jesus by Pilate and the frantic outburst of the mob, lies at the crux of the work and outlines a theology of the cross. Highlights in part 2 include the alto aria (30/58) *Es ist vollbracht!* ("It is finished!"), which is a meditation on Christ's final words, and the nine notes of the tenor recitative *Und neiget das Haupt und verschied* ("And bowed his head and was gone") (31/59), recounting Christ's actual death. The work concludes with the chorus *Ruht wohl, ihr heiligen Gebeine* ("Rest well, gentle bones") (39/67) in a major tonality, reminiscent of a lullaby as Jesus is laid to rest in the tomb, and the final chorale (40/68) with a reference to the **Bosom of Abraham** (Lk. 16:19–31) and the promise of eternal life. Other well-known settings include works by Orlando de Lassus (1580), William Byrd (1605), Heinrich Schütz, Arvo Pärt (1982), Mørk Karlsen (1992), Sofia Gubaidulina (2000), and James McMillan (2007). *See* ST. JOHN PASSION.

ST. JOHN PASSION. Oratorio in two parts and 10 movements for baritone, chamber choir, large chorus, orchestra, and chamber organ by James McMillan, commissioned by the London Symphony Orchestra (2007). Alongside the biblical text, the work draws on texts from the **Seven Last Words** of Christ, the **Stabat Mater**, the **Coventry Carol**, and the **Reproaches** sung by Christ (Bar), with a response from the crowd in the words of the **Sanctus**. Following the announcement of Christ's death, the work concludes with an orchestral epilogue entitled *Sanctus Immortalis, miserere nobis*, described by the composer as a "song without words."

ST. JOHN THE BAPTIST. Oratorio by George Alexander Macfarren with a libretto by William H. Monk, first performed at the Bristol Musical Festival on 23 October 1873 and one of the composer's most enduring works. In two parts entitled "The Desert" and "The Machaerus" (Herod's fortress where John was beheaded), it is scored for five soloists, a chorus of Pharisees, and full orchestra, with a shofar salutation at the beginning and end to herald the coming of the Messiah. In addition to the main Gospel narrative (Mt. 3; Mk. 6; Jn. 1, 3), the libretto draws on numerous other biblical texts, including Malachi (Mal. 3:1; 4:6), Psalms (Pss. 94:3–4; 132:18; 68:23), Ecclesiastes (Eccl. 2:10; 11:9–10), Proverbs (Prov. 14:13; 16:14–15; 19:12), Esther (Esth. 15:5), Judges (Judg. 11:35), Zechariah (Zech. 13:7), and Ezekiel (Ezek. 21:28). Memorable moments include John's baptism of Christ, sung as an aria ("I indeed baptize you with water"), and God's words "This is my beloved Son," sung by a female chorus to the accompaniment of violins and harp.

ST. LUKE PASSION. *See* PASSIO ET MORS DOMINI NOSTRI JESU CHRISTI SECUNDUM LUCAM.

ST. MARY MAGDALENE. (*Sainte Marie-Magdalene*). Short cantata in two parts by Vincent D'Indy (op. 23, 1905) scored for soprano solo, female chorus, and piano/organ accompaniment. Based on the story of the anointing of the feet of Jesus by a sinful woman in the house of Simon the Pharisee (Lk. 7:36–38, 48), part 1 describes the woman as wearing "a modest veil shading her stooping forehead" and with "tresses loose and long," underscored by a romantic-sounding arpeggiated accompaniment. Jesus' words to the Pharisee, "Her sin shall be forgiven for her love has been great," is preceded and followed by the chorus, "Weep thou no more but hope, O Magdalene." Part 2 highlights the Magdalene's conversion and the inspiration given to the Church by her humble yet significant act and closes with the chorus "Pray that our ship the Church," accompanied by arpeggiated chords to suggest the waves of the sea. It may be compared to Stainer's sacred cantata *St. Mary Magdalene* (1883).

ST. MATTHEW PASSION. (*Matthäuspassion*). Oratorio passion in two parts for double chorus, double orchestra, and soloists by J. S. Bach, premiered at the Thomaskirche in Leipzig on 11 April 1727 for the Good Friday Vespers Service (BWV 244) and revised by Bach in 1736 to the version known today. It is regarded universally as a masterpiece of sacred music and was described by Mendelssohn as "the greatest of all Christian works" following its revival in Berlin in 1829. Based on the passion narrative in Matthew 26–27, from the anointing in Bethany and his arrest in Jerusalem to his trial and crucifixion, part 1 opens with a monumental double chorus, *Kommt, ihr Töchter, helft mir Klagen* ("Come daughters, help me lament"), and concludes with the chorale fantasia *O Mensch bewein dein Sünde gross* ("O man, your grievous sin bemoan") (29/35). In the final double chorus of part 2, *Wir setzen uns mit Tränen* *nieder* ("We seat ourselves with tears") (68/78), both choirs sing together as though present at the poignant scene of Christ being laid to rest in the tomb. The libretto is interspersed with poetic texts by the poet/librettist Christian Fredrich Henrici, known by the pseudonym Picander, along with familiar Lutheran chorales. The Gospel narration is recounted by the evangelist as well as other biblical characters, including Pontius Pilate, in recitativo secco (speech-like narrative style accompanied by the continuo). This is followed by arioso recitatives and arias sung by soloists commenting reflectively on the biblical text. Jesus' words, however, are sung to an expressive "halo" of string accompaniment, apart from his final words, "My God, my God, why have you forsaken me," which are in recitativo secco. The passion chorale tune **O Sacred Head, Sore Wounded** (*O Haupt voll Blut und Wunden*) is sung five times (15 [21], 17 [23], 44 [53], 54 [63], 62 [72]), perhaps a reference to the five wounds inflicted on Christ's body, and also appears in instrumental parts underscoring numbers 29 (29), 35 (41), 29 (47), and 57 (66). The work opens with a large choral-based movement, cast as a dialogue between a chorus of Christian believers and one of the allegorical daughters of Zion sung by a tenor, evoking references to the Song of Songs (Cant. 1:5; 3:5; 11, 5:16; 8:4) and featuring the bridegroom as a witness to the passion of Christ. The accompanying chorale that follows, *O Lamm Gottes unschuldig*, a German setting of the **Agnus Dei** in *siciliano* rhythm and sung by ripieno sopranos, alludes to the passion of Christ and to the Lamb, who rules in Jerusalem (Rev. 5:12). Similarly, part 2 opens with a dialogue between an alto solo, perhaps representing Mary Magdalene, *Ach, nun ist mein Jesus hin!* ("Ah, now my Jesus is gone!") (30/36), and chorus 2 (30/36), with text based on the Song of Solomon (Cant. 5:6–8). To the rhythm of a saraband, the alto asks the whereabouts of her lover, and the onlookers from chorus 2, the daughters of Zion, offer to go with her and find him: *So wollen wir mit dir ihn suchen* ("We will go with you to seek him"). The next scene (31/37), featuring the trial of Jesus, is narrated by the Evangelist in recitativo secco. At the heart of the work, the soprano aria *Aus Liebe will mein Heiland sterben* ("Out of love my Saviour is dying") (49/58) focuses on Christ's loneliness, marked by the conspicuous absence of a continuo, while the triple meter and flowing semiquavers suggest the joyfulness brought to believers by Christ's sacrificial death. The alto aria *Erbarme Dich, mein Gott* ("Have mercy, my God") (39/47), with a violin obbligato, regarded by Yehudi Menuhin as "the most beautiful piece of music ever written for the violin," expresses the overwhelming emotional intensity of Peter's passionate pleas for God's mercy following his denial of Christ. The tenor recitative and chorus (63a,b/73) *Und siehe da, der Vorhang im Tempel zerriß in zwei Stück von obenan bis untenaus* ("And behold, the veil of the temple tore in two pieces, from top to bottom"), based on Mt. 27:51–58, features a series of ascending and descending scale-like passages in the bass line to represent lightning bolts, along with a dramatic use of tremolo that ascends chromatically to underscore the tenor's words *Und die Erde erbebete* ("and the earth did quake"). The final bass aria, *Mache dich, mein Herze, rein* ("My heart, purify yourself"), set in a major tonality to a lilting rhythm (12/8), expresses the joy of salvation in union with Christ. The Italian film director Pier Paolo Pasolini incorporated the final chorus and violin obbligato from the aria "Erbarme dich" into his film *The Gospel according to St. Matthew* (1964). The final chorus also appears as the opening and closing sound track of *Casino* (1995), directed by Martin Scorsese.

ST. PAUL. Oratorio for soloists, chorus, and orchestra by Mendelssohn (op. 36, 1834–1836) to a libretto by Julius Schubering, premiered on 22 May 1836 (Pentecost) at the Lower Rhine Music Festival in Düsseldorf and performed at the Birmingham Festival in 1837. Inspired by the Book of Acts (Acts 4–21) with allusions to Paul's letters (1 Cor. 3:16; 2 Tim. 4:6–8, 17; Rom. 11:36), Psalms (Pss. 51:3, 13, 19, 15, 17; 59:14; 86:12–13; 89:2, 19) and other biblical texts, part 1 begins, after a recitative and chorus, with the memorable soprano aria *Jerusalem! die du tötest die Propheten* ("Jerusalem! Thou that killest the Prophets") (Lk. 13:34) and then tells the story of the martyrdom of St. Stephen and Saul's persecution of the Christians and his conversion on the road to Damascus. The chorus acts both as the crowd in the dissonant *Steiniget ihn* ("Stone him to death") and as the voice of Jesus, *Ich bin Jesus von Nazareth, den du verfolgst!* ("I am Jesus of Nazareth whom thou persecutest"). The rage of Saul (B) against the Christians is expressed in the aria *Vertilge sie, Herr Zebaoth* ("Consume them all, Lord Sabaoth!") (Pss. 59:14; 83:19; 31:19) and his prayer for forgiveness in the aria *Gott, sei mir gnädig nach deiner Güte* ("O God have mercy upon me") (Ps. 51), while the chorale *Dir, Herr, dir will ich mich ergeben* ("To thee, O Lord, I yield my spirit") is sung as a prayer by Stephen (T) before his death. Part 2, which begins with Paul's first missionary journey and ends with his visit to Ephesus, includes four chorales and a hymn by Martin Luther. The famous ***Wachet Auf*** ("Sleepers awake"), intoned by the strings and clarinets in the orchestral overture, reappears again when Paul's faith is awakened on the road to Damascus. Other chorales include *O Jesu Christe, wahres Licht* ("O Thou, the true and only Light!") by Johann Heermann (1630) and the Lutheran hymn sung by the chorus, *Aber unser Gott ist im Himmel* ("But our God abideth in Heaven") (Ps. 115:3).

ST. PAUL'S VOYAGE TO MELITA. Cantata in one movement by Dyson for tenor (St. Paul), chorus, orchestra, and organ, first performed at the Three

Choirs Festival, Hereford Cathedral, on 7 September 1933. Based on Acts 27, it describes St. Paul's journey to Rome up to the point of his shipwreck on the island of Melita with excessive storm music in the middle section describing the tempestuous wind, "the Euroclydon." Noted for its use of timpani rolls, the work concludes with the sound of pealing bells to celebrate the crew's survival. *See also* EUROCLYDON.

ST. PETER. Oratorio in two parts by John Knowles Paine (op. 20) for soloists (SMezTBar), chorus, and orchestra, premiered in the Boston Music Hall on 3 June 1872. Compiled from numerous biblical texts, the libretto is subdivided into four parts: "The Divine Call" (Mk. 1:15–18; Mt. 16:4–8), "The Denial and Repentance" (Mt. 26), "The Ascension" (Acts 1), and "Pentecost" (Acts 2; 12:17). It is scored for 12 male voices representing the apostles and a bass soloist (Peter). There is a memorable orchestral "Lament" representing Peter's grief over his denial of Christ, followed by his aria "O God, my God, forsake me not" (Ps. 25:16, 11, 20). The work includes three chorales from the Lutheran Chorale Book: "How lovely Shines the Morning Star" (Nicolai), "Jesus My Redeemer Lives" (Crüger), and "Praise to the Father" (Neander). Other notable settings of the same story include an oratorio by Julius Benedict, premiered on 2 September 1870 at the Birmingham Festival.

SALOME. Opera in one act and four scenes by Richard Strauss (op. 54, 1905) to a libretto in German by Hedwig Lachmann based on Oscar Wilde's *Salomé* (1891). Inspired by the biblical story (Mt. 14:3–12; Mk. 6:17–29), principal roles are assigned to Salome (S), portrayed as the archetypal femme fatale in her attempted seduction and murder of John the Baptist; Jokanaan the Prophet ("John") (T); and Herod (B). Based on a complex system of leitmotifs representing the various characters and their emotions, the opera is renowned especially for Salome's seductive oriental "Dance of the Seven Veils" and for her kiss of the severed head of John the Baptist in the final scene, which ends on a highly dissonant chord known as "the most sickening chord in all opera." Other musical interpretations of the story include the song "Salome" by Peter Doherty (1979) and a ballet in two acts by Peter Maxwell Davies (1982). *See also* LA TRAGÉDIE DE SALOMÉ.

SAM AND DELILAH. Song by George Gershwin with lyrics, based loosely on the biblical story (Judg. 16), by Ira Gershwin and sung in a debut performance by Ethel Merman in the musical comedy *Girl Crazy* (1930). A slow blues tempo evokes an image of Delilah as the archetypal femme fatale whose excessive jealousy, depicted musically by an array of guttural consonants in verse 3, led to the death of Samson and Delilah's execution by hanging. It was performed by Duke Ellington and His Orchestra (1931), Louise Carlyle (1951), Ella Fitzgerald with Nelson Riddle and His Orchestra (1959), Debbie Gravitte (1994), and Klea Blackhurst (2004).

SAMSON. Popular oratorio by Handel (HWV 57, 1741; rev. 1742) with a libretto by Newburgh Hamilton (1712–1759) adapted from John Milton's *Samson Agonistes* (1671) and other poems after the biblical story in Judg. 13–16. Telling of the final hours of Samson before his destruction of the Temple of Dagon, it begins just before his imprisonment in Gaza, where he is already blinded and bound in chains by the Philistines following the revelation of the secret of his strength to his wife, Delilah. Containing music borrowed from Carissimi, Telemann, and others, two numbers, "Let the Bright Seraphim," for soprano, and Samson's air, "Total Eclipse," for tenor, are still popularly performed at concerts today. *See also* ALL WOMEN ARE BAD; HAIR; HALLELUJAH; RUN SAMSON RUN; SWINGIN SAMSON.

SAMSON. Song by Jewish artist and songwriter Regina Spektor from the album *Begin to Hope* (2006). It is a poignant lament with piano accompaniment based on the story of the Timnite woman from Judg. 14–15. In first-person narration, she speaks from beyond the grave to tell of her passionate love affair with her first husband, Samson (Judg. 14:1–3, 15:1), and of Samson's subsequent liaison with Delilah. She loved him first, and Samson, despite his father's words, was besotted by her beauty (Judg. 15:1–2) and trusted her to cut his long hair. She contrasts her uneventful relationship, which the history books forgot, with that of Samson and Delilah, which caused the temple columns to fall (Judg. 16:29–30). The lyrics of the plaintive chorus allude to her violent death at the hands of her own people (Judg. 15:6).

SAMSON ET DALILA. ("Samson and Delilah"). Grand opera in three acts by Saint-Saëns (op. 47, 1877) with a libretto by Ferdinand Lemaire, premiered in a German translation at the Grossherzogliches Hoftheater in Weimar, Germany, on 2 December 1877. An intensely passionate interpretation of the biblical story involving the use of leitmotifs, it is scored for eight soloists; a chorus of Philistines and Israelites; and large orchestral forces. One of the most famous arias in all opera is *Mon coeur s'ouvre à ta voix* ("Softly awakes my heart"), describing Delilah's seduction of Samson. Samson's cries of *Dalila! Dalila! J'aime!* ("Delilah! Delilah! I love!") are usually omitted from concert performances. Sung by many great sopranos, including Maria Callas, Elina Garancą, Marilyn Horne, Jessye Norman, and Shirley Verret, the aria is characterized by long melodic lines requiring legato singing ("Surrender to my tender caresses, fill me with esctasy") in the lush tonality of D-flat major and accompanied by flute, oboe, English horn, clarinet, harp, and strings. Another piece often performed on its own is the bacchanal inside the Temple of Dagon after Samson's incarceration in act 3, which describes the Philistines' celebrations in florid oriental melodies with sensual harmonies, hypnotic rhythms, and percussion. *See* SAMSON.

SAMUEL THE PRIEST. Funeral anthem in A minor for SATB a cappella chorus by William Billings, published in *Suffolk Harmony* (1786). Inspired by the story of the death of the prophet Samuel (1 Sam. 25:1), the verses are variously intoned by basses, tenors, and sopranos, and the final verse, "The Lord gave and the Lord taketh away; blessed be the name of the Lord," from Job 1:21, is sung in homophony by the chorus. Samuel's refrain "Have pity on me, O ye my friends for the hand of God hath touched me" is not biblical.

SAMUELE. *Azione sacra*/oratorio in two parts for soloists (SSTB), chorus, and orchestra by Simon Mayr, commissioned by the Congregazione della Carità for the ordination of Bishop Pietro Mola in Bergamo in 1821. The libretto by Bartolomeo Merelli contains 66 footnotes with references to texts from Deuteronomy, Leviticus, 1 Samuel, Ecclesiasticus, and Psalms as well as contemporary biblical commentators, such as Augustin Calmet. Part 1 opens with the journey of Samuel's parents, Hannah (S) and Elkanah (T), with their small children to the Temple at Shiloh to visit their son Samuel (S). In an accompanied recitative, they remember their grief when she was barren and in a duet recall their subsequent sadness at the loss of their son when he was offered up to the Lord ("Do you hear the sad sheep bleat through the fields. . . . Do you hear the lonely sparrow that weeps in sorrow?") (1 Sam. 1). The climax of part 1 is Hannah's song of thanksgiving (1 Sam. 2:1–10), a march depicting the Israelites' journey to the Temple, and a hymn of praise sung by the chorus. Part 2 tells of the call of Samuel (1 Sam. 3) and the melodrama of his prophetic ecstasy, spoken by Samuel to the accompaniment of solo violin, cello, and harp. It concludes with the chorus "All Israel will see how you make us happy."

SANCTA CIVITAS. ("The Holy City"). Oratorio in 10 parts for tenor and baritone soloists, chorus, semichorus, distant chorus, and orchestra by Vaughan Williams (1925) based on verses from the Book of Revelation. It opens with an account of the rejoicing in heaven (Rev. 19) as a backdrop to the account of the fall of Babylon (Rev. 18) and the vision of the new heaven and the new earth (Rev. 21), including the salvation of the "great multitude" (Rev. 7:9, 15–17) and the joy with God forever (Rev. 22:1–7). The voice of John is scored for baritone solo, and the sound of rejoicing is sung by the choruses, with the distant chorus accompanied by a distant trumpet, depicting the choir of angels. The semichorus and distant chorus join forces to sing "For the Lord God Omnipotent Reigneth." It concludes with a setting of **Holy, Holy, Holy** (Isa. 6:3, 5; cf. Rev. 4:8) with "Glory be to thee O Lord" sung fortissimo and in homophony, followed by the solo tenor voice representing Christ, "Behold I come quickly, I am the bright and the morning star" (Rev. 22:12, 16), with the semichorus and full chorus singing "**Amen**, even so come" (Rev. 22:20).

SANCTUS. ("Holy"). Benjamin Britten's setting for soprano and baritone soloists, chorus, and orchestra in his *War Requiem* (1962). It opens with a soprano soloist accompanied by bells recalling the consecration during Mass, followed by choral murmuring on *Pleni sunt caeli et terra gloria tua*, which crescendos to a triumphant *Hosanna* fortissimo calling for large orchestral forces, including brass. The gentle **Benedictus** sung by the soprano is answered by the chorus singing in parallel fifths and a reprise to the *Hosanna*. The movement closes in a dark mood, colored by diminished triads, the tritone, and dramatic word painting, with a setting of Wilfred Owen's *The End*, sung by a baritone.

SANCTUS. ("Holy, Holy, Holy"). There are numerous musical settings of this prayer from the Mass Ordinary in chant, polyphony, and settings by composers from every period of music history. The first half of the text (*Sanctus Sanctus, Sanctus Dominus Deus Sabaoth . . . Pleni sunt caeli*) derives from Isa. 6:1–3 and the second, the **Hosanna** (*Hosanna in excelsis*) and the **Benedictus** (*Benedictus qui venit in nomine Domini*), from Mt. 21:9 (cf. Ps. 118:26). A notable example is Bach's setting for six-part chorus (SSAATB) and orchestra in his Mass in B Minor. The first part of the text, originally composed for performance on Christmas Day 1724, opens with a majestic chorus recalling the seraphim in Isaiah's vision (Isa. 6:1–3) and is followed by a jubilant fugue (*Pleni sunt caeli et terra gloria tua*) with melismas on "gloria" exalting God's glory in heaven and on earth. The numbers 3 and 6 feature prominently (e.g., six-part chorus, three trumpets, triplets on "Sanctus," and 3/8 meter) to symbolize the presence of the triune God and the six wings of the seraphim. The **Hosanna**, scored for double eight-part chorus (SSAATTBB), is an adaptation of a secular Cantata no. 215 (1734), originally composed to celebrate the anniversary of the coronation of Polish King Augustus III in 1733. The **Benedictus** is scored as an aria in ternary form for tenor voice and wind obbligato. *See also* HOLY, HOLY, HOLY.

SARAH WAS NINETY YEARS OLD. Minimalist work for soprano, two tenors, organ, and percussion (1976/1990) by Arvo Pärt. Inspired by passages from Genesis, the first five minutes evoke the period of Sarah's protracted barrenness (Gen. 16:1–2), opening with the repetition of four slow timpani blows and bouts of silence, followed by a three-minute tenor vocalize, perhaps to reflect Sarah's sighs as she waited. The work continues in this way, alternating between timpani and vocalize for a further 16 minutes until the four-minute climax, during which the soprano sings a dramatic vocalize accompanied by organ and timpani, followed by a tender lyrical vocalize to suggest Sarah's joy at Isaac's birth (Gen. 21:1–7).

SAUL. Oratorio in four acts for soloists, chorus, and large orchestra by Handel (HWV 53, 1738). The libretto by Charles Jennens is based on the story of Saul's derangement and tragic downfall as told in the Bible (1 Sam. 9 to 2 Sam. 1) and two secular texts, *Davideis,* a verse epic by Abraham Cowley (1656), and *The Tragedy of King Saul,* by Lord Orrery (1703), both of which defended the concept of the divine right of kings. Despite being the focus of the work, Handel did not assign any da capo arias to the character of Saul and played down the relationship between Jonathan and David by embedding the words "more than women's love thy wondrous love to me" within a solo-choral number so that both the nation of Israel and David mourn the loss of Jonathan, not just David. Act 1 includes many fine numbers, including "Along the monster atheist strode" (i.e., Goliath), a plaintive air sung by David; "O Lord, whose mercies numberless," followed by a harp solo (Symphony) aimed at soothing Saul's rage; and Saul's air "A serpent in my bosom warm'd would sting me to the heart" with descending demisemiquavers depicting him hurling his javelin at David. Act 2 opens with the chorus "Envy, eldest born of Hell" and concludes with "Oh, fatal consequence of rage," describing Saul as a "furious monster." It also includes a love duet by David and Michal ("O fairest of ten thousand"), a "Wedding Symphony," and an organ concerto. Act 3 opens with the scene of the Witch of Endor ("Infernal spirits, by whose pow'r") and the appearance of Samuel ("Why hast thou forced me from the realms of peace back to this world of woe"). The Battle Symphony, featuring trumpets and drums, depicts Saul's final battle with the Philistines, and this is followed by the famous "Dead March" in C major for strings, organ, trombones, flutes, oboes, and timpani. The great solo-choral complex "Elegy on the death of Saul and Jonathan" includes solos by the high priest ("O, let it not in Gath be heard") (2 Sam. 1:20) and Michal ("In sweetest Harmony they lived") and several choruses, such as "Eagles were not so swift as they" and "O fatal day! How the mighty lie!" (cf. 2 Sam. 1:19). The work concludes with a recitative by the high priest ("For pious David will restore what Saul by disobedience lost") and a chorus in C major ("Gird on thy sword, thou man of might"). The "Dead March" was played at the state funerals of George Washington and Winston Churchill.

SAUL. Incidental music by Honegger (1922), commissioned by the poet René Morax for the play by André Gide (1898). It focuses on the homosexual relationship between David and Jonathan (2 Sam. 1:26) and King Saul's attraction to the young harpist David. Milhaud also composed incidental music to the play text in 1954, followed by its setting as an opera in three acts by the Italian composer Flavio Testi (2003). *See also* SCENES FROM THE LIFE OF DAVID AND JONATHAN.

SAUL OG DAVID. ("Saul and David"). Opera in four acts by Carl Nielsen (1902) to a libretto by Einar Christiansen, premiered in the Royal Danish Opera House on 28 November 1902. Based loosely on the stories told in 1 Samuel, act 1 opens at Gilgal, where Saul and his army await the arrival of the prophet Samuel (1 Sam. 13). When Samuel arrives, he announces the arrival of the evil spirit who will trouble Saul's soul, illustrated by tremolo in the strings. When Saul turns against God ("Wicked is God and wicked am I"), Jonathan invites his shepherd friend David into his house to comfort his father with his singing and harp music ("Sing Praises to God") (Ps. 104:1, 2, 10, 11). Act 1 concludes with a duet in which David and Michal declare their love for each other. Act 2 opens with the well-known martial prelude and recounts the story of David and Goliath (1 Sam. 17), ending with the people's song of victory (1 Sam. 18:6–7), Saul's jealous outburst against David ("Banished! Accursed! Out of my house!"), and David's departure ("God shall pass sentence! We meet again, King Saul!"). Act 3 begins with David's entry into Saul's camp and the removal of the spear and cruse of water from the sleeping Saul, punctuated by quavers in the strings, clarinets, and bassoons to depict their tiptoe movement. This is followed by the reunion of David and Saul (extrabiblical), the anointing of David as king, and the death of Samuel (1 Sam. 16:21), but the act ends with Saul's curse expressing his hope of killing David and regaining power. After a prelude, act 4 begins with the story of the Witch of Endor ("Sheol! Sheol! Mighty Sheol") and the dead Samuel's prophecy (1 Sam. 28), followed by "battle music" (*allegro violento*) depicting the battle between Saul's armies and the Philistines. With the chorus "All hope is vanished," Jonathan's death and Saul's suicide are followed by David's lament (2 Sam. 1:17–27; Ps. 93, 99; Jer. 18; Sir. 33:13) and the choruses "Thou art our hope" and "'Tis thou art chosen by God." David, Abner, and Michal sing a hymn of praise to God as the chorus proclaim David as the one who will found God's kingdom on earth.

SAUL! WAS VERFOLGST DU MICH? ("Saul! Why Do You Persecute Me?"). *Concertato* motet for six-voice ensemble and two four-voice choruses, two violins, brass, and continuo by Schütz (op. 12, no. 18, SWV 415) from *Symphoniae sacrae III*, regarded as one of his masterpieces. Christ's words to Saul on the road to Damascus (Acts 9:4, 26:14) are sung repeatedly by all 14 voices in homophony and in polyphony.

SCENES FROM THE LIFE OF DAVID AND JONATHAN. Chancel opera in five scenes for three male soloists and piano accompaniment with optional tambourine by Susan Hulsman Bingham (1993), inspired by the story of David's relationship with Jonathan (1 Sam. 17:55–20:42). Scene five includes a dramatic farewell scene in which Jonathan (T), son of Saul (B), sings a song of consolation to David based on Jer. 31: 8–9 and David (T) sings of his love for Jonathan: "Very pleasant have you been to me. Your love for me was wonderful, surpassing the love of women" (2 Sam. 1:26). *See also* SAUL.

SCHELOMO: HEBREW RHAPSODY. ("Solomon"). Concerto for cello and orchestra and best-known work of Ernest Bloch (1915–1916), dedicated to Russian cellist Alexander Barjansky. Inspired by the Book of Ecclesiastes (Eccl. 1:2–9) and composed against the backdrop of World War I, it was written, according to the composer, in the spirit of many books of the Bible to include the freshness of the patriarichs, the violence evident in the Prophetic Books, the sorrow of Job, and the sensuality of the Song of Songs. In three movements ("Largo Moderato," "Allegro Moderato," and "Andante Moderato"), the solo cello represents the voice of Solomon or his inner thoughts, while the orchestra depicts his world and the outward expression of his thoughts. It opens and closes with a cello cadenza, a melismatic lamentation of five measures based on Eccl. 1:1, "Vanity of Vanities, all is vanity," a theme that pervades the entire work. It has been performed by almost every major virtuoso cellist.

SEACHT NDÓLÁS NA MAIGHDINE MUIRE. ("The Seven Sorrows of the Virgin Mary"). Irish medieval carol and one of the oldest numerical carols in the Irish song tradition, it is performed by Nórín Ní Riain and the Monks of Glenstal Abbey on the album *Caoineadh na Maighdine* (2012) and also by Katie McMahon on the album *Lights in the Dark* (1998) to a haunting arrangement by Hector Zazou featuring chorus, oud, cello, and percussion. Sung in traditional *sean nós* style, it lists the seven sorrows of Mary as she witnesses her son die on the cross. The sorrows include Christ's lowly birth, the flight into Egypt (Mt. 2:13–21), Christ's passion (Christ stripped of his garments, the crowning of thorns, and Christ nailed to the cross), the Deposition, and Christ laid in the tomb. *See also* STABAT MATER DOLOROSA.

SEACHT SUÁILCE NA MAIGHINE MUIRE. ("The Seven Joys of the Virgin Mary"). Irish medieval carol known also as "The Seven Comforts of Mary," recounting moments of great joy in the life of Mary based on significant events in the life of Christ, including his birth, two healing miracles (healing the lame and the blind), raising the dead, reading the Scriptures in the Temple, the Resurrection, and wearing the crown of heaven (nonbiblical). It has been performed by Irish folksingers Nórín Ní Riain and Mary McLaughlin, English folksingers Maddy Prior and June Tabor, and the Good Shepherd Band, and in special arrangements by American composer Kirke Mechem and English composer Geoffrey Bush.

SEEK YE FIRST. A well-known praise song by Karen Lafferty (1972) for voices and folk guitar, based on Mt. 6:33 and 7:7, with four repetitions of the **Alleluia** as a refrain.

SENNACHERIB. Cantata by George Arnold to a libretto by the Rev. F. H. Arnold, composed for the Three Choirs Festival at Gloucester, where it was premiered in 1883. Inspired by the biblical narrative (Isa. 36–37), the work begins with an orchestral introduction, "The Besieged City," followed by the "March of the Assyrians" and a duet by Abi (S) and Hezekiah (T), "O House of Jacob," urging the Israelites to trust in God. Other notable numbers include Hezekiah's prayer "O Lord God of Hosts" (Isa. 37:16 –20), a song of praise sung by Abi and then by the chorus ("The sword of the enemy"), and the choral recitative "Then the Angel," sung by tenors and basses with the accompaniment scored in demisemiquavers and semiquavers to mark the destruction of 185,000 Assyrians (Isa. 37:36).

SEPT CHORALES-POÈMES D'ORGUE POUR LES SEPT PAROLES DU CHRIST. ("Seven Chorale Poems for Organ Based on the Seven Last Words of Christ"). Seven chorales for organ based on Christ's **Seven Last Words** by Charles Tournemire (op. 67, 1935). Each movement is based on a number of themes, most notably the "thirst theme," which comprises two harsh augmented second intervals and appears in all seven movements. In movement 1 (Lk. 23:34), the pedal line, marked with dissonant intervals and stark interruptions, evokes the stations of the cross. Movement 2 begins with a piercing cornet stop and concludes pianissimo to depict the thief's entry into paradise (Lk. 23:43). A two-part canon represents Christ's mother Mary and his beloved disciple John (Jn. 19:26), and the cry of dereliction (Mk. 15:34; cf. Ps. 22:1) is expressed by a passacaglia with the theme opening in the pedals and increasing in intensity in each variation. Movement 5 opens with the thirst theme (Jn. 19:28), and a fugue in movement 6, marked by a tutti, is followed by stark silence depicting Christ's death and a coda that contains the fugal theme in ascending motion depicting the movement of Christ's soul to heaven (Lk. 23:46). The final movement, *Consummatum est* ("It is finished") (Jn. 19:30), is a funeral dirge, and the work concludes on bare open fifths depicting the sense of desolation following Christ's death.

SEPT PAROLES DE NOTRE SEIGNEUR JÉSUS-CHRIST SUR LA CROIX, LES. ("The Seven Last Words of Our Lord Jesus Christ on the Cross"). Cantata for SATB/SATB chorus and organ by Gounod (1855). The sayings of Jesus on the cross (see preceding entry) are preceded by a prologue for SATB, largely homorhythmic, based on words spoken on his way to Golgotha (Lk. 23:28). Other settings include those of César Franck (1859) and François-Clément Théodore Dubois (1867). *See also* SEVEN LAST WORDS FROM THE CROSS, THE.

SET ME AS A SEAL UPON THY HEART. Wedding anthem for a cappella SATB chorus and tenor and soprano solos composed by William Walton for the wedding of the Honorable Ivor Guest to Lady Mabel Fox-Strangways in 1938. Based on the Song of Solomon (Cant. 8:6–7), it opens with an exquisite tenor solo ("Set me as a seal upon thine heart"), followed by a choral repetition of the same words and lush harmonies to evoke the lovers' tender feelings toward each other. The lyric "Love is strong as death" is repeated throughout to music that moves from uncertainty to certainty, from an open fifth to a major seventh on "death," and the work concludes on a major chord to reinforce the strength of love.

SEVEN DAYS OF THE PASSION. A cycle of 13 hymn arrangements in Church Slavonic by Alexander Tikhonovich Grechaninov (op. 58, 1911) from the Holy Week liturgy of the Eastern Orthodox Church. It begins with two hymns from the Bridegroom Matins Service, "Behold the Bridegroom" (Mt. 25:1–13) and "I See thy Bridal Chamber" (Mt. 22:1–14), followed by two hymns from the vespers liturgy of the Presanctified Gifts, including "Let My Prayers be set forth" (Ps. 141). Hymns from the Vespers of the Great and Holy Friday include the "Hymn of the Wise Thief" (Mt. 27:38) and the well-known **"The Noble Joseph"** (Mt. 27:57–60), based on a Bulgarian chant melody and usually sung to accompany the procession of the Holy Shroud. After Christ's words of comfort to his mother spoken from the grave, "Weep not for me O Mother," the cycle ends with the Cherubic Hymn of the Great and Holy Saturday, **"Let all Mortal Flesh keep silence"** (Hab. 2:20) (EH 318).

SEVEN DEADLY SINS, THE. (*Die sieben Todsünden*). Satirical *ballet chanté* ("sung ballet") in nine scenes by Kurt Weil with a libretto by Bertold Brecht, translated into English by W. H. Auden, Chester Kallman, and Michael Feingold. The last collaboration between Brecht and Weill, it was premiered at the Théâtre des Champs Elysées on 7 June 1933, produced, directed, and choreographed by George Balanchine with visual scenes by Caspar Neher. It is cast for Anna I (S), Anna II (dancer), the Family (TT-BarB), corps de ballet, and orchestra. Featuring Lotte Lenya as Anna I and Tilly Losch as Anna II in the original production, the two Annas represent two facets of one personality. On the advice of their family, they travel to different American cities in order to make enough money to build a house on the banks of the Mississippi River, and in each of the seven cities, they encounter a deadly sin: Sloth (city unnamed), Pride (Memphis), Wrath (Los Angeles), Gluttony (Philadelphia), Lust (Boston), Covetousness (Tennessee/Baltimore), and Envy (San Francisco). The list of seven deadly sins was formulated by Pope Gregory the Great (590 CE) but alludes also to biblical lists (Gal. 5:19–21; Prov. 6:16–19).

SEVEN LAST WORDS FROM THE CROSS, THE. Cantata for SSAA-TTBB chorus and strings by James MacMillan, commissioned by the BBC and broadcast a year later over seven nightly episodes during Holy Week (1994). The biblical texts (Mt. 27:39, 46; Mk. 15:33–34; Lk. 23:34, 39, 42, 43, 46; Jn. 19:26–30) are interpolated into other liturgical texts. Regarded by many as a masterpiece, the work has many poignant moments, such as the singing of the third sentence ("Verily, I say unto thee, today thou shalt be with me in Paradise") by two sopranos with violins, pitched at a high tessitura, to depict Christ's pain, followed by the Good Friday versicle "Behold the Wood of the Cross" (*Ecce lignum crucis*), sung in turn by basses, tenors, and altos, to mirror the Good Friday ritual. The bare and desolate harmonic accompaniment in the fifth sentence ("I Thirst") is heard against the backdrop of the Good Friday **Reproaches**, chanted as if in the distance ("I gave you to drink of life-giving water from the rock: and you gave me to drink of gall and vinegar"). The work concludes with the final sentence "Father into your hand I commend my Spirit" (Lk. 23:46), followed by a long instrumental postlude.

SEVEN LAST WORDS OF OUR REDEEMER ON THE CROSS, THE. (*Die Sieben letzte Worte unseres Erlösers am Kreuze*). Orchestral work by Joseph Haydn (op. 51), commissioned for the Good Friday Service at the Oratorio de la Santa Cueva in Cádiz, Spain, in 1783. Initially scored for flutes, oboes, bassoons, trumpets, drums, four horns, and strings and revised three days after the premiere for larger orchestral forces, it comprises seven sonatas, based on the sayings of Jesus on the cross. The work begins with an introduction in D minor and ends with the Finale *Il terremoto* ("The Earthquake") in C minor based on Mt. 27:51–53. At its premiere in Cádiz, each of the bishop's seven prostrations before the altar, after his sermon on the "**Seven Last Words**," was accompanied by the relevant sonata. Other versions of this work include a string quartet (op. 51, 1787), an oratorio (H. 20/2,1796), and a piano arrangement approved by the composer. *See also* SEVEN LAST WORDS FROM THE CROSS, THE.

SEVEN LAST WORDS OF OUR SAVIOUR ON THE CROSS, THE. (*Die Sieben letzte Worte unseres Erlösers am Kreuze*). Well-known cantata for SAATB chorus, five instruments, and continuo by Schütz, first performed in Dresden (SWV 478, 1645). It begins (Introitus) and ends (Conclusio) with the chorus singing the opening and closing stanzas of the Passiontide hymn *Da Jesus an dem Kreuze stund* ("As Jesus hung upon the Cross") by Johann Böschenstein and includes two instrumentals played immediately after the first verse of the hymn and just before the last. All Jesus' words are sung by the tenor and accompanied by strings, an unusual feature for the time, while the narrator's words are sung by several voices, including the chorus. *See also* SEVEN LAST WORDS FROM THE CROSS, THE.

SEVEN LETTERS. Choral work for seven soloists and chorus by Anthony Pitts (1998), it is dedicated to the seven members of Tonus Peregrinus, an ensemble founded in 1990 by Pitts while studying at New College, Oxford, and based on the seven letters of St. John to the churches in Asia Minor, modern-day Turkey, in Ephesus (Rev. 2:2–7), Smyrna (Rev. 2:8–11), Pergamum (Rev. 2:12–17), Thyatira (Rev. 2:18–28), Sardis (Rev. 2:29–3:1–6), Philadelphia (Rev. 3:7–13), and Laodicea (Rev. 3:14–22). Each letter begins on a different note of the scale, beginning on A and ascending through B-flat–C–D–E–F and finally G, and is declaimed by each of the seven members of Tonus Peregrinus (alto, soprano, soprano, countertenor, tenor, bass, and tenor) over a cyclical choral backdrop. The final letter incorporates the melody of **Amazing Grace** within the second alto part as a reference to the text "you can see" (Rev. 3:18).

SEVEN SEALS, THE. String quartet by Karel Goeyvaerts (1986), commissioned by the Royal Opera House De Munt–La Monnaie, Brussels. A revision of the finale was later incorporated into the composer's opera **Aquarius**. Scored in seven sections, each representing one of the seven seals from the Book of Revelation (Rev. 6:1–17, 8:15), it is cyclical in tonality, beginning and ending in B-flat.

SHADRACH. Rap pastiche by American hip-hop trio the Beastie Boys, produced by the Dust Brothers on the album *Paul's Boutique* (1989). Its title and references to "Shadrach, Meshach, and Abednego" at the end of each verse stem from the story of the three children in the fiery furnace from Dan. 3. A classic example of postmodernism in popular music, it samples nine songs by well-known artists, including "Loose Booty" by Sly and the Family Stone (1974), from whose lyrics the song takes its title. Characterized by fragmented lyrics, it includes references to other songs, such as **Amazing Grace**, as well as personalities, literary artists, musicians, the composer Arnold Schoenberg, consumer products, and copious references to hyperreality. Possibly identifying themselves with the three children in the fiery furnace, the trio (Ad Rock, MCA, and Mike D) composed unconventional music that dominated the rap scene for years.

SHADRACK. Song (1930) by Robert MacGimsey written in the style of a spiritual and based on the story of the three children in the fiery furnace (Dan. 3). It was performed by the Ames Brothers, Louis Armstrong, Jack Teagarden, Brook Benton, and many others and features in the movie *The Strip* (1951). In an arrangement for baritone and orchestra by opera singer Robert Merrill (1946), the cornet, flute, and harp are sounded to illustrate King Nebuchadnezzar's command to the Children of Israel to bow down to the idol (Dan. 3:5, 7, 10, 15), and staccato notes played on violins depict the raging flames of the fiery furnace (Dan. 3:19).

SHEEP. Progressive rock song on the album *Animals* (1977), originally entitled "Raving and Drooling," by the English rock band Pink Floyd. The lyrics, by Roger Waters, speak of the violence and greed of a capitalist society. The track opens and closes with the sound of bleating sheep as a setting for the parody of Ps. 23 which is spoken midway through the song using a vocoder. Here, the "Lord" represents corrupt leaders who have been overthrown by "sheep" who revolted and became just as evil as their leaders.

SHEPHERD'S CAROL, THE. One of the earliest American carols, written in 1778 by William Billings (1746–1800) to the tune "Shiloh" and first published in *The Suffolk Harmony* (1786).

SICUT CERVUS. ("Like as the Hart"). Well-known motet in two parts for SATB a cappella by Palestrina based on Ps. 42. Plaintive melismas on *aquarum* ("water"), *desiderat* ("longs for"), and *Deus* ("God"), together with syncopation on *ita desiderat*, describe the soul's longing for God. *See also* LIKE AS THE HART.

SILENT NIGHT. (*Stille Nacht*). Popular Christmas carol originally written in German by Franz Xavier Gruber (1816) and set to music by Joseph Mohr (1818). Later translated into English by American hymnologist John Freeman Young, it was published in John Hollister's *Sunday School Service and Tune Book* (1863). Inspired by Lk. 2:8–11 and sung as a gentle lullaby in compound duple time, it was first performed at a Midnight Mass in St. Nicholas Church in Oberndorf, Austria, to a guitar accompaniment in place of the organ, which legend tells had broken down. It was famously sung during the unofficial Christmas truce of World War I, after which English and German soldiers exchanged presents and played a game of football in no-man's-land.

SING JOYFULLY. Well-known anthem for six voices (SSAATB) by William Byrd based on Ps. 81:1–4. Thought to have been his last surviving anthem, it was performed at the christening service of Mary, daughter of James I, in 1605, where extended references to Jacob most likely allude to James I. Set in joyful imitative counterpoint and madrigalian in its text setting, the use of syncopation on "bring forth the timbrel, the pleasant harp" paints the sound of dancing, and the largely homophonic setting of "Blow the trumpet in the New Moon," sung antiphonally, evokes the sound of a trumpet fanfare.

SING UNTO GOD. Wedding anthem (HWV 263) for SATB soloists and chorus by Handel written for the marriage of Prince Frederick, the prince of Wales, to Princess Augusta of Saxe-Coburg on 27 April 1736. The first two movements are scored for alto solo, chorus, and full orchestra ("Sing unto God, ye kingdoms of the earth") (Ps. 68:32) and soprano solo ("Blessed are all they that fear the Lord") (Ps. 128:1). The third movement is scored for bass soloist and cello obbligato ("Thy wife shall be as the fruitful vine") (Ps. 128:3), and the work concludes with a joyful setting of Ps. 106:48 ("Blessed be the Lord God of Israel") for chorus and tenor solo in the style of a typical Handelian chorus.

SING YE TO THE LORD. Full anthem for Easter for SATB chorus and organ by Edward Cuthbert Bairstow to a text by Robert Campbell (1911). Inspired by the **Song of Miriam** (Exod. 15:21), the work begins and ends with a triumphant trumpet call and celebrates Christ's resurrection with the full chorus singing about the Lord's victory over Pharaoh and his chariots. References to the Resurrection are sung at a high tessitura, and it concludes in C major with a joyful **Alleluia**.

SINGET DEM HERRN EIN NEUES LIED. ("Sing unto the Lord a New Song"). Motet in three sections for double chorus (SSAATTBB) by J. S. Bach

(BWV 225, Leipzig, 1726/1727). It is based on two Psalms (Pss. 149:13, 150:2, 6) with a hymn text by Johann Gramann in the middle section. The final movement concludes with a lively fugue for two unison choruses reflecting the mood of Ps. 150 ("Let everything that breathes praise the Lord").

SINNERMAN. African American spiritual dating from the turn of the 20th century. It portrays the image of sinners trying to hide from the wrath of God in the rocks and the mountains. Derived indirectly from Isaiah (Isa. 2:10, 19, 20) via the Apocalypse (Rev. 6:15–16), it has been performed by numerous artists, including Les Baxter (1956), Nina Simone (1965), and Peter Tosh and Bunny Wailer (1970). A more recent version by Religious Souls on the album *Good God! Apocryphal Hymns* (2013) features a fusion of soul, funk, and rock as the sinner man lays bare his sins for all to hear.

SIRE OF SORROW, THE (JOB'S SAD SONG). Song by folksinger/songwriter Joni Mitchell (1994) on the album *Turbulent Indigo* (1994). Inspired by the story of Job and his friends, it repeats some of Job's bitter words addressed to God ("Can you see what mankind sees?" [Job 10:4]; "And still you torture me with visions. You give me terrifying dreams!" [Job 7:14]). His friends, called "Antagonists" throughout, interject moralizing arguments, such as "God is correcting you" (Job 5:17), "evil is sweet in your mouth hiding under your tongue" (Job 20:12) , and "you have no name now" (Job 18:17).

SIRENS. Song by the neoprogressive rock group Arena on the album *Pride* (1996). Unlike Hubert Parry's **Blest Pair of Sirens** who unite with the heavenly choirs of Seraphim (Isa. 6:2–3), the sirens here, based on the Greek myth about beautiful creatures who lured sailors to shipwreck with their enchanting, mystical voices, are symbols of female temptation. It includes the sound of women's voices singing, "Spare me from those sirens' lies . . . spare me those weeping eyes and promises of absolution."

SLEEP, ADAM, SLEEP AND TAKE THY REST. Sacred song for soprano/ countertenor and continuo by Henry Purcell (1693). One of the composer's earliest sacred songs, inspired by Gen. 2:21–24, it opens in the lower registers to represent Adam's deep sleep, apart from three occasions when "waking" is referred to. Following a seven-measure arioso on "Flesh of thy flesh . . . bone of thy bone," the song concludes with an extrabiblical warning about the woman: "But in the midst of thy delights beware, Lest her enticements prove thy snare."

SMALL AXE. Reggae song from the album *Burnin* by Rastafarian Bob Marley (1973). Inspired by biblical language and imagery (cf. Mt. 3:10; Isa.

10:34; Prov. 26:7), the song's title is an allusion to the righteous who will be victorious over their oppressors.

SOLDIER OF THE CROSS. Bluegrass gospel song by American country and bluegrass singer/songwriter Ricky Skaggs. It is performed by Skaggs and Kentucky Thunder on the album *Soldier of the Cross* (1999). The song's title refers to Christ's passion from the Gospels. The soldier in the song's title alludes to Christ the centurion at the cross (Mt. 27:54; Mk. 15:39; Lk. 23:47), and a modern follower of Christ.

SOLOMON. Oratorio by Handel (HWV 67, 1748; rev. 1759), regarded as a masterpiece, with a libretto by an unknown writer based on 1 Kgs. 3–11 and 2 Chron. 1–9 and Josephus's *Antiquities of the Jews,* first performed at the Theatre Royal in Covent Garden, London, on 17 March 1749. Scored for Solomon (A); Solomon's Wife and Queen (S); Nicaule, Queen of Sheba (S); First Harlot (S); Second Harlot (Mez); Zadok the high priest (T); a Levite (B); an Attendant (T); a chorus of Priests; and a chorus of Israelites, it tells three stories from the life of King Solomon. Act 1 opens with a song of praise by the Priests celebrating the opening of the Temple ("Your harps and cymbals sound to great Jehovah's praise") and depicts Solomon as a loving husband with his recitative "And see my Queen, my wedded love." Act 2 tells the story of the two harlots, both of whom claim the baby as their own, and Solomon's wisdom (1 Kgs. 3:16–28), concluding with a chorus of Priests praising Solomon's judgment ("Swell, swell the full chorus to Solomon's praise"). Act 3 opens with the well-known sinfonia "The Arrival of the Queen of Sheba," which is often performed as a concert piece in its own right, and concludes with a moralizing chorus of Israelites singing, "The name of the wicked shall quickly be past/But the fame of the just shall eternally last."

SOLOMON: A SERENATA. Serenata in three parts by William Boyce (ca. 1741) for two voices, mixed chorus, and orchestra to a libretto by Edward Moore (1712–1757), most likely based on the extended poem *The Fair Circassian* by Samuel Croxall (1720). It was extremely popular in the 18th century, performed in both Dublin and London, and the earliest existing word book was published by George Faulkner for the annual benefit concert in Mercers' Hospital, Dublin (1741). Inspired by the Song of Songs, it consists of recitatives and airs entitled "He" and "She," which abound in sexual allusions, as in the tenor air (part 2) "Softly arise, O Southern Breeze, and kindly fan the blooming trees, upon my spicy garden blow, that sweets from every part may flow." One of the most popular numbers, still performed today, is the soprano air "Tell Me, Gentle Shepherd!" The work opens and closes with the choruses "Behold Jerusalem thy king" and "In vain we trace the globe to try."

SONG FOR ATHENE. ("May Flights of Angels Sing Thee to Thy Rest"). Elegy in memory of the actress Athene Hariades, who died in a cycling accident, written for four-part chorus a cappella (SATB) by John Tavener (1993) to lyrics by Mother Thekla. Commissioned by the BBC, it was heard by millions of people all over the world at the funeral service of Diana, Princess of Wales, in 1997 and is one of the composer's best-known works. Inspired by words from Shakespeare's *Hamlet* (5, 2; 2, 2), Luke's Gospel (Lk. 23:42), and the Orthodox Funeral Service, it is characterized by the intonation of an **Alleluia** (cf. Rev. 19:1, 3, 4, 6) before each of the six verses and a continuous drone (*ison*), a notable feature of Byzantine music that underscores the entire work. A seventh reiteration of the **Alleluia** concludes the work.

SONG OF GOMER, THE. Song by American singer/songwriter Michael Card from the album *The Word: Recapturing the Imagination*, telling of Hosea's suffering in first-person narration by his wife, Gomer (Hos. 1–3). The tender lyrical melody reflects Hosea's love for his wife and Gomer's pity for her husband, who suffered silently because of her infidelity. The three verses tell of his loving qualities ("fondness of a father," "tenderness of a friend," and "understanding smile") and continuing forgiveness, and the refrain mocks Hosea, calling him a "fool" for loving someone like her and suffering in silence. Even though she delights in his company when he welcomes her back, she could never be as faithful as Hosea. *See* HOSEA'S WIFE.

SONG OF SIMEON. Nativity masque by Malcolm Arnold with words by Christopher Hassall, premiered at the Theatre Royal, Drury Lane, London, under the auspices of the vicar of St. Martin-in-the-Fields on 5 January 1960. Seen through the eyes of the aged Simeon (Lk. 2:22–38), the story of the Annunciation and the Nativity is told mainly in recitative, combined with a reflective commentary sung by the chorus and extended to include the Feast of the Purification. The main action occurs at the Inn, where Simeon (T) is also looking for a room and the shepherds (BBBB) are accused of being drunk. The work concludes outside the Temple at Jerusalem, where Simeon with the Christ child sings the **Nunc Dimittis** followed by the lesser doxology.

SONG OF SOLOMON, THE. Song by Kate Bush on the album *The Red Shoes* (1993), telling of a lovesick woman who, like the woman in the Song of Solomon, is alone and weary of her lover's lies. All she wants is his "sexuality" (Cant. 2:6). Alluding to the fruit of the apple tree (Cant. 2:3), she says that she will be for him "the Rose of Sharon . . . the Lily of the Valley" (Cant. 2:1).

SONG OF TWO WIDOWS. Hymn in D minor (1997) by Mary Nelson Keithahn to the tune "Two Widows" by John D. Horman based on the story of two nameless widows: the widow of Zarephath who baked a loaf of bread for Elijah out of the last ingredients in her cupboard (1 Kgs. 17:18) and the widow who put her last two coins into the Temple treasury (Lk. 21:1–4).

SONGS FROM THE LION'S CAGE. Debut album (1995) by British progressive rock group Arena, it features song titles with biblical themes, including "Out of the Wilderness," "Jericho," and "Solomon." The album's front cover alludes to Daniel in the lion's den (Dan. 6).

SONGS OF BATHSHEBA. Oratorio for soprano, choir, and orchestra by Gil Shohat (2005). In it, Bathsheba, now the queen mother after David's death, gives her side of the story (2 Sam. 11–12), while the choir sings a kind of reflective commentary. Bathsheba's words are an English translation of a text written by the Israeli poet Shin Shifra, while the choir sings verses from Ps. 51 in Hebrew, thus combining a modern feminist interpretation of the biblical text with a liturgical use of the Psalm. Bathsheba's words are unrelentingly bitter, as when she cynically quotes a verse from the Psalm herself, accusing David of trying to blame primeval sin for his own wicked deeds (Ps. 51:5).

SONGS OF SYON: A COLLECTION OF HYMNS AND SACRED PO-EMS MOSTLY TRANSLATED FROM ANCIENT GREEK, LATIN, AND GERMAN SOURCES. A collection of hymns edited by George Ratcliffe Woodward and Charles Wood, first published in 1904 and in an enlarged edition in 1908. The collection concentrated on plainsong Lutheran hymns and 16th- to 17th-century metrical Psalms sung to tunes mainly from before 1800 with some exceptions, including two composed by Wood and four by Wagner. A third edition (1910) was described by the writer of Woodward's *Church Times* obituary as "the finest hymn book, both as regards words and music, ever produced in England" but was overshadowed by the much more successful **English Hymnal** published in 1907.

SOUNDING THE LAST TRUMPET. Debut album by American rock band Avenged Sevenfold (2011). Inspired by the angel blowing the seventh and final trumpet (Rev. 11:15–19), it describes the third woe (v. 14), signifying the end of the world, and includes the songs "To End the Rapture," "Forgotten Faces," and "Shattered by Broken Dreams."

SPEM IN ALIUM. ("I Have Hope in None Other"). Motet (ca. 1568) for 40 voices comprising eight five-part choirs by English Catholic composer Thomas Tallis. It is based on a response for matins from the Sarum rite, adapted from Judith's prayer (Jud. 9). Perhaps inspired by Alessandro Striggio's 40-part motet *Ecce beatam lucem* ("Behold the blessed light"), it was composed around 1568 either for the 40th birthday of the Protestant Queen Elizabeth I or to honor the memory of the Catholic Queen Mary. There may also be an allusion to biblical periods of trial, such as Israel's 40 years (Deut. 8:2, 4) or Jesus' 40 days in the wilderness (Mk. 1:13), in reference to the plight of English Catholics. The composition opens with a single voice from choir 1, followed by imitative voice setting, moving on to choir 2 to choir 8. At the 40th breve, all parts enter together and repeat the opening pattern in reverse. Following a series of antiphonal exchanges, it concludes with a 40-voice chord. The first performance is thought to have taken place in the octagonal banqueting hall of Nonesuch Palace, which accommodated the eight choirs and enabled a sound evoking a sense of God's majesty (*Domine Deus Creator caeli et terrae*). A contrafactum was performed for the investiture of Henry, Prince of Wales, in 1610, and more recently it reached the top of the charts in the United Kingdom following its appearance in the film *Fifty Shades of Grey* by E. L. James.

SPIRIT OF THE PSALMS, THE. Collection of hymns written by Henry Francis Lyte (1793–1847) and published in 1834. Based mostly on the Book of Psalms, they include *Praise my soul the King of heaven* (Ps. 103), *Pleasant are thy courts above* (Ps. 84), *Praise the Lord his glories show* (Ps. 150), and, his most famous hymn, **Abide with me** (Lk. 24:29).

SPIRITUS SANCTUS. ("Holy Spirit"). Antiphon of the Holy Spirit from "Symphony of the Harmony of Celestial Revelations" by Hildegard of Bingen (1098–1179). Perhaps inspired by Jn. 6:63, 1 Cor. 6:11 and 19, and Titus 3:5, it was arranged for SATB a cappella.

STABAT MATER DOLOROSA. ("The Mother Stood Grieving"). A popular medieval Latin hymn describing the suffering of Mary the mother of Jesus at the Crucifixion that found its way into the liturgy in the later Middle Ages. Often attributed to Jacopone da Todi, the 20 stanzas make direct reference to the biblical text only once (Lk. 2:35). Among numerous musical settings, the most notable are those of Pergolesi for women's voices, Vivaldi for alto solo and strings, Haydn (1767), Schubert (in German) (D. 383, 1833), Rossini (1841), Dvořák (1877), Stanford in five movements (1907), and Pärt for soprano, countertenor (or alto), and tenor solos with string trio (1985).

STAIRWAY TO HEAVEN. Song by Jimmy Page and Robert Plant of the English rock group Led Zeppelin on their untitled fourth studio album, *Led Zeppelin IV* (1971), regarded as one of the greatest rock songs of all time. Inspired by the story of Jacob's ladder (Gen. 28:10–19), the song tells of two paths that lead to heaven and to hell and the "piper" (i.e., Christ) who leads and calls the faithful. It is composed in a number of sections, ranging from a gentle folk-style introduction with finger-plucked guitar, four recorders, and voice to a slow electric middle section with voice and solo guitar to a more animated hard-rock section concluding with solo vocals. Every episode of the Australian comedy talk show *The Money or the Gun* on the ABC network began with the song performed by a different artist (1989–1990), resulting in a compilation album entitled *Stairway to Heaven*, featuring 12 performances by Australian artists (1995).

STAIRWAY TO HEAVEN. Hit song by Neil Sedaka and Howard Greenfield on the album *Neil Sedaka Sings Little Devil and His Other Hits* (1960). The singer tells of his intention to build a "stairway to heaven," like Jacob's ladder (Gen. 28:10–19), to enable him to reach his girl, imagined as a heavenly angel. It was later recorded with Stan Applebaum and His Orchestra on the RCA Victor label (1960).

STAR OF BETHLEHEM. Christmas hymn by John Williams with words by Leslie Bricusse, arranged by Tom Fettke, for the movie *Home Alone II* (1990). It is based on the reference to a star in the East that guided the Magi to Bethlehem to worship the Christ child (Mt. 2:2). *See also* DER STERN VON BETHLEHEM.

STIFF-NECKED FOOLS. Reggae song by Rastafarian Bob Marley (1973), performed by Marley and the Wailers and released posthumously on the album *Confrontation* (1983). Inspired by a variety of biblical words and phrases (cf. Exod. 3:3, 5; Prov. 10:15, 21; 18:11; Rom. 1:21), the song's title is an allusion to those who reject righteousness in favor of vanity.

STROPHES. Short work for soprano soloist, reciting voice, and ensemble (10 instruments) by Penderecki, dedicated to Andrzej Markowski (1959). Brief fragments of ancient texts about the mystery of death and the plight of human nature are sung in the manner of *Sprechstimme* in the original languages of each text: Greek, Hebrew, and Persian. Pointillist in texture, it begins with a fragment in Greek by the dramatist Menander, introduced by the speaker ("What charming creatures men can be as long as they are still human"), followed by the last few lines of Sophocles' tragedy *Oedipus Rex* ("So while we wait to see that final day,/we cannot call a mortal being happy/before he's passed beyond life free from pain"), sung by the soprano and then spoken by the speaker. This is followed by texts from the biblical prophets (Isa. 5:20; Jer. 17:9) in Hebrew with the speaker echoing the soprano, and the work concludes with a piece by the mathematician and Sufi poet Omar Khayyám (1048–1131) ("From the depth of black soil to the planet's summit,/I have answered all questions in the universe./I have solved all puzzles and all complex cases/But I have not managed to untangle the secrets of death!").

SULAMITH, THE SONG OF SONGS. Oratorio by Leopold Damrosch, first performed by the Oratorio Society of New York in 1882. The 10 movements are settings of love poetry from the Song of Solomon, beginning, after an orchestral prelude, with a passionate duet sung by Sulamith (S) and Solomon (T) (Cant. 1:7). In movement 4, Solomon's words to Sulamith, "Arise come away with me" (Cant. 2:13), are sung vivace by the chorus, and then movement 5 portrays Sulamith's anticipation when she hears of Solomon's arrival and disappointment when she realizes that it was only a dream (Cant. 5:2–6) with a variety of tempi (*agitato assai, poco lento, allegro con fuoco*, and *poco lento espressivo*). Movement 6 is a march in C major painting the procession of the bridal couple to the banqueting hall (Cant. 2:4) followed by a tender love song in movement 7 describing Sulamith's ravishing beauty. The next two movements comprise an octet of female voices representing the maidens of Jerusalem as they search for Solomon (Cant. 6:1) and a duet sung by the couple as they return to Sulamith's vineyard (Cant. 7:10–13), while the final chorus is a fugue set in C major celebrating the durability of married love (Cant. 8:6–7).

SUPER FLUMINA BABYLONIS. ("By the Waters of Babylon"). Offertory antiphon from the traditional Latin Mass, sung on the 20th Sunday after Pentecost. Inspired by Ps. 137, it was set to music by numerous composers, most notably in the 16th and 17th centuries by Palestrina, Lassus, and Victoria. In 1583, Flemish composer Philippe de Monte, who was Kapellmeister to the Holy Roman emperor, sent William Byrd a copy of his eight-part setting of the first four verses, rearranged for added poignancy (vv. 1, 3, 4, 2) as an expression of concern for a fellow Catholic composer living in England during the repression of Catholics under Elizabeth I. Byrd responded a year later with an eight-part motet (SSAATTBB) based on the same Psalm but beginning where de Monte had left off: *Quomodo cantabimus* ("How shall we sing the Lord's song in a foreign land?") (Ps. 137:4). As a striking example of intricate contrapuntal writing, Byrd's defiant motet includes a three-part canon in inversion in the first of two sections, as the number 3 is symbolic of Christ's victory over death "on the third day." There is also a 19th-century setting of the text for piano by Charles-Valentin Alkan (1813–1888). *See also* BY THE WATERS OF BABYLON.

SUPPER'S READY. Concept piece in seven sections by the British rock band Genesis on their album *Foxtrot* (1972). Taking under 27 minutes to perform, it tells of two lovers who, on their travels to different worlds, are witnesses of the Apocalypse. In "Apocalypse in 9/8," which is a type of mini-organ concerto in varying meters, played by Tony Banks alternating with stirring vocals by Peter Gabriel, the lyrics describe the battle of Armageddon (Rev. 16:16) with references to the number of the beast, 666 (Rev. 13:18); the seven trumpets (Rev. 8:6–15); and Magog (Rev. 20:7–8). Staged performances employ orange lights to signify the destruction of humankind in fire, smoke, and brimstone (Rev. 9:17–18) and a backdrop of flames representing the lake of fire into which the devil and the false prophet were cast forever (Rev. 19:20). Peter Gabriel wears a number of quirky costumes throughout the piece, including one depicting Magog that he throws off at the end of section 6 to signify the death of the Antichrist. In section 7, "As Sure as Eggs Is Eggs (Aching Men's Feet)," he wears a glowing-white costume and fluorescent makeup to represent the angel of Rev. 19:17, who, having defeated the Beast, invites all the birds of the sky to the celebration of the Great Supper of the Lord in the New Jerusalem (Rev. 19:5–21). The piece ends with the lyric "King of Kings . . . and Lords of Lords" (Rev. 19:16; 1 Tim. 6:15).

SURGE, ILLUMINARE. ("Arise, Shine"). Antiphonal motet for double chorus a cappella by Palestrina, published in the third book of motets (1581). Based on Isa. 60:1–2 and written for the Feast of the Epiphany, the opening is characterized by rising scale-like passages on *Surge* in all voice parts, while a change to triple meter and homophony on *et Gloria domini* produces a dance-like effect praising God. There are numerous other 16th-century settings, including one by William Byrd and a more recent one for SATB with *divisi* and organ by Frank Boles (1993).

SUSANNA. Oratorio in three acts for SSATBB soloists, chorus, and string orchestra with oboes, bassoons, and trumpets by Handel (HWV 66, 1749). Inspired by the story of Susanna and the Two Elders (Dan. 13), the oratorio highlights the themes of virtue and vice. In act 1, Susanna's Husband (A) and Father (B) describe her virtue, and Susanna (S) joins in the love duet "Art thou Nigh, my pulse beats high," while in scenes 3 and 4, the Two Elders (TB) describe their lust for Susanna ("Tyrannic Love! I feel thy cruel dart") and plot to defile her. In act 2, Susanna seeks relief from the heat of the day in a stream ("Crystal streams in murmurs flow"), and as she bathes, the Elders approach and attempt to seduce her. When they fail, they accuse her of adultery, after which Susanna sings the air "If guiltless blood be your intent." Following her trial and the saving intervention of Daniel (S) ("Thou artful wretch" and "False is thy tale") in act 3, the oratorio concludes with a duet sung by Susanna and Joacim (alto) and a chorus that praises Susannah's virtue and chastity ("A virtuous wife shall soften fortune's frown"). Other works include the *oratorio erotico La Susanna* by Alessandro Stradella (1681), the one-act opera *Sancta Susanna* by Hindemith (op. 21, 1921), and the opera **Susannah** by Carlisle Floyd (1955).

SUSANNAH. Opera in two acts by Carlisle Floyd, premiered at Florida State University in 1955 and staged by the New York City Opera in 1956. Based loosely on the story of Susannah and the Two Elders (Dan. 13), it was inspired by the anticommunist witch hunt of Senator Joseph McCarthy in the 1950s. Set in New Hope Valley, Tennessee, in the Bible Belt, it features the beautiful Susannah Polk (S), an unmarried 19-year-old virgin who was discovered bathing naked in a creek used for baptisms; her drunkard brother Sam (T); and the itinerant preacher Rev. Olim Blitch (B), who seduces Susannah ("I'm a lonely man, Susannah") and is murdered by Sam. The opera opens with the prediction that Susannah will come to no good ("She's a shameless girl, she is") and the elders of an Evangelical congregation and their wives ostracize Susannah for driving her brother crazy to commit murder. Highlighting the themes of hypocrisy and mistrust, it is one of the most frequently performed operas in the United States today.

SUSANNE UN JOUR. ("One Day Susanna"). *Chanson spirituelle* (sacred song). One of the most famous songs of the 16th century, inspired by the apocryphal story of Susanna and the Elders (Dan. 13). Written by the poet Guillaume Guéroult, it was first set to music by Didier Lupi Second (1548) and subsequently by numerous composers. The most famous by Lassus, for five voices and two lutes (1560), became the basis for his parody Mass *Missa Susanne un jour* (1577), later transcribed for keyboard by Andrea Gabrieli (1605). William Byrd composed two settings in English entitled *Susanna Fair*, one for five voices published in *Psalmes, Sonnets and Songs* (1588) and the other for three voices in *Songs of Sundrie Natures* (no. 8, 1589). Giles Farnaby also composed a setting in English for four voices (SSTB) in *Canzonets to Foure Voyces* (1598).

SWING LOW, SWEET CHARIOT. Traditional African American spiritual attributed to Wallace Willis, inspired by the story of Elijah's ascension to heaven in a chariot of fire (2 Kgs. 2:11). The song's descending melody describes the arrival of the angels on the banks of the River Jordan who come to bring the souls of the dead home to heaven. First performed by the Fisk Jubilee Singers in 1909, it has been performed by a host of performers, including Johnny Mathis (1958), Johnny Cash (1959), the Grateful Dead (1970), Joan Baez (1970), and, more recently, Beyoncé in the film *Fighting Temptations* (2003). It was incorporated by Dvořák into his New World Symphony (1893), adopted as the unofficial anthem of the English Rugby Union (1988), and sung at the funeral of President Ronald Reagan on 10 June 2004 at Washington National Cathedral.

SWINGIN SAMSON. Cantata for children's unison voices, narrator, and piano accompaniment with words and music by Michael Hurd (1973). First performed by the Southend Boys' Choir, it is a child-friendly version of the story of Samson and Delilah (Judg. 14–16) and includes popular numbers, such as "Clip clip went the clippers," set in a barber's shop; "Weak as a Kitten," sung by a soloist and chorus in lilting compound duple time to depict Samson's weakening; and "Everybody came to the Philistine's Party," for chorus and soloist set as a square dance. *See also* SAMSON AND DELILAH.

SYMPHONIAE SACRAE. ("Sacred Symphonies": Vocal-Instrumental Concertos). A collection of three volumes of motets and cantatas for voices, instruments, and continuo by Heinrich Schütz (op. 6, SWV 257–276, 1629; op. 10, SWV 341–67, 1647; op. 12, SWV 398–418, 1650). Based mostly on texts from the Old Testament—the second volume in particular, on Psalms—the collection includes well-known works such as *Fili mi, Absalom* ("My Son, Absalom") (2 Sam. 18:33) (op. 6, SWV 269, no. 13), *Mein Herz ist bereit, Gott* ("My heart, O God, my heart is steadfast") (Ps. 57:7) (op. 10, SWV 341, no. 1), and *Saul! Was verfolgst du mich?* (**Saul! Why are you persecuting me?**) (Acts 26:14) (op. 12, SWV 415, no. 18).

SYMPHONIE-PASSION FOR ORGAN. Symphonic poem for organ in four movements by Marcel Dupré (op. 23, 1924). It began as an improvisation on **Adeste Fideles** and three Gregorian plainchants during a concert at Wanamaker's Department Store (currently Macy's) in Philadelphia in 1921. The first movement (*Le monde dans l'attente du Sauveur*) describes the restless world awaiting the birth of Christ, illustrated musically by changing time signatures and the chant *Jesu Redemptor omnium* ("Jesus redeemer of all"), played on the oboe stop, as a plea for deliverance. The second movement describes the Nativity, from the Virgin's lullaby and the march of the Magi to Bethlehem to their adoration of the Christ child; Adeste Fideles and distant **Alleluias** represent the choirs of angels. In movement 3, a syncopated one-measure ostinato and ascending elongated notes depict Christ's agonizing steps on the way to Golgotha, culminating in a series of chords representing the nails driven into Christ's flesh. Descending chords ending on a single soft pedal note, followed by a fragmented version of the **Stabat Mater**, illustrate Christ's death and the presence of his grieving mother at the foot of the cross. The final movement (*Résurrection*) is highly contrapuntal and features the plainchant Eucharistic hymn *Adoro te devote*.

SYMPHONY NO. 7: "SEVEN GATES OF JERUSALEM." Choral symphony in seven movements by Penderecki for five soloists (SSATB), narrator, three mixed choruses, and orchestra, commissioned to celebrate the Holy City's third millennium (1996). The number 7 features prominently in the seven movements: the seven-note repetition on a single pitch in the passacaglia in the second and fourth movements and in the septuple meters that occur throughout, including seven fortissimo chords on E major at the close of the final movement. The first three movements, inspired by Psalms, are "Great is the Lord" (Ps. 48), "If I forget thee" (Ps. 137), and "Out of the depths" (Ps. 130). Movement 4 repeats "If I forget thee" but continues with "Open the gates" (Isa. 26:2) and "Awake, awake, put on your strength, O Zion" (Isa. 52:1). Penderecki constructed two entirely new instruments (tubaphones) for the fifth movement, "Praise the Lord, O Jerusalem" (Ps. 147:12–14), and movement 6, "The hand of the Lord was upon me" (Ezek. 37:1–10), scored for speaker and orchestra, is in Hebrew and includes solo bass trumpet in place of a shofar to symbolize the "voice of God." The work concludes with a return to Ps. 48 combined with quotations from Ps. 96 ("O Sing to the Lord a new song") and the prophets (Jer. 21:8; Dan. 7:13; Isa. 59:19; 60:1–2, 11).

SYMPHONY OF PSALMS. Symphony in three movements for mixed chorus and orchestra without violins, violas, or clarinets by Igor Stravinsky. Commissioned by Serge Koussevitzky to celebrate the 50th anniversary of the Boston Symphony Orchestra, it was premiered in Brussels on 13 December 1930. Based on the text of three Psalms to be sung in Latin, the first movement, a prelude, composed in a "state of religious and musical ebullience," is a prayer of lamentation based on the words *Exaudi orationem meam, Domine* ("O Lord hear my prayer") (Ps. 39:13–14). The second movement, *Expectans expectavi* ("I waited patiently for the Lord") (Ps. 40:1–3), is a double fugue. Movement 3, *Laudate Dominum* ("Praise the Lord") (Ps. 150), is "a prayer to the Russian image of the infant Christ with orb and scepter," beginning with the whispered intonation of the **Alleluia** followed by an allegro middle section inspired by the "vision of Elijah's chariot climbing into the heavens." The work concludes with a return to the whispered **Alleluia**.

• T •

TÁLADH CHRÍOSDA. ("Christ's Lullaby"). Scottish Gaelic lullaby, popularized in English as "The Christ Child's Lullaby" by Marjory Kennedy-Fraser. Written by Fr. Ranald Rankin (ca. 1855) and traditionally sung at Midnight Mass on Christmas Eve in Barra, South Uist, and Eriskay in the Outer Hebrides, Scotland, it comprises 29 verses telling of the Virgin's lullaby to the Christ child, sung to the tune "Cumha Mhic Árois" ("Lament for the son of Árois").

TE DEUM LAUDAMUS. ("We Praise You, God"). Also known as the *Te Deum*. This hymn of praise, sung at the end of matins, is traditionally attributed to St. Ambrose but almost certainly existed earlier, perhaps the work of Niceta of Remesiana (fourth century). It follows the pattern of the Apostles' Creed, drawing on Isaiah's vision (Isa. 6) and some of the Psalms, such as Ps. 145. Well-known settings include Handel's *Utrecht Te Deum*, written, with the **Jubilate** (Ps. 100), to celebrate the Treaty of Utrecht (1713), and his *Dettingen Te Deum* (HWV 28, 1743), written to celebrate the British victory at the Battle of Dettingen (1743). Charpentier composed six settings, four of which exist, including the grand polyphonic motet in D major (H. 146, 1868) for SSATB soloists, SATB chorus, two flutes, two oboes, bassoon, two trumpets, timpani, two violins, viola, and basso continuo. The rondo prelude to this work features as the signature theme of the Eurovision song contest. Other popular settings are those of Mozart, Berlioz, Bruckner, Kodály, and Britten. The English hymn "Holy God we praise thy name" is a translation of the 18th-century German version of the *Te Deum* by Ignaz Franz (1771). A contemporary setting of the Te Deum in English and Latin for SATB chorus *divisi*, two soloists (MezBar), and orchestra by American composer Mark Hayes is a monumental work of great beauty. *See also* UTRECHT JUBILATE.

TEHILLIM. ("Psalms"). A setting by Steve Reich of four Psalms (Pss. 19:2–5; 34:13–15; 18:26–27; 150:4–6) scored for three sopranos (one high and two lyric sopranos), alto, strings, percussion, and keyboards (1981). Minimalist in character and sung in Hebrew, the work makes extensive use of percussion, including small tuned tambourines with no jingles, hand clapping, maracas, marimba, vibraphone, and crotales, representing biblical instruments, such as the small drum, or "timbrel" (Hebrew *tof*), and cymbals (Hebrew *şelşelim*) (Ps. 150:4–5). The settings are not based on any Jewish tunes.

TELL ME SOME PITYING ANGEL. *See* BLESSED VIRGIN'S EXPOSTULATION, THE.

TELL OUT MY SOUL. Well-known hymn by Tim Dudley-Smith (1962), a paraphrase of the **Magnificat** (Lk. 1:46–56), telling, in first-person narration, of Mary's joy following the announcement of the birth of Christ by the angel Gabriel. Sung to the popular tune "Woodlands" by Walter Greatorex (1916), it is published in over 40 hymnals.

TEMPLE, THE. Oratorio in two parts for soprano, tenor, and baritone soloists, chorus, orchestra, and organ by Walford Davies (op. 14, 1902) with a libretto compiled by the composer. It was inspired by biblical accounts of David's desire to build a temple (1 Chron. 17) and Solomon's fulfillment of his father's wish (1 Chron. 28–29; 2 Chron. 2–7; cf. 1 Kgs. 6–8) with reflective movements based on the Psalms (Pss. 96, 100, 71, 65, 31, 132, 136) and Acts (Acts 7:47, 48). Memorable moments include David's prayer for baritone solo ("Thou art my hope, O Lord God") (Ps. 71), the solemn interlude following the announcement of David's death sung as a recitative by a soprano soloist ("And David Died"), and the double chorus celebrating the completion of Solomon's Temple ("O give thanks unto the Lord") (Ps. 36).

TEN COMMANDMENTS, THE. Musical in two acts by Patrick Leonard (2006) with lyrics by Maribeth Derry, based on the biblical story of **Moses** but adding a nonbiblical account of his relationship with his brother Ramses and their rivalry over the beautiful Nefertari. Filmed live at the Hollywood Kodak Theater, highlights include "Is Anybody Listening," sung by *American Idol* contestant Adam Lambert (**Joshua**), and "Let Them Go," sung by Val Kilmer (**Moses**).

TEN COMMANDMENTS, THE. Sole album by progressive rock group Salamander (1971), comprising 10 tracks, one for each of the commandments, entitled as follows: "Prelude" (incorporating "He's my God"), "Images," "People," "God's Day," "Honour thy Father and thy Mother," "Kill," "Thou shalt not Commit Adultery," "Steal," "False Witness," and "Possession."

TEN COMMANDMENTS, THE. A cycle of 10 a cappella canons for three, four, and five voices by Joseph Haydn (Hob. XXVIIa:1–10, 1791, published posthumously 1809). Dedicated to Count Hans Moritz von Brühl, the Saxon minister to England, the work as a whole was composed during Haydn's first visit to England (1791–1792). The music of the first canon, *Canon cancrizans, a tre,* known as a "crab canon," was submitted as an exercise for the honorary degree of doctor of music by Oxford University (1791) to the words "Thy voice, O Harmony is Divine." Other notable numbers include the fifth ("Thou shalt not kill") with striking dissonances and the sixth ("Thou shalt not commit adultery") in a flighty 6/8 meter. Haydn's student Sigismund Ritter von Neukomm later composed an oratorio based on the **Ten Commandments**, dedicated to the king of Prussia, that was later translated into English for SATB soloists, chorus, and piano under the title *Mount Sinai, or The Ten Commandments An Oratorio,* in two parts, taken from the Holy Scriptures, translated from the German (London, 1832).

TEN COMMANDMENTS, THE: SOUND TRACK SUITE. The sound track of Cecil B. DeMille's epic movie (1956), starring Charlton Heston (**Moses**), Yul Brynner (Rameses), and Anne Baxter (Nefretiri). Composed and conducted by Elmer Bernstein, it is based on a series of leitmotifs, of which the most prominent denotes deliverance from bondage, featuring instruments such as the *tiple,* finger cymbals, and a sistrum during the Egyptian dance scene; a theremin in the scene of the plagues; and a shofar (ram's horn) to announce the Israelites' departure from Egypt.

TERRE PROMISE, LA. ("The Promised Land"). Oratorio for narrator, chorus, and large orchestra by Jules Massenet (1899) to a libretto compiled by the composer, premiered at the Church of St. Eustache, Paris, on 15 March 1900. Based on chapters from Deuteronomy and **Joshua** (Josh. 6:22), the work is in three parts entitled "Moab: The Alliance," "Jericho," and "Canaan," each prefaced with a biblical text. It is scored for a narrator ("La Voix") who narrates text from the speeches of **Moses** and Joshua, a chorus representing the Israelites and the Levites, and an orchestra. Another notable work with the same title was composed by Saint-Saëns to a libretto by Hermann Klein (op. 140, 1913). *See also* PROMISED LAND, THE.

TEST OF FAITH, THE. Chamber opera/pulpit opera in one act by Lawrence Goldberg (1987) to a libretto by poet and author Marcia Hain Engle, prize winner in a competition organized by the Jewish Music Commission of Los Angeles (1987). Based on the Akedah, or "binding of Isaac" (Gen. 22:1–19) and inspired by Shalom Spiegel's *The Last Trial: On the Legends and Lore of the Command to Abraham to Offer Isaac as a Sacrifice* (1969), it is scored for a Narrator (Spoken/Bar), Abraham (T), Isaac (Tr), an Angel of God/God (Spoken/Bar), and a seven-piece instrumental ensemble, including a harp and a shofar that play the final instrumental number.

THE ANGEL GABRIEL. A Basque folk carol known also by the title "Gabriel's Message," arranged and harmonized by Edgar Pettman in *Modern Christmas Carols* (1892). It tells of the Annunciation to the Virgin Mary by the angel Gabriel (Lk. 1:26–38, 46–55). Notable contemporary arrangements include performances by Sting on the album *A Very Special Christmas* (1987) and in a performance at Durham Cathedral (2009) by Jars of Clay on the album *Christmas Songs* (2007).

THE EARTH IS YOURS. Song by American singer/songwriter Michael Gungor inspired by Ps. 29 and performed by the liturgical postrock band Gungor, formerly known as the Michael Gungor Band, on the album *Beautiful Things* (2010). Celebrating the majesty of God as King and Lord of Creation, the upbeat chorus praises God with an allusion to the **Sanctus** (Isa. 6:3). *See also* HOLY, HOLY, HOLY.

THE HEAD THAT ONCE WAS CROWNED WITH THORNS. Hymn by Thomas Kelly (1769–1854), inspired by Heb. 2:9 (cf. Ps. 8:5) and perhaps influenced by the poem "One Thing Is Needful" (1964) by John Bunyan. The tune "St. Magnus" (or "Nottinghan") is attributed to Jeremiah Clarke in W. Riley's *Parochial Harmony* (1762).

THE HEAVENS DECLARE YOUR GLORY. Hymn based on Ps. 19 by Thomas R. Birks, published in the *Companion Psalter* (1874). The tune "Faithful" is an adaptation of Bach's well-known soprano aria *Mein gläubiges Herze* ("My heart ever faithful") from his cantata **Also Hat Gott Die Welt Geliebt** (BWV 68).

THE KING OF LOVE MY SHEPHERD IS. Hymn based on Ps. 23 by Henry W. Baker (1821–1877). It was first published in the appendix to *Hymns Ancient and Modern* (1868). Rendered explicitly Christian by references to the "Cross" and the "Good Shepherd," it is normally sung to the tune "Dominus Regit Me" by John Bacchus Dykes (1823–1876) but also to the traditional Irish tune "St. Columba" from George Petrie's collection *Ancient Irish Music of Ireland* (1855).

THE KING SHALL REJOICE. Coronation anthem based on Ps. 21 in four movements for mixed chorus (SAATBB), orchestra, and organ by Handel (no. 2, HWV 260), performed at the coronation of King George II and Queen Caroline in 1727 at the moment when the monarch receives the crown (v. 3). It opens with a majestic, ceremonial setting of verse 1 with melismas on "rejoice," followed by "Exceeding Glad shall he be" in triple meter with notable suspensions on "thy salvation." The third section, "Glory and Worship" (v. 5), builds in instrumental texture and color, and the final movement, an **Alleluia**, is an exuberant double fugue.

THE LORD BLESS YOU AND KEEP YOU. Anthem for SATB chorus and organ by John Rutter (1981), composed for the memorial service of Edward T. Chapmen, director of music at Highgate School, London. Based on the Priestly Blessing (Num. 6:24–26), it begins with sopranos singing "The Lord bless you and keep you, the Lord make his face to shine upon you," followed by unison singing and then harmony on "The Lord make his face to shine upon you." It concludes with a series of sublime **Amens** that crescendo and then decrescendo to a *molto rallentando*.

THE LORD IS MY LIGHT AND MY SALVATION. Setting of Ps. 27 for SATB, solo clarinet, and organ/orchestra by John Rutter (1990s), written at the request of a friend who was dying from AIDS. It features a melancholic clarinet obbligato, capturing the Psalmist's devotion and trust in the Lord. Other settings of this Psalm include anthems by Lassus (1562), Handel (**Chandos anthem** no. 10, 1718), and Boyce (1790); a chorus in Honegger's oratorio **Le Roi David** (1921); and hymns by Frances Allitsen (1897) and David Haas (1983).

THE LORD IS MY ROCK AND MY SALVATION. Choral anthem for SATB chorus, orchestra, and drums by Americans Dan and Heidi Goeller. Based on Ps. 18:2–3, it is written in Spanish style to convey the Psalm's fiery proclamation of faith and in lilting compound duple time to convey God's steadfast love for his people. The chorus syncopation on "attack me" and "against me" is contrasted with dotted crotchets on "my faith will not," followed by a sustained note for a measure and a half, rising to a climax on "swayed." It has also been arranged as a song by the Christian group Elevation Media.

THE LORD'S MY SHEPHERD. Popular hymn based on a paraphrase of Ps. 23 published as a metrical Psalm in the *Scottish Metrical Psalter* (1650). Commonly sung in England at weddings and funerals to the tune "Crimond" (1872) by Jessie Seymor Irvine (1836–1883), it featured in the wedding service of Princess Elizabeth and Prince Philip (1947) and the 10th-anniversary memorial service for the late Diana, Princess of Wales (2007). It is sung to other traditional Scottish Psalm tunes, such as "Wiltshire" and "Martyrdom," and to the "Brother James Air" by Scottish hymn writer James Leith Macbeth Bain (1860–1925). *See also* NEW 23RD PSALM, THE.

THE MAN COMES AROUND. Title track from the album *American IV* (2002), one of the last songs written by Johnny Cash before his death in 2003. Sung to the accompaniment of two guitars, piano, and electric organ, it opens and closes with a spoken recitation from Rev. 6:1–2 and Rev. 6:8, respectively. Numerous references to death and the afterlife include allusions to Mt. 25:1–13, 2 Kgs. 2:11, Acts 26:14, and Job 10:8–9, as well as Rev. 1:8, 10; 4:1, 10; 8:13, and 21:6–7. The song's title and the last line of each verse refer to Christ and his Second Coming.

THE OLD ARK'S A MOVERIN'. African American spiritual known also by the title "Keep the Ark Movin'" and "Keep the Old Ark Rollin'." Inspired by the story of Noah's ark (Gen. 6–9), the lilting melody in all versions paints the movement of the ark over the floodwaters. It appears on the George Mitchell Minstrel album *Another Black and White Minstrel Show* (1961).

THE OLD MASTER PAINTER. Song inspired by the biblical story of creation with allusions to the temptation of Eve (Gen. 3) and the rainbow (Gen. 9). The title refers to God as the "Old Master Painter from the hills faraway" who created not only the "violets and the daffodils" but also the songwriter's sweetheart and the devil in her eyes. Written by James Lamont Haven Gillespie and Beasley Smith, it was first performed in 1949 by Snooky Lanson, Beasley Smith and His Orchestra, and numerous artists, including Frank Sinatra and the Modernaires (1949), Peggy Lee, Mel Tormé with the Mellomen (1949), and, more recently, Brian Wilson (2004).

THE SPACIOUS FIRMAMENT ON HIGH. Hymn inspired by Ps. 19:1–3, written by Joseph Addison (1672–1719). First published in *The Spectator* on 23 August 1712, it was later appended to *The Scottish Paraphrases* (1781). The tune "Firmament" was composed by Walford Davies in 1908.

THE WAYS OF ZION DO MOURN. Funeral anthem for Queen Caroline by Handel (HWV 264, 1737) for mixed chorus, soloists, and orchestra. The libretto mourns her loss in texts from Lamentations (Lam. 1:4, 11; 2:10) and 2 Samuel (2 Sam. 1:19, 27); quotes verses from Job (Job 29:14, 11, 12), Psalms (Pss. 103:17, 112:6), Ecclesiasticus (Sir. 36:23), and Philippians (Phil. 4:8) to extol her virtues; and celebrates her reward in heaven in the words of Ben Sira (Sir. 44:14), Solomon (Wisd. 5:15), and Daniel (Dan. 12:3). The theme of the opening chorus comes from the Lutheran hymn *Wenn mein Stündlein vorhanden ist* ("When my final hour is close at hand") by Nikolaus Herman (1560) and was also used by Mozart in the opening movement of his *Requiem*. Handel later reworked this anthem for the opening of his oratorio **Israel in Egypt** (1739). *See also* ECCE, QUOMODO MORITUR JUSTUS.

THE WILDERNESS AND THE SOLITARY PLACE. Anthem in five parts for SATTB and organ by Samuel Sebastian Wesley (1832), composed for the opening of the rebuilt Hereford Cathedral and revised with orchestral accompaniment for a performance in Birmingham (1852). Based on verses from Isa. 35, the opening chorus ending "and blossom as the rose" (vv. 1–2) is followed by a bass solo ("Say to them of a fearful heart, Be strong") (v. 4) and a setting for SATB soloists of verse 6 ("For in the wilderness shall waters break out"). The work concludes with an extended SATTB chorus beginning *allegro moderato* ("And the ransomed of the Lord shall return to Zion") and ending softly in a slower tempo with the words "and sorrow and sighing shall flee away" (v. 10).

THEN DAVID MOURNED. Anthem for a cappella chorus by Thomas Tomkins based on David's lament over Saul and Jonathan (2 Sam. 1:17–27). It is thought to have been composed as a tribute to Prince Henry, son of James I, who died possibly from typhoid following a swim in the River Thames (1612). A preponderance of descending melodic lines describes David's lamentation over the bodies of **King Saul** and his son Jonathan. *See* O JONATHAN.

THEY SAW THAT THE STONE HAD BEEN ROLLED AWAY. Fanfare for percussion and brass (1993) by Scottish composer James MacMillan. It is dedicated to his former school music teacher Bert Richardson. Deriving from MacMillan's music theater piece *Visitatio Sepulchri*, it describes the women's encounter with the three angels at the entrance to Christ's tomb (Mt. 28:1–10). The women's bewilderment and quiet reflection are expressed by extreme contrasts between brass and percussion and by the use of timbales, cowbells, and tubular bells, along with an atmospheric crescendo roll on a large tam-tam at the end.

THEY THAT GO DOWN TO THE SEA IN SHIPS. Anthem for SATB chorus and organ by Herbert Sumsion, written for the Repton Preparatory School Choir (1979). Based on Ps. 107:23–30, it is characterized by a rocking accompaniment and undulating chorus lines to paint the rise and fall of the sea. Other settings of the same text include a verse anthem for bass and countertenor soloists, chorus, strings, and continuo by Purcell (Z. 57, 1685/1685), the anthem **Euroclydon** for mixed chorus (SATB) by William Billings (1781), and, more recently, Sean Street's anthem *Shipping Forecast* for SSATB chorus and piano or strings (2011).

THIS IS THE DAY WHICH THE LORD HATH MADE. Wedding anthem based on Pss. 118:24 and 27:14 and other biblical texts for mixed chorus, soloists, and orchestra by Handel (HWV 262), composed for the wedding of the eldest daughter of King George II to Prince William of Orange in St. James Chapel in 1734. Opening with trebles, it features an atmospheric a cappella section toward the end, "Be strong, and he shall comfort thine heart" (Ps. 27:14), as an instruction to the married couple to keep the faith. A hymn by Isaac Watts with the same first line, first published in *The Psalms of David* (1719) and sung to the tune "Arlington" by Thomas A. Arne or "Bishop-thorpe" by Jeremiah Clarke, features in many modern hymnbooks. A setting for mixed chorus and organ by John Rutter, based on texts from the Psalms (Pss. 118:24; 148:1–3, 5a; 91:4a, 11; 121:5–8; 27:16b), was commissioned by the Dean and Chapter of Westminster Abbey for the wedding of Prince William to Catherine Middleton in 2011.

THIS IS THE RECORD OF JOHN. Verse anthem by Orlando Gibbons for countertenor/tenor soloist and five-part chorus (SAATB) to the accompaniment of viols. Written for the feast day of John the Baptist, the genre of the verse anthem, which alternates between soloist and chorus voices, describes the dialogue between John the Baptist and the priests and Levites from the **Temple** who were sent by the Jews to question him about his identity (Jn. 1:19–23). The soloist's quasi-declamatory lines are echoed by the chorus in all three sections, while madrigalian effects include John's florid response on "I am not the Christ" and a rising figure on the question "Who art thou?"

THIS IS THE TRUTH SENT FROM ABOVE. Traditional carol sung to the tune "Herefordshire" and sometimes known as the "Herefordshire Carol," arranged by Vaughan Williams to a harmonization adapted from "Fantasia on Christmas Carols" in *Eight Traditional Christmas Carols* (1919). Four of the five stanzas draw on the story of Adam and Eve, and the final stanza looks to the promise of salvation brought about by Christ's death and resurrection. Another version of the carol, known as the "Shropshire Carol," was published in *A Good Christmas Box* (1847).

THIS LITTLE LIGHT OF MINE. Popular gospel song by American composer Harry Dixon Loes (ca. 1920) inspired by Mt. 5:14–16. The lyrics "Let it shine, let it shine, let it shine" repeated in the chorus and the verses are a response to Christ's words in Mt. 5:16. Featuring as a popular civil rights anthem in the 1950s and 1960s, it has been performed by numerous artists, including Bruce Springsteen in 2006, and, more recently, has appeared remixed as a hip-hop, rap, and soul sound track in Disney Channel's original movie *Let it Shine* (2012).

THOU WHO WAST RICH BEYOND ALL SPLENDOR. Christmas hymn by British Missionary Bishop Frank Houghton, written while he was bishop of East Szechwan in China to the music of the French carol *Quelle Est Cette Odeur Agréable*. The text was inspired by 2 Cor. 8:9.

THOU WILT KEEP HIM IN PERFECT PEACE. Anthem for SATTB by Samuel Sebastian Wesley (ca. 1850), included in the order of service for the coronation of Queen Elizabeth II in 1953. The opening words (Isa. 26:3) are contrasted with the next section, sung by basses, "The darkness is no darkness with thee," with the gradual addition of tenors and altos, "The darkness and the light to thee are both alike" (cf. Ps. 139:12). The work reaches a climax on "thine is the kingdom and the power and the glory" (Mt. 6:13) and concludes with the words from Isaiah.

THREE HOLY CHILDREN, THE. Oratorio in two parts for soloists, choruses, and orchestra by Stanford (op. 22, 1885), dedicated to Queen Victoria. Set during the time of the captivity of the Jews under Nebuchadnezzar, king of Babylon, it is based on the biblical story of Daniel; his three friends Ananias, Azarias, and Mishael (also known as Shadrach, Meshach, and Abednego) (Dan. 1:6–7), who refused to worship the image of Bel (Dan. 3); and the *Song of the Three Children* (Dan. 3:51–90). Scored for King Nebuchadnezzar (B), the Three Children (STB), a Herald (B), and various choruses representing Assyrian worshippers, Assyrian nobles, and Jewish women, part 1 is set by the waters of Babylon with text from the Psalms (Pss. 137; 79:1, 9; 102:15–16) and Baruch (Bar. 4:36–37). Part 2 is set "On the Plain of Dura" and includes text from an Assyrian inscription ("Bel! Great is thy name among all gods most honoured thou") and from Dan. 3 and Isa. 43:10. The work concludes with a double chorus inspired by the Song of the Three Children ("O all ye works of the Lord, bless ye the Lord, praise and exalt him above all for ever") and Ps. 148.

THREE KINGS, THE. Carol by Jonathan Dove for a cappella chorus (SATB) to a text by Dorothy L. Sayers, commissioned by King's College, Cambridge, for the Festival of Nine Lessons and Carols for Christmas Eve (2000). After the simple refrain "O balow balow la lay," two soprano soloists sing three stanzas telling of the **Three Kings** (the first is very young, the second is in his prime, and the third is very old) and their gifts of myrrh, incense, and gold. The carol concludes, "O Balow, balow la lay, Gifts for a baby King O."

THREE KINGS, THE. Christmas cantata for SATB soloists, chorus, and orchestra by Maxwell Davies (1995) to a text by George Mackay Brown and an anonymous medieval text, commissioned by the London Symphony Chorus to commemorate its 30th anniversary. Written in simple modal style, it opens with the word "Lullabye" and a reference to the skin color of each king (yellow, ebony, and ivory) and concludes with a reference to the dove from Noah's ark: "What hands will take the branch from the dove's beak?"

THREE PSALM PRELUDES (SET 1). Three miniature tone poems for organ by Herbert Howells (op. 32) based on an incipit from each of three Psalms. Composed between 1915 and 1916 against the backdrop of World War I, first published in 1921, and characterized by a minor tonality, an introspective mood, and a common structural formula, each one opens quietly, crescendos to an impassioned climax, and concludes with a diminuendo in the major tonality to suggest an air of hope for the downtrodden (Ps. 34:6), justice for the meek (Ps. 37:11), and the promise of everlasting life for the faithful departed (Ps. 23:4).

THREE PSALM PRELUDES (SET 2). Three miniature tone poems for organ by Herbert Howells (1938) based on an incipit from each of three Psalm texts. They were composed during a time of great sorrow following the death of the composer's nine-year-old only son, Michael, in 1935. The first, scored in D minor and based on a similar structural formula to that of the preludes in set 1, echoes the Psalmist's cries of despair to the Lord (Ps. 130:1) with two poignant rests in the music (mm. 64 and 68) and concludes in a mood of resigned tranquillity in the tonality of D major. The second is a quiet reflection on Ps. 139:12, while the third begins and ends in C major and is the only one to end "with a loud noise" as directed by the Psalmist (Ps. 33:3).

THRENI, ID EST LAMENTATIONES JEREMIAE PROPHETAE. Cantata in Latin for six soloists (SATTBB), four-part mixed chorus, and orchestra by Igor Stravinsky (1958), one of the composer's first and longest works in twelve-tone serialism. Part 1, *De elegia prima* (Lam. 1:1, 2, 5, 11, 20), opens with a brief orchestral introduction, followed by *Incipit lamentatio Jeremiae Prophetae*, sung by the soprano and accompanied by the alto singing its inversion, which provides the foundation for the entire work. The second part,

De Elegia Tertia, is divided into three sections: *Querimonia* ("Complaint") (Lam. 3:1–6, 16–22), *Sensus spei* ("Sense of Hope") (Lam. 3:22–27, 34–36, 40–45, 49–57), and *Solacium* ("Solace") (Lam. 3:58–64). After the words *Oratio Jeremiae Prophetae* ("Prayer of the Prophet Jeremiah"), sung by the bass soloists, the last section, *De Elegia Quinta*, the shortest movement, is a setting of Lam. 5:1, 19, and 21. The Hebrew letters of the acrostic in Lam. 1 and 3 are incorporated into the score and sung by the chorus. *See* LAMENTATIONS OF JEREMIAH, THE.

TIMOR ET TREMOR. ("Fear and Trembling"). Motet in two parts for six voices (SAATTB) a cappella by Orlando de Lassus based on verses from the Psalms (Pss. 55:5; 57:1, etc.), published in *Thesauras Musicus* (1564). Composed in the style of *musica reservata* with hauntingly beautiful chromaticisms, cross relations, and syncopations, alternating polyphony and homophony express the penitent's request for mercy (*miserere mei*) in part 1 (Ps. 56:1; Vulg. 55:2) and a prayer of petition (*Exaudi, Deus*) in part 2 (Ps. 61:12; Vulg. 60:2). In a striking conclusion, *non confundar* ("let me not be confounded") (Ps. 71:1; Vulg. 70:1) is scored in syncopation to highlight the sense of confusion brought about by God's absence.

TOBIAS AND THE ANGEL. Church opera in one act by Jonathan Dove to a libretto by David Lan, premiered at Christ Church, Highbury, London, on 7 July 1999. Inspired by the Book of Tobit, the folk character of the story is reflected in the klezmer band that appears onstage, and a supernatural atmosphere is created by children's choruses of sparrows and fish and the use of a vibraphone to accompany the angel Raphael, a timpani for the wicked demon Ashmodeus, and an extended glockenspiel solo to herald the return of Tobit's sight. Other works based on this theme include *Tobias and the Angel* by Mario Castelnuovo-Tedesco (1965) and *Tobias and the Angel*, an opera for television, by Arthur Bliss (1960). *See also* TOBIE.

TOBIE. ("Tobias"). "Little oratorio" in one act for soloists, chorus, and orchestra by Gounod (CG31, 1854; published 1865) to a libretto by Hippolyte Lefèvre, premiered in Lyons in April 1854. Scored for Tobias (T); Tobit, his father (B); Anne, his mother (A); and the angel Raphael (S), the work focuses on the closing sections of the Book of Tobit, contrasting the weak faith of his mother, Anne, who believes that she will never see her son again ("Why in my old age, oh son, dids't thou leave me"), with the steadfast faith of her husband ("Woman! And thou blasphemest! Meekly listen and obey the words of God the Lord"). Notable numbers include the air sung by Tobias on his return ("Father, thine arms about me throw!"), accompanied by muted strings, the Tobias prayer for the restoration of his father's sight, and the finale, a joyful hymn of praise for soloists and *divisi* chorus. *See also* RITORNO DI TOBIA, IL.

TÖCHTERLEIN DES JAIRUS, DAS. ("The Little Daughter of Jairus"). Cantata for female voices or children and orchestra by Josef Rheinberger (op. 32, 1863) to a libretto by Franz Bonn (1830–1894). Inspired by the story of the raising of Jairus's daughter (Mt. 9:18–25), it comprises four choruses, of which one is scored for keening women (no. 7), four solos (A), a duet (SA) for two women (neighbors of Jairus), and a trio for the family of Jairus. The work concludes with a chorus of **Hallelujahs** praising God for his good works. It was adapted and translated into English by William Alexander Barrett (1879).

TOMORROW SHALL BE MY DANCING DAY. English carol first published in William B. Sandy's *Christmas Carols Ancient and Modern* (1833). There are numerous versions, the original having 11 verses punctuated by a refrain, "Sing O my love, O my love," narrated by Christ in the first person, covering the major events in his life and ministry and concluding with his ascension into heaven (Acts 1:9–11). The last line of each refrain includes a reference to Christ's "true love," that is, to his Church, and an invitation to all to celebrate God's saving grace on Christmas Day. There are numerous arrangements by Holst, Stravinsky, David Willcocks, John Gardner, and others, and an anthem by John Rutter for SSA voices and harp accompaniment that concludes his song cycle *Dancing Day: Cycle of Christmas Carols* on a joyful, upbeat note. *See* LORD OF THE DANCE.

TORCHES. Traditional Spanish carol translated into English by J. B. Trend and arranged for SATB chorus and organ by John Joubert (op. 7a, 1951). A joyful call to celebrate Christ's birth, it is scored in a lively march tempo in E minor.

TOWER OF BABEL. Song by Sir Elton John from the album *Captain Fantastic and the Brown Dirt Cowboy* (1975). Inspired by the biblical story (Gen. 11), the chorus tells of a party in the Tower of Babylon, a place renowned for its evil acts (Cain's murder of Abel), lowly characters ("call girls"), and inhabitants of evil lands (Sodom and Gomorrah). There is no hope of redemption for those living within the walls of the Tower.

TOWER OF BABEL, THE. (*Der Thurm zu Babel*). Sacred opera (*geistliche Oper*) in one act by Rubinstein (op. 80, 1869), first performed in Königsberg in 1870. The libretto by Julius Rodenberg (translated by Fitz William Rosier, 1883) is based loosely on Gen. 11 and possibly influenced by midrashic literature that recounts Nimrod's confrontation with Abraham. After an orchestral overture, a chorus of workers roused from sleep by the master builder sings, "To work, to work. . . . Soon our glorious Tower shall rise, beyond the skies. . . . Ply the strong hammers," mimicking the bustling sound of their enthusiastic activity. In a recitative, Nimrod (B) admires the construction from afar and boasts that it would enable him to see God face-to-face in "majesty arrayed." When Abram (T) rebukes Nimrod, "And how wilt thou attain his presence! Thou art but a man," and implores him to give up the Tower, Nimrod replies, "Insolent Shepherd," and hurls him into a fiery furnace. Dotted rhythms highlight the barbaric nature of the workers ("Seize him! Death be his lot") and their violence and polytheism (Baal, Dagon, and Astaroth). But after Abram's redemption, a chorus of angels, invisible to the audience, sing in a mystical chant on a B major chord of their intention to destroy the Tower and confound the language of the people. Thunder breaks out, represented by a tremolo effect in the accompaniment, and the Tower crashes to the ground, illustrated by downward scale-like passages. At the end, the audience gets a glimpse of heaven, earth, and hell as the angelic hosts sing "**Hallelujah**" before the throne of God and mortals pray that, through their sins, they may find their way back to God while demons before the throne of Satan celebrate the power they gain through human error.

TRAHE ME POST TE. ("Draw Me after you"). Canonic motet for five a cappella voices (SSATB) by Spanish composer Francisco Guerrero (1528–1599), adapted from a Marian antiphon and published in *Sacrae Cantiones* (1555). Inspired by verses from the Song of Solomon (Cant. 1:4; Vulg. 1:3), it is the third of eight canonic motets, incorporating a canon at the third between soprano 1 and soprano 2 to symbolize the Virgin Mary as mother, daughter, and spouse. There is also a setting by Palestrina and a parody Mass based on the motet by Victoria.

TRIUMPHLIED. ("Song of Triumph"). Cantata for chorus, baritone solo, orchestra, and organ by Brahms (op. 55, 1872). Based on the celebration of the fall of Babylon in Rev. 18–19, it was written as a thanksgiving for German victory in the Franco-Prussian War. Scored in the tonality of D major, it is in three movements (fast, slow, and fast), beginning with a choral setting of Rev. 19:1, a **Hallelujah** chorus based on a theme from the old German national anthem *Heil dir in Siegerkranz* ("Hail to Thee with Victor's Laurels"), familiar today as the melody of the British national anthem, "God Save the Queen." This movement ends with a triumphant eight-part Hallelujah. The second movement in G major (Rev. 19:5–7) is quieter and incorporates the Lutheran hymn *Nun Danket Alle Gott* (**Now Thank We All Our God**). The third movement, sung by the baritone, is inspired by St. John's vision of the rider on a white horse (Rev. 19:11, 13, 16) and concludes with a four-part fugue and a final **Hallelujah** chorus.

TSAR SAUL: PES'N SAULA PERED BOYEM. ("King Saul: Song of Saul before Battle"). Song for bass and piano (1863) in B-flat minor by Mussorgsky with words taken from a poem by Lord Byron and translated into Russian by Pavel Kozlov (1841–1891). The 12th song in a collection of early works entitled *Youthful Years* (1857–1866), it is based on Saul's words to his armor bearer in the final battle against the Philistines (1 Sam. 31:4). It was later rewritten and orchestrated by the composer himself.

TU ES PETRUS. ("Thou Art Peter"). Motet in C major for SATB chorus, baritone soloist, and organ by Fauré (1872), first published in 1884. The words of Christ (Bar) to Peter (Mt. 16:18–19) are first sung by the soloist and then reiterated by the chorus in imitative polyphony, concluding with all voices singing in homophony the words *Tu es Petrus*. *Tu es Petrus* is a Gregorian chant used by Palestrina in a Mass and in motets by numerous composers, including Byrd (1607), Haydn (1785), Mendelssohn (1827), Charles Marie-Widor (1876), Duruflé (1914), and Saint-Saëns (1914). More recently, it features in James Macmillan's *Introit* for SATB chorus, organ, brass, and percussion (2010). *See also* HYMN TO ST. PETER.

TURN TURN TURN. Song by folksinger/songwriter Pete Seeger (1965), adapted from Eccl. 3:1–13 and number 1 on the American Billboard charts in 1966. The addition of the words "Turn, Turn, Turn" transforms the original pessimism of Ecclesiastes into a cheerful acceptance of how things are, reminiscent of the Beatles' "Let It Be" (1969). The tonality of C major and the melody based around C is imbued with the symbolism of new beginnings. The performance by the Byrds, an American folk rock group, was made famous by the jangle accompaniment of a twelve-string Rickenbacker guitar and appeared more recently in the movie *Forest Gump* (1994). Other notable covers include versions by Judy Collins, Johnny Cash, Joan Baez, and Dolly Parton.

TWELVE, THE. Anthem and mini-cantata for four soloists, choir, and organ, intended to be performed on the feast day of any of the 12 apostles. Premiered at Christ Church, Oxford, in May 1965, the text is by W. H. Auden and the music by William Walton. Lasting just under 11 minutes, it is divided into three parts. Section 1, based loosely on the Acts of the Apostles, opens with a declamatory text sung by a bass recounting the call of the apostles, followed by an eight-part chorus telling of their missionary work and, at the end of the final part, a poignant section sung a cappella that tells of the apostles' martyrdom "one by one." Section 2 is a penitential poem sung by a mezzo-soprano solo, "O Lord my God," and later sung as a duet with the addition of a soprano solo. Section 3 opens with an alto recitative, "Children play about the ancestral graves," and concludes with a jubilant fugue of praise.

TWELVE DAYS OF CHRISTMAS, THE. Popular Christmas carol celebrating the 12 days of Christmas, from Christmas Day (25 December) to Epiphany (6 January). Thought to have been written in the 16th century for English Catholics prohibited from practicing their religion, it apparently contains 12 coded references to Christian tradition, such as Christ on the cross ("Partridge in the Pear Tree"), the Old and New Testaments ("Two Turtle Doves"), and faith, hope, and love ("Three French Hens") (1 Cor. 13:13).

TWELVE GATES TO THE CITY. Gospel song by singer/songwriter Thelma Davis (1955), based on Rev. 21:12–13. A theme song and hit of the Davis Sisters of Philadelphia, founded by Thelma Davis in 1945, it features as the title song on their first album (1955) and later on the album *The Best of the Famous Davis Sisters* (1978). The "12 gates" are the gates of the New Jerusalem, protected by angels, through which the faithful followers of Christ gain access to the heavenly city. Covered by the Weavers and also by Ralph Stanley, it was arranged with additional words and music by American southern gospel singer/songwriter and guitar and harmonica player Buddy Greene on the album *A Few More Years* (2010).

TWO BY TWO. Broadway musical by Richard Rogers with lyrics by Martin Charnin, based on the play *The Flowering Peach* by Clifford Odets. It was first performed on Broadway on 10 November 1970, featuring Danny Kaye as Noah and Joan Copeland as Noah's wife. Popular numbers included Noah's song "Why Me?," "The Gitka's Song," and "The Golden Ram."

• U •

UBI CARITAS ET AMOR. ("Where Charity and Love"). Gregorian chant based on 1 Cor. 13. The antiphon was traditionally sung at the washing-of-feet rite on Maundy Thursday, but today it is reassigned to the offertory (*Roman Catholic Missal*, 1970) with words adapted (*Ubi caritas est vera, Deus ibi est*). The chant was incorporated into choral works by Maurice Duruflé, Morten Lauridsen, and Paul Halley (*Angel on a Stone Wall*, 1991). In the well-known Taizé chant by Jacques Berthier (1978) in Anglican and Lutheran hymnals, *Ubi caritas et amor, ubi caritas Deus ibi est*, in ostinato form, is the refrain; the verses come from 1 Cor. 13:2–8. Other modern settings include choral works by Ola Gjeilo, David Conte, and, more recently, Paul Mealor for the wedding of Prince William and Catherine Middleton (2011).

UNE CANTATE DE NOËL. ("A Christmas Cantata"). Cantata by Honegger (H. 212, 1952–1953) for baritone soloist, SATB chorus, children's chorus, orchestra, and organ. It brings together the Psalm texts **De Profundis** (Ps. 130) and **Laudate Dominum** with a host of festive Christmas carols, such as **O Come, O Come Emmanuel** and *Vom Himmel hoch* ("From Heaven High"), including an **Alleluia** and a Gloria. It is reputed to have been the last composition by the composer before his death.

UNICORN, THE. Song from the album *The Unicorn* (1968) and signature tune of the Canadian folk group the Irish Rovers. It sold over 8 million copies worldwide. Originally written as a poem by the American singer/songwriter and cartoonist Shel Silverstein (1930–1999) and published in a collection of children's poetry, *Where the Sidewalk Ends* (1974), it is an etiological tale, based loosely on the biblical account of Noah's flood (Gen. 6–7), explaining why unicorns became extinct.

UNTIL THE END OF THE WORLD. Song from the album *Achtung Baby* (1991) by singer songwriter Bono from U2. It tells of a fictitious conversation between Jesus and Judas in the afterlife and Judas's remorse, which resulted in his taking his own life (Mt. 27:3–10; Acts 1:15–20).

UTRECHT JUBILATE. ("O Be Joyful in the Lord"). Anthem for six soloists, orchestra, and basso continuo by Handel, written to celebrate the Treaty of Utrecht, which ended the War of the Spanish Succession (HWV 279,

1713). Often preceded by the *Utrecht Te Deum* (HWV 278), the Jubilate is a setting of Ps. 100:1–5 for a combination of solo, duo, trio, and choral numbers scored in the ceremonial key of D major. Characterized by melismatic writing on "joyful," "gladness," and "praise," it concludes with a doxology in eight parts. Other well-known settings of the Jubilate include those of Gabrieli, Purcell (1697), and Benjamin Britten (1961).

UTRENJA. PART 1. ZLOZENIA CHRYSTUSA DO GROBU. ("The Entombment of Christ"). Work for five voices (SSMTB), mixed chorus, and orchestra by Penderecki (1970) commissioned by West German Radio. It is a lament for Christ's death inspired by the Holy Saturday liturgy of the Eastern Orthodox Church. Subdued choral chanting highlights the solemnity of Christ's entombment, and at the end, a tutti for voices and instruments only fades away into silence, marking the silence of the grave.

UTRENJA. PART 2. ZMARTWYCHWSTANIE PANSKIE. ("The Resurrection of Christ"). Work in seven parts by Penderecki (1971), commissioned by West German Radio. It is based on the account of the resurrection of Christ in old Slavonic texts of the Easter Sunday liturgy. The first part, *Ewangelia* ("The Gospel"), appeared in the horrific climax of the British American psychological horror movie *The Shining* (1980).

VADEM ET CIRCUIBO CIVITATEM. ("I Will Rise and Go about the City"). Motet in two parts for six voices (SSATTB) by Victoria (published 1572, 1583, 1589, 1603). Inspired by the Song of Songs, it is one of the composer's longest motets. There are multiple examples of text painting, most notably at the beginning, where a maze of dense counterpoint represents the bride's search for her beloved in the streets and squares of the city (Cant. 3:2). Other notable examples include a descending melody line on *Quo declinavit* (Cant. 6:2; Vulg. 5:17), a leap of either a fourth or a fifth on *ascendit* to depict her beloved climbing the palm tree, and melismas on *fructus eius* ("its fruit") (Cant. 7:8).

VALE OF TEARS. Song on the album *Epilogue* (2001) by To/Die/For, featuring the place-name "Land of Nod," that is, the place to the East of Eden where Cain was exiled following his murder of Abel (Gen. 4:16). This place also occurs in Bob Dylan's song "Tweedle Dee & Tweedle Dum" on the album *Love and Theft* (2001).

VANGELO SECONDO MATTEO, IL. ("The Gospel according to St. Matthew"). Film in black and white by film director, writer, and poet Pier Paolo Pasolini (1964). The theme music includes Bach's B Minor Mass and his **St. Matthew Passion**; the spiritual "Sometimes I feel like a Motherless Child," sung by Odetta Holmes ("the voice of the civil rights movement"); a blues number, "My Oh My"; selections from the African *Missa Luba* (1965); and Prokofiev's musical score to Sergei Eisenstein's film *Alexander Nevsky* (1938).

VANITY OF VANITIES, THE. Choral symphony for twelve-part a cappella mixed chorus by Granville Bantock (1913), inspired by the Book of Ecclesiastes. Written before the outbreak of World War I, it appears to foretell the dark days that would lie ahead (Eccl. 11:8) and, in the last two numbers, beckons the young to rejoice and live life to the fullest. The work is in seven movements: "Vanity of Vanities, said the Preacher" (Eccl. 1:2–11), "I said in mine heart" (Eccl. 2:1, 4–5, 7–8, 10–11), "Then I saw that wisdom excelleth folly" (Eccl. 2:13–18, 23), "To everything there is a season" (Eccl. 3:1–4, 6, 8), "I returned and saw under the sun" (Eccl. 9:11–12; 6:4; 5:15; 6:12), "Go thy way" (Eccl. 9:7–10, 5–6; 11:8), and "Rejoice, O young man" (Eccl. 11:9–10; 12:1–8).

VANITAS VANITATUM I: LA VANITÉ DES HOMMES. Motet for two voices by Giacomo Carissimi, inspired by the Book of Ecclesiastes. It opens with the refrain *Vanitas vanitatum et omnia vanitas* (Eccl. 1:2), which is sung at the end of each of the verses. Verse 1 speaks about the fate of the foolish rich man, known also as Dives, from the parable of the rich man and Lazarus (Lk. 16:19–31) and verse 2 about Nebuchadnezzar's molten image of gold (Dan. 3:1–7), which, according to Carissimi's extrabiblical addition, was crushed by a rock "in the mud, in the dust, in the shadows, into nothing." The composition concludes with a prayer of petition for guidance in this life of "mortal darkness." Ildebrando Pizzetti also composed a setting of *Vanitas vanitatum* in 1959.

VATER UNSER. ("Our Father"). Setting of **The Lord's Prayer** (Mt. 6:9–13) in German for boy soprano and piano/organ by Arvo Pärt, performed in the Vatican in 2011 to mark the 60th anniversary of Pope Benedict's ordination to the priesthood. Sixteenth- and 17th-century settings include an a cappella motet for SSAT/ATTB by Michael Praetorius from *Musae Sioniae* (1. Pars., no. 7, 1605) and a motet by Heinrich Schütz from ***Symphoniae Sacrae III*** (op. 12, SWV 411, 1650). Another is Martin Luther's hymn *Vater unser im Himmelreich*, based on a chorale melody (1538) used by J. S. Bach both in compositions for keyboard (e.g., *Orgelbüchlein* BWV 636; Clavier-Übung III BWV 682 and BWV 683) and in choral settings, including the Neumeister Chorales (BWV 737), three cantatas (BWV 90, BWV 101, and BWV 102), and the **St. John Passion** (BWV 245/5, 1724). The melody also features in chorale preludes by Pachelbel (*Erster Theil etlicher Choräle*), Telemann (TWV 31:1–2, 1735), and Reger (op. 67, 1903?) and in an organ sonata by Mendelssohn (op. 65, no. 6, 1844–1845). It also appears in the song cycle in nine movements for voice and piano by Peter Cornelius (op. 2, no. 1, 1854–1855), translated into English by Mabelle Shapleigh. *See also* LORD'S PRAYER, THE; PATER NOSTER.

VEIL OF THE TEMPLE. All-night vigil by John Tavener, scored for soprano (Mary Magdalene), tenor, baritone, and bass soloists; large SATB chorus; children's voices; and orchestra and premiered in two overnight concerts at the Temple Church, London, on 27 June and 1 July 2003 as part of the City of London Festival. Regarded by the composer as "the supreme achievement of my life," it draws inspiration from the music of the Orthodox vigil service and its subject matter from the sepulchral shape of the Temple's Round Church. In the words of the composer, it was constructed as a "gigantic prayer wheel of eight cycles, each one ascending in pitch," beginning and ending in C major, with verses from St. John's Gospel at the center of cycles

1 to 7 (Jn. 13–17). Other biblical texts are cited, such as Pss. 3, 38, 63, 88, 103, and 143 and a setting of Ps. 104 as an anthem, "You mantle yourself in light, stretch out the skies as a curtain" (Ps. 104:2). The rest of the piece is made up of the "Our Father," **"Alleluia,"** the Acclamations, *Maranatha* (1 Cor. 16:22), "Awake thou that sleepest" (Eph. 5:14), "Surely I come quickly" (Rev. 22:20), and other texts, including "What shall we say then?" (Rom. 6:1–10), "It was early in the morning on the first day of the week" (Jn. 20:1) (sung by children's voices), and "Shine, Shine O Jerusalem, for the glory of the Lord hath arisen upon thee" (Isa. 60:1). The work is a journey from darkness to light, from death to rebirth, and from the first day of the Old Creation (Gen. 1:5) to the first day of the New Creation on Easter Sunday (Jn. 20:1) and to the revelation of the mystery of Christ's cosmic ascent (Acts 1:9). It incorporates texts from Christianity, Islam, Hinduism, and Buddhism, written in Aramaic, Church Slavonic, English, Greek, and Sanskrit, and with instruments from a variety of traditions, including the *duduk*, Indian harmonium, Tibetan temple bells, tubular bell, and tam-tam and a Tibetan horn used to mark the divisions of cycles 1 to 7.

VENI CREATOR SPIRITUS. ("Come Creator Spirit"). Gregorian hymn attributed to Rabanus Maurus, archbishop of Mainz (ninth century), traditionally sung at the Feast of Pentecost to commemorate the descent of the Holy Spirit on the apostles (Ps. 103:30; Acts 2:1–13) but also at the sacrament of Confirmation, the ordination of priests, the consecration of bishops, the coronation of monarchs, and the election of a new pope. There is a well-known English version by Richard Mant (*Ancient Hymns*, 1837), "Come Holy Ghost, Creator Blest," sung to the tune "Melcombe" by Samuel Webbe Sr. (1782) or to "Mendon" by Samuel Dyer (1828). The Gregorian melody has been included in numerous works, including Martin Luther's chorale *Komm, Gott Schöpfer, Heiliger Geist* ("Come Creator God, Holy Spirit") (1524), a motet for eight voices and a hymn for five voices by Palestrina (1589 collection), a chorale prelude for organ by Bach (Leipzig Chorales, no. 17, BWV 667), Symphony no. 8 in E-flat Major ("Symphony of a Thousand") by Mahler (1906), a motet for female voices and chorus (SSA) by Berlioz (H. 141, 1861–1868), a hymn for a cappella double chorus (SSAATTBB) by Penderecki (1987), the fourth movement of Hindemith's organ concerto (1963), *Prélude, Adagio et Choral varié sur le thème du "Veni Creator"* by Duruflé (1930), and an organ prelude by Kenneth Leighton (1987). The last of three settings by Peter Maxwell Davies (1963, 1972, 2002) was performed at the royal wedding of Prince William and Catherine Middleton in 2011. *See also* VENI SANCTE SPIRITUS.

VENI SANCTE SPIRITUS. ("Come Holy Spirit"). Sequence for the Feast of Pentecost, inspired by Acts 2:1–13, also known as the "golden sequence." It is attributed to various people, including King Robert II the Pious of France, Pope Innocent III, and Stephen Langton, archbishop of Canterbury. There are settings by Palestrina, John Dunstable, Johann Michael Haydn, Sir Peter Maxwell Davies (1980), John Rutter (1997), Eric Pazdziora (2013), and many others. Memorable settings include a sacred motet for SATB solos and SATB chorus and orchestra by Mozart (K. 47), composed when he was just 12 years old, and a Taizé chant, based on a lilting ostinato in compound duple time with verses superimposed. The hymn "Come Thou Holy Paraclete" is an English version of the sequence by John M. Neale in *The Hymnal Noted* (2nd ed., 1854), sung to music by Samuel Webbe (1782). This further inspired an anthem of the same name for SATB chorus and organ by Francis Jackson (op. 85, 1993).

VENI, VENI EMMANUEL. ("O Come, O Come Immanuel"). Hymn of unknown origin based on the **O Antiphons**. The English translation by John Mason Neale (1818–1866) was originally published in *Medieval Hymns and Sequences* (1851) under the title "Draw nigh, draw nigh," with the addition of the refrain "Rejoice, rejoice, Immanuel shall come to thee, O Israel" (*Gaude, Gaude, Emmanuel nascetur pro te, Israel*). *Veni, veni Emmanuel* inspired a choral work by Kodály (1943) and a percussion concerto by James Macmillan (1959). It is also the basis of the U2 lyric "White as Snow" from the album *No Line on the Horizon* (2009).

VENI, VENI, EMMANUEL. ("Come, Come, Emmanuel"). Concerto for percussion and orchestra in one movement by Sir James MacMillan (1992) premiered at the Royal Albert Hall, London, on 10 August 1992 with percussion soloist Dame Evelyn Glennie. Inspired by the 15th-century Advent plainchant and Lk. 21:25–27, the percussion represents the noise and chaos of the world, and the plainsong, performed by the orchestra, depicts the "human presence of Christ" in the world. The work is divided into five seamless sections, rising to a climax in section 4, entitled "Dance—Chorale," featuring the ethereal plainsong as a chorale and concluding with an allusion to the Gloria of the Easter Vigil in the sound of Easter bells, which bring together the Incarnation and the Resurrection.

VENITE. ("Come"). A hymn of praise and call to worship based on Ps. 95, sung as an invitatory prayer at matins and as a morning prayer in the Book of Common Prayer. Well-known settings of the Latin, *Venite exultemus Domino,* include a sacred motet for nine voices (SSAATBTTB) by Michael Praetorius (1607) and a Taizé chant. Settings in English include a "Canticle of Praise to God" in C major (vv. 1–7) by William Boyce and a largely homophonic setting for SATB chorus and organ by Benjamin Britten (1961), the composer's last sacred work and published posthumously. The metrical three-stanza hymn "Come, Let Us Sing for Joy: A Morning Prayer setting" by Marty Haugen, commissioned by Luther College in Iowa in honor of Professor Weston Noble, is a joyful song of praise in common time.

VERITAS HYMNAL. Irish Catholic hymnal containing hymns in Irish and English, commissioned by the National Commission for Sacred Music and approved by the Irish Church Music Association in 1973. Among the best-known hymns in Irish, it includes *Ag an bPóasadh Bhí i gCána* ("The Marriage in Cana"), Ár nAthair ("Our Father"), **Caoineadh na dTri Muire** ("The Lament of the Three Marys"), **Don Oíche úd i mBeithil** ("That Night in Bethlehem"), *Rug Muire Mac do Dhia* ("Mary Gave Birth to the Son of God"), and *Suantraí Na Maighdine* ("The Virgin's Lullaby"), among others.

VESPERAE DE DOMINICA. ("Sunday Vespers"). Work for soloists, chorus, orchestra, and organ by Mozart (K. 321, 1779) based on five Psalms (Pss. 110–113, 117) and the **Magnificat** (Lk. 1:46–55). Each movement ends with a setting of the lesser doxology (*Gloria Patri*). The Laudate Dominum (Ps. 117) in A major, scored for soprano soloist, violins I and II, cello, bassoon, and organ, is an extended aria featuring melismas on *confirmata* ("bestowed"), *semper* ("forever"), and *Amen*. *See also* VESPERAE SOLENNES DE CONFESSORE.

VESPERAE SOLENNES DE CONFESSORE. ("Solemn Vespers of the Confessor"). Work for soloists, mixed chorus, strings/organ, trumpets, trombones, bassoon, and timpani by Mozart (K. 339, 1780), composed in honor of an unnamed confessor saint for a Sunday Vespers Service at the court of Prince-Archbishop Hieronymus Colloredo of Salzburg. It comprises five settings of the Psalms (Pss. 110–113, 117) and the **Magnificat** (Lk. 1:46–55), each movement lasting under five minutes, originally performed without a break. The work opens with a setting of **Dixit Dominus** ("The Lord Said") (Ps. 110) with festive-sounding trumpets and drums and colorful chromatics on *confregit in die irae suae reges* ("crushes kings in the day of his wrath"). In *Confitebor* ("I will Praise") (Ps. 111), the soloists sing in a call-and-response manner, while **Beatus Vir** ("Blessed is the Man") (Ps. 112) alternates between sections for chorus and the soloist quartet and *Laudate Pueri* ("Praise O Ye Servants") (Ps. 113) is scored as a fugue. The fourth movement is the hauntingly beautiful *Laudate Dominum* ("Praise the Lord") (Ps. 117) for soprano solo, chorus, strings, organ, and bassoon, and the work concludes with the **Magnificat** and a return of the festive sound of trumpets and drums. Today, individual movements, notably *Laudate Dominum*, are performed as separate concert pieces. *See also* VESPERAE DE DOMINICA.

VESPRO DELLA BEATA VERGINE. ("Vespers for the Blessed Virgin Mary," also known as "Vespers of 1610"). Monumental work for mixed chorus, soloists, solo violin, cornet, and ripieno by Monteverdi (SV 206 and 206a, 1610), regarded as a Venetian masterpiece. It is based on biblical texts used in the liturgy for Marian feasts, including settings of Ps. 110 (*Dixit Dominus* ["The Lord said"]) and Ps. 122 (*Laetatus sum* [I was glad]) for six voices and instruments and the motets **Nigra sum** ("I am black") for solo tenor and *Pulchra es* ("thou art beautiful") for soprano duet from the Song of Solomon (Cant. 1:5; 2:3, 11–12, 15). The motet *Duo Seraphim* ("Two Seraphims"), a duet for two voices with a third on "these three are one," is based on Isaiah's vision of the Trinity (Isa. 6:3; 1 Jn. 5:7–8). **Nisi Dominus** ("Unless the Lord") is a setting of Ps. 127 for 10 voices, and *Lauda Jerusalem* ("Praise O Jerusalem"), for two choruses of three voices with the tenor voice acting as a cantus firmus, is a setting of Ps. 147:12–20. The work concludes with two nonbiblical pieces (the *Sonata sopra Sancta Maria*, an instrumental with soprano solo, and the hymn *Ave maris stella*) and two settings of the **Magnificat** (Lk. 1:46–55).

VEXILLA REGIS. ("The Royal Banner"). Gregorian vespers hymn sung on Passion Sunday through Maundy Thursday and at the Feast of the Triumph of the Cross. It tells of Christ's glorious passion and death on the cross. It was written by the sixth-century poet Venantius Honorius Fortunatus (530–609 CE) to celebrate the arrival in Poitiers of a precious relic, a fragment of the True Cross, presented as a gift from the Byzantine emperor Justinian II to the Merovingian queen, Radegunda, who was known for her good works and miracles. A favorite hymn of the Crusaders, it was incorporated into numerous 19th-century compositions, including, among others, the **Rédemption** by Charles-François Gounod, **Via Crucis** by Franz Liszt, and **The Hymn of Jesus** by Gustav Holst.

VIA CRUCIS. ("Way of the Cross"). Oratorio in 15 movements for SATB soloists, chorus, and organ by Liszt (S. 53, 1876–1879), published in Leipzig in 1936. Sung in Latin, it tells the story of Christ's passion through the 14 **stations of the cross**. The introduction opens with a three-note motif representing the cross, taken from the first three notes (F, G, B-flat) of the Gregorian vespers hymn **Vexilla Regis** ("The banners of the King"). This is followed by the hymn sung in unison by the choir and then by the soloists (SATB), who enter imitatively on *O crux ave*, based on the cross motif. The 14 movements include solos by Pilate (B) (I) and Jesus (B) (VIII: "Weep not for me"; Lk. 23:28), a tender setting for solo organ (IV: "Jesus meets his mother"), and the chorales *O Haupt voll Blut und Wunden* ("**O Sacred Head, Sore Wounded**") (VI: "Saint Veronica") and *O Traurigkeit, O Herzeleid* ("O Darkest Woe, Ye Tears Forth Flow") (XII: "Jesus Dies on the Cross"). There is a meditative setting of the *Stabat Mater* sung by SSA voices in III ("Jesus falls for the first time"), and chromatic harmony is used to paint Christ's pain (IX). Jesus' last words are sung a cappella by the bass, beginning with *Eli Eli lama Sabach-thani* (XII), and the work concludes with a return to the opening hymn, *Ave Crux spes unica*, and the three-note cross motif played again in unison by the organ. The work was also arranged for organ (S. 669b, 1886), piano (S. 504a, 1880), and four hands (S. 583, 1887). More recently, the stations of the cross were set to music by an eclectic blend of metal artists on the album *Via Crucis: The Way of the Cross* (2012), featuring Katholicus, Cradle Catholic, Seven Sorrows, Malchus, and others.

VIA DOLOROSA. ("The Way of Suffering"). Song by Billy Sprague and Niles Borop telling of Christ's journey to Calvary on the Via Dolorosa with details of the Passion and references to his titles as the Lamb of God, Messiah, and Christ the King. A dramatic song with orchestral accompaniment, it was performed by Sandi Patti in English and in Spanish.

VIDERUNT OMNES FINES TERRAE. ("All the Ends of the Earth"). Well-known *organum duplum* from the *Magnus Liber Organi de graduali et antifonario* ("The Great Book of Graduals and Antiphons"), the principal collection of two-voice polyphony during the 12th century, ascribed to Léonin (ca. 1170). Based on Ps. 98:2–4, this ancient Christmas gradual for two voices opens with a respond in three parts: *viderunt* (v. 3) is a cantus firmus in three separate syllables, each one sung as a sustained note by the tenor voice set against the upper voice in unmeasured, melismatic polyphony; *omnes* is sung by the two voices as a *discant clausula* and concludes with a cadence (*organum*) on the second syllable; and (*viderunt*) *fines terrae salutare dei nostri iubilate deo omnis terra* ("the ends of the earth have seen the salvation of our God. Sing joyfully to God all the earth") (vv. 3–4) is chanted by the two voices. The verse follows the same pattern, concluding with *justitiam suam* ("his righteousness") (v. 2) sung by the two voices and a repetition of the respond. Léonin's successor, Pérotin, another great master of the Notre

Dame school who made revisions to Léonin's *Magnus Liber*, set this piece as a *duplum triplum* for three additional voices above the cantus firmus.

VIDETE MIRACULUM. ("Behold the Miracle"). Responsory at first vespers of Candlemas, it serves as a processional during the Feast of the Visitation of the Virgin and celebrates the arrival of Mary at the house of her cousin Elizabeth (Lk. 1:39–45). Among various settings, there is a popular motet by Thomas Tallis.

VIDI SPECIOSAM. ("I Saw the Fair One Rising Like a Dove"). Responsory at matins on the Feast of the Assumption, arranged by Victoria as a motet for six a cappella voices (SSATTB) in two parts in the form AB-CB, the second of which (*Quae est ista* ["who is this?"]) (Cant. 3:6) is rarely performed today. The first is not biblical but is based loosely on the language and imagery of the Song of Solomon and illustrates musically the assumption of the Virgin Mary into heaven, likened to a dove rising over the river surrounded by roses and lilies (cf. Cant. 2:1, 14).

VIER ERNSTE GESÄNGE. ("Four Serious Songs"). Song cycle for bass and piano accompaniment by Johannes Brahms (op. 121, 1896), his last choral composition before his death in 1897. Thought to have been inspired by the death of Clara Schumann, if not his own impending death, each song is based on a biblical text. The first song, *Denn es gehet dem Menschen* ("It is for a person as it is for an animal"), is sung in the manner of a dirge, with bare octaves and open fifths in the piano accompaniment contributing to its bleak funereal sound, concluding with "Who knows if the human spirit rises upwards?" (Eccl. 3:19–22). The second song, *Ich wandte mich und sahe*, is solemn in mood and features offbeat chords in the accompaniment and descending melodic lines with an emphasis on *Unrecht* ("oppressions") and *Tränen* ("tears") (Eccl. 4:1–3). The third song, *O Tod, O Tod, wie bitter bist du* ("O Death, how bitter you are") (Sir. 41:1–2), is structured around the "death motif" of falling thirds, and the final song, *Wenn ich mit Menschen* ("Though I speak with the tongues") (1 Cor. 13:1–3, 12–13), which stands apart from the other three and is characterized by a lyrical melody and rising arpeggios in the accompaniment, has been described as a paean for love.

VIERGE, LA: LÉGENDE SACRÉE. ("The Virgin: A Sacred Legend"). Oratorio in four acts by Massenet to a libretto by Charles Grandmougin. While the work as a whole failed to gain popularity, the prelude to act 4, *Le Dernier Sommeil de la Vierge* ("The last sleep of the Virgin"), in which a solemn lullaby played by muted strings and cello depicts the Virgin's final sleep before her assumption into heaven, enjoyed numerous concert performances.

VINGT REGARDS SUR L'ENFANT JÉSUS. ("Twenty Contemplations on the Infant Jesus"). Solo piano cycle by Messiaen written between 23 March and 8 September 1944 during the German occupation of France, dedicated to the young pianist Yvonne Loriod, who would later become his wife. Now regarded as one of the most important works for piano of the 20th century, the work is a meditation on the Nativity of Christ based on a number of leitmotifs, such as God, the Star and the Cross, Mystical Love, and Chords. The "contemplations" move from the gaze of God the Father (I), the Star (II), the Virgin (IV), and the Cross (VII) to Silence (XVII) and the Church of Love (XX).

VIRGIN MARY HAD A BABY BOY. West Indian carol inspired by the biblical narrative (Lk. 2:7–20; Mt. 2:1–12), sung by Dame Kiri Te Kanawa, Michael George, and the choirs of Coventry and Lichfield on the album *Christmas with Kiri Te Kanawa* (1995). It tells of Christ's lowly birth in the AAAB verse form sung by the soloists representing the voice of God's angel (Lk. 2:9–12) and of his divinity in a refrain sung by the choir representing the angel choir ("He came from the Glory, He came from the Glorious kingdom") (Lk. 2:13–14). There is a piano arrangement for four hands by Mack Wilberg.

VIRGIN'S SLUMBER SONG, THE. (*Maria Wiegenlied*). Art song for voice and piano, organ, or orchestral accompaniment by Max Reger (op. 72, no. 52, 1904). The text is by Martin Boelitz, translated into English by Edward Teschemacher, and the work is dedicated to Princess Elizabeth Sachsen-Meiningen. Originally a folk song, "Joseph Dearest, Joseph Mine" (*Josef Lieber, Josef Mein*), its lilting melody and compound duple meter recall the cradle-rocking scene, a conversation between Joseph and Mary, and the Virgin's lullaby in 15th-century medieval mystery plays in Leipzig. In the 13th and 14th centuries, it was sung as a traditional carol, *Resonet in Laudibus*, later incorporated into polyphonic settings by Orlando de Lassus, Jacob Handl, Michael Praetorius, and Peter Cornelius, and in the 19th century as a viola obbligato by Brahms in the art song **Geistliches Wiegenlied** (op. 91).

VIRI GALILAEI. ("Men of Galilee"). Introit and motet for the Ascension (Acts 1:11; Pss. 46:5, 102:19) set to music by numerous 16th-century composers. One of the best known is a work for six voices by Palestrina, originally published in the lost *Motetta festorum totius anni* (1563) and later in the *Liber primus motettorum* (1569). It is noted for its dramatic use of different groupings of voices and homophony on *Viri Galilaei* ("men of Galilee"), *quid statis* ("Why are you standing?"), and *sic veniet* ("so he will come"). A Mass based on the motet, *Missa Viri Galilaei*, was published in the *Missarum liber duodecimus* (1601). The text was recently set to music by Patrick Gowers as a commission for the ordination of Richard Harries as bishop of Oxford in St. Paul's Cathedral (1987).

VISIONS DE L'AMEN. ("Visions of the **Amen**"). Seven-movement suite for two pianos by Messiaen (1943). Written for a performance by the composer himself and his 19-year-old student Yvonne Loriod, who later became his second wife, it is regarded as a masterpiece of the 20th century. Inspired by the Bible as well as speaking of Messiaen's passionate relationship with Loriod, it opens with the creation theme, rising from the depths of piano II to a dance depicting the orbiting planets (no. 2). A somber three-note theme (C-sharp, D, E-flat) reflects Christ's agony in the Garden of Gethsemane (no. 3), and dance rhythms, combined with Messiaen's characteristic birdsong, represent the heavenly dance of the angels and saints (no. 5), concluding with the entry into heaven to the sound of pealing bells (no. 7).

VISITATIO SEPULCHRI. ("Visit to the Tomb"). Sacred opera for seven-part chorus and chamber orchestra (1993) by Scottish composer James Macmillan based on the text of the 14th-century liturgical drama from Notre Dame Cathedral in Paris, also known as the *Quem quaeritis?* ("Whom do you seek?"). Originally enacted during matins on Easter Sunday morning, it tells of the women's encounter with the angel at the entrance to the empty tomb of (Mt. 28:1–7; Mk. 16:2–7; Lk. 24:1–18). The first act opens with an orchestral prelude and captures musically the violence of the Crucifixion with asymmetrical rhythms and abrasive dissonances. The second is a stylized dialogue between the three angels and the three women, opening with a bass voice intoning the question "Whom do you seek?" to a melody reminiscent of a Tibetan Buddhist chant, while a cantor, representing the onlookers in the drama, speaks, shouts, and chants in *Sprechstimme* style. The opera concludes with the Easter sequence *Victimae Paschali laudes* ("Praise of the Paschal Victim") and a rousing setting of the **Te Deum** ("We praise you, O God") celebrating Christ's resurrection.

VIVA LA VIDA. ("Long Live Life"). Song written and performed by Coldplay, included on their fourth album, *Viva la Vida or Death and All His Friends* (2008), and released as the band's second single, reaching number 1 on the U.K. and U.S. charts. In first-person narration, it tells the story of a dispossessed king who reflects on his loss of power, dishonest governance, past life as a warlord, and the prospect of eternal damnation, using biblical imagery as illustrations, such as the parable of the foolish builder (Mt. 7:26–27), the story of Lot's wife (Gen. 19:26), and the beheading of John the Baptist (Mt. 14:1–12). The song, sung by lead vocalist Chris Martin, is characterized by its upbeat riff played by strings, bass drum, and bass guitar, with the addition of a bell during the chorus to represent the tolling church bells in the city of Jerusalem.

VOM HIMMEL HOCH. ("From Heaven Above"). Well-known Christmas hymn based on Lk. 2:1–18 by Martin Luther, thought to have been composed for his young son, Hans. First published in *Geistliche Lieder* (Wittenberg, 1535), it was later set to music as a motet by Hans Leo Hassler, Michael Praetorius, and others. It features in Bach's **Christmas Oratorio** and **Magnificat** and is the basis for a chorale prelude (BWV 738) and a set of five canonic variations (BWV 769) for organ, later transcribed for chorus and orchestra by Igor Stravinsky (1956). Other well-known settings include a work for soprano, violin, and organ (op. 78, no. 20) by Sigfrid Karg-Elert (Prae-und Postludien für Orgel, 1912) and a choral arrangement of stanzas 13 and 14 in Benjamin Britten's **Ceremony of Carols** (op. 28, 1942).

VOX IN RAMA AUDITA EST. ("A Voice Is Heard in Rama"). Motet for a cappella SATB chorus by Jacobus Clemens non Papa (ca. 1553) composed for the Feast of the Holy Innocents and inspired by Jer. 31:15. The text, which employs imitation, expressive leaps, and downward stepwise movement on *ploratus et ululatus*, evokes the harrowing sound of Rachel "weeping and wailing" for her children, lost in exile according to Jewish tradition or, according to Christian tradition, massacred by Herod the Great (Mt. 2:18). The text was also set by several Renaissance composers, such as Claude de Sermisy, Mikołaj Zieleński, and Giaches de Wert.

• W •

WACHET AUF. ("Sleepers Awake"). One of Bach's best-known cantatas (BWV 140, 1599), based on the hymn *Wachet auf, ruft uns die Stimme* ("Awake, the voice is calling us") by Philipp Nicolai, composed for the 27th Sunday after Trinity, the last Sunday of the Church year. As the 27th Sunday occurs only when Easter falls exceptionally early, this cantata was performed only twice when Bach was in Leipzig (1731 and 1742). It is also frequently performed on the first Sunday of Advent because of the reference at the end to the Second Coming of Christ (Parousia). Scored for soprano, tenor, bass, orchestra, and continuo, it is inspired by the Gospel reading for the day, which was the parable of the wise and foolish virgins (Mt. 25:1–13), together with words from the Song of Songs allegorically applied to Christ's search for his bride, the Church. The cantata is in seven movements, of which the first, middle, and last incorporate the three verses of Nicolai's hymn. The first movement opens with a stately orchestral introduction in dotted rhythm heralding the arrival of the bridegroom, followed by a cantus firmus on the chorale tune calling on the wise virgins to wake up and get ready to meet the bridegroom. Long polyphonic melismas on **Alleluia** reflect the jubilant nature of the forthcoming wedding. Following the tenor's recitative announcing the bridegroom's arrival, a florid melody played by a solo violin opens movement 3 and continues as a countermelody during the dialogue between Jesus and his bride to represent the flickering flame of the lamp held by the bride/soul as she awaits her savior. The second chorale movement, "Zion hears the watchmen sing" (Isa. 52:8), sung by a tenor, is characterized by unison strings playing a joyous melody and later a countermelody, and this is followed by an accompanied recitative sung by the bass ("So come in to me, you my chosen bride"). Movement 6 opens with a lively, dance-like melody played on an oboe, followed by a sublime dialogue between the bride and groom, beginning with the soprano ("My Friend is mine") and answered by the bass ("And I am thine") (Cant. 2:16), followed by the two voices in harmony ("love will never part us"). The cantata concludes with the final verse of the chorale, which alludes to the Song of Heaven's Triumph (Rev. 19:6–9), sung in homophony by the chorus. Felix Mendelssohn incorporated an arrangement of *Wachet Auf* in his oratorio *St. Paul* (1836).

WADE IN THE WATER. African American spiritual alluding to the deliverance of the Israelites from slavery during the time of the Exodus and the saving waters of baptism. The chorus points to the "Underground Railroad" and the plight of slaves escaping north by wading through the river to avoid detection by sniffer dogs. First published in the *New Jubilee Songs as Sung by the Fisk Jubilee Singers* (1901), it has been performed by many, including Big Mama Thornton (1968), Eva Cassidy, and Bob Dylan (2001).

WALKING BACK TO JESUS: III. The third in a trilogy of songs with the same title by British American rock band the Broken Family Band on the mini-album *Jesus Songs* (2004). Perhaps inspired by Jn. 6:66, the narrator is one of the many disciples who walked away from Jesus and finds himself returning after leading a wayward life.

WAS GOTT TUT, DAS IST WOHL GETAN. ("What God Does, That Is Well Done"). Cantata by J. S. Bach (BWV 100) composed between 1732 and 1735 in Leipzig. One of the last of Bach's surviving cantatas, the libretto is based on the chorale *Was Gott tut, das ist wohlgetan*, which was composed by Samuel Rodigast to a melody by the composer Severin Gastorius (1674). Scored for SATB soloists, SATB chorus, orchestra, and continuo, the work is in six movements, each one opening with the first line of the chorale. The chorale also features in Cantatas BWV 98, first performed on the 21st Sunday after Trinity (10 November 1726), and BWV 99, first performed on the 15th Sunday after Trinity (17 September 1724), both of which have the same title. The libretto was inspired by the prescribed Epistle and Gospel readings (Gal. 5:25–6:10; Mt. 6:23–34). The chorale also features in the last movement of the cantata **Weinen, Klagen, Sorgen, Zagen** (BWV 12).

WATCHER OF MEN. Song by Sinead O'Connor from the album *Theology*. The title is derived from Dan. 4:13, 17, and 23, and the song is inspired by Job's cry "Why did I not die at birth?" (Job 3:11), sung in a weary, husky-sounding voice.

WAY OVER IN BEULAH LAN'. African American spiritual for SATB chorus a cappella, arranged by Stacey Gibbs based on Isa. 62:4. The phrase "way over in Beulah lan'," which is repeated throughout, refers to the Promised Land, that is, heaven. Other notable compositions based on the same text include the gospel hymn "Beulah Land" by Edgar Page Stites (1876) to music by John Sweney and the southern gospel song "Sweet Beulah Land" by Squire Parsons (1973).

WAYFARING STRANGER, THE. Nineteenth-century American folk song that became the signature song of American actor, writer, and folksinger Burl

Ives and appeared on an album of the same name in 1944. It tells of the soul's journey homeward, over Jordan, back to its loved ones (v. 1) and his Savior (v. 3). There are many versions, but most refer to the crown of glory that awaits the faithful in heaven (1 Pet. 5:4) and the souls washed in the blood of the Lamb (Rev. 7:14). The song appeared in the movies *How the West Was Won* (1963) and *Cold Mountain* (2003) and was covered by Johnny Cash (2000), American alternative country group 16 Horsepower (2000), and the Norwegian progressive death metal band In Vain (2000).

WE ARE CLIMBING JACOB'S LADDER. African American spiritual inspired by Gen. 28:12, an ascending melody suggestive of a spiritual ascent to heaven on Jacob's ladder. It has been performed by many, including Paul Robeson, Pete Seeger, Arlo Guthrie, and Bruce Springsteen.

WE ARE CROSSING THE JORDAN RIVER. Traditional American folk song arranged by Bob Gibson, performed by Bob Gibson and Joan Baez at the Newport Folk Festival (1959). The River Jordan in the song's title, chorus, and verses symbolizes the passageway for the souls of the dead from an earthly existence to eternal life in heaven. The final verse mentions Jacob's ladder (Gen. 28:10–19) as a **Stairway to Heaven**, and there are references to "my golden crown" (cf. 2 Tim. 4:8; 1 Pet. 5:4) and "my golden throne" (Mt. 19:28; Lk. 22:30) that await the faithful in heaven. *See also* JERICHO ROAD.

WE THREE KINGS. Popular Christmas carol by John Henry Hopkins Jr. (1857) inspired by the story of the visit of the Magi to Bethlehem (Mt. 2:1–12), written for a Christmas pageant in New York City and published in *Carols, Hymns and Songs* (1862). Verses 2 to 4 detail each of the gifts of gold, frankincense, and myrrh brought by the kings, while the chorus extols the beauty of the **Star of Bethlehem** (Mt. 2:2).

WEDDING CANTATA. Cantata for SATB chorus and piano by Daniel Rogers Pinkham, written to celebrate the marriage of his friends Lotje and Arthur Loeb (1956). It is in four movements based on verses from the Song of Songs. Movement 1 is a setting of "Arise my love" (Cant. 2:10–12) for chorus, tenor, and soprano soloist. Movement 2, "Many Waters cannot Quench Love" (Cant. 8:7), is a canon in unison, and movement 3, "Awake O North Wind" (Cant. 4:16), is striking for its rollicking accompaniment. The final movement is a slow, serene setting of "Set me as a Seal" (Cant. 8:6).

WEINEN, KLAGEN, SORGEN, ZAGEN. ("Weeping, Wailing, Lamenting, Fearing"). Jubilate cantata for ATB, SATB chorus, orchestra, and continuo by J. S. Bach for the third Sunday after Easter (BWV 12, 22 April 1714, Weimar; rev. 30 April 1724). The libretto, inspired by the Epistle and Gospel readings for the day (1 Pet. 2:11–20; Jn. 16:16–23), is by Salomo Franck. It is one of only a few cantatas that open with a sinfonia. The choral first section of the second movement, like the *Crucifixus* in the B Minor Mass (BWV 232), is based on a chromatic fourth ostinato (*lamento bass*) to depict intense sorrow turning to joy (Jn. 16:20, 22). The same thought is expressed in the alto recitative in movement 3 (Acts 14:22). The tenor aria in movement 6 is accompanied by a trumpet/oboe obbligato from the chorale melody *Jesu meine Freude* ("Jesus my joy"), and the work concludes with the chorale **Was Gott tut, das ist wohlgetan** set for four-part chorus. Liszt composed a work for piano solo (S. 179, 1859) based on a theme from the sinfonia (first movement).

WERE YOU THERE? African American spiritual sung as a slow, meditative hymn since it first appeared in the Episcopal Hymnal of 1940. First published in William Barton's *Old Plantation Hymns* (1899), the verses relate various stages in Christ's passion, death, burial, and resurrection, and the refrain "Oh, sometimes it causes me to tremble, tremble, tremble" ends with the question "Were you there when they crucified my Lord?" It is all the more chilling when one realizes that African American slaves regularly witnessed members of their community hanged and lynched in trees. Traditionally sung on Good Friday, it has been performed by Johnny Cash and arranged for solo voice by H. T. Burleigh and for SATB chorus by Christopher Norton.

WEXFORD CAROL, THE. Christmas carol originating in Enniscorthy, County Wexford. One of the oldest existing carols in European tradition, it was discovered by William Grattan Ford (1859–1928), organist and musical director of St. Aidan's Cathedral, who, after hearing it sung by a local singer, sent it for publication to the editors of the *Oxford Book of Carols* (1928). The carol was previously published in two collections: *Pious Garlands* (Ghent, 1864; reprint, London, 1728, 1731) by Bishop Luke Wadding of Ferns (1631–1687) and *A New Garland Containing Songs for Christmas* (1728) by Rev. William Deveraux of Drinagh, County Wexford (1696–1771). This carol, with its haunting melody in the Dorian mode, wide leaps, and flattened sevenths, evokes the sound of a poignant lament that points musically to the passion and death of Christ. It has been performed by numerous choirs and artists, including the Irish Chamber Choir, Anúna, American bluegrass/country singer Alison Krauss, and American folksinger Nanci Griffith with the Dubliners.

WHALE, THE: A BIBLICAL FANTASY. Dramatic cantata in two parts and eight sections by John Tavener (1965–1966), scored for soloists (Mez-Bar), mixed chorus, speaker, organ, orchestra, non-orchestral instruments (e.g., a whip and a football rattle), and electronic tape (1966). Based on the Book of Jonah, it was premiered at the London Sinfonietta debut concert on 24 January 1968 and performed a year later at the Proms (1 August 1969). Released by the Beatles' Apple Records label (1970), it was re-released on Ringo Starr's label Ring'O Records (1977), followed by its release as a CD on Apple Records in 1992 and 2010. Ringo Starr participated in the original recording, contributing voices, noises, and percussion. It opens rather unconventionally with an encyclopedia entry on the sea mammal "of the order of the cetacea" read by BBC Radio newsreader Alvar Lidell. Noted for its use of percussion and dramatic sound effects, such as an improvised section in part 7, "In the Belly," in which the chorus "clap hands, neigh, grunt, snort, yawn, make vomiting noises, whisper, cough, shuffle, hum and talk to each other in any order."

WHAT CHILD IS THIS? Popular Christmas carol with words by William Chatterton Dix (1865) sung to the 16th-century English folk song tune *Greensleeves*. It appeared in *Christmas Carols New and Old* (1871) to a harmonization by Stainer. The lyrics recount the birth, passion, and death of Christ. The lilting compound duple time calls to mind the Virgin's imagined lullaby to the Christ child, while the modal folk melody points to Christ's joyful birth, his death on the cross, and his glorious resurrection. The carol has enjoyed performances by numerous classical and popular artists and choirs, including arrangements by Vaughan Williams and, more recently, Paul Hayley, performed by Gaudeamus on the album *What Child Is This?* (2006). *See also* NIÑO, EL.

WHAT SWEETER MUSIC. Christmas carol anthem for chorus and orchestra/organ by John Rutter, commissioned for the annual Festival of Nine Lessons and Carols in 1987, based on a poem by Robert Herrick (1591–1674). Intended for performance after the reading recounting the journey of the Three Wise Men (Mt. 2), this lavish carol with its exquisite melody highlights the gift of music presented to Jesus at the time of his birth.

WHEN CAIN KILLED ABEL IN A FIGHT. Hymn (1997) by Mary Nelson Keithahn to the tune "Absolution" by John D. Horman (1997). It is a lament by God for Abel (Gen. 4:8–10), Esau (Gen. 27), and Joseph (Gen. 37) and also for Christians who suffer the effects of jealousy and rivalry at home and in the world today. The final verse urges Christians to join in this song as a prayer for forgiveness.

WHEN DAVID HEARD. Anthem for SATB choir by American composer Norman Dinerstein for the Hartt Chamber Singers (1975). Based on David's lament on hearing of his son Absalom's death (2 Sam. 18:33), it begins with a chorus in five, six, and then eight parts, repeating "Oh Absalom my son, oh my son." In the last two measures, David's wailing cry "O my son" is sung pianissimo, as if in the distance, by a solo soprano on high B-flat over a sustained E-flat major chord by the chorus.

WHEN DAVID HEARD. Polyphonic anthem/sacred madrigal in two parts for six voices (SSAATB) by Thomas Weelkes, probably written in response to the untimely death of Prince Henry, son of King James, in 1612. David's outpouring of grief when he heard the news of his son Absalom's death (2 Sam. 18:33) is depicted by poignant dissonances, silences punctuated by musical rests, sighs on "O (my son)," and descending melodic lines on "(would God) I had died for thee" and "Absalom," including one instance of homophony at the end for all eight parts, and on "my son," punctuated by rests before and after. Other settings include those of Thomas Tomkins, a student of Weelkes; F. Melius Christiansen (1925); Castelnuovo-Tedesco (1953); George McKay (organ, 1963); León Schidlowsky (orchestra, 1996); Alexandra Du Bois (violin and prepared piano, 2001); and Patricia Alessandrini (contrabass and percussion with live electronics, 2005).

WHEN DAVID HEARD. Choral work for SSAATTBB chorus a cappella by Eric Whitacre, based on David's lament for his son Absalom (2 Sam. 18:33). The work, which lasts for approximately 15 minutes, is built around a series of variations that evoke the sound of wailing and weeping with poignant silences and pregnant pauses. It opens in A minor with a six-part chorus chanted in recitative style, with movement on "he went up," to eight parts on "up into his chamber over the gate and wept," with cluster chords built around intervals of a third, fifth, seventh, ninth, and 11th. David's words "my son, my son" are repeated by the sopranos on a single A in a section marked "adagio," rising in intensity with the addition of 17 voice parts from the bass up to measure 13 and dissonances on Absalom's name.

WHEN DAVID'S LIFE BY SAUL. Lute song for solo voice or four voices (SATB) with lute and viol accompaniment by John Dowland, the second of three religious songs published in Dowland's fourth book, *A Pilgrimes*

Solace (1612). It is a setting of the second of three stanzas of a sonnet by Nicholas Breton about patience and hope, beginning with Job, whose "Patience asswaged his excessive paine," and ending with "the poore Criple by the Poole" (Jn. 5). It recalls Saul's desperate attempts to have David killed and how, "in his griefes, Hope still did help him out" (1 Sam. 19–24). It begins with a four-part canon, alluding perhaps to Saul's search for David, and emphasizes David's sorrow with chromaticisms and word painting on "woes" and "griefs."

WHEN I SURVEY THE WONDROUS CROSS. Hymn based on Gal. 6:14 by Isaac Watts (1707), considered by Matthew Arnold to have been the finest in the English language. The tune "Rockingham" (1790) is also known as "Communion" because the hymn is almost invariably sung on Communion occasions.

WHEN ISRAEL WAS IN EGYPT'S LAND. *See* GO DOWN MOSES.

WHEN JESUS WENT INTO SIMON THE PHARISEE'S HOUSE. Anthem/contrafactum for five voices (SATBarB) a cappella by Thomas Tallis based on the story of the woman wiping Christ's feet with her hair (Lk. 7:36–38). It is set to the music of his motet *Salvator mundi II*.

WHEN JESUS WEPT. Round for four voices by American composer William Billings, first published in the *New England Psalm Singer* (Boston, 1770). Composed in the minor tonality, the four-line stanza recounts the scene of Jesus weeping at the grave of Lazarus (Jn. 11:35), a lilting effect mimicking the rising and falling contours of the sound of Christ weeping and groaning, while the polyphonic texture of the round paints the keening of Lazarus's sister Mary and the Jews who accompanied her (Jn. 11:33), and a descending melody line represents Christ's "falling tear." American composer William Shumann composed a "Prelude for Band" (1958) with the same title based on this composition, as did Ralph McTell in the album *Sand in Your Shoes* (1995). *See also* JESUS WEPT.

WHEN THE SAINTS GO MARCHING IN. American gospel hymn by Luther G. Presley set to music by Virgil Oliver Stamps. Inspired by verses from the Book of Revelation (Rev. 6:12, 13, 7, 8–11; 14:1–5; 19:12; 1:14), the last two lines of each verse allude to the "144,000" (Rev. 7:4–8; 14:1–5), "the saints" entering heaven's gateway. Traditionally sung at jazz funerals in New Orleans, it was popularized by Louis Armstrong in the 1930s and performed by numerous artists, including Dixieland artist Fats Domino, Judy Garland, Elvis Presley, Mahalia Jackson, the Beatles and Tony Sheridan, and Bruce Springsteen with the Seeger Sessions Band. Popular as a football anthem, it features as the unofficial anthem of New Orleans.

WHEN THE SHIP COMES IN. Folk song by Bob Dylan on his third album, *The Times They Are A-Changin'* (1964). Written after a dispute with a hotel clerk, the song points to a time "when the ship comes in," when all oppressors will be vanquished, with allusions to the Three Wise Men and the destruction of other oppressors, such as Pharaoh's army (Exod. 15) and the Philistine Goliath (1 Sam. 17). It was performed by the Clancy Brothers and Tommy Makem at Dylan's 30th Anniversary Concert Celebration in Madison Square Garden in New York City in 1992.

WHEN THE WEARY, SEEKING REST. Hymn by Horatius Bonar, based on 2 Chron. 6:29–30 and inspired by the tune "Intercession," of which the last two lines recall the prayer for rain in Mendelssohn's *Elijah* (1846).

WHEN YOU BELIEVE. Song from the animated movie *The Prince of Egypt*, written by Stephen Schwartz in 1998. It is sung by Miriam (Michele Pfeiffer) and Zipporah (Sally Dworsky), Moses' sister and wife, respectively, and a chorus of women and children who sing God's praises in Hebrew (Exod. 15:1, 11, 13). It was also performed as a duet by Mariah Carey and Whitney Houston during the end credits of the film. In 1999, the song was awarded an Academy Award for Best Original Song.

WHICH WAS THE SON OF . . . Work for a cappella chorus (SATB) by Arvo Pärt, commissioned by Reykjavík European City of Culture 2000 for Voices of Europe. The 76 ancestors of Christ are listed, all the way back to "Seth which was the son of Adam which was the son of God" (Lk. 3:23–38). The texture becomes fuller and richer (SATB *divisi*) with the patriarchs Abraham, Isaac, and Jacob, and the work concludes on an open fifth chord on "God." Having opened momentarily in E minor, the work concludes on an E major triad.

WHILE SHEPHERDS WATCHED THEIR FLOCKS BY NIGHT. Christmas carol inspired by Lk. 2:4–8, written by Nahum Tate and first published in the supplement (1700) to the **New Version of the Psalms of David** (1696) by Nicholas Brady and Nahum Tate. In Europe, it is commonly sung to the tune "Winchester Old" by Christopher Tye and in the United States to the tune "Jackson" from Handel's opera *Siroe, King of Persia* (1728).

WHITHER THOU GOEST. Popular song written by Guy Singer (1954), inspired by Ruth 1:16–17 and Jn. 13:36. It has been performed by numerous artists, including Les Paul and Mary Ford, Perry Como, Bing Crosby, Mahalia Jackson, and Leonard Cohen. The text was also set as a wedding song for high voice and piano/organ (*Wo du hingehst, da will auch ich hingehen*) by the Belgian composer Flor Peeters (op. 103a, 1962) and translated into English by Hugh Ross. *See also* I WILL FOLLOW; I WILL GO WHERE YOU WILL GO; RUTH.

WINGS OF A DOVE. Country song by Bob Ferguson (1958) inspired both by the dove in the story of Noah's flood (Gen. 8:6–12) and by the dove at the baptism of Jesus (Mt. 3:16). The song's title comes from Ps. 55:6–8. Recorded by Ferlin Husky (1960), it was covered by many artists, including the Jordanaires, Dolly Parton, and Ricky Skaggs and the Whites. It appears in the movie *Tender Mercies* (1983), sung by lead actor Robert Duval, and, with Gail Youngs, as a duet in the background.

WIR DANKEN DIR, GOTT. ("Unto Thee, O God Do We Give Thanks"). An "election" cantata for SATB soloists, SATB chorus, and orchestra, with organ obbligato and continuo, by J. S. Bach, composed for the so-called election of new members to the town council in Leipzig (BWV 29) on 27 August 1731. It is one of five election cantatas, the others being BWV 69, BWV 119, BWV 120, and BWV 193. Festive in character, it opens, rather unusually, with an orchestral sinfonia, followed by a motet-like chorus (*Wir danken dir, Gott*) based on Ps. 75:1, and concludes with the final verse of the well-known hymn *Nun lob mein Seel' den Herren* ("Now Praise my Soul, the Lord") with festive trumpets and timpani added to create an air of splendor.

WISE VIRGINS, THE. Ballet in nine movements by William Walton (1940), choreographed by Frederick Ashton and premiered at Sadler's Wells Theatre, London, on 26 April 1940, featuring Margot Fonteyn and Michael Somes as the bride and bridegroom. Inspired by the parable of the wise and foolish virgins (Mt. 25:1–13), it was later adapted as a ballet suite in six movements, first performed in September 1940. Based on orchestrations of various movements from Bach's cantatas, it opens with the final four-part chorale from *Wachet Auf* (BWV 140), followed by an orchestration of the bass aria *Dein Geburtstag ist erschienen* ("Your birthday has appeared") from the Christmas Cantata (BWV 142) and the opening chorus of **Was Gott tut, das ist wohlgetan** ("What God does is well done") (BWV 99). Movement 7 is based on the well-known recitative and soprano aria "Sheep may safely graze" from the secular cantata Was mir behagt ist nur die muntre Jagd ("The lively hunt is all my heart's desire") (BWV 208), and the work ends with *Gelobet sei der Herr, mein Gott* ("Praised be the Lord, my God") (BWV 129). The theme from the fourth movement, based on the chorale prelude for organ **Herzlich tut mich verlangen** (BWV 727), later featured in *The Five Foolish Virgins*, an opera by Jan Meyerowitz (1953).

WITCH OF ENDOR, THE. One-act ballet by American composer William Schumann, commissioned by Martha Graham (1965) and later reworked by Moondog (Thomas Hardin) into a six-minute "minisym," that is, a short symphonic-style work for orchestra (1969). Based on 1 Sam. 28:8–20, it begins and ends with a dance featuring atmospheric percussion depicting the witch as she conjures up the spirit of the prophet Samuel and a trio comprising an adagio ("Prophecy") with tremolo strings, an andante ("The Battle"), and an agitato ("Saul's Death") with tremolo strings again. *See also* IN GUILTY NIGHT.

WITH OR WITHOUT YOU. Lead single from the album *The Joshua Tree* (1987) and one of U2's most popular songs. It is sung by Bono at every live concert to a woman from the audience invited up on to the stage. The lyric "See the thorn twist in your side," perhaps alluding to an autobiographical reference by St. Paul (2 Cor. 12:7), refers to Satan as the thorn in every woman, and the title states that the songwriter cannot live "with or without" the woman in his life.

WODE PSALTER, THE. A collection of 16th-century part books, also known as the St. Andrew's Psalter, featuring Psalms, anthems, hymns, and other sacred and secular vocal and instrumental music. The heart of the collection is a set of four-part harmonizations (SATB) of 106 metrical Psalm tunes from the Anglo-Genevan Psalm Book (1556), composed mainly by Scottish composer David Peebles at the request of the composer's protestant patron, Lord James Stewart, earl of Moray. Thomas Wode, a former monk and later vicar of St. Andrew's, compiled the collection between 1562 and 1592, including works by known and less well known Scottish, English, French, and Italian composers. Highly illustrated, it contains the largest body of annotations found in any early modern British musical manuscript. The album *The Wode Collection* (2011) includes a rich selection of music from the work, including *Susanne un Jour* by Lassus, an arrangement of the ever-popular Ps. 124 by Peebles, and *Hosanna* by Palestrina.

WOMAN OF SAMARIA. Cantata in one act for soloists, chorus, and orchestra by William Sterndale Bennett (op. 44, 1867). Inspired by the biblical story (Jn. 4:1–26), it tells of the dialogue between Jesus (B) and the Samaritan woman at the well (S) and the revelation of his messianic identity, with reflective comments from the chorus based on texts from the Psalms (Pss. 36:9; 139:1, 3; 18:1, 3, 27; 85:9, 12; 18:3; 72:18), prophets (Isa. 30:21; Jer. 31:12), Gospels (Lk. 1:68–69), and Paul's Letters to the Colossians (Col. 1:15). It opens with a brief instrumental overture and the chorale "Ye Christian People, Now Rejoice" (*Nun freut euch, lieben Christen g'mein*), based on a text and melody published by Martin Luther in *Geistliche Lieder* (1523), and also includes the hymn **Abide with Me** and the well-known anthem "God is a Spirit" (Jn. 4:24–26).

WOMAN WITH THE ALABASTER BOX, THE. Choral work in English for SATB a cappella chorus by Arvo Pärt, composed for the 350th anniversary of the Karlstad Diocese of the Church of Sweden (1997). Telling of the anointing of Jesus' feet by a woman traditionally identified as Mary Magdalene (Mt. 26:6–13), it is characterized by a largely homophonic texture, changing meters, and reflective pauses.

WOMEN OF VALOR. Oratorio by American composer Andrea Clearfield (2000) based on biblical texts and translations of modern Hebrew and Yiddish writings by Jewish women, including Rivka Miriam, Ellen Frankel, Alicia Ostriker, Isidor Lillian, and Andrea Clearfield. The three movements present 10 biblical examples of the "woman of valor" (Hebrew *eshet ḥayil* [Prov. 31:10]): Sarah (Gen. 17:15), Leah and Rachel (Gen. 29:16–21), Jocheved (Exod. 6:20) (movt. 1), Miriam and Hannah (1 Sam. 1–2), Jael (Judg. 5:24–27) (movt. 2), Michal (1 Sam. 18), and Ruth and Esther (movt. 3). In movement 2, the text of Prov. 31:10–31 is sung in Hebrew to synagogue chants and other Jewish traditional melodies woven together. To reflect the text's acrostic form, each line is sung on a consecutive degree of a 22-note scale, preceded by a chime tone, derived from three synagogue prayer modes. The incorporation of traditional instruments, Jewish dance forms, and cantorial ornamentation lends a Middle Eastern ambience to the composition. *See also* ESHET CHAYIL.

WORMWOOD: CURIOUS STORIES FROM THE BIBLE. Concept album by the Residents, released in 1998 to explore the meaning of 18 "curious" biblical texts. The title comes from the Book of Revelation (Rev. 8:11), and the work begins and ends with instrumentals based on Gen. 1–3 and Rev. 4–22. The sequence of songs begins with "Fire Fall," on the story of Sodom and Gomorrah (Gen. 19), and then ranges freely over the Pentateuch with "Cain and Abel" (Gen. 4), "Spilling the Seed" (Gen. 38), "The Seven Ugly

Cows" (Gen. 41), and "The Bridegroom of Blood" (Exod. 4:24–6); the histories with "Tent Peg in the Temple" (Judg. 4–5), "David and Bathsheba" (2 Sam. 11), and "Hanging by his Hair" (2 Sam. 13:20–30; 16:20–22; 18:9–15); and the prophets with "Mr Misery" (Lamentations), "They Are the Meat" (Ezek. 4:4–15), and "God's Magic Finger" (Dan. 5). The Dark Bride from the Song of Solomon (Cant. 1:5) sings "I hate Heaven," and there are two songs from the New Testament: "How to Get a Head" (Mk. 6:17–29), which is Salome's account of reactions to her dance for Herod and her obsession with John the Baptist's decapitated head, and "Judas Saves," where Judas argues that it was to save humanity that he betrayed Jesus (Mk. 14:17–46). But the two most disturbing songs in the cycle are undoubtedly Abraham's "Kill him" (Gen. 22) and Jephthah's "Burn Baby Burn" (Judg. 11:31–40).

WRESTLER, THE. One-act opera by Samuel Adler (1971) with a libretto by Judah Stampfer, commissioned by the American Guild of Organists. Inspired by the biblical story of Jacob wrestling the angel (Gen. 32:22–32), it tells, in a series of flashbacks, the story of his fractious relationship with his brother Esau, the stolen birthright, and a meeting with Esau. It is scored for soloists and four choruses: a children's chorus representing his children, a choir of angels ascending and descending the ladder, a women's chorus representing Jacob's wives and concubines, and a men's chorus representing Esau's army.

• Y •

YAHWEH. Song by U2, featuring as the 11th track on the album *How to Dismantle an Atomic Bomb* (2004) and performed live during the Vertigo Tour (2005–2006). The song's title, which also features in the chorus, is a reference to the Tetragrammaton, the four consonants of the mysterious and unpronounceable sacred name of Israel's God (YHWH) (Exod. 3:13–15).

YERUSHALAYIM SHEL ZAHAV. ("Jerusalem of Gold"). Popular Hebrew song composed by Israeli musician Naomi Shemer in 1967, the year when the Israelis defeated Jordan and took the Old City of Jerusalem. Poignant biblical allusions include "How lonely sits the city" (Lam. 1:1), "If I forget thee, O Jerusalem" (Ps. 137:5), and perhaps the "gold . . . bronze . . . and light" of the refrain from Isa. 60, "Arise, shine for your light is come" (vv. 1, 6, 17, 19). In an orchestral arrangement by John Williams, the song features on the sound track of the film *Schindler's List* (1993).

YOU RAISE ME UP. Song composed by Rolf Løvland from the group Secret Garden to lyrics written by Irish songwriter Brendan Graham, popularized by lead singer Brian Kennedy, the Irish boy band Westlife, and later the American singer/songwriter Josh Groban. Based on the melody of "The Londonderry Air" and inspired by verses from the Psalms (Pss. 41:10; 30:1; 61:2), it opens with an ascending melody illustrating the hope of new life brought about by God's saving grace. Sung as a hymn in church services, it has been performed at the 9/11 Official Ground Zero and Pentagon Commemorations, the NASA Tribute, Nobel Peace ceremonies, the opening of the Northern Ireland Peace Assembly, Queen Elizabeth's visit to Ireland, and the closing ceremony of the Eucharistic Congress as well as many sporting events.

• Z •

ZADOK THE PRIEST. One of four coronation anthems (HWV 258) composed by Handel for the coronation of George II in Westminster Abbey on 11 October 1727 and performed during the anointing ceremony at every subsequent British coronation service. In an arrangement by the English composer Tony Britten, it is the official anthem of the UEFA Champions League. Based on the account of the anointing of Solomon by Zadok the priest (1 Kgs. 1:38–40), it is scored for SSAATBB chorus and orchestra in D major, the baroque tonality of glory. It opens with a stately orchestral prelude in 4/4 meter, building in anticipation and excitement through a trommel bass accompaniment and rising arpeggios in the strings to the majestic homophonic entry of the choir. Section 2 opens in 3/4 meter, like a dance, with dotted rhythms in the accompaniment to represent the people rejoicing, and in the last section, chorus and orchestra in homophony proclaim Solomon as king, "God Save the King, Long Live the King, May the King Live Forever," followed by a series of jubilant **Amens** and **Alleluias**.

ZELOPHEHAD'S DAUGHTERS. The third of three monologues titled *Sisters* (1989) for soprano with chamber jazz ensemble or piano by Jewish composer Leonard Lehrman. Based on the biblical narrative (Num. 27:1–11; 36:1–12; Josh. 17:3–4; 1 Chron. 7:15), it is sung by Tirzah, who tells the story of how she and her four sisters, Mahlah, Noah, Hoglah, and Milkah, after the death of their father Zelophehad in the wilderness, with God's help, won the right to inherit their father's property in the land of Israel.

ZION TRAIN. Reggae song by Rastafarian Bob Marley (1973), performed by Marley and the Wailers on the album *Uprising* (1980). Inspired by numerous biblical texts (Mt. 16:26; Prov. 8:19; 16:16), "Zion Train," also called the "Soul Train," is an allegory for freedom from slavery in Babylon (the West) back to "self-control" and liberation in Zion (a united Africa).

ZUM SANCTUS. Fifth movement of Schubert's *Deutsche Messe* ("German Mass," D. 872, 1826–1827), inspired by Isa. 6:3 and Rev. 7:8–11. It is one of Schubert's last works, commissioned by Johann Philipp Neumann of the Polytechnic School of Vienna, who also wrote the words. A work for SATB chorus, wind ensemble, brass, timpani, organ, and double bass, it is largely homophonic in texture and intended for a church congregation. Today, it is a popular choice at weddings.

Glossary of Technical Terms

a cappella	Italian "singing without instrumental accompaniment"
accidental	a sharp, flat, or natural not in the key signature
accompagnato	Italian "recitative accompanied by the orchestra"
accompanied recitative	a type of monody that imitates the accents, rhythms, and declamation of spoken speech, as found in oratorios and operas and accompanied by orchestra
ad lib.	impromptu, improvised
adagio	Italian "slowly"
adiastematic neumes	known also as "unheightened neumes"; a form of early notation that records approximate rather than exact pitch
African American spiritual	unaccompanied monophonic songs of enslaved African Americans created during the 17th century
agitato assai	Italian "quite agitated"
aleatoric music	also known as "aleatory" or "chance music" in which elements of the composition are left to chance
allegretto	Italian "moderately fast tempo"
allegro con fuoco	Italian "fast/lively with fire"
allegro guerriero	Italian "fast war-like"
anabasis	a musical rhetorical device or figure that describes a rousing emotion in an ascending musical passage
andante	Italian "at a walking pace," that is, moderately slow
anthem	a polyphonic setting of a religious/biblical text in English scored for several voices
antiphon	a responsory by a choir or congregation in the form of a Gregorian chant sung before and after a psalm verse
Apache dance	a term associated with Parisian street gangs at the end of the 19th century; a dramatic type of ballroom dance with close contact, jerks, and spins
appoggiatura	a grace note that receives one half the value of the note that follows
aria	a solo song with orchestral accompaniment, commonly found in an oratorio, opera, or cantata
arioso	a vocal style that falls between an aria and a recitative

275

arpeggio	the articulation of successive notes of a chord
augmentation	a compositional device in which the notes of a melodic phrase are lengthened
ballad	derived from medieval French dance songs, or "ballades"; a form of verse set to music
bar	synonymous with measure, it denotes a segment of time defined as a given number of beats of a given duration
basso continuo	known also as the continuo, figured bass or thorough-bass; in the 18th century, a harpsichord, double bass, or cello played a bass line figured with numbers to indicate specific harmonic progressions
beat	pulse in music
bel canto	Italian "beautiful singing," that is, virtuoso legato singing
berimbau	a Brazilian percussion instrument used to accompany the capoeira
binary form	music divided into two contrasting parts (AB)
bluegrass	a subgenre of country and western inspired by the music of Appalachia, incorporating Irish, Scottish, Welsh, and English traditional music as well as elements of jazz
cadence	a series of chords marking the end of a phrase, section, or piece of music
cadenza	a passage in music that occurs before the end of a composition, usually a concerto, to allow a soloist to demonstrate technical brilliance and agility
canon	a polyphonic technique in which the initial melody is played or sung and then imitated by subsequent voices either exactly (strict canon) or with modifications (free canon)
cantata	a genre of sacred music for voices comprising solos, duets, recitatives, and choruses sung to an instrumental accompaniment
canticle	a song of praise deriving from a biblical text other than the psalms
cantilena	a smooth flowing, lyrical passage of vocal or instrumental music
capoeira	a Brazilian martial art that combines elements of dance and acrobatics
carol	from the Old French "carole," that is, a circular dance; a festive song sung at Advent, Christmas, and, to a lesser extent, Easter

chalumeau	an 18th century woodwind instrument associated primarily with pastoral scenes
chancel opera	a short opera based on a biblical theme for performance in a church; it can also be performed in a synagogue
Charleston	a dance named after the harbor city of Charleston, South Carolina, characterized by alternating forward and backward steps and a rotation of the knees
chiaro e solenne	Italian "clear and solemn"
chorale	a homophonic setting of a German Lutheran hymn
chorale prelude	a work for organ based on a chorale
chromatic	a half step interval
circulatio	a musical rhetorical device representing Christ's crucifixion
coloratura	elaborate ornamentation of a vocal line, especially by a soprano
compound duple time	music with two beats in the bar, for example, in 6/8 time; music is divided into two groups of three beats
concept album	studio album organized around an overarching theme
concerto	an instrumental work in three movements for solo instrument and orchestral accompaniment
concerto grosso	type of baroque concerto for soloists (concertino) and ensemble (ripieno)
continuo	*See* basso continuo
contra danse	French folk dance
contrafactum	the substitution of one text for another without any major alteration to the music, as in a parody
counterpoint	the art of combining two or more independent melodic lines
country and western	a genre of popular music originating in Atlanta, Georgia, in the 1920s
crab canon	a canon in which the imitating voice sings the tune backward
crescendo	a dynamic marking indicating a gradual increase in volume
cross-relation	known also as a false relation, that is, a type of chromatic dissonance that occurs in close proximity between two vocal parts or melodic lines, such as G sharp in the tenor voice and G natural in the soprano
crotchet	known also as a quarter note that has the value of a quarter of a semibreve, that is, one beat
da capo aria	a solo song in ternary form (ABA), common during the 18th century

dialogue	a musical genre common in the 16th century and an important antecedent of 17th-century oratorio; a setting of dialogue text between two or more characters
diatonic scale	a musical scale with seven pitches comprising whole tones and semitones
diminuendo	a dynamic marking meaning "diminishing of sound"
discant clausula	a type of early polyphony in which two voice parts move together in strict modal rhythm
dissonance	two or more harsh tones that demand resolution to a consonance
divisi	Italian "divided"
dodecaphonic	*See* twelve-tone serialism
duduk	a traditional woodwind instrument indigenous to Armenia
English oratorio	oratorio in English developed by Handel in the 18th century and scored in three parts
erhu	Chinese two-stringed instrument played with a bow
espressivo	Italian "expressively"
false relations	known also as cross relations; a chromatic contradiction between two notes in close proximity, employed for an expressive effect
falsobordone	*See* fauxbourdon
fauxbourdon	a technique of harmonization used by composers of the late Middle Ages and early Renaissance
flat	the lowering in pitch by a semitone as indicated by a "b" sign in the key signature or preceding the note being flattened
fortissimo (*ff*)	a dynamic marking meaning "very loud"
fugue	from the Italian *fugare*, "to put to flight"; a contrapuntal compositional technique in which a subject, that is, a short melody, is played or sung in one voice and answered by another
galliard	a 16th-century French dance characterized by leaps, jumps, and hops
glissando	Italian; a gliding technique articulated by the performer up and/or down an instrument
gospel music	a genre of Christian music that began in the 17th century among African Americans; the term "gospel song" first appeared in 1874
heavy metal	a genre of rock music originating in the United States and the United Kingdom in the late 1960s and early 1970s

Heldentenor	a tenor voice that sings heroic roles in German opera
hip-hop	a genre of popular music arising out of hip-hop culture characterized by stylized rhythmic music that accompanies rapping and chanted speech; it is associated with rapping, deejaying, break dancing, and graffiti writing
historicus	a term found in oratorio *Latino* to signify the narrator
homophonic	a musical texture where two or more melodic lines move together in harmony
hymn	a religious song of praise, adoration, or prayer, it is strophic
ieratico	Italian "sacred, solemn"
imitative counterpoint	the art of combining independent melodies to form a homogeneous texture, with the first voice leading and second and subsequent voices following at the same pitch or transposed, as in a canon or fugue
incipit	Latin "it begins," that is, the first words of a chanted liturgical text
intermezzo	a short movement in a work that separates other, larger movements
interval	the distance in pitch between two notes
inversion	when the root of a given chord is not in the bass
Kaddish	an ancient Jewish prayer of praise
katabasis	written also as catabasis; a musical-rhetorical device or figure that describes a negative emotion in a descending musical passage
klezmer	a musical tradition of the Ashkenazi Jews of Eastern Europe, consisting of dance tunes and festive instrumentals for weddings and other celebrations
kontakion	a poetic form in Byzantine hymnography, attributed to Romanos the Melodist (6th century CE)
largo	Italian "very slow tempo"
leitmotif	German "leading motif"; pioneered by Wagner, it is a short musical idea associated with a character or event in a given work
lento	Italian; a tempo marking meaning "slow"
libretto	the literary text of an oratorio and opera
macaronic	a type of verse that combines two or more languages
madrigal	an unaccompanied song in the vernacular, first from the 14th century, later developed in the 16th century as a setting of a poetic text for four to six voices
maestoso	Italian "in a stately and dignified manner"

mariachi	a bass guitar used primarily in Mexican folk music
masque	festive courtly entertainment in the 16th and 17th centuries involving dancing, singing, and acting on an elaborate stage
maximalism	the period of modernism from 1890–1914
measure	synonymous with "bar" and denotes a segment of time defined as a given number of beats of a given duration
melisma	an ornate vocal passage sung on one syllable of text
melodic leap	leaps within a melody comprising consonant intervals of the degree of a major/minor third, perfect fourth, perfect fifth, major/minor sixth, and octave and dissonant intervals of diminished, augmented, major/minor seconds, and seventh degrees of the scale
meter	the grouping together of beats into twos, threes, or fours; the time signature at the beginning of a composition indicates the number and value of beats in a bar
minim	known also as a half note and articulated for two beats
minimalism	an approach to composition in the 1960s as a reaction against serialism and aleatoric music
minuet	from the French *menuet*, "small"; a stately 17th-century French dance in triple meter
moderato con moto	Italian "a moderate speed with movement"
modulation	a change of key(s) in a composition, for example, C major modulating to the relative minor
molto agitato	very agitated
monody	unaccompanied solo song of the early 17th century
monophonic	where individual vocal parts in an ensemble or chorus sing one melodic line in unison
motet	a polyphonic setting of a religious/biblical text in Latin scored for several voices
motif	a short musical idea developed during a composition
musica reservata	Latin "reserved music"; a 16th century style of vocal music noted for its intense emotional expression
musical	a theatrical performance combining song, spoken dialogue, acting, and dance
natural	an accidental that cancels a sharp or a flat in the same measure
neume	the notation of pitch in Gregorian chant, written in square notation on a staff with four lines and three spaces
obbligato	an instrumental countermelody to a vocal part

octave	the interval of eight diatonic degrees between two tones of the same name, for example, C–C
opera	an extended dramatic composition for soloists, chorus, and orchestra, staged with action, costumes, and scenery
opera seria	also called *dramma per musica*, referring to the "serious" style of Italian opera that dominated the 18th century
oratorio	an extended dramatic composition for soloists, chorus, and orchestra, based on a biblical or hagiographical story, performed without any staged action, costumes, or scenery
oratorio *Latino*	17th-century oratorio in Latin developed by Carissimi at the Oratorio del SS. Crocifisso in Rome, scored in one part
oratorio *volgare*	an oratorio of the mid-17th century, scored in Italian and in two parts
organum triplum	an early form of polyphony from the School of Notre Dame comprising three voices: the tenor voice, which sings the cantus firmus, and two additional voice parts, a duplum and a triplum
ostinato	known also as a basso ostinato or ground bass; a musical pattern (rhythmic or melodic) repeated in the bass line, for example, Tallis's Canon
oud	an Arab stringed instrument resembling a lute
palindrome	a musical phrase that sounds the same when played in reverse
parody mass	a 16th century setting of the mass based on music derived from a motet, chanson, or madrigal
pastiche	an opera or oratorio composed of works by different composers
pastorale	an instrumental or vocal work suggestive of rural life and/or the music of shepherds
pianissimo (*pp*)	a dynamic marking "very soft"
Picardy third	*See* tierce de Picardie
pizzicato	an instrumental technique in which a stringed instrument is plucked instead of bowed
plainsong	also known as plainchant; monophonic in texture, it is written on a four-lined staff and notated with neumes
poco	Italian "a little"
polyphonic	a musical texture consisting of two or more melodic lines set against the other

qawwali	devotional sufi music popular in South Asia
quaver	known also as an eighth note, played and articulated for one-eighth of a whole note
rap	spoken or chanted rhyming lyrics associated with hip-hop, alternative rock, and Kwaito music that originated in Johannesburg, South Africa
rapido e selvaggio	Italian "fast and wild"
recitative	known also as recitative secco, a type of monody that imitates the accents and rhythms of spoken speech, found in oratorio and opera to the accompaniment of a basso continuo, such as a harpsichord
recitative semplice	Italian "simple recitative"; a type of eighteenth century recitative accompanied only by continuo instruments
reggae	a genre of music originating in Jamaica in the late 1960s
reprise	a repeated passage in music
respond	a refrain portion of a responsorial chant sung before the verse
rest	an interval of specified silence in music
retrograde	in serialism, a technique in which a musical motif is notated in reverse
rhapsody	a one-movement, free-flowing work featuring a range of contrasting moods, color, and tonality
riff	a short, repeated musical phrase played on a guitar
rock and roll	a genre of popular music originating in the United States in the late 1940s
rude e bene ritmato	Italian "rough and rhythmical"
saraband	a slow, stately dance in triple meter popular in Spain and France in the 17th and 18th centuries
sean nós	Irish "old style"; highly ornamented style of unaccompanied traditional singing
semiquaver	known also as a 16th note and articulated for a quarter of a crotchet beat
semitone	the smallest musical interval, known as a half step or half tone
serialism	*see* twelve-tone serialism
sharp	raising pitch by a semitone as indicated by the # sign in the key signature or preceding the note being raised
siciliana	a slow style of music in 6/8 or 12/8 time with lilting rhythms often used in arias in baroque operas to evoke a pastoral mood

sinfonia	an orchestral introduction, interlude, or postlude in a 17th- or 18th-century oratorio, opera, cantata, or suite
Singspiel	German "Sing-play"; a genre of opera characterized by spoken dialogue alternating with songs, ballads, arias, and ensembles
ska	a genre of popular music originating in Jamaica in the late 1950s, a precursor to reggae
sonata	a musical form for solo or instrumental ensemble; in the 18th century, there were two types of sonata: the *sonata da chiesa* (for use in a "church") and the *sonata da camera* (for use at "court")
sonorism	a movement associated with Polish composers of the 1950s; an approach to composition that uses novel types of sounds and new textures played on traditional orchestral instruments
Sprechstimme	German "speaking voice"; a vocal style that contains elements of speech and song in rhythm without any precise pitch
staccato	Italian "detached"; signifying a note of shortened duration
stepwise movement	the fluid movement of a melodic line in ascending or descending movement by the degree of a tone or semitone
stile concertato	Italian; a musical style in which a group of instrumentalists or voices share a melody in alternation
strophic	the same music for each verse of a song
style gallant	elegant, graceful style of music from the mid- to late 18th century noted for its simplicity in contrast to the complex counterpoint of baroque music
subito forzando (*sfz*)	Italian "suddenly with force"
suite	a collection of dances or dance-like movements for solo instrument or instrumental ensemble
suspension	the prolongation of one or more notes of a chord into the following chord to create a dissonance
symphonic poem	term coined by Liszt; a one-movement programmatic work for orchestra
symphony	an extended work for orchestra in four movements with the first based on sonata form
tarantella	a group of various folk dances accompanied by tambourines
tempo	time, that is, the speed or pace of a given composition

tenuto	a horizontal line above or below a note indicating it is to be held for its full length or a slightly longer duration
ternary form	music divided into three parts (ABA) with a contrasting middle section
tessitura	the consistent range of pitches found in a melodic line or vocal part; tessitura can be high, medium, or low
texture	the richness or thinness of the music; texture can be monophonic, homophonic, or polyphonic
theorbo	a plucked string instrument of the lute family
theremin	an electronic musical instrument patented by Léon Theremin in 1928
thrash/death metal	a subgenre of heavy metal employing distorted and low-tuned guitars, screaming, deep growling, and powerful, aggressive drumming
through-composed	a continuous stream of music devoid of any section repetitions
tierce de Picardie	the final triad of a cadence in the minor tonality played in the major tonality
timbales	shallow single-headed drums with metal casing
time signature	indicates the number and value of beats in a measure of music
tintinnabulation	the sound of the bells; a compositional style first created by Estonian composer Arvo Pärt in 1976; the triadic movement of one voice combined with the diatonic motion of another
tiple	a small plucked string instrument of the guitar family used in the traditional music of Spain and Latin America
tonality	the scale on which a composition is based; in Western European art music, tonalities are major and minor
tone poem	a programmatic work in one movement for instrument, instrumental ensemble, or orchestra
tonus peregrinus	Latin "wandering tone"; a plainchant reciting tone that employs two pitches rather than the more usual single pitch
tranquillo	Italian "quiet"
tremolo	the trembling effect articulated by a musical instrument or singer
triad	a group of three notes (root, third, and fifth) a third apart played simultaneously

tritone	known also as a diminished fifth (e.g., C–G flat) or augmented fourth (e.g., C–F sharp) and in medieval times as the *diabolus in musica* ("devil in music"); comprising three whole tones, it is characterized by a grating, dissonant sound
trommel bass	a bass part consisting of steady repeated notes in ascending and descending motion to animate music; employed primarily in 18th century music
troparion	a short hymn of one stanza or one of a series of stanzas found in Byzantine music
trope	a musical or textual addition to a plainchant
twelve-tone serialism	known also as dodecaphonic and twelve-note serialism; the organization of all twelve notes of the chromatic scale into tone rows
verse anthem	a polyphonic setting of a religious/biblical text in English scored for several voices, alternating passages for choir, soloists, and instrumental accompaniment
vielle	a medieval hurdy gurdy
virelay	a short lyric poem that originated in France in the 14th century
vivo e tumultuoso	Italian "lively and tumultuous"
vocoder	an electronic device that distorts speech

Bibliography

Alfonso, Barry. *The Billboard Guide to Contemporary Christian Music.* New York: Billboard Books, 2002.

Allison, Dale C., C. Helmer, T. Römer, C. L. Seow, B. D. Walfish, and E. Ziolkowski, eds. *Encyclopedia of the Bible and Its Reception.* 30 vols. Berlin: de Gruyter, 2010–.

Allison, John. *Edward Elgar: Sacred Music. Border Lines Series.* Bridgend: Seren, 1994.

Aniol, Scot. *Worship in Song: A Biblical Approach to Music and Worship.* Winona Lake, IL: BMH Books, 2009.

Bailey, Albert E. *The Gospel in Hymns.* New York: Charles Scribner's Sons, 1950.

Billig, Michael. *Rock and Roll Jews.* Syracuse, NY: Syracuse University Press, 2001.

Blumhofer, Edith Waldvogel. *Her Heart Can See: The Life and Hymns of Fanny J. Crosby.* Grand Rapids, MI: Eerdmans, 2005.

Boer, Roland. *Knockin' on Heaven's Door: The Bible and Popular Culture.* New York: Routledge, 1999.

Bohlman, Philip V., Edith Blumhofer, and Maria Chow. *Music in American Religious Experience.* New York: Oxford University Press, 2006.

Bossius, Thomas, Andreas Häger, and Keith Kahn-Harris. *Religion and Popular Music in Europe: New Expressions of Sacred and Secular Identity.* New York: Tauris, 2011.

Boyd, Kari, David L. Orvis, and Linda Austern, eds. *Psalms in the Early Modern World.* Farnham: Ashgate, 2011.

Boyd, Malcolm. *Bach.* New York: Oxford University Press, 2000.

Boyd Brown, Christopher. *Singing the Gospel: Lutheran Hymns and the Success of the Reformation.* Cambridge, MA: Harvard University Press, 2005.

Boynton, Susan, and Diane J. Reilly. *The Practice of the Bible in the Middle Ages: Production, Reception, and Performance in Western Christianity.* New York: Columbia University Press, 2011.

Bradley, Ian. *You've Got to Have a Dream: The Message of the Musical.* Louisville, KY: Westminster John Knox, 2004.

Brower, Jeffrey E., and Kevin Guilfoy, eds. *The Cambridge Companion to Abelard.* Cambridge: Cambridge University Press, 2004.

Burrows, David, ed. *The Cambridge Companion to Handel.* Cambridge: Cambridge University Press, 1997.

Butt, John. *Bach's Dialogue with Modernity: Perspectives on the Passions.* Cambridge: Cambridge University Press, 2010.

——, ed. *The Cambridge Companion to Bach*. Cambridge: Cambridge University Press, 1997.

Cameron, Euan. *The New Cambridge History of the Bible*, Vol. 2, *From 600 to 1450*. Cambridge: Cambridge University Press, 2016.

Campbell, Ted. *The Gospel in Christian Traditions*. Oxford: Oxford University Press, 2009.

Carpenter, Humphrey. *Benjamin Britten*. London: Faber, 2003.

Carter, Tim, and John Butt, eds. *The Cambridge History of Seventeenth Century Music*. Cambridge: Cambridge University Press, 2005.

Cessac, Catherine. *Marc-Antoine Charpentier*. Translated by E. Thomas. Glasgow, OR: Amadeus Press, 1982.

Chafe, Eric. *Analyzing Bach Cantatas*. New York: Oxford University Press, 2000.

Charlton, David, ed. *The Cambridge Companion to Grand Opera*. Cambridge: Cambridge University Press, 2003.

Chase, Gilbert. *America's Music, from the Pilgrims to the Present*. 3rd rev. ed. Urbana: University of Illinois Press, 1987.

Christianson, Eric S. *Ecclesiastes through the Centuries*. Oxford: Blackwell, 2007. Paperback, 2012.

Clancy, Ronald. *Sacred Christmas Music: The Stories behind the Most Beloved Songs of Devotion*. New York: Sterling, 2008.

Clines, David J. A. *The Bible and the Modern World*. Sheffield: Sheffield Phoenix, 2005. Continuum, 1997.

Cohen, Leonard. *Book of Mercy*. Toronto: McClelland and Stewart, 1984.

Collins, Ace. *Stories behind the Hymns that Inspire America*. Grand Rapids, MI: Zondervan, 2003.

——. *Turn Your Radio On: The Stories behind Gospel*. Grand Rapids, MI: Zondervan, 1999.

Collins, J. J. *The Bible after Babel: Historical Criticism in a Postmodern Age*. Grand Rapids, MI: Eerdmans, 2005.

Coogan, Michael D. *The Oxford Encyclopedia of the Books of the Bible*. 2 vols. New York: Oxford University Press, 2011.

Cooke, Mervyn. *Britten: War Requiem*. Cambridge: Cambridge University Press, 1996.

——, ed. *The Cambridge Companion to Benjamin Britten*. Cambridge: Cambridge University Press, 1999.

Cross, Jonathan, ed. *The Cambridge Companion to Stravinsky*. Cambridge: Cambridge University Press, 2003.

Culbertson, Philip Leroy, and Elaine Mary Wainwright, eds. *Bible in/and Popular Culture: A Creative Encounter*. Atlanta: Society of Biblical Literature, 2010.

Cusic, Don. *Encyclopedia of Contemporary Christian Music: Pop, Rock, and Worship*. Santa Barbara, CA: Greenwood Publishing Group, 2010.

——. *The Sound of Light: A History of Gospel and Christian Music*. Milwaukee, WI: Hall Leonard, 2002.

Danielou, J. *The Bible and the Liturgy*. Notre Dame, IN: University of Notre Dame Press, 1956.

Dawn, Maggi. *The Writing on the Wall: High Art, Popular Culture and the Bible*. London: Hodder and Stoughton, 2010.

Daye, Stephen. *The Bay Psalm Book: The Whole Booke of Psalmes Faithfully Translated into English*. New York: Cosimo Classics, 2007.

Di Grazia, Donna Marie, ed. *Nineteenth-Century Choral Music*. New York: Routledge, 2013.

Dowling Long, Siobhán. *The Sacrifice of Isaac: The Reception of a Biblical Story in Music*. Sheffield: Sheffield Phoenix, 2013.

Dürr, Alfred. *The Cantatas of J. S. Bach: With Their Librettos in German-English Parallel Text*. Oxford: Oxford University Press, 2006.

Dyas, Dee, and Esther Scott Hughes. *The Bible in Western Culture: The Student's Guide*. Abingdon: Routledge, 2005.

Ehrlich, Carl S., and Marsha C. White, eds. *Saul in Story and Tradition*. Tübingen: Mohr Siebeck, 2006.

Elliott, Graham. *Benjamin Britten: The Spiritual Dimension*. Oxford: Oxford University Press, 2000.

Evans, Peter. *The Music of Benjamin Britten*. London: J. M. Dent, 1979.

Evans, Robert. *Reception History, Tradition and Biblical Interpretation: Gadamer and Jauss in Current Practice*. London: Bloomsbury T & T Clark, 2014.

Everett, William A., and Paul R. Laird. *The Cambridge Companion to the Musical*. Cambridge: Cambridge University Press, 2008.

Exum, J. Cheryl, ed. *Plotted, Shot, and Painted: Cultural Representations of Biblical Women*. Sheffield: Sheffield Academic Press, 1996.

————, ed. *Retellings: The Bible in Literature, Music, Art and Film*. Leiden: Koninklijke Brill NV, 2007.

Fish, S. *Is There a Text in This Class? The Authority of Interpretive Communities*. Cambridge, MA: Harvard University Press, 1980.

Forbes, Bruce, and Jeffrey H. Mahan, eds. *Religion and Popular Culture in America*. Berkeley: University of California Press, 2005.

Frühauf, Tima. *The Organ and Its Music in German-Jewish Culture*. New York: Oxford University Press, 2009.

Gallagher, Sean, James Haar, John Nádas, and Timothy Striplin, eds. *Western Plainchant in the First Millennium: Studies in the Medieval Liturgy and Its Music*. Aldershot: Ashgate, 2003.

Gatens, William J. *Victorian Cathedral Music in Theory and Practice*. Cambridge: Cambridge University Press, 1986.

Gerbrandt, Carl. *Sacred Music Drama: The Producer's Guide*. 2nd ed. Bloomington, IN: Author House, 2006.

Gillingham, Susan. *Jewish and Christian Approaches to the Psalms: Conflict and Convergence*. Oxford: Oxford University Press, 2013.

————. *A Journey of Two Psalms: The Reception of Psalms 1 & 2 in Jewish and Christian Traditions*. Oxford: Oxford University Press, 2013.

————. *Psalms through the Centuries*. Vol. 1. Oxford: Blackwell, 2012.

Gilmour, Michael J. *The Gospel according to Bob Dylan: The Old, Old Story for Modern Times*. Louisville, KY: Westminster John Knox, 2011.

——. *Tangled Up in the Bible: Bob Dylan and Scripture*. New York: Continuum, 2004.

Gloag, Kenneth. *A Child of Our Time*. Cambridge: Cambridge University Press, 1999.

Goodman, William. *Yearning for You: Psalms and the Song of Songs in Conversation with Rock and Worship Songs*. Sheffield: Sheffield Phoenix, 2012.

Gowler, David B. *James through the Centuries*. Oxford: Blackwell, 2014.

Hamlin, Hannibal, and Norman W. Jones, eds. *The King James Bible after Four Hundred Years: Literary, Linguistic, and Cultural Influences*. Cambridge: Cambridge University Press, 2010.

Harley, John. *The World of William Byrd: Musicians, Merchants and Magnates*. Farnham: Ashgate, 2010.

Harris, Michael, W. *The Rise of Gospel Blues: The Music of Thomas Dorsey in the Urban Church*. New York: Oxford University Press, 1992.

Hauerwas, Stanley. *Unleashing the Scripture: Freeing the Bible from Captivity to America*. Nashville, TN: Abingdon Press, 1993.

Herissone, Rebecca, ed. *The Ashgate Research Companion to Henry Purcell*. Farnham: Ashgate, 2012.

Heskes, Irene. *Passport to Jewish Music: Its History, Traditions, and Culture*. Westport, CT: Greenwood Press, 1994.

Hillier, Paul. *Arvo Pärt*. New York: Oxford University Press, 1997.

Idelsohn, Abraham Z. *Jewish Liturgy and Its Development*. New York: Dover, 1995.

——. *Jewish Music: Its Historical Development*. New York: Schocken Books, 1967.

Iser, Wolfgang. *The Act of Reading: A Theory of Aesthetic Response*. London: Routledge and Kegan Paul, 1978.

Jaffe, Kenneth. *Solo Vocal Works on Jewish Themes: A Bibliography of Jewish Composers*. Lanham, MD: Scarecrow Press, 2011.

Janssen, David, and Edward Whitelock. *Apocalypse Jukebox: The End of the World in American Popular Music*. Berkeley, CA: Soft Skull Press, 2009.

Janssen, Geert H., Alexandra Bamji, and Mary Laven. *The Ashgate Research Companion to the Counter-Reformation*. Farnham: Ashgate, 2013.

Jauss, H. R. *Toward an Aesthetic of Reception*. Translated by T. Bahti. Minneapolis: University of Minnesota Press, 1982.

Joyce, Paul M., and Diana Lipton. *Lamentations through the Centuries*. Oxford: Blackwell, 2013.

Joynes, Christine E. *Perspectives on the Passion: Encountering the Bible through the Arts*. New York: T & T Clark, 2008.

Keefe, Simon P. *Mozart's Requiem: Reception, Work, Completion*. Cambridge: Cambridge University Press, 2012.

Kendrick, Robert L. *Singing Jeremiah: Music and Meaning in Holy Week*. Bloomington: Indiana University Press, 2014.

Kermode, F. *The Genesis of Secrecy: On the Interpretation of Narrative*. Cambridge, MA: Harvard University Press, 1979.

Kirkpatrick, Robin. *The European Renaissance 1400–1600*. London: Pearson, 2002.

Kovacs, Judith, and Christopher Rowland. *Revelation: The Apocalypse of Jesus Christ*. Oxford: Blackwell, 2004.

Kung, H., and J. Moltmann. *Conflicting Ways of Interpreting the Bible*. Edinburgh: T & T Clark, 1980; New York: Seabury, 1980.

Langston, Scott M. *Exodus through the Centuries*. Oxford: Blackwell, 2006.

Larkin, Colin, ed. *The Encyclopedia of Popular Music*. London: Omnibus Press, 2007. 5th ed., 2011.

Laster, James H. *Catalogue of Choral Music Arranged in Biblical Order*. Rev. ed. Lanham, MD: Scarecrow Press, 1996.

Lau, Stella Sai Chun. *Popular Music in Evangelical Youth Culture*. New York: Routledge, 2012.

Leaver, Robin A. *Luther's Liturgical Music: Principles and Implications*. Grand Rapids, MI: Eerdmans, 2007.

Leneman, Helen. *Love, Lust, and Lunacy: The Stories of Saul and David in Music*. Sheffield: Sheffield Phoenix, 2010.

———. *The Performed Bible: The Story of Ruth in Opera and Oratorio*. Sheffield: Sheffield Academic Press, 2007.

Lieb, Michael, Emma Mason, Jonathan Roberts, and Christopher Rowland, eds. *The Oxford Handbook of the Reception History of the Bible*. Oxford: Oxford University Press, 2011.

Lord, Suzanne, and David Brinkman. *Music from the Age of Shakespeare: A Cultural History*. Westport, CT: Greenwood Press, 2003.

Lyons, W. J., and J. Økland. *The Way the World Ends? The Apocalypse of John in Culture and Ideology*. Sheffield: Sheffield Phoenix, 2009.

MacNeil, Dean. *The Bible and Bob Marley: Half the Story Has Never Been Told*. Eugene, OR: Cascade Books, 2013.

Marsden, Richard, and E. Ann Matter, eds. *The New Cambridge History of the Bible*. Vol. 2, *From 600 to 1450*. Cambridge: Cambridge University Press, 2012.

McFarland, Jason J. *Announcing the Feast: The Entrance Song in the Mass of the Roman Rite*. Collegeville, MN: Liturgical Press, 2011.

McKim, Donald K., ed. *The Cambridge Companion to Martin Luther*. Cambridge: Cambridge University Press, 2003.

McNeil, W. K., ed. *Encyclopedia of American Gospel Music*. New York: Routledge, 2005.

Melamed, Daniel, R. *Hearing Bach's Passions*. New York: Oxford University Press, 2005.

Metzger, Bruce M., and Michael David Coogan, eds. *The Oxford Companion to the Bible*. Oxford: Oxford University Press, 1993.

———, eds. *The Oxford Guide to Ideas and Issues of the Bible*. Oxford: Oxford University Press, 2001.

Minear, Paul Sevier. *Death Set to Music: Masterworks by Bach, Brahms, Penderecki and Bernstein*. Atlanta: Westminster John Knox, 1987.

Moffat, J., ed. *Handbook to the Church Hymnary*. Oxford: Oxford University Press, 1927.

Morehen, John. *English Choral Practice, 1400–1650*. Cambridge: Cambridge University Press, 1995.

Moskowitz, David Vlado. *The Words and Music of Bob Marley*. Westport, CT: Praeger, 2007.

Musgrave, Michael. *Brahms: A German Requiem*. Cambridge: Cambridge University Press, 1996.

Music, David W., and Paul Akers Richardson. *"I Will Sing the Wondrous Story": A History of Baptist Hymnody in North America*. Macon, GA: Mercer University Press, 2008.

Newton, John, and Charles J. Doe. *John Newton's Olney Hymns*. Minneapolis: Curiosmith, 2011.

Ogasapian, John. *Church Music in America, 1620–2000*. Macon, GA: Mercer University Press, 2007.

Olleson, Philip. *Samuel Wesley: The Man and His Music*. Woodbridge: Boydell Press, 2003.

Osbeck, Kenneth W. *101 Hymn Stories*. Grand Rapids, MI: Kregel Publications, 1982.

———. *101 More Hymn Stories*. Grand Rapids, MI: Kregel Publications, 1985.

Paget, James Carleton, and J. Schaper, eds. *The New Cambridge History of the Bible*. Vol. 1, *From the Beginnings to 600*. Cambridge: Cambridge University Press, 2013.

Palisca, Claude. *Baroque Music*. Englewood Cliffs, NJ: Prentice Hall, 1968.

Partridge, Christopher, ed. *Anthems of Apocalypse: Popular Music and Apocalyptic Thought*. Sheffield: Sheffield Phoenix, 2012.

Pelikan, Jaroslav. *Bach among the Theologians*. Minneapolis: Fortress, 1986.

Pesce, Dolores. *Hearing the Motet: Essays on the Motet of the Middle Ages and Renaissance*. Oxford: Oxford University Press, 2007.

Powell, M. A. *Chasing the Eastern Star: Adventures in Biblical Reader-Response Criticism*. Louisville, KY: Westminster John Knox, 2001.

———. *Encyclopedia of Contemporary Christian Music*. Peabody, MA: Hendrickson, 2002.

Range, Matthias. *Music and Ceremonial at British Coronations: From James I to Elizabeth II*. Cambridge: Cambridge University Press, 2012.

Riches, John. *The New Cambridge History of the Bible*, Vol. 4, *From 1750 to the Present*. Cambridge: Cambridge University Press, 2015.

Rischin, Rebecca. *For the End of Time: The Story of the Messiaen Quartet*. Ithaca, NY: Cornell University Press, 2003.

Roncace, Mark, and Patrick Gray, eds. *Teaching the Bible: Practical Strategies for Classroom Instruction*. Atlanta: Society of Biblical Literature, 2005.

———, eds. *Teaching the Bible through Popular Culture and the Arts*. Atlanta: Society of Biblical Literature, 2007.

Sawyer, John F. A., ed. *The Blackwell Companion to the Bible and Culture*. Oxford: Blackwell, 2006.

———. *A Concise Dictionary of the Bible and Its Reception*. Louisville, KY: Westminster John Knox, 2009.

———. *The Fifth Gospel: Isaiah in the History of Christianity*. Cambridge: Cambridge University Press, 1996.

Scharen, Christian. *Broken Hallelujahs: Why Popular Music Matters to Those Seeking God*. Grand Rapids, MI: Brazos, 2011.

Schippe, Cullen, and Chuck Stetson. *The Bible and Its Influence*. Fairfield, VA: Bible Literacy Project, 2005.

Schulenberg, David. *Music of the Baroque*. Oxford: Oxford University Press, 2001.

Seow, C. L. *Job 1–21: Interpretation and Commentary*. Grand Rapids, MI: Eerdmans, 2014.

Shenton, Andrew. *Olivier Messiaen's System of Signs: Notes towards Understanding His Music*. Aldershot: Ashgate, 2008.

Shrock, Denis. *Choral Repertoire*. Oxford: Oxford University Press, 2009.

Smith, Ruth. *Handel's Oratorios and Eighteenth-Century Thought*. Cambridge: Cambridge University Press, 1995.

Smither, Howard E. *A History of the Oratorio: Oratorio in the Classical Era*. Vol. 2. Oxford: Clarendon, 1987.

———. *A History of the Oratorio: Oratorio in the Classical Era*. Vol. 3. Oxford: Clarendon, 1987.

———. *A History of the Oratorio: The Oratorio in the Nineteenth and Twentieth Centuries*. Vol. 4. Chapel Hill: University of North Carolina Press, 2000.

———. *The Oratorio in the Baroque Era: Italy, Vienna, Paris*. Vol. 1. Chapel Hill: University of North Carolina Press, 1977.

Spiegel, Shalom. *The Last Trial: On the Legends and Lore of the Command to Abraham to Offer Isaac as a Sacrifice*. New York: Schocken Books, 1969.

Spinks, B. D. *The Sanctus in the Eucharistic Prayer*. Cambridge: Cambridge University Press, 1991.

Stapert, Calvin R. *Handel's Messiah: Comfort for God's People*. Grand Rapids, MI: Eerdmans, 2010.

Stern, Max. *Bible and Music: Influences of the Old Testament on Western Music*. Jersey City, NJ: KTAV Publishing House, 2011.

———. *Psalms and Music: Influences of the Psalms on Western Music*. Jersey City, NJ: KTAV Publishing House, 2013.

Sternberg, Meir. *The Poetics of Biblical Narrative*. Bloomington: Indiana University Press, 1985.

Stevens, John. *Words and Music in the Middle Ages: Song, Narrative, Dance and Drama, 1050–1350*. Cambridge: Cambridge University Press, 1986.

Strimple, Nick. *Choral Music in the Nineteenth Century*. Milwaukee, WI: Amadeus Press, 2007.

———. *Choral Music in the Twentieth Century*. Milwaukee, WI: Amadeus Press, 2002.

Swain, Joseph Peter. *The A to Z of Sacred Music*. Lanham, MD: Scarecrow Press, 2006.

———. *Sacred Treasure: Understanding Catholic Liturgical Music*. Collegeville, MN: Liturgical Press, 2012.

Symynkywicz, Jeffrey. *The Gospel according to Bruce Springsteen: Rock and Redemption, from Asbury Park to Magic*. Louisville, KY: Westminster John Knox, 2008.

Taff, Tori, and Christa Farris. *100 Greatest Songs in Christian Music: The Stories behind the Music That Changed Our Lives Forever*. Nashville, TN: Integrity Publishing, 2006.

Tarling, Nicholas. *Choral Masterpieces: Major and Minor.* Lanham, MD: Rowman & Littlefield, 2014.

Taruskin, Richard. *The Oxford History of Western Music* [in six volumes: 1: *The Earliest Notations to the Sixteenth Century*; 2: *The Seventeenth and Eighteenth Centuries*; 3: *The Nineteenth Century*; 4: *The Early Twentieth Century*; 5: *The Late Twentieth Century*; 6: *Resources: Chronology, Bibliography, Master Index*]. New York: Oxford University Press, 2005.

Temperley, Nicholas. *Haydn: The Creation.* Cambridge: Cambridge University Press, 1991. Reprint, 1994.

———. *The Music of the English Parish Church.* Cambridge: Cambridge University Press, 2005.

Terrien, Samuel L., and Bruce Gebert. *The Magnificat: Musicians as Biblical Interpreters.* New York: Paulist Press, 1995.

Til, Rupert. *Pop Cult: Religion and Popular Music.* London: Continuum, 2010.

Todd, R. L., ed. *Mendelssohn and His World.* Princeton, NJ: Princeton University Press, 1991.

Twomey, Jay. *The Pastoral Epistles through the Centuries.* Oxford: Blackwell, 2009.

Unger, Melvin P. *Handbook to Bach's Sacred Cantata Texts: An Interlinear Translation with Reference Guide to Biblical Quotations and Allusions.* Lanham, MD: Scarecrow Press, 1996.

———. *Historical Dictionary of Choral Music.* Lanham, MD: Scarecrow Press, 2010.

Warren, Gwendolin Sims, ed. *Ev'ry Time I Feel the Spirit: 101 Best-Loved Psalms, Gospel Hymns, and Spiritual Songs of the African American Church.* New York: Henry Holt, 1999.

Wellesz, E. *A History of Byzantine Music and Hymnography.* Oxford: Clarendon, 1949.

White, Eric Walter. *Stravinsky: The Composer and His Works.* Berkeley: University of California Press, 1966.

Wilson-Dickson, Andrew. *The Story of Christian Music: From Gregorian Chant to Black Gospel.* Minneapolis: Augsburg Fortress, 2003.

Wimbush, Vincent L., with the assistance of Rosamund C. Rodman, ed. *African Americans and the Bible: Sacred Texts and Social Textures.* New York: Continuum, 2000.

List of Authors, Composers, and Musicians

10,000 Maniacs. American alternative rock group formed in 1981 in Jamestown, New York.

Abelard, Peter (1079–1142). French philosopher and monk, famous for his love of Heloise.

Abram, John (1959–). Anglo-Canadian composer of electroacoustic music.

Adams, John (1947–). American composer and Pulitzer Prize winner.

Adams, Sarah Flower (1805–1848). English poet and hymn writer.

Addison, Joseph (1672–1719). English essayist and politician.

Adler, Samuel (1928–). American Jewish composer and conductor.

Agnew, Todd (1971–). American Christian musician and songwriter.

Alexander, Cecil Frances (née Humphreys) (1818–1895). Irish poet and hymn writer.

Alfvén, Hugo (1872–1960). Swedish composer, conductor, and painter.

Allegri, Gregorio (1582–1652). Italian priest and composer who lived and died in Rome.

Allen, William Francis (1830–1889). Classicist. Worked with Charles Ware on slave songs.

Angel Voices. *See* **Libera**.

ApologetiX. Christian parody band formed in Pittsburgh, Pennsylvania, in 1992.

Arasimowicz, George (1954–). American composer and conductor.

Arcade. American glam metal band formed in 1992.

Arcadelt, Jacob (ca. 1505–1568). Flemish singer and composer at St. Peter's, Rome, until 1551.

Arena. British neoprogressive rock band founded in 1995.

Ares Kingdom. Heavy metal band formed in Kansas City, Missouri, in 1996.

Argento, Dominick (1927–). American composer of operatic and choral music.

Arlen, Harold (1905–1986). American composer of popular music.

Armes, Philip (1836–1908). English composer and organist.

Arne, Thomas (1710–1778). English composer.

Arnold, George Benjamin (1832–1902). English organist and composer.

Arnold, Sir Malcolm (1921–2006). English composer.

Arnold, Samuel (1740–1802). English composer and organist.

Auber, Daniel François Esprit (1782–1871). French composer.

Avenged Sevenfold (A7X). American rock band formed in 1999.

Avshalomov, Aaron (1894–1965). Russian-born Jewish composer. Lived in Shanghai from 1917 to 1947.

Bach, Johann Christoph Friedrich (1732–1795). German chamber musician and composer.

Bach, Johann Sebastian (1685–1750). German Lutheran organist and composer.

Bad Religion. Punk rock band founded in Los Angeles in 1979.

Badings, Henk (1907–1987). Dutch composer.

Baez, Joan (1941–). American songwriter and political activist.

Bairstow, Sir Edward Cuthbert (1874–1946). English composer.

Baker, Henry W. (1821–1877). English vicar and hymn writer.

Bantock, Granville (1868–1946). British composer.

Barnby, Joseph (1838–1896). English organist, conductor, composer, and hymn writer.

Bartholomew, William (1793–1867). English librettist and composer.

Barton, William Eleazer (1861–1930). American Congregational pastor and writer.

Bassano, Giovanni (ca. 1558–1617). Venetian composer.

Beastie Boys. American hip-hop trio formed in New York City in 1981.

Beatles, The. English rock band formed in Liverpool, England, in 1960.

Beckwith, John (1927–). Canadian composer and writer.

Beethoven, Ludwig van (1770–1827). German romantic composer.

Belafonte, Harry (1927–). Caribbean singer, songwriter, and social activist.

Bennett, William Sterndale (1816–1875). British pianist, conductor, and composer.

Berkeley, Lennox (1903–1989). British composer.

Berlinski, Herman (1910–2001). German-born American Jewish composer.

Berlioz, Hector (1803–1869). French romantic composer and music critic.

Bernstein, Leonard (1918–1990). American Jewish composer.

Berton, Henri-Montan (1767–1844). French composer and writer.

Biber, Heinrich Ignaz Franz von (1644–1704). Bohemian violinist and composer.

Bieber, Justin (1994–). Canadian singer and songwriter.

Billings, William (1746–1800). Composer and hymn writer. First American choral composer.

Bingham, Judith (1952–). British composer.

Bitton, Eyal. Contemporary Canadian Jewish composer and lyricist.

Blake, Howard (1938–). English composer.

Bliss, Sir Arthur (1891–1975). English composer.

Bliss, Philip Paul (1838–1876). American gospel singer and hymn writer.

Bloch, Ernest (1880–1959). Swiss composer of Jewish origins. Lived in the United States from 1917.

Bolcom, William (1938–). American composer and pianist.

Bonar, Horatius (1808–1889). Scottish clergyman and hymn writer.

Boney M. Jamaican-born vocal group formed in Germany in 1976.

Bourgeois, Louis (ca. 1510–1560). French Calvinist composer and music theorist.

Bowie, David (1947–). English musician and songwriter.

Boyce, William (1711–1779). English organist and composer.

Bradbury, William Batchelder (1816–1868). American organist and composer.

Brady, Nicholas (1659–1726). Irish Protestant clergyman and poet.

Brahms, Johannes (1833–1897). German composer. Lived in Vienna from 1862.

Bridges, Matthew (1800–1894). English hymn writer. Lived in Canada from 1848.

Bridges, Robert (1844–1930). English poet. Poet laureate from 1913.

Bristow, George Frederick (1825–1898). American composer and choral conductor.

Britten, Benjamin (1913–1976). English composer.

Broken Family Band. British indie rock band formed in Cambridge, England, in 2001.

Brooke, Jonatha (1964–). American folk rock singer and songwriter.

Brooks, Elkie (1945–). English singer; the "British queen of blues."

Brooks, Garth (1962–). American singer and songwriter.

Bruce, Michael (1746–1767). Scottish poet and hymn writer.

Bruch, Max (1838–1920). German romantic composer.

Bruckner, Anton (1824–1896). Austrian composer and organist.

Buck, Dudley (1839–1909). American organist and composer.

Buckley, Jeff (1966–1997). American singer/songwriter and guitarist.

Burleigh, Harry T. (1866–1949). African American classical composer and singer.

Bush, Kate (1958–). British singer/songwriter.

Butler, Geezer (1949–). English musician and songwriter.

Buxtehude, Dietrich (1637–1707). Danish German organist and composer.

Byrd, William (1543–1623). English Catholic composer, greatest of the Tudor composers.

Cale, John (1942–). Welsh experimental rock musician and producer.

Campbell, Glen (1936–). American country singer and songwriter.

Campbell, Hilary. Contemporary English choral composer, arranger, conductor, and singer.

Campbell, Ian. English folk artist, cofounder of the Ian Campbell Folk Group in 1956.

Card, Michael (1957–). American Christian singer and songwriter.

Carissimi, Giacomo (1605–1974). Italian composer, pioneer of the early baroque style.

Carman (Carmelo Domenic Licciardello) (1956–). American evangelist and musician.

Carmichael, Ralph (1927–). American composer. Pioneer of contemporary Christian music.

Carter, Sydney (1915–2004). English poet, performer, and songwriter.

Casals, Pablo (1876–1973). Spanish cellist and composer.

Cash, Johnny (1932–2003). One of the greats of American country music.

Castelnuovo-Tedesco, Mario (1895–1968). Italian composer, mainly of guitar music.

Cavalieri, Emilio de' (ca. 1550–1602). Italian renaissance composer and choreographer.

Cave, Nick (1957–). Australian singer, composer, writer, and actor.

Celan (Antschel), Paul (1920–1970). German Jewish poet and translator.

Céline, Louis-Ferdinand (1894–1961). French novelist noted for his black comedy.

Celtic Woman. All-female Irish musical ensemble formed in 2004.

Charpentier, Marc Antoine (1643–1704). French baroque composer.

Cher (1946–). American singer and actress.

Chesnutt, Cody (1968–). American soul and rhythm-and-blues musician.

Chumbawamba. British alternative rock band formed in 1982 and social activists.

Clancy Brothers, The. Irish folk group formed in 1956.

Clarke, Jeremiah (ca. 1674–1707). English composer and organist.

Clearfield, Andrea. Contemporary American composer of choral and ensemble music.

Clemens non Papa, Jacobus (ca. 1510–ca. 1555). Flemish baroque composer.

Cohen, Leonard (1934–). Canadian poet, novelist, singer, and songwriter.

Coldplay. British rock band formed in 2006.

Collins, Judy (1939–). American singer, songwriter, and political activist.

Collins, Shirley (1935–). English folk singer.

Como, Perry (1912–2001). American singer and television host.

Coolio (1963–). American rap musician, producer, and actor.

Copland, Aaron (1900–1990). American composer, born in Brooklyn, New York, to Jewish parents.

Corelli, Arcangelo (1653–1713). Italian baroque composer. Influenced Bach and Handel.

Costa, Michael (1808–1884). Italian-born conductor and composer who settled in England.

Couperin, François (1668–1733). French baroque composer and musician.

Cowper, William (1731–1800). English poet and hymn writer.

Cramps, The. American punk band formed in 1976.

Creston, Paul (Giuseppe Guttoveggio) (1906–1985). Italian American composer.

Croft, William (1678–1727). English composer and organist.

Crosby, Bing (1903–1977). American singer and actor.

Crosby, Fanny (1820–1915). American Protestant hymn writer.

Crotch, William (1775–1847). English composer and organist.

Crozier, Eric (1914–1994). British theater director and librettist long associated with Britten.

Cruger, Johann (1598–1662). German composer and writer.

Cullum, Jamie (1979–). English jazz/pop singer and songwriter.

Cummings, William Hayman (1831–1915). English singer and writer on music.

Czerny, Carl (1791–1857). Austrian composer and pianist of Czech origin.

Dallapiccola, Luigi (1904–1975). Italian composer of lyrical, 12-tone music.

Damon, William (ca. 1540–ca. 1591). Organist of the Chapel Royal under Queen Elizabeth.

Darin, Bobby (1936–1973). American singer, songwriter, and actor.

Davies, Sir Peter Maxwell (1934–). British composer.

Davis, Katherine Kennicott (1892–1980). American pianist and composer.

Davy, Richard (ca. 1465–1507). English Renaissance composer and organist.

de André, Fabrizio (1940–1999). Italian singer/songwriter.

de Binche, Gilles (Binchois) (ca. 1400–1460). Franco-Flemish composer of the Burgundian school.

de Burgh, Chris (1948–). British Irish singer, songwriter, and musician.

De la Guerre, Elisabeth-Claude Jacquet (1665–1729). French composer and musician.

De Monte, Philippe (1521–1603). Flemish composer of madrigals and sacred works.

Debussy, Achille-Claude (1862–1918). French composer, often linked with impressionism.

Destiny's Child. American hip-hop/rhythm-and-blues/soul group formed in 1996.

D'Humières, Robert (1868–1915). French poet, translator, and theater director.

Diemer, Emma Lou (1927–). American composer.

Dietrich, Marlene (1901–1992). German American actress and singer.

Dinerstein, Norman Myron (1937–). American composer.

Dix, William Chatterton (1837–1898). English hymn writer.

DJ Muggs (1968–). Stage name of Lawrence Muggerud, American deejay and producer.

Doddridge, Philip (1702–1751). English nonconformist leader, educator, and hymn writer.

Donizetti, Gaetano (1797–1848). Italian operatic composer in the bel canto style.

Dorsey, Thomas Andrew (1899–1993). American jazz pianist and gospel music composer.

Dowland, John (ca. 1563–1626). English Renaissance lutenist and composer.

Draper, William Henry (1855–1933). English clergyman and hymn writer.

Dudley, Anne. Contemporary British composer, arranger, and pop musician.

Dudley-Smith, Timothy (1926–). Anglican bishop and hymn writer.

Dufford, Robert J. (1943–). Jesuit priest and composer of Catholic liturgical music.

Duffy, John (1926–). Irish American composer, mainly for theater, film, and television.

Dulot, Francois. Sixteenth-century French composer.

Dun, Tan (1957–). Chinese American composer. Best known for his film scores.

Dunkerley, William Arthur (1852–1941). English journalist and poet.

Dunstable, John (ca. 1390–1453). English Renaissance composer.

Dupré, Marcel (1886–1971). French composer and organist.

Duruflé, Maurice (1902–1986). French composer and organist.

Dvorak, Antonin (1841–1904). Czech "nationalist" composer.

Dykes, John Bacchus (1823–1876). English clergyman and composer of hymn tunes.

Dylan, Bob (1941–). American singer and songwriter of Jewish origins.

Dyson, George (1883–1964). English musician and composer.

Eaton, Chris (1958–). British contemporary Christian singer and songwriter.

Eben, Petr (1929–2007). Czech Catholic composer of Jewish origins.

Edwards, Julian (1855–1910). Anglo-American composer of light opera.

Effinger, Cecil (1914–1990). American composer and oboist.

Eisenstein, Judith Kaplan. Contemporary American Jewish composer.

Elgar, Sir Edward (1857–1934). English composer.

Ellerton, John (1826–1893). English writer, compiler, and translator of hymns.

Ellington, Duke (1899–1974). American composer, pianist, and jazz bandleader.

Engle, Marcia Hain. Contemporary American Jewish poet.

Ewing, Donald "Skip" (1964–). American country singer and songwriter.

Falvetti, Michelangelo (1642–1692). Italian priest and baroque composer.

Farber, Sharon (1965–). Los Angeles–based Israeli American composer.

Farjeon, Eleanor (1881–1965). English author and poet.

Farnaby, Giles (ca. 1563–1640). English composer.

Feuchtwanger, Lion (1884–1958). German Jewish novelist and playwright. Lived in the United States from 1941.

Finzi, Gerald Raphael (1901–1956). British composer, mainly of choral music.

Flaherty, John. Contemporary American liturgist, composer, and educator.

Fleischer, Tsippi (1946–). Israeli composer.

Floyd, Carlisle (1926–). American operatic composer.

Francis, Connie (1938–). American pop singer.

Franck, César (1822–1890). Flemish/French composer, pianist, and organist.

Franck, Johann (1618–1677). German politician, poet, and hymn writer.

Franklin, Aretha (1942–). American singer and musician; the "queen of soul."

Fraser, Brooke (1983–). New Zealand singer and songwriter.

Freed, Isadore (1900–1960). Jewish American composer and musicologist.

Friedman, Debbie (1951–2011). Jewish American singer/songwriter and feminist.

Gabriel, Peter Brian (1950–). English musician, songwriter, and political activist.

Gabrieli, Andrea (ca. 1532–1585). Italian composer of the Venetian style.

Gabrieli, Giovanni (1554–1611). Italian baroque composer.

Gagnebin, Henri (1886–1977). Belgian composer. Lived mostly in Lausanne, Switzerland.

Gaither Vocal Band, The. American southern gospel group formed in 1992.

Gallico, Paola (1868–1955). Italian pianist, composer, and teacher.

Gardner, John Linton (1917–2011). English composer.

Garland, Judy (1922–1969). American actor and singer.

Gauntlett, Henry John (1805–1876). English organist and hymn writer.

Genesis. English progressive rock band formed in 1967 with Peter Gabriel.

Gershwin, George (1898–1937). American composer of jazz-influenced classical works.

Gesualdo, Carlo (1560–1613). Italian composer, known for his "tortured" chromatic style.

Gibbons, Orlando (1583–1625). English composer of church music and madrigals.

Gilchrist, William Wallace (1846–1916). American composer.

Gill, Fionnuala. Contemporary Irish folk musician.

Gipps, Ruth (1921–1999). English composer, conductor, oboist, and pianist.

Glass, Philip (1937–). American composer, often described as a minimalist.

Glick, Srul Irving (1834–2002). Canadian Jewish composer and conductor.

Goeller, Dan and Heidi. Contemporary American composers of biblically inspired music.

Goeyvaerts, Karel (1923–1993). Belgian composer, friend of Stockhausen.

Goldmark, Karl (1830–1915). Hungarian Jewish composer and writer.

Golijov, Osvaldo (1960–). Argentinian Jewish composer.

Goodall, Howard (1958–). English composer and television host.

Gorecki, Henryk Mikolaj (1933–2010). Polish composer; "sacred minimalist."

Goss, John (1800–1880). English organist, teacher, and composer.

Goudimel, Claude (ca. 1514–1572). French composer and writer.

Gounod, Charles-François (1818–1893). French composer.

Graham, Brendan (1945–). Irish novelist, lyricist, and songwriter.

Graun, Carl Heinrich (1704–1759). German composer of Italian opera.

Greatorex, Walter (1877–1949). English composer and musician.

Gréban, Arnoul (ca. 1420–ca. 1485). French composer and organist at Notre-Dame de Paris.

Grechaninov, Alexander (1864–1956). Russian composer. Lived in the United States from 1939.

Greene, Buddy. Contemporary American singer, songwriter, and harmonica player.

Greenfield, Howard (1936–1986). American lyricist and songwriter.

Gregorian. German band performing popular songs in Gregorian style.

Griffin, Patty (1964–). American singer and songwriter.

Grosjean, François (1844–1936). French organist and composer.

Gruber, Franz Xavier (1787–1863). Austrian schoolteacher and organist.

Guerrero, Francisco (1528–1599). Spanish composer of the high Renaissance.

Guinand, Edouard (1838–1909). French poet, librettist, and professor of law.

Gungor, Michael (1980–). American singer and songwriter.

Hairston, Jester (1901–2000). American composer, songwriter, and actor.

Hamilton, Newburgh (1691–1761). Irish playwright and librettist.

Handel, Georg Frideric (1685–1759). German-born composer. A British subject from 1729.

Handl, Jacob (Gallus) (1550–1591). A Slovenian composer influenced by Venetian music.

Harbison, John (1938–). American composer.

Harvey, PJ (1969–). British singer and songwriter.

Hassler, Hans Leo (1564–1612). German organist and composer. Studied in Venice.

Haydn, Joseph (1732–1809). German composer, chief architect of the classical tradition.

Hayes, Philip (1738–1797). Eighteenth-century English composer and organist.

Heber, Reginald (1783–1826). English clergyman and hymn writer.

Herms, Bernie. Contemporary Canadian songwriter and producer.

Hildegard of Bingen (ca. 1098–1179). German composer, mystic, intellectual, and poet.

Hillsong Kids. Music label of the Australia-based Hillsong Church.

Hoffmann, Elizabeth. Contemporary American composer of electroacoustic music.

Hogan, Moses (1957–2003). American composer and arranger of Afro-American spirituals.

Holst, Gustav (1874–1934). British composer and teacher.

Honegger, Arthur (1892–1955). Swiss composer, lived in Paris. A member of Les Six.

Hooters, The. American rock band; played folk, ska, and reggae music.

Houston, Whitney (1963–2012). African American singer and actress.

Howe, Julia Ward (1819–1910). American poet and social activist.

Howells, Herbert (1892–1983). English composer, organist, and teacher.

Hulsman Bingham, Susan (1944–). American pianist and composer.

Humfrey, Pelham (1647–1674). Influential young English composer.

Hurd, Michael (1928–2006). British composer of choral music.

Impressions, The. American music group formed in 1958 in Chicago.

Indy, Vincent d' (1851–1931). French composer and teacher.

Ireland, John (1879–1962). British composer.

Iron & Wine (Samuel Beam) (1974–). American folk singer and songwriter.

Iron Maiden. British heavy metal band formed in 1975.

Isaacson, Michael (1946–). American Jewish composer of synagogue music.

Islam, Yusuf (Cat Stevens) (1948–). British singer/songwriter and humanitarian.

Ives, Charles (1874–1954). American experimental composer.

Jackson, Mahalia (1911–1972). African American gospel singer; the "queen of gospel music."

Jacopone da Todi (ca. 1230–1306). Italian Franciscan friar and satirical writer.

Jagger, Mick (1943–). British singer, actor, and producer; founder of the Rolling Stones.

Jenkins, Karl (1944–). Welsh musician and composer.

Johnson, James Weldon (1871–1938). American writer, lawyer, and civil rights activist.

Joio, Norman Dello (1913–2008). American composer, most famous for his choral works.

Jommelli, Niccolò (1714–1774). Italian composer, primarily of operas and sacred oratorios.

Jones, Roger. Contemporary British composer and director of Christian Music Ministries.

Josquin des Prez (ca. 1450–1521). Franco-Flemish Renaissance composer.

Joubert, John (1927–). British composer, born in South Africa.

Joy Division. English postpunk band formed in 1976, re-formed as New Order in 1980.

Judd, Wynonna (1964–). American country music singer.

Kapp, Artur (1878–1952). Estonian composer.

Karg-Elert, Sigfrid (1877–1933). German composer of works for organ and harmonium.

Keiser, Reinhard (1674–1739). German composer.

Keithahn, Mary Nelson (1934–). American minister, journalist, and hymn writer.

Kellogg, Daniel (1976–). American composer.

Kelly, Thomas (1769–1854). Irish evangelical clergyman and hymn writer.

Keyes, Aaron. Contemporary American songwriter and worship leader.

Klashnekoff (Darren Kandler) (1975–). British rap artist.

Kleiberg, Ståle (1958–). Norwegian classical composer.

Klein, Hermann (1856–1934). English music critic, writer, and translator.

Kodály, Zoltán (1882–1967). Hungarian composer, musicologist, and teacher.

La Rocca, Frank (1951–). American composer of orchestral, choral, and electronic music.

Lady Gaga (Stefani Germanotta) (1986–). American singer, songwriter, and actress.

Laine, Frankie (1913–2007). American singer, songwriter, and actor.

lang, k.d. Contemporary Canadian country singer and political activist.

Lang Zaimont, Judith (1945–). American pianist and composer.

Langgaard, Rued (1893–1952). Danish composer and organist.

Langlais, Jean (1907–1991). French composer of sacred music.

Lassus, Orlando de (ca. 1530–1594). Franco-Flemish composer of the Counter-Reformation.

Lauridsen, Morten (1943–). American composer.

Laurie, Hugh (1959–). British comedian, actor, writer, and musician.

Lawless, Blackie (1956–). American songwriter and musician, lead singer in W.A.S.P.

Ledger, Philip (1937–2012). British composer and choirmaster.

Lehrman, Leonard (1943–). American composer of vocal music.

Leighton, Kenneth (1929–1988). British composer and pianist.

Leonard, Patrick (1955–). American songwriter and producer.

Léonin (Leoninus) (ca. 1150–ca. 1200). The first named composer in the Notre Dame school of polyphony.

Libera (Angel Voices). English vocal group formed out of the choir of a London church.

Lichine, David (1910–1972). Russian ballet dancer and choreographer. Lived in Paris from 1917.

Liszt, Franz (1811–1886). Hungarian pianist, composer, and conductor.

Lloyd Webber, Andrew (1948–). British composer and producer of musical theater.

Loes, Harry Dixon (1895–1965). American composer and teacher.

Lotti, Antonio (ca. 1667–1740). Italian baroque composer.

Loveless, Patty (1957–). American country singer.

Løvland, Rolf (1955–). Norwegian composer.

Lowry, Mark (1958–). American Christian singer, songwriter, and comedian.

Luther, Martin (1483–1546). German reformer, amateur musician, and hymn writer.

Lyte, Henry Francis (1793–1847). Scottish clergyman, hymn writer, and poet.

MacClean, Don (1945–). American singer and songwriter.

Macfarren, George Alexander (1813–1887). British composer and musicologist.

MacGimsey, Robert (1898–1979). American composer of music in African American style.

MacLellan, Gene (1938–1995). Canadian singer/songwriter.

MacMillan, Sir James (1959–). Scottish classical composer and conductor.

Macpherson, Jean Jay (1931–2012). Canadian poet.

Malotte, Albert Hay (1895–1964). American composer, organist, and pianist.

Manson, Marilyn (1969–). Controversial American musician and songwriter.

Mäntyjärvi, Jaakko (1963–). Finnish choral composer and translator.

Manz, Paul (1919–2009). American composer and organist.

Markland, Gerald (1953–). American musician and composer.

Marley, Bob (1945–1981). Jamaican reggae musician and songwriter.

Marsalis, Delfeayo (1965–). American jazz trombonist and record producer.

Martin, Frank (1890–1974). Swiss composer, influenced by Schönberg.

Martinez, Marianna (1744–1812). Austrian composer of Spanish descent.

Martynov, Vladimir (1946–). Russian composer and avant-garde musician.

Massenet, Jules (1842–1912). French composer of operas, oratorios, and over 200 songs.

Mathias, William (1934–1992). Welsh composer and pianist.

Mattea, Kathy (1959–). American country musician and social activist.

Maxwell Davis, Sir Peter. *See* **Davies, Sir Peter Maxwell.**

May, Brian (1947–). English singer/songwriter, lead guitarist in the rock group Queen.

Maybrick, Michael (Stephen Adams) (1841–1913). British composer and singer.

Mayr, Johann Simon (1763–1845). German Italian composer.

McDaniels, Gene (Eugene) (1935–2011). African American singer and songwriter.

McFerrin, Bobby (Robert Keith) (1950–). American singer and conductor.

McKim Garrison, Lucy (1842–1877). American collector of African American spirituals.

McTell, Ralph (Ralph May) (1944–). English singer/songwriter and guitarist.

Mechem, Kirke (1925–). American composer, mainly of choral pieces and operas.

Méhul, Etienne Nicola (1763–1817). French romantic opera composer.

Mendelssohn(-Bartholdy), Felix (1809–1847). German musician and composer.

Menotti, Gian Carlo (1911–2007). Italian American composer and librettist.

Mercer, Johnny (1909–1976). Singer/songwriter and composer.

Merritt, Stephin (1965–). American singer/songwriter. Lead singer of the Magnetic Fields.

Merula, Tarquinio (1594–1665). Italian composer and organist.

Messiaen, Olivier (1908–1992). French composer. A major 20th-century musical influence.

Metallica. American heavy metal band formed in Los Angeles in 1981.

Metastasio (Pietro Antonio Domenico Trapassi) (1698–1792). Italian poet and librettist.

Meyerbeer, Giacomo (1791–1864). German Jewish composer.

Meyerowitz, Jan (1913–1998). German American Jewish composer.

Miami Boys Choir. Choir formed in 1977 to perform contemporary Jewish music.

Milhaud, Darius (1892–1974). French Jewish composer. Member of Les Six.

Molique, Bernhard (1802–1869). Belgian violinist and composer.

Monk, Edwin George (1819–1900). English organist and composer.

Monk, William Henry (1823–1889). English organist and composer of hymns and anthems.

Monteverdi, Claudio (1689–1755). Italian priest and early baroque composer.

Montgomery, James (1771–1854). British poet, hymn writer, and political activist.

Morales, Cristóbal (ca. 1500–1553). Spanish composer and priest.

Morley, Thomas (ca. 1557–1602). English Renaissance musician and composer.

Moultaka, Zad (1967–). Lebanese composer and pianist.

Mouskouri, Nana (1934–). Greek singer and pacifist.

Mozart, Wolfgang Amadeus (1756–1791). Austrian composer, major influence on Beethoven.

Mullins, Rich (1955–1997). American contemporary Christian singer/songwriter.

Mussorgsky, Modest Petrovich (1839–1881). Russian composer.

Mysliveček, Josef (1737–1781). Czech composer.

Neale, John Mason (1818–1866). Anglican priest, scholar, and hymn writer.

Neander, Joachim (1650–1680). German Calvinist theologian and hymn writer.

Nefarium. Black metal band formed in northern Italy.

Newton, John (1725–1807). English evangelical clergyman and hymn writer.

Nicolai, Philipp (1556–1608). German Lutheran pastor, poet, and composer.

Nielsen, Carl (1865–1931). Danish composer and conductor.

Nowowiejski, Feliks (1877–1946). Polish composer.

Nusrat Fateh Ali Khan (1948–1997). Pakistani singer, interpreter of *Qawwali* music.

Oakely, Frederick (1802–1880). English Catholic priest and writer.

Oasis. English rock band formed in Manchester, England, in 1991 with Liam and Noel Gallagher.

Ockeghem, Johannes (ca. 1420–1497). Flemish composer at the court of Louis XI.

O'Connor, Sinéad (1966–). Irish singer/songwriter and campaigner for social justice.

O'Donnell, Daniel ("Wee Daniel") (1961–). Irish singer and television host.

Ogden, William Augustine (1841–1897). American composer, conductor, and hymn writer.

One Bad Pig. American Christian punk and metal crossover band formed in 1985.

Ord, Boris (1897–1961). Organist and choirmaster at Kings College, Cambridge.

Osbourne, John Michael ("Ozzy") (1948–). English singer/songwriter.

Owen, David (1953–). British pianist and composer.

Pachelbel, Johann (1653–1706). German composer and organist.

Paine, John Knowles (1839–1906). American composer, organist, and choirmaster.

Palestrina, Giovanni Pierluigi da (1525–1594). Italian Renaissance composer, mainly in Rome.

Panufnik, Roxanna (1968–). British Catholic composer.

Parker, Matthew (1504–1575). Scholar, editor, and archbishop of Canterbury.

Parry, Sir Hubert (1848–1918). English composer and musicologist.

Pärt, Arvo (1935–). Estonian composer.

Parton, Dolly (1946–). American singer/songwriter and film actor.

Penderecki, Krzysztof (1933–). Polish composer.

Pergolesi, Giovanni Battista (1710–1736). Italian composer.

Persichetti, Vincent Ludwig (1915–1987). American composer and teacher.

Picander (Christian Friedrich Henrici) (1700–1764). German poet and librettist.

Pink Floyd. British progressive rock band formed in 1965.

Pinkham, Daniel (1923–2006). American composer and organist.

Pitts, Antony (1969–). British composer and radio producer.

Pixies, The. American indie/alternative rock band formed in Boston, Massachusetts, in 1986.

Pizzetti, Ildebrando (1880–1968). Italian composer and musicologist.

Porter, Cole Albert (1881–1964). American composer and songwriter.

Poston, Elizabeth (1905–1987). English composer and writer.

Poulenc, Francis (1899–1963). French composer and pianist. One of Les Six.

Pousseur, Henri (1929–2009). Belgian composer and musicologist.

Praetorius, Hieronymus (1560–1629). Late Renaissance German organist and composer.

Praetorius, Michael (1571–1621). German musician, composer, and writer.

Pratten, Catharina Josepha (Madame Sidney Pratten) (1821–1895). German guitarist, composer, and teacher.

Presley, Elvis (1935–1977). American singer and actor; the "king of rock and roll."

Presley, Luther G. (1887–1974). American songwriter.

Prince Allah (Ras Allah) (Keith Blake) (1950–). Jamaican-roots reggae singer.

Prince Far I (1944–1983). Jamaican reggae musician, deejay, and producer.

Prokofiev, Sergei (1891–1953). Russian composer.

Quarles, Frances (1592–1644). English poet, author of *Emblems*.

Rachmaninov, Sergei (1873–1943). Russian romantic composer and pianist.

Ramsey, Robert (1590–1644). Scottish composer and organist.

Raphael (Fred Sharpe) (1948–). American avant-garde composer and San Francisco hippie.

Reger, Max (1873–1916). German composer, mostly of songs and keyboard pieces.

Reich, Steve (1936–). American philosopher and composer.

Renville, Joseph (1779–1846). American explorer and translator.

Residents, The (1972–). American art collective based in California.

Respighi, Ottorino (1879–1936). Italian composer and musicologist.

Rheinberger, Josef (1839–1901). German organist and composer, mostly for organ.

Rice, Tim (1944–). British songwriter; worked with Andrew Lloyd Webber.

Richards, Keith (1943–). British singer/songwriter; original member of the Rolling Stones.

Rihm, Wolfgang (1952–). German composer, seen as a reaction against Stockhausen.

Rilke, Rainer Maria (1875–1926). Bohemian Austrian poet and novelist.

Rimsky-Korsakov, Nikolay Andreievich (1844–1908). Russian composer.

Rinkart, Martin (1586–1689). German pastor and hymn writer.

Ritter, Josh (1976–). American singer/songwriter.

Rodgers, Richard Charles (1902–1979). American composer, with Oscar Hammerstein II.

Rogers, Kenny (1938–). American country music superstar.

Root, George Fredrick (1820–1895). American songwriter during the American Civil War.

Rossetti, Christina (1830–1894). English romantic poet.

Rossi, Camilla de (fl. 1707–1710). Italian composer of sacred music.

Rossi, Salomone (ca. 1570–1630). Italian Jewish violinist and early baroque composer.

Rozs, Miklos (1907–1995). Hungarian composer. Lived in the United States from 1940.

Rubbra, Edmund (1901–1986). British composer.

Rubinstein, Anton Gregorevich (1829–1894). Russian pianist and composer.

Runestad, Jake (1986–). American composer.

Rutter, John (1945–). British composer, conductor, and editor.

Sacer, Gottfried Wilhelm (1635–1699). German poet, satirist, and hymn writer.

Saint-Saëns, Camille (1835–1921). French romantic composer, conductor, and organist.

Sampson, Don. Contemporary American country music artist.

Scarlatti, Alessandro (1660–1725). Italian baroque composer.

Scheidt, Samuel (1587–1654). German baroque composer and organist.

Schein, Johann Hermann (1586–1630). German early baroque composer.

Schmitt, Florent (1870–1958). French composer in the post-Wagnerian French tradition.

Schoenberg, Arnold (1874–1951). Austrian composer, painter, and writer. Lived in the United States from 1934.

Schubert, Franz (1797–1828). Austrian early romantic composer.

Schumann, Robert (1810–1856). German composer and writer.

Schutte, Dan (1947–). American songwriter and composer of Catholic liturgical music.

Schütz, Heinrich (1585–1672). German composer, influenced by Gabrielli in Venice.

Schwartz, Stephen (1948–). American composer and lyricist in music theater.

Scott, K. Lee (1950–). American conductor and composer of sacred music and hymns.

Sears, Edmund (1810–1876). American Unitarian minister and theologian.

Second, Didier Lupi (ca. 1520–1559). French composer of Italian origin.

Sedaka, Neil (1939–). American singer and songwriter.

Seeger, Pete (1919–2014). American folk musician and activist.

Sermisy, Claudin de (ca. 1490–1562). French Renaissance composer of vocal music.

Seter, Mordecai (1916–1994). Russian-born Israeli composer.

Seward, Theodore F. (1835–1902). American choirmaster, arranger, and musicologist.

Shaw, Knowles (1834–1878). American evangelist, author and composer of gospel hymns.

Sheppard, John (ca. 1515–1558). One of the finest Tudor composers of sacred music.

Sheriff, Noam (1935–). Israeli composer and conductor.

Shilkret, Nathaniel (1889–1982). American clarinetist, composer, pianist, and conductor.

Shohat, Gil (1973–). Israeli composer.

Sila, Edouard (1827–1909). Dutch composer and organist.

Simon and Garfunkel. Paul Simon and Art Garfunkel. Formed a folk rock duo in the 1960s.

Sinatra, Frank (1915–1998). American singer, producer, actor, and director.

Siouxsie and the Banshees. British rock band formed in 1976.

Sjostrand, Janice. Contemporary American Christian pastor and writer.

Skaggs, Ricky (1954–). American bluegrass singer, songwriter, and producer.

Smith, Andrew (1970–). English composer of sacred choral music living since in Norway from 1984.

Smith, John Christopher (1712–1795). English composer, Handel's amanuensis.

Smith, Timothy. Contemporary American composer of Christian music.

Smiths, The. British indie band formed in 1982.

Sorley, Charles Hamilton (1895–1915). British poet of World War I.

Spektor, Regina (1980–). Russian American singer, songwriter, and pianist.

Spohr, Louis (1784–1859). Early romantic German violinist, composer, and conductor.

Springsteen, Bruce (1949–). American singer and songwriter; "the Boss."

Stainer, John (1840–1901). British composer, organist, and academic.

Stanford, Sir Charles Villiers (1852–1924). Irish conductor, composer and teacher.

Starer, Robert (1924–2001). Austrian-born American composer and pianist.

Stevie Wonder (1950–). American singer/songwriter, producer, and political activist.

Strauss, Richard (1864–1949). German late romantic composer.

Stravinsky, Igor (1882–1971). Russian composer, pianist, and conductor.

Striggio, Alessandro (ca. 1536–1592). Italian Renaissance composer.

Stroope, Z. Randall (1953–). American conductor and composer, mainly of sacred works.

Strozzi, Barbara (1619–1677). Italian Baroque singer and composer.

Sweelinck, Jan Pieterszoon (1562–1621). Dutch composer, mainly of keyboard music.

Tal, Josef (1910–2008). Israeli composer, pioneer of Israeli classical music.

Tallis, Thomas (ca. 1505–1585). English composer; the "father of English cathedral music."

Tansman, Alexandre (1897–1986). Polish Jewish composer and pianist, working in Paris.

Tas, Rudi (1957–). Belgian composer, primarily of choral music.

Tate, Nahum (1652–1715). Irish poet, author, and hymn writer.

Taylor, James (1948–). American singer, songwriter, and guitarist.

Tchaikovsky, Pyotr Ilyich (1840–1893). Russian composer.

Telemann, Georg Philipp (1681–1757). German baroque composer.

Theodorakis, Mikis (1925–). Greek composer and political activist.

Thompson, Randall (1899–1984). American composer, primarily of choral music.

Thomson, Virgil (1896–1989). American writer and composer.

Timberlake, Justin (1981–). American singer, songwriter, and actor.

Tippett, Sir Michael (1905–1998). Major British composer.

To/Die/For. Finnish gothic metal band formed in 1999.

Toch, Ernst (1887–1964). Austrian avant-garde composer.

Tomkins, Thomas (1572–1656). English composer.

Toolan, Sr. Suzanne (1927–). American composer and musician.

Toplady, Augustus Montague (1740–1778). English Calvinist preacher and hymn writer.

Torke, Michael (1961–). American "postminimalist" composer.

Tusser, Thomas (1524–1580). English poet and farmer.

Tye, Christopher (ca. 1505–1573). English composer and organist.

U2. Irish rock band formed in 1976.

Valls, Francisco (1665–1747). Spanish composer and music theorist.

Van Morrison (1945–). Northern Irish singer, songwriter, and musician.

Verdi, Giuseppe (1813–1901). Italian operatic composer.

Verve. British psychedelic rock band formed in 1990.

Victoria, Tomas Luis de (ca. 1548–1627). Spanish composer, organist, and priest.

Villette, Pierre (1926–1998). French composer in the tradition of Poulenc and Messiaen.

Violent Femmes. American alternative rock band formed in 1980.

Vivaldi, Antonio (1678–1741). Italian composer and priest.

Vox Dei. Argentinian rock band formed in 1967.

Wagner, Richard (1813–1883). German romantic composer, writer, and nationalist.

Wainwright, Rufus (1973–). Canadian American singer, songwriter, and environmentalist.

Walford Davies, Henry (1869–1931). British composer and radio personality.

Walton, Sir William (1902–1983). English composer.

Ware, Charles Pickard (1840–1921). American abolitionist, editor of American folk music.

Warlock, Peter (1894–1930). British composer and music critic.

Warner, Anna Bartlett (1819–1885). American novelist and hymn writer.

Warren, Elinor Remick (1900–1991). American pianist and composer.

W.A.S.P. American "shock rock" heavy metal band formed in 1982.

Watts, Isaac (1674–1748). English hymn writer.

Weavers, The. American folk band formed in 1948, based in Greenwich Village, New York.

Weelkes, Thomas (1576–1623). English composer and organist.

Weill, Kurt (1900–1950). German composer. Fled to Paris in 1933 and New York in 1935.

Weinberg, Jacob (1879–1956). Russian-born Jewish composer and pianist.

Weir, Judith (1954–). British composer.

Werdyger, Mordechai Ben David (1951–). American Jewish singer and songwriter.

Wesley, Charles (1707–1788). English preacher and hymn writer.

Whitacre, Eric (1970–). American composer.

White, Robert (ca. 1538–1574). English Tudor composer.

Whittier, John Greenleaf (1807–1892). Journalist and hymn writer; the "Quaker poet."

Wilkins, Reverend Robert (1896–1987). African American blues guitarist and singer.

Willan, Healey (1880–1968). Anglo-Canadian composer and organist.

Willcocks, David (1919–). British conductor, organist, and composer.

Williams, Robbie (1974–). British singer and songwriter.

Wilson, Brian (1942–). American singer and songwriter; cofounder of the Beach Boys.

Winans, Priscilla (CeCe) Marie (1964–). American gospel singer.

Winfrey, Gillitte (1961–). American hymn writer and Presbyterian pastor.

Wolcott, John Truman (1869–?). American composer.

Wood, Charles (1866–1926). Irish composer and teacher.

Work, John Wesley (1901–1967). African American composer and musicologist.

Wuorinen, Charles (1938–). American composer of 12-tone music.

Zelenka, Jan Dismas (1679–1745). Czech composer.

Ziegler, Christiana Mariana von (1695–1760). German poet and writer.

Zutons, The. English indie band formed in 2001.

Zytowski, Carl. Contemporary American composer and academic.

Index of Biblical Names and Subjects

Index of Biblical References

Note: an asterisk (*) denotes apocryphal additions

OLD TESTAMENT

321

NEW TESTAMENT

APOCRYPHA